German Colonial Wars and the Context of Military Violence

German Colonial Wars and the Context of Military Violence

SUSANNE KUSS

Translated by Andrew Smith

Harvard University Press

Cambridge, Massachusetts
London, England
2017

First printing

An earlier version of this work was first published as *Deutsches Militär auf kolonialen Kriegsschauplätzen: Eskalation von Gewalt zu Beginn des 20. Jahrhunderts* © Christoph Links Verlag GmbH, Berlin 2010.

The translation of this work was funded by Geisteswissenschaften International—Translating Funding for Humanities and Social Sciences from Germany, a joint initiative of the Fritz Thyssen Foundation, the German Federal Foreign Office, the collecting society VG WORT, and the Börsenverein des Deutschen Buchhandels (German Publishers & Booksellers Association).

Library of Congress Cataloging-in-Publication Data
Names: Kuss, Susanne, author.
Title: German colonial wars and the context of military violence / Susanne Kuss ; translated by Andrew Smith.
Other titles: Deutsches Militär auf kolonialen Kriegsschauplätzen. English
Description: Cambridge, Massachusetts : Harvard University Press, 2017. | "An earlier version of this work was first published as Deutsches Militär auf kolonialen Kriegsschauplätzen: Eskalation von Gewalt zu Beginn des 20. Jahrhunderts (c) Christoph Links Verlag GmbH, Berlin 2010"—Title page verso. | Includes bibliographical references and index.
Identifiers: LCCN 2016040430 | ISBN 9780674970632 (alk. paper)
Subjects: LCSH: Germany—History, Military—20th century. | Militarism—Germany—History—20th century. | Maji Maji Uprising, 1905–1907. | Namibia—History—Herero Revolt, 1904–1907. | Namibia—History—Nama Revolt, 1904–1908. | China—History—Boxer Rebellion, 1899–1901. | Imperialism.
Classification: LCC DD104 .K8713 2017 | DDC 909/.09712430821—dc23
LC record available at https://lccn.loc.gov/2016040430

Contents

Part III: Evaluation and Memory

German Colonial Wars and the Context of Military Violence

Introduction

T H E A I M of this study is to analyze the causes and forms of the violence perpetrated by the German Empire within the context of three major colonial wars fought at the turn of the twentieth century: the Boxer War in China (1900–1901), the Herero and Nama War in German South-West Africa (1904–1907), and the Maji Maji War in German East Africa (1905–1908). Although long sidelined in German historiography, the issues raised by these conflicts touch on some of the central and abiding questions of modern German history: development from imperial Germany to the Third Reich and the continuities between these two systems. Intricately associated with the so-called *Sonderweg* thesis, first postulated by Fritz Fischer and Hans Ulrich Wehler, later proponents of this highly controversial theory argued that the seeds of Nazism lay within these minor conflicts.[1] They claimed the level and nature of violence meted out in China and Africa not only were commensurate with those witnessed on the Eastern front after 1941 but indeed were nourished from one and the same wellspring. According to such an approach, the seeds of Operation Barbarossa and even the Holocaust were sown and the atrocities foreshadowed within the smaller conflicts. In summary such an approach posits a direct path from Windhoek to Auschwitz.[2]

Despite originating at the interface between military and colonial history, historical treatments of the colonial wars remained the preserve of scholars of imperial and commonwealth history. Colonial studies in Germany grew out of Hannah Arendt's appreciation that, far from being a twentieth-century phenomenon, totalitarianism had first developed in the European colonies.[3]

I

Although not considering Germany or the military and its practices in any great detail—the literature focused on British administrators, technocrats, and bureaucrats—the theory remained flexible enough to be applied to the German context. The end of the 1960s saw the development of a number of specialist studies concentrating on the former German colony of South-West Africa. Studies conducted in both East and West Germany identified continuities in the system of rule spanning Wilhelmine colonialism to the expansive policies of the Third Reich; the latter was identified in nascent form in the administration of German South-West Africa.

The postcolonial turn in history in general and the cultural turn in military history in particular also had an impact on research into the German colonial wars. Previous studies of the conflicts examined in this book restricted themselves to a straightforward analysis of their genesis, course, and aftermath. A new approach now widened the focus to incorporate such disparate aspects as the influence of the press, propaganda, and military literature on the course of the wars; the question of gender in East Africa; the participation of African and Chinese auxiliaries; and the significance of the Herero war for the history of the Herero people and the Namibian nation. The development of a number of comparative studies contrasting the German wars with those conducted by their imperial rivals added an international component to what had previously been an exclusively national debate.[4]

These developments provided the backdrop to the emergence of a new generation of historians advocating the continuity from German South-West Africa to National Socialism in the way in which violence was exercised against subject populations.[5] The discussion of the interrelationship between the colonies and the metropole raised questions of colonial and European practices of violence and National Socialism as a form of colonial rule. Within this debate, the Herero and Nama War was repurposed as the hinge between imperialism and National Socialism, the crimes of the fathers committed in a much smaller and non-European framework merely anticipating those perpetrated by their sons some forty years later.

The concept of a specifically German collective military disposition, born in 1871 and documented for both the colonial wars and the First World War, was seen to reach its apogee in the war of racial destruction unleashed in Central and Eastern Europe after 1939. Advancing the existence of a putative German "military culture" consisting of a range of unarticulated dispositions—assumptions, principles, values, standards, tenets of faith, and formal knowledge—and expressed in stated doctrines, some scholars argued that it formed a clear mindset influencing or even determining military behavior.[6] This construct was advanced by American historian Isabel Hull as the basis of a model that identified a general tendency on the part of the German military to make swift recourse to violence in the pursuit of radical, absolute solutions. Genocide and extermination were thus not the product of extreme ideologization, but the outcome of institutionalized yet unformulated standard military practices. According to this model, the specifically "German" form of extreme violence unleashed in its colonies may well have been given first expression in this environment, but its presence in latent form long predated the colonial wars.[7]

Others viewed the path from Windhoek to Auschwitz as much less direct, advancing three arguments to this effect.[8] Comparison of the Herero and Nama massacres with the events in other colonial contexts soon dashed all claims of their uniqueness and historical significance. A German colonial *Sonderweg* was conspicuous only by its absence. Moreover, it was pointed out that the temporal gap between 1904 and 1941 not only was too large but had not been bridged by any continuity in personnel.[9] The youngest of the empire builders were sixty years of age in 1941. Indeed, the indirect transmission of genocidal practices via a putative institutionalized military "memory" specific to Germany was not only extremely difficult to demonstrate but nearly impossible to assess. This personnel argument was augmented by the realization that the mass murder committed in 1904 was the immediate responsibility of a number of small units consisting of only a few thousand men. This raised the question as to the true significance for later German wars of the experiences of only a handful of soldiers.

Neither the Wehrmacht nor Hitler attempted to justify the Eastern campaign by reference to the German colonial wars.[10] An important precondition for the continuity theory is the preservation and transmission of such experiences within the military establishment in the form of reports or doctrines. However, the opposite is the case—neither the Reichswehr nor the Wehrmacht commissioned or made recourse to any study of the German colonial wars from which to learn lessons for the future. Although advancing a range of arguments striking in their clarity, resting on analogy and assumption, the advocates of the continuity theory fail to demonstrate that the extreme violence practiced in the Second World War actually derived its central causal impetus from the war in German South-West Africa.

The continuity thesis is based on a number of assumptions. Positing a disposition to violence rooted in an inherently violent military culture not only denies the perpetrators of this violence any measure of free agency but absolves them from all responsibility. Functioning as the agents of an all-encompassing military culture, the soldiers prosecuting these wars are depicted as incapable of choosing an alternative course of action. Moreover, the courses taken by all three German colonial wars must necessarily have exhibited considerable similarities in order to give credence to the continuity theory.

The divergent patterns of violence manifested in all three conflicts belie any attempt to press them into a common framework. Whereas the random violence unleashed in the Chinese campaign was exercised within the scope of a number of punitive expeditions, it was the collapse of a carefully planned orthodox military strategy in German South-West Africa that resulted in a genocidal spiral. German East Africa reveals yet another pattern of violence, the prominent use of a scorched earth policy. Moreover, the three conflicts were perpetrated by different actors drawn from a number of agencies: a volunteer expeditionary corps, Protection Forces, naval units, and native contingents. With entirely different training and distinctive motivations, they exhibited differing forms of military behavior.

The deployment of native auxiliaries indicates that European practices and mentalities—in whatever form—could not have exercised the sole decisive influence in the conduct of the colonial wars. Colonial campaigns should instead be understood as an extreme form of cultural encounter, a framework within which the extermination of an entire ethnicity represented only the most radical form of dealing with the "other."[11] That this was regarded as a feasible course of action is demonstrated by discussions conducted in Britain and France in the 1830s, examining the "correct" approach to colonizing. Centering on two different answers—the mixing of white and native populations versus extermination—a similar debate began in Germany in 1884.[12]

Those advancing the continuity thesis have tended to base their arguments on the identification of similarities in the events, from which they proceed to extrapolate an identity of attitude. Whatever the apparent appeal of such arguments, they are not supported by the sources. Moreover, focusing on the Herero and Nama War in German South-West Africa, proponents of this thesis make no reference to the other colonial wars. None have posed or even attempted to answer the question as to why the war in German South-West Africa culminated in genocide but those in China and German East Africa did not. What was different about South-West Africa? Moves to posit a putative German military culture of extreme violence expressed in wars conducted in both a colonial and a European context involves the argument that a specifically "German" mode of behavior had been forged by institutional factors. The question is raised, however, as to whether the behavior of the colonial soldiers corresponded to the standards and rules established for Europe and if not, which factors were decisive in conditioning such an outcome. Both claims overlook the fact that the genesis of extreme violence in war is associated with the conditions experienced in each individual theater of war.

This book seeks to demonstrate not only that the violence unleashed within the context of the three colonial wars was rooted in the mental or psychological disposition of the soldiers conducting them but that the soldiers responsible for the violence were themselves subject to the influence of the specific set of circumstances in which they found themselves, and that their response was conditioned by the possibilities for action presented by each environment. Any effort to understand the different patterns of extreme violence unleashed within the three wars requires a close examination of their development during the course of the conflict. War involves the employment of violence; combatants seek to kill and destroy in order to achieve a set of defined military objectives. Violence, on the other hand, is an anthropological constant manifesting itself at all times; its incidence is in no way restricted to times of war. Some scholars even view it as an entirely natural phenomenon. The discussion of violence in the social sciences tends to focus on its causes, which themselves are associated with the wishes and intentions of its perpetrator. Despite the widespread nature of this often implicit assumption of intention and agency, a further profitable approach has come to focus on the situational and sociocultural context of the violent act. Such an understanding does not reduce the phenomenon to causes beyond violence but rather presents it as an imminent process developing from a specific set of circumstances: "the key to violence is to be found in the form which it assumes."[13] In order to understand exactly what unleashes violence, it is necessary to consider its individual practices.

Violent action represents the crossing of a very clear border. This also applies to violence perpetrated in the context of war. The German military theorist Carl von Clausewitz did not invent the understanding of war as the "attempt to destroy or overcome an opponent by inflicting death or serious wounding"; this consideration was all too familiar to the ancients.[14] Even if he accepted the existence of different levels of intensity in the application of violence, however, in writing his famous book *On War*, Clausewitz still established the main aim of all warlike encounters as the destruction of enemy forces.[15] Nevertheless, his conception of war still rested on the necessity of deploying military power in an organized and calculated—and thus restricted—fashion, with the aim of breaking the will of the opponent and seizing victory. For Clausewitz, even unbounded violence remained a strategic (and thus controlled) instrument.

"Extreme violence" applied within the context of a war—sometimes referred to as "excessive" or "barbaric"—represents a level of violence uncoupled from military objectives. Such violence is perpetrated following the realization of the immediate aims for which it was unleashed. As such, this violence is strategically superfluous. Extreme violence can also be aimed against land and property in the form of theft, plunder, requisitions, or extortion. Taken to its extreme, such a phenomenon often results in the total destruction of all traceable resources—an approach that has become known as a policy of "scorched earth." Its application can mean sure death for the population of a territory to which it has been applied, or at the very least can force them to take flight. The concept of extreme violence also encompasses wars exhibiting a very high incidence of violent actions concentrated in a single location (massacres) and the applications of military technology to produce abnormally high levels of casualties. Despite such considerations, the levels of violence perpetrated in a war and its labeling as "extreme" cannot be derived alone from the number of civilian or military casualties incurred.

In war, extreme violence can escalate into the total destruction of an opponent, thus assuming the characteristics of a genocide. The term "genocide" refers to the killing of a specific group of people. Although there is no linear relationship between genocide and the degree of destruction perpetrated in the war that produces it, the two processes are linked by the extreme violence they involve. War is a form of collective killing that exhibits a "multitude of genocidal 'family traits.'"[16] A war can also be unleashed and conducted as a state-sanctioned program of racial extermination. The most famous example was the program of genocide launched against the Jewish and Soviet population in 1941 under the aegis of Operation Barbarossa. A war without limit does not use killing as an instrument to achieve military victory but sets the death of enemy soldiers, the civilian population, and prisoners of war as an aim in itself.

Under colonial rule, war and peace were never clearly demarcated. The wide expanse of every colonial territory and the restricted administrative and military resources available to police it exercised a constitutive impact on the nature of the colonial state. Inherently weak and exhibiting a pronounced disposition to violence, colonialism was infused by the ever-present threat of extreme force that was given constant expression in colonial decision making, routine, institutions, and even its representation in architecture and contemporary scholarly treatments.[17] The regular use of corporal punishment and military action in the fabric of colonial rule demonstrates its inherently violent nature. Contemporaries classified such events not as "war" but in terms of "actions," "risings," "expeditions," "operations," "police operations," "disruption," "punitive expeditions," "campaigns," and the response to "unrest."[18] As such, the imposition of a lasting peace is referred to in such contexts as the "pacification" of the colonial area. Never achieved in a single act, it rather involved a continuing process of violent interaction.

Close analysis of colonial wars reveals a number of differences from European wars. Dispatched to far-flung areas, the intervention forces were forced to endure a long sea passage (a month to six weeks), during which time they were prepared for alien environments by a range of addresses, songs, and instructions. The inhomogeneity of the newly raised units sent to China and Africa was thus offset. Inculcating soldiers in the aims of the war they were about to fight, this unique group dynamic had a considerable impact on the way in which they operated. Once arrived in what amounted to an entirely unfamiliar setting, for which their previous training and experience had done nothing to prepare them, European troops were often forced to rely on middlemen in order to facilitate their survival and movement in the colony. Indeed, this principle was often taken to the extreme to the extent that some wars were conducted almost exclusively by native mercenary formations. Clear cultural divisions between the colonizers and the colonized thus could easily become blurred in extreme situations, with implications for the conduct of the war.

Given the disparity in equipment and local knowledge between the belligerents, colonial wars almost invariably descended into guerilla warfare conducted on an asymmetric scale. As such, western commanders were often forced to improvise a response at variance with established European military doctrine. This was complicated by the absence of the extensive and reliable infrastructure on which modern warfare relied, which introduced a level of uncertainty into military planning. Operating across sizeable territories terrifying in their unfamiliarity and hostile climates and facing unfamiliar diseases served to transform the military experience of the western troops, almost to the extent of presenting new "enemies" to fight.

Such a situation had significant implications for the view of the enemy held by the colonial military forces, both commanders and troops alike. The German troops were worn down by the conditions under which they were forced to conduct campaigns, as well as by the failure on the part of the native forces to conform to European conceptions of warfare, which was taken as an affront amounting to a "flouting of the rules of civilized warfare and conduct" and testament to their lack of humanity. This situation was compounded by the legal context. The conduct of colonial wars was not subject to the rules of war established by the Hague Convention, as the humanitarian principle of the *ius in bello* applied only to military conflicts conducted between "civilized" nations, a category that excluded Africans and Chinese.[19] This dehumanizing of the enemy and their status as an "invisible other" conditioned the nature of the military response, which unbounded by the recently established precepts of international law was now able to plumb the depths of behavior deemed commensurate to a colonial setting.

Seeking to do justice to the range and impact of this new military experience, the analysis in this book relies on the concept of the *Kriegsschauplatz* theater of war. Although enjoying considerable academic currency, the German term suffers from the paucity of its definition.[20] Another established term is the German *Kriegstheater* (a literal rendering of the English "theater of war" and French *théâtre de la guerre*), which evokes the image of an enclosed site in which an event is provided to the spectators who surround it. Indeed, the customary understanding of the term "theater of war" refers to the setting for a set of actions comparable to the acts of a play and staged within a narrowly defined time and space. In short, two armies march onto the scene; the attack is sounded and the battle conducted to its logical end, leaving a clear outcome and a multitude of dead and wounded.[21] It is this understanding that provides the foundation for the concept underpinning the analysis of this study, which describes the site of battle as a clearly delimitable geographical area in which the warring parties conduct hostile operations. In its function as an analytical term, *Kriegsschauplatz* should be understood differently, specifically as the result of a combination of a number of factors encountered by the warring parties during the course of a conflict. The course of this investigation will reveal the extent to which the term facilitates a better understanding of the development of extreme violence than previous explanations.

The following factors combine to constitute the *Kriegsschauplatz* in the three colonial wars under investigation. The first relates to geophysical conditions, in particular the geography, topography, and climate of an area. The second is cultural geography, that is, the culture of human settlement and population density, infrastructure, and economy. Special attention will be accorded to the regional prevalence of either arable production or animal husbandry. The third factor is indigenous actors as one of the warring parties. With their knowledge and perceptions, social traditions, customs and habits, weapons, experience of war, and strategic and tactical knowledge, indigenous peoples were closely associated with the site of each war.

A fourth factor to be investigated is the predominantly, if not exclusively, foreign actors, represented by the military personnel dispatched to the colonies by the German Empire. Their attitudes and conduct, perceptions, and experiences were shaped by the following factors: (a) their origin and socialization, with considerable differences between officers, noncommissioned officers (NCOs) and enlisted men, sailors and Marine Infantrymen, medical personnel, and possibly also civil servants; (b) their affiliation with a specific operational unit, in particular the branch of the services in which the actors had been trained and to which authority they were subject—their training in terms of a theoretical understanding of warfare, weaponry, and military technology was also imparted within this framework; (c) ideological considerations and self-conceptions such as racism or assumptions of Western superiority, which were also characteristic of this group.

The actions of the colonial soldiers were also shaped by a fifth factor: external requirements. These consisted of the political goals of the campaign, such as punishment, retribution, settlement, or occupation; political expectations of the military timetable and the limits placed on funding for the war, whether based on restricted or unrestricted funds; and the legitimization of colonial wars in the court of public opinion. The fora in which this process was conducted included Parliament, the military and nonmilitary press, and the veterans' associations *(Kriegervereine)*. This category also includes official concerns to uphold a favorable international image through compliance with international conventions and agreements pertaining to the conduct of warfare, as well as pressures exerted by foreign press coverage of each individual war.

In addition to the political, social, mental, and institutional conditions influencing the conduct of a war, its course is also affected by a sixth factor: what Clausewitz called "friction." It is friction that differentiates between military planning and the actual conduct of a war. Even the most well-laid plans cannot anticipate a range of contingent developments such as changes in weather, failure to keep to timetable, or faulty intelligence. These random or even coincidental events can decide the course of a war. The combination of all these conditions determined the patterns of war in each colony and theater. The course assumed by each war, furthermore, was conditioned by the response of the German military to a new set of circumstances experienced in what for them was an entirely new environment. Thus it was the interaction of the German military with local conditions that produced a unique dynamic, not the imposition of a preestablished mindset on a static situation.

Part 1 of the book opens with a general treatment of the three major colonial wars conducted by the German Empire at the beginning of the twentieth century: the Boxer War in China, 1900–1901; the Herero and Nama War in German South-West Africa, 1904–1907; and the Maji Maji War fought in German East Africa, 1905–1906. Beyond a narrative of the significant military engagements themselves, this section also focuses on acts of violence that blur the line between orthodox military strategy and wanton violence, such as plundering and requisition, the impact of epidemics; the issuing of war proclamations, and the establishment of prisoner camps. All three campaigns are then evaluated through an identical analytical prism in order to establish the similarities and differences each conflict exhibits in terms of the aims and conduct of the war and the forms of violence within their scope. Beginning with a brief outline of the causes of the war, the account moves to establish a short overview of the periodization leading through the war and toward the postwar period. This is followed by a detailed account of the course of the war, undertaken in two steps. Analysis of the Boxer War also provides the opportunity to contrast the approach to colonial warfare assumed by the various nations. This raises the question as to whether the conduct and behavior of the German military differed in any respect from those of other intervention powers.

The narrative reconstruction of the events of the three wars establishes the different forms they took and the violence exercised within their scope, but does not explain the genesis. This requires a close analysis of the factors determining the actions of the officers, medical officers, NCOs, other ranks, and native auxiliaries who conducted the German military actions, offered in Part 2 of the book. The concept of the *Kriegsschauplatz* requires us to investigate the individual aspects of the three wars in a systematic and diachronic fashion. Working with seven multiperspective clusters, the investigation proceeds to establish the factors that influenced the course of the war.

The systematic analysis begins with a discussion of the conditions of life in the German Empire, providing the context for the actions of all the white participants in the various colonial wars under scrutiny. Chapter 4 assesses the motivation of white and native colonial soldiers across the various military formations—Protection Force, army volunteers, sailors, Marine Infantry, and native troops—and the reasons that moved them to participate in a colonial war. Chapter 5 investigates the various programs of military training through which colonial soldiers passed as well as the weapons with which they were armed. This chapter continues by establishing the knowledge they had of warfare in general and colonial warfare in particular as well as the degree of their understanding and acceptance of military law. Chapter 6 investigates the conceptions of the enemy and the ideological constructions circulating in the ranks of the German armed forces. Working in this context, the analysis establishes the role played by the long sea passage to the colonial theater during which the soldiers prepared themselves mentally for the impending campaign, thus acquiring an ideologically reinforced confidence in their mission.

After their arrival in China or Africa, the German colonial soldiers were forced to deal with demands placed on them by an alien environment—factors outlined in Chapters 7 and 8. Climate and geography, population, and infrastructure of the colonial regions exercised just as decisive an influence on the course of the war as the military tactics employed and the illnesses suffered by the troops. After establishing the ways in which the German military conceived of colonial rule and the resulting forms assumed by the punitive expeditions, an analysis follows of the way in which enemy tactics and the geography and topography of the various colonial environments influenced the conduct of the colonial wars. In doing so, it is necessary to appreciate not only the immediate impact of the geographical space and cultural geography on military operations but also the way in which these phenomena were perceived and incorporated into a vision of a postconflict colony—a vision that then went on to influence subsequent military plans. In understanding the influence of illness on the performance of the colonial soldiers, it is necessary first to determine the specific character of the diseases presented in the context of colonial wars. Only then is it possible to establish the circumstances under which the incidence of disease and illness acted not only to impair military operations but to change the conduct of a war.

The colonial theater of war was also influenced by national and international discussions of the three wars. This relationship constitutes the focus of Chapter 9, on foreign reactions to the German colonial wars and the German practice of violence. A question of particular interest is whether international military commentators from other colonial powers identified anything approaching a specifically "German" form of violence and if so, the way in which it was reported. The final issue to be addressed involves the reports of the war published in the international military press. Did they subject

German colonial violence to equally weighted comment or did they exhibit specific national patterns of interest? In contrast, Chapter 10, the final chapter of Part 2, turns to the German debates on the wars in the Reichstag and the carefully censored military journalism that played a part in forming the bellicose popular attitude to colonial wars. The focus of this analysis rests on the attempts made by the German government to legitimize the colonial wars and the violence employed in their prosecution. The chapter poses the question as to whether the parties of the various and hostile political camps were able to reach anything approaching a national consensus regarding the wars. A further line of inquiry is the level of partisanship exhibited by the military press and the manner in which it reported the colonial violence—as an inherent character of imperialism or something requiring specific justification.

After subjecting the genesis, practice, and escalation of the violence meted out within the scope of the German colonial wars to analysis based on the concept of *Kriegsschauplatz,* Part 3 examines the impact of the war on the military establishment of the German Empire and its soldiers. The primary focus rests on the way in which the colonial wars were stored in military "memory." To this end, the analysis centers on the discussions of the strictly confidential military commission of investigation and the report it produced. How did the inner circle of military planners conceive of the colonial war of the future? What, if any, lessons were taken as relevant for a war in Europe? This approach is supplemented by an examination of the colonial war associations and Scouting movement founded by former colonial soldiers. Here the focus rests on the ways in which remembrance of the colonial wars was lived out, cultivated, and passed on. The question will be addressed as to the possible existence of a form of memorial culture specific to each war and how and whether the violence exercised in these wars was reckoned with or appropriated. This is followed by a short overview of the lives and professional history of former colonial soldiers in the First World War and the Freikorps. In this way, the investigation broaches the question of the continuity of wartime violence between the three colonial wars and the events of 1914–1918 and 1939–1945.

Part I

THREE WARS

CHAPTER 1

The Boxer War

THE CHARACTER of the military intervention launched to crush the Boxer rebellion in China (1900–1901) was as new as it was unusual. The "old" colonial powers of Great Britain, France, and Russia made common cause with their ambitious arriviste competitors Germany, Italy, Austria-Hungary, the United States, and Japan to form the first multinational intervention force in military history. Despite pursuing contrasting war aims, the powers were united by the common resolve not to invade the Chinese Empire. Instead, military planning focused on a short and geographically limited intervention designed to force China into accepting the "rules of the game" established by the so-called Western, civilized world. Those powers engaged in East Asia viewed the war as a necessary measure to protect their economic interests. The Boxer War, then, was a coalition war fought with German participation.

Origins and Phases

In 1897, Germany established her protectorate at Qingdao, in the northern province of Shandong—and so began her imperialist policy of *Weltpolitik*. Two years later, the same province was to see the birth of the Boxer movement. The name "Boxer" was derived from a grouping inspired by the traditions of a number of pugilist movements; the groups referred to themselves as *yihequan* (The Society of Righteous and Harmonious Fists). They subsequently changed their name to *yihetuan* (The Righteous and Harmonious Militias), and this appellation has been adopted by modern Chinese historiography and a number of Western scholars. The movement was characterized by their practice of callisthenic rituals—believed to bring invulnerability—and flat hierarchies.[1]

Reflecting the almost exclusively agrarian nature of China, the Boxer movement principally recruited its followers from the young peasantry. The northern provinces with their monsoon climate specialized in the cultivation of cereals; famine periods during droughts led to increasing support for the Boxer movement, support for which grew in reaction to a capricious administration and a crippling tax burden. In addition to its peasant foundation, the Boxer movement also drew support and membership from a number of local civil servants, the so-called gentry.

The grievances of the Boxer movement focused primarily on the presence and economic significance of foreign nationals. The German colonization of Qingdao and the subsequent program of railway building served only to increase such resentments.[2] The ultimate source of foreign influence was identified, however, in the cultural sphere, with the Boxers expending considerable vituperation on the system of Jesuit missions which had been established as early as the seventeenth century.[3] Although an earlier historiographical consensus focused on tensions between Christians and non-Christians in explaining the Boxer rebellion, modern scholarship emphasizes the importance of social change and the dissolution of traditional social bonds, a process that the missionary presence only intensified. Any explanation for the Boxer uprising should not be reduced to a "clash of civilizations."[4]

The term "Boxer uprising" presents a number of difficulties. With its connotations of a seditious political movement aimed at overthrowing an existing system of rule, the term "uprising" is perhaps ill-suited to what was essentially a movement hostile to foreign religious and political influences and which alternated between opposition and loyalty to the ruling Qing dynasty. With the formal authority of the colonial powers restricted to their small coastal bases, the war of liberation that the Boxer movement unleashed can be viewed as an uprising only if viewed from the imperialist perspective. Although the Boxers directed their energies against the symbols of imperial rule such as foreign-built railroads, their movement remained an essentially Chinese matter.[5]

In early 1900, the Boxer movement spread from Shandong to the neighboring province of Zhili, in the center of which lay the Chinese capital. Mobilizing considerable support, the Boxers made for Peking and Tianjin, leaving a path of destruction—focusing on churches, houses, and railroads—in their

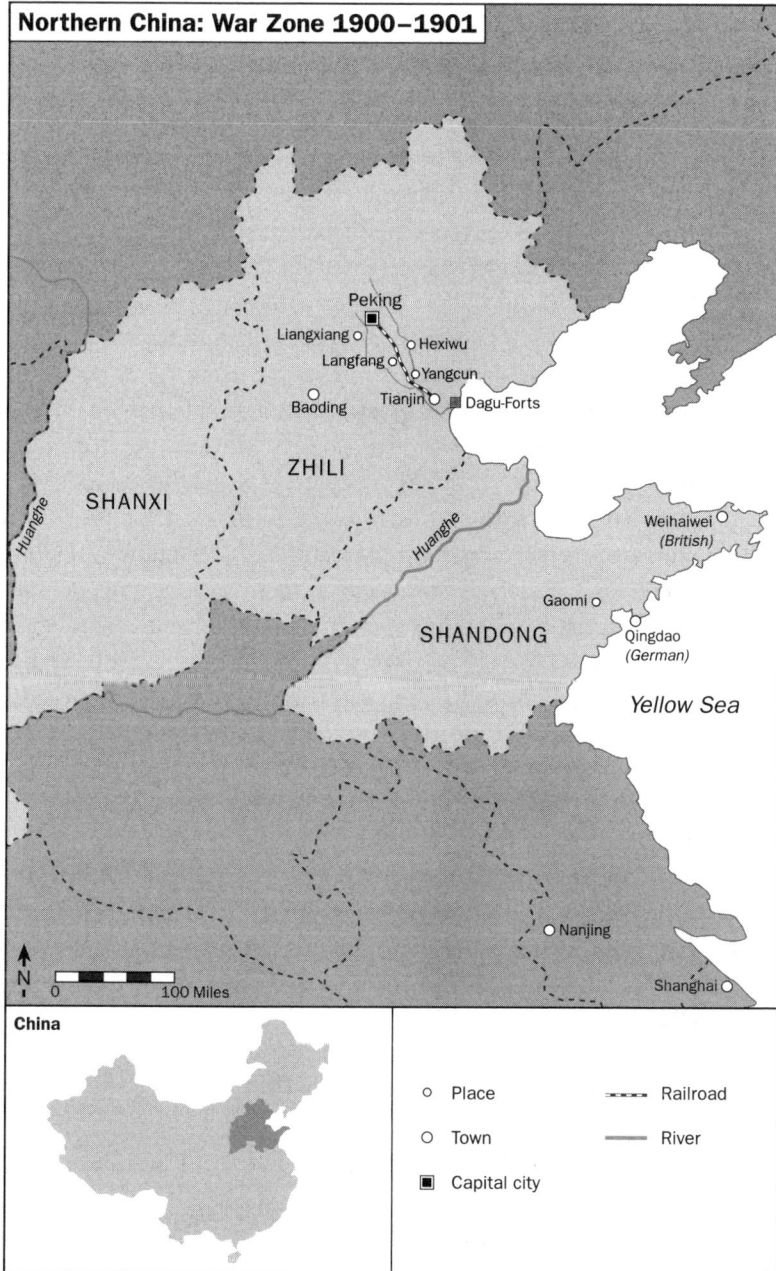

Northern China: War Zone 1900–1901

China

○ Place	▬▬▬ Railroad
○ Town	▬▬ River
■ Capital city	

wake. Those Chinese Christians that they found were robbed and murdered on the way. European and American nationals living in China were unsettled, especially in view of the official Chinese disinclination to take any measures against the unrest. Western observers blamed the Chinese government of the dowager Empress Cixi for its indecisive management of the crisis and amateurish attempts to quell the uprising.

Viewed from the Chinese perspective, however, such inaction was entirely rational, as Western displeasure represented far less a threat than domestic discontent. Tied up with questions of legitimation and the need to balance competing ethnic, regional, factional, and professional interests at court, in the bureaucracy and the Chinese military establishment, the threat to royal power from internal unrest was far greater than international pressure. The limited and primarily defensive official response to the uprising (culminating in the eventual flight of the Chinese government) was designed more to appease international pressure than as a serious effort to put down the insurrection. This situation was compounded by western misunderstanding of Chinese cultural conventions. The delay, evasion, obfuscation, prevarication, deception, and flight, characteristic of a traditional Chinese response to conflict situations, were interpreted merely as an unwillingness to confront the Boxer movement. Moreover, Chinese inaction was partially the result of divisions at court regarding both the ultimate goal of policy and the most expedient means of its realization. Many senior policy makers even advocated cooperation with the Boxers in order to take advantage of the situation and expel the foreign powers and their nationals from the country.[6]

Not only did the majority of the rural population provide at least passive support for the Boxers, the movement even split the local authorities, raising the specter of civil war in a number of provinces. The Chinese units sent to engage the Boxers were not of the first order and often either accepted their defeat or joined the ranks of the Boxer movement. Made up of a number of separately organized Manchurian and Chinese formations, the army serving the Manchurian Qing dynasty was supplemented after 1890 by what was known as the "New Army," equipped with modern weaponry and having enjoyed Western training. In 1900, 68,000 of its number were stationed in the insurgent province of Zhili. The international coalition force eventually dispatched to the region was thus (at least initially) faced by a larger and entirely modern opponent.[7]

The conflict came to a head in April and May 1900 as the Boxer force attacked a group of foreign railway engineers in Baoding, destroying the railway embankment and telegraph lines in the process. The dangerous proximity of the insurgents to the Chinese capital and the alarming news of their violent actions mobilized the Western Powers into what emerged as the first phase of confrontation with the Chinese government. Characterized by threats and sabre rattling, this phase, beginning in April 1900, saw an international naval force of significant size converge in international waters off the coast by the Dagu forts, the fortified maritime entry point to inland China. This move was followed in May by the reinforcement of the legation troops in Peking by a number of contingents, drawn from various nations. The German mission was reinforced with an additional fifty members of the III Sea Battalion (Marine Infantry) stationed at Qingdao.[8]

The second phase of the intervention began on 17 June 1900 with the shelling of the Dagu forts. Despite these bellicose actions, there was no official declaration of war from the Western Powers, as such a step would have provoked the whole of China into entering a conflict that the Great Powers hoped could be restricted to its northern provinces. Indeed, the *Times* believed in the possibility of conducting "military operations" against mixed groups of Boxers and Chinese soldiers without provoking (or indeed requiring) a declaration of war and the associated financial consequences involving increased pay and pensions claims. Contemporary opinion was clear in its assessment that a state of war, as defined by international law, did not exist between China and the Great Powers.[9] Despite such legal gymnastics, the soldierly mindset viewed the action as a war. Even Alfred Graf von Waldersee (subsequently commander in chief of the allied intervention force) wrote in his diary of the "diplomatic fiction" that the campaign did not amount to a war with China.[10]

Not all of the allied forces engaged in the intervention participated in the assault on the Dagu forts. Arguing that until the morning of 17 June 1900, the Chinese government had not committed any acts of aggression toward the multinational force assembled off its coast, Rear Admiral Louis Kempff, commander of the American flagship *Newark*, held his forces back from the assault. Fearing that an allied attack would endanger the lives of American citizens in inland China, he viewed what he saw as precipitate and aggressive action as counterproductive.[11] Whereas naval personnel from the German ship *Iltis* participated in the storming of the Dagu forts, the American contingent restricted itself to rescuing women and children from merchant ships in the immediate vicinity of the battle zone.[12]

In northern China, the storming of the Dagu forts was followed by an escalation of the situation on three fronts. In Tianjin (population 700,000), fierce fighting in the international settlement between 17 and 23 June was only brought to a final end in mid-July following its relief by a mixed force of German, Russian, and British troops. With 1,800 Russian and 400 British troops involved in the relief of Peking, the German contribution of 190 Marine Infantrymen was comparatively modest.[13] The preponderance of Russian and Japanese forces in the early phase of the war can be explained by their geographical proximity to China and the corresponding speed with which they were able to dispatch a large body of troops. Great Britain was able to establish a presence of similar significance in an equally short time by dispatching troops from their garrisons (predominantly in India), while the American force was deployed in June 1900 from the Philippines.[14]

The international force dispatched to Tianjin was highly heterogeneous, in terms of not only its military composition but also the ethnic backgrounds of its constituent troops. Consisting mainly of units of the Indian army, the British contingent also included a number of troops from the Chinese-manned Weihaiwei Regiment. They were joined later by the Zouaves and *chasseurs d'Afrique* of the French army. It was not just the presence of Japanese forces that indicates the impossibility of delimiting this war along racial lines of "white" versus "yellow" or "colored" and thus precludes any interpretation of the Boxer War as a clash of civilizations.[15]

The conquest of Tianjin was followed by extensive looting. With each of the Western Powers blaming its allies for the unrest, many Chinese also took the opportunity to abscond with large quantities of silk and works of art. The widespread thieving focused on not only private property but also Chinese state and imperial possessions. In particular, the American troops purloined a number of silver bars from the safe of the Tianjin state treasury. The silver was deposited in the (British-owned) Hong Kong Bank, and it is unclear whether this represents a further act of theft or an attempt to protect it from loss.[16]

The second area of conflict centered on Peking. The murder of the German ambassador Clemens Freiherr von Ketteler on 19 June 1900 (three days after the storming of the Dagu forts) was committed not by a Boxer, but by a Chinese imperial soldier. The exact reasons for the murder of the German ambassador remain unclear. His unpopularity probably rested on his reputation as a supporter of the division of China and his provocative behavior toward the Boxers.[17] Whoever held ultimate responsibility for ordering the murder, the act was followed two days later by an official Chinese declaration of war on the imperial powers. Having altered its stance to one of support for the Boxers, the government launched the now-legendary siege of the diplomatic quarter in the Chinese capital lasting until 14 August 1900. After destroying the telegraph lines to Tianjin, Chinese forces managed to isolate and encircle the area around the foreign embassies for a full fifty-five days. Coming under daily fire from both Boxers and imperial soldiers, the legation quarter provided refuge not only to allied diplomats and their families, but to thousands of Chinese Christians seeking the protection of ramshackle barricades made of household furniture, brocade draperies, and sandbags. Sustaining casualties— of 450 soldiers from eight nations, sixty-five, including twelve Germans, were killed and 156, including fifteen Germans, were wounded—and an alarming supply situation, the garrison waited for relief.

The area of operations of the expedition force sent to relieve the besieged diplomats represents the third area of conflict in the Boxer War. A force of 2,117 allied soldiers under the command of the British admiral Edward Seymour left Tianjin for Peking on 10 June 1900. Although Seymour's force registered victory in a number of minor engagements, its progress was slowed by stiff resistance from a numerically superior opponent and the destruction of the railway line between Peking and Tianjin. Succeeding only in reaching Langfang, Seymour was forced to abandon the advance on 18–19 June. Indeed, threatened with the breakup of his force, Seymour opted to retreat to Tianjin. The official German account of this abortive advance established a myth surrounding Admiral Seymour's order that the German contingent adopt a position at the head of the advance. This account interpreted the order "The Germans to the front" as an appreciation of superior German military prowess. In a speech given on 27 July 1900, Kaiser Wilhelm II informed his listening troops, "It is a source of no little pride to hear the highest possible praise from the foreign General [Seymour] to our troops."[18] A much less flattering interpretation portrays this order as an attempt to redress a situation in which the Germans spent most of the time bringing up the rear.

Only a second joint expedition by a mixed force of British, Russian, American, and Japanese troops was able to end the fifty-five-day siege of Peking, liberating the legation quarter on 13 August 1900. The German Marine Infantry stationed in Qingdao shared the ignominy with their French and Italian counterparts of arriving too late to contribute to the action. Arriving in Dagu on 15 August, the soldiers of the I and II Sea Battalions dispatched from Germany were also unable to realize their hopes of contrib-uting to the relief of Peking. Reaching the Chinese capital on 23 August, approximately a week after the siege had been broken, they found the city to be under the control of the British, Americans, Russians, and Japanese. Although a German zone of control was later established, it remained clear that German forces did not make a decisive contribution to the outcome of the war.

Surprisingly, the second allied expedition to Peking met with no resis-tance, from either Boxer or imperial Chinese forces. This was the result of the ill-coordinated conduct of the war on the part of the Chinese military and political elite, which remained divided as to aims of the war, and the expedience of conducting hostilities against such a large and powerful co-alition. Their inability to reach a consensus on these questions resulted in considerable variations in policy. Indeed, only after their liberation did those barricaded in the diplomatic quarter realize the extent of their peril: had the Chinese forces organized a concerted attack, it is unlikely that they would have survived. Chinese military performance was hampered by poor coop-eration between the Boxers and imperial Chinese forces, who often turned on each other after defeats.[19]

The entrance of the allied troops into Peking was followed by an orgy of plunder and rape. A number of Chinese women and even whole families com-mitted suicide rather than fall into the hands of foreign troops, who razed entire quarters. Eyewitnesses reported a cloud of soot and smoke hanging over the city days after the ceasefire, later to be replaced by a pervasive smell from the rotting corpses that littered the diplomatic quarter long after its liberation. As an American officer commented, "The feeling toward the Chinese was, of course, exceedingly bitter."[20]

The capture of Peking altered the political and military situation funda-mentally. The Boxers were made responsible for the military catastrophe by Dowager Cixi and the imperial court (which had flown to the regional capital of Shaanxi), and an edict issued on 7 September 1900 declared the Boxers to be enemies of the Chinese state. The regional governors were now instructed to proceed against them. With the exception of a few minor skir-mishes, the imperial army ceased all hostilities with the Western troops. The allied intervention force had won the war. The third phase of the Boxer War, lasting from the end of August 1900 to mid-1901, was characterized by the establishment of a zone of occupation between the northern Chinese cities of Peking, Tianjin, and Baoding. Arriving in Dagu at the end of September 1900, the German field marshal Graf von Waldersee assumed supreme command of the international force; both he and Berlin hoped that this office would bring a great deal of international prestige. Composed of volunteers drawn from the German army, the German East Asian Expedition Corps reached the northern Chinese harbors in a number of transports. Numbering some 22,000 men, the German contingent represented the largest single contribution to the international undertaking, followed by the British and French with around 17,000 men, respectively; 16,000 Japanese; and 16,000 Russians.[21] The relative size of the German contingent increased even further following the reduction by the other nations of their troop presence. With the gradual end of the hostilities, the United States began withdrawing troops on October 1900; the Japanese, British, Russians, and Italians followed suit at the end of December. The considerably smaller Austro-Hungarian contingent was deployed for the last time on 29 January 1901.

Although nominally able to draw on a force of some 90,000 allied soldiers, von Waldersee was not granted unrestricted authority over the Japanese and Russian contingents, while the United States and France rejected his command altogether.[22] His position was made even more difficult by the nature of his task, involving, as it did, conduct of a war that had largely been concluded. Seeking an activity, he organized a number of punitive expeditions to find and punish Boxers. Not conspicuous in the early stages of the war, the German forces soon became very active in its third and final phases. They even opened up a new front in the German protectorate of Qingdao, where the Marine Infantry stationed in the area was dispatched to suppress resistance in a number of insurgent villages to the construction of a railroad in Shandong. On 15 October 1900, over 200 sailors and Marine Infantrymen advanced on the town of Gaomi and a number of other villages. Nevertheless, this new front was never more than a sideshow.[23]

The proliferation of small and large engagements launched within the course of the war and within the scope of the subsequent punitive expeditions prevents reliable estimates of the total number of Chinese dead. Conservative estimates place the number of dead in Peking alone at more than 100,000.[24] The level of suffering of the population of northern China was so high that the Chinese representative to the interventionist powers, Li Hongzhang, raised the matter in his meetings with the allied representatives in November 1900. His entreaties fell on deaf ears.[25]

Negotiations between the interventionist powers and Chinese representatives regarding the end of the conflict began in late October. Concluded just under a year later on 7 September 1901, the negotiations were brought to an end with the signing of the so-called Boxer Protocol. This was accompanied by the publication by the Great Powers of a note accusing China of crimes against international law, humanity, and civilization.[26] Following this analysis, the Boxer Protocol imposed a catalogue of sanctions of both a preventative and symbolic nature. The range of penalties and proscriptions that it imposed did not mark an end of the occupation of northern China but rather extended it to cover the treaty ports, the Yellow Sea, and the Yangzi, all of which were placed under the control of the East Asian Brigade of Occupation.

Chinese Towns under German Administration

Captured by an international military force, Tianjin and Peking and their hinterlands were divided into a number of zones of occupation, the command of which was distributed among the interventionist powers. These zones were sometimes guarded, but often just demarcated with a flag or pennant in the various national colors of the occupying nations. The reproduction of this practice in the various district towns and villages throughout the area of occupation transformed northern China into a rich vexilogical tapestry leaving no doubt as to the presence and pattern of foreign authority.[27]

Both Tianjin and Peking, cities of more than a million people before the war, had been almost entirely destroyed by the end of summer 1900, and some quarters had been entirely depopulated. Those residents remaining were subject to continuing incidents of assault and plunder, the fruits of which were often put to auction. Everything imperial China had to offer was now available in large quantities: porcelain, cloisonné, bronzes, red lacquered objects, furs, silks, embroideries, watches, pearls, gemstones, and other valuables. One excuse for the plundering was the claim that the acts of plunder committed by the Boxers had set an example for the troops of the Great Powers. The German Army High Command sought to portray the actions as an attempt to protect the works of art from destruction and theft.[28]

Following the end of hostilities, the occupying forces introduced a number of measures to win the trust of the local population and reassure residents that they could return safely to their homes. The Japanese practice of providing protection to the civilian population meant that shops and businesses reopened in the Japanese sector as early as the end of August. This was emulated in the British and American sectors soon afterward. The streets of Peking and Tianjin soon returned to their usual level of bustle, in which a number of (unarmed) soldiers spent their off-duty time. The long duration of the occupation developed into what some described as approaching "garrison life."[29]

Allied troops occupied Baoding, the provincial capital of Zhili, in the fall of 1900.[30] With its good strategic position, the city served the allies as a military base and victualing station from which to secure the border to the northwest province of Shaanxi. Baoding was divided among Great Britain, France, Germany, and Italy; each power received its own city gate. Awaiting the judgment of an international inquiry (made up of a military officer from each national contingent and a British diplomat) convened to investigate the murder of missionaries, the British and Italians withdrew from Baoding in October 1900, leaving it under joint German-French administration.[31] The northern half of the city was placed under German administration, the southern half under French authority. Neither the northern Chinese zone of occupation as a whole nor the three large cities Peking, Tianjin, and Baoding were provided with anything approaching a unified system of administration, although the regulations published by the powers for their respective zone of occupation did exhibit a certain degree of similarity. The Chinese authorities in Baoding were placed under the supervision of a military commission that vetted each and every one of its decisions. Similarly, the provisional government of Tianjin was subject to supervision by a military commission, the composition of which (a Russian, British, and Japanese officer) reflected the makeup of the intervention force.[32] Peking, on the other hand, was placed under the direct administration of the military and diplomatic representatives of the occupying powers.

Surveying this multiplicity of jurisdictions, one of the first acts of the recently arrived field marshal von Waldersee was an attempt to install a single unitary administration for Peking, which in his view the "conventions of war of all nations" required.[33] Moreover, he demanded that this administration be placed under military control. Assembling a military committee to this end (which was later to include a representative of the Chinese municipal authorities), his quest for complete administrative unity was scuppered by French refusal to submit to the joint administration. As a result, the joint proclamations regulating Chinese behavior were not enforced in the French sector of occupation or section of the diplomatic quarter under French control.[34]

Meeting for the first time on 10 December 1900, the "Committee for the Administration of Peking" passed a number of measures and rules governing the behavior of the Chinese population, the socially controlling nature of which far exceeded its initial aims of establishing order. Instructed to hand over any remaining weapons to their nearest police station, the civil population was also to report any crimes or incidences of blackmail, theft, violence, denunciation or false testimony.[35] A further catalogue of proscriptions regulated all other aspects of public life. Thus it was forbidden to set off any fireworks without prior police permission, as was the running or frequenting of opium dens and casinos. Infringements of these provisions were subject to a catalogue of punishments. Individual freedom of movement was restricted by the closure of the city gates between six P.M. and five A.M. No Chinese were permitted to walk the streets after eight P.M. without a lantern and without a good reason, which they were to state upon closer questioning. Any gathering of more than three Chinese in a public place was forbidden and infringement of this provision could be punished with any sentence up to and including death. "Those Chinese found breaking the law have only themselves to blame if they are subsequently forced into submission or even killed."[36] These provisions were clearly based on the so-called Chinese Order promulgated in the German protectorate of Qingdao on 14 June 1900. Indeed, these highly provocative formulations had themselves contributed to the spread of the Boxer movement in the first place.[37]

This plethora of prohibitions and regulations necessitated a comprehensive organization of the justice and police systems during the constitutive sitting of the public committee. It was arranged that crimes involving allied soldiers and Chinese civilians would be heard by a military court, while crimes involving only Chinese citizens came under the jurisdiction of a special court. Fears of restrictions to national sovereignty moved the occupying powers to block the institution of an international court. As a result, in the German section of Peking—for which Major General Lothar von Trotha was responsible—the court hearing purely Chinese crimes was composed entirely of German soldiers. "Adapting to the Chinese understanding of law," the German military authorities deemed it expedient to "make relatively wide use of capital punishment."[38] Requiring a judge to hear such cases, the German authorities sent for the German judge advocate general, who was rushed over from Qingdao. In their sector, the Americans set up a Chinese criminal court to dispense Chinese law. All death sentences were to be confirmed by the general commanding, who was also responsible for all judicial appointments.[39]

Working closely with the allied-controlled committee, the sectors of occupation were divided into a number of police districts in which the allied military and Chinese auxiliary police kept order. Both wore a distinctive white band on their left upper arm, indicating their function in a number of languages. Seeking to avoid conflict between the Chinese auxiliaries and allied troops, the former were not permitted to arrest allied soldiers, but were to report any untoward activities involving soldiers to an allied officer, who would arrange for action to be taken.[40]

Following the establishment of a functioning criminal justice and police system, the most pressing concern of the committee was the organization of health care provision. The storming of Peking had generated a large number of corpses and the need to recover and bury them was acute. A standing military conference agreed on a number of measures to improve sanitary conditions in the Chinese capital including street cleaning, the emptying of latrines, and improvements to water pipes. The speed with which the first brothels reopened (in November 1900) moved the military authorities to issue orders for the registration and medical control of all prostitutes.[41] The committee also addressed a number of questions involving traffic and tax collection. Those Chinese seeking to move from one section to the next now required a multilingual passport. The military authorities then conducted negotiations with the Chinese communal administrators (soon seconded as civilian members of the committee) regarding tax revenues and the municipal budget.[42] Measures to deal with the impending winter were also drawn up; the distribution of rice, fuel, and food for the needy and the establishment of a network of shops constituted the most immediate concerns.

The Chinese experience of the allied occupation involved not just daily restrictions and controls, but repeated humiliation and debasement. In contrast, the regime established in some sections of Peking permitted a relatively free life; so grateful were the residents of the American sector that they sent a deputation to the American commanding officer, Major General Adna R. Chaffee, to thank him for the protection that his administration afforded. They also criticized the conduct of the other allies: "He dwelt on the contrast between Americans and European soldiers, saying that America appeared to the Chinese as a sort of heaven; that the Americans did not come here to seize territory, but to protect all the people, and that the Chinese were proud to be under the shelter of the American flag. He also remarked that if the civilized nations were to be judged by what had been seen here of the acts of European soldiers, then the Chinese must prefer to remain barbarians."[43]

Punitive Expeditions

A further aspect of the military occupation of northern China was the concern of the allies to pacify the rural areas not subject to a constant military presence. The instrument chosen to achieve this was the punitive expedition. Implemented immediately after the liberation of the diplomatic quarter in Peking, this policy was developed with the aim of eliminating the last hotbeds of Boxer resistance. While waiting for the arrival of von Waldersee, a number of operations were conducted in September in the areas to the southwest of Tianjin and the north and south of Peking. Many of these expeditions were performed as joint undertakings involving a number of the international contingents. Sometimes marching together, a number of opportunities were taken to place some of the units under a foreign command. These undertakings were characterized by a high level of solidarity between the soldiers of various nationalities who cooperated to overcome food shortages. An Anglo-American expedition conducted in September 1900 saw the storming of a hill conducted as a sporting contest between the British-officered Sikh troops and the (eventually victorious) Americans.[44]

According to records of the Army Supreme Command, December 1900 and May 1901 saw fifty-three expeditions, thirty-five of which were performed by German troops working alone. One was conducted as a joint Franco-German undertaking.[45] As the British colonel James Grierson remarked, the conduct of the war in northern China was dominated by German forces: "The entire conduct of the war is, and this, I cannot think was ever intended, exclusively in German hands."[46] He complained bitterly and at length that the Expedition Command consisted entirely of German officers, who degraded the officers of other nations to mere recipients of their orders. A further criticism was leveled at the Germans by the Japanese and Italian forces, who found the German information policy as insufficient for their purpose. The Chinese civilian population also suffered greatly under what it regarded predominantly as "German violence," the punitive expeditions conducted in the main by German forces, to whom they referred as "brutal" "cruel," and "criminal" in their methods.[47]

Shortly after his arrival in China in September 1900, von Waldersee defined the aims of the punitive expeditions as the subjugation of the Chinese imperial court. Should the Chinese government not accept and fulfill the allied demands, the military pressure would be increased without delay. He listed his specific aims as the removal of Chinese forces from the province of Zhili; pacification of the insurgent areas; the protection of the peaceful populace, Christian missionaries, and Chinese Christians; and the punishment and ruthless pursuit of the "Boxers and robbers."[48]

Many German officers were highly dissatisfied with the restriction of their mission to the province of Zhili: "Had we been permitted to take a closer look around in the neighboring province, we could have achieved in a number of weeks what negotiations were unable achieve in months."[49] As von Waldersee's command over the allied troops was no more than nominal, he was forced to cooperate with the commanders of the other allied contingents in order to organize larger punitive expeditions. According to Grierson, von Waldersee sought to avoid any action that would "arouse in the minds of the Chinese people the belief that there is discord among the Powers, and that our views on the situation are not harmonious."[50] The numerous small expeditions that the Germans organized were conducted in retaliation to attacks by Chinese snipers on German units or the ambush of individual soldiers. The German officer Arnold von Lequis noted in his diary that reprisals were taken against a number of villages in retaliation for attacks on the pioneer corps.[51] Indeed, when conducting operations in proximity to villages classified as "hostile," individual commanders were permitted to decide on the scope and course of action that they followed so that "Boxer nests" could be "smoked out" at any time.[52] This level of independence served merely as a license for officers and NCOs to decide the extent to which their men were permitted to plunder, destroy, and kill. As far as the surviving evidence shows, none of the commanders of the individual contingents issued any orders for such willful destruction or execution, restricting themselves to issuing battle orders. As one war reporter put it, "the high spirits and influence of the NCOs was more decisive than the plan of attack."[53] Many of the actions undertaken by the German troops in northern China were thus the result of neither central military planning in Peking nor political guidelines from Berlin.

The punitive expeditions followed a similar pattern. After collecting intelligence concerning the whereabouts of Boxers responsible for the deaths of missionaries, or regarding villages harboring members of the resistance, a plan of action was drawn up. Much of this information came from locals or foreign missionaries, some of whom the allied commanders regarded with no little suspicion. Indeed, many locals tried to exploit the allied military presence for their own ends. Many Chinese, often Christian, denounced their neighbors as "Boxers" to gain an advantage in preexisting

local conflicts. The suppliers of such unreliable information often then offered their services as scouts and sometimes even as combatants. Despite
being aware of these machinations, allied commanders valued the wide and
impenetrable local network to which the Chinese had access, and as a result, they viewed this form of collaboration with them as indispensable.[54]

After receiving reliable (or at least credible) intelligence regarding the
location of Boxers, the allied commanders advanced against the villages or
towns implicated by their informants. The usual procedure was to interro-
gate the most senior officials or local notables as to the local whereabouts of
the former Boxers, usually exercising some form of pressure in the process.
The soldiers conducting such operations had a very clear if rudimentary
conception of Chinese society: "In such cases, we make use of the Chinese
principle of responsibility, not only of the official for his district, but his
local area, of the family for its members, neighbors for each-other and the
landowner for the crimes committed on his land, for which he is also liable
with his life and property. If exploited without scruple, such an approach
can only have sweeping success."[55] If this approach yielded any information,
"ideal" procedure dictated that suspects were either executed following a
drumhead court marital or handed over to local officials. Many suspected
Boxers were simply shot out of hand.

The chief problem experienced during the expeditions was the difficulty
of identifying Boxers. After removing their characteristic symbols—a red
headband and banner—they were entirely indistinguishable from the rest of
Chinese society. Reacting to this situation, allied commanders developed a
particular approach to identifying a Boxer: "suspects should be forced to . . .
undress to the waist. If their right shoulder is bruised or reveals a pressure
mark, we can be sure that this man has carried a gun as a 'Boxer' and deserves
to die."[56] The line between the peaceful population and the violent Boxer
movement was fluid and membership of the latter was often a matter of
short-term personal expedience.

Despite the absence of a popular guerilla insurgency directed against the
allied forces, the allied soldiers persisted in their considerable fear of harmless peasants. Growing levels of insecurity and nervousness were reflected in
the order issued to German troops that "every Chinese" found to be carrying
a weapon or an object resembling a weapon was to be "regarded as an enemy"
and "shot on sight."[57] That such an approach could tempt the soldiers into rash
and counterproductive action was demonstrated in December 1900. After
passing through Yongqing, a town that had previously been pacified by the

British, the German forces disarmed the Chinese police, released six Boxers, plundered the locality, and extorted a fine of 7,000 taels, on top of the fine previously levied by the British.[58] Grierson, the British representative to the Supreme Command, tried to persuade von Waldersee that not every Chinese found with a weapon in hand should be shot. The province of Zhili would collapse into anarchy, he argued, if the local mandarins were shorn of support from the local police. Moreover, flighty and light-fingered international troops were not going to enforce order.[59]

Finds of weapons or Boxer banners in a village sufficed as conclusive proof of the guilt of the entire village. The punishment notice, requiring a list of items—foodstuffs, means of transport, ponies—to be surrendered and/or fines to be paid by a specific deadline, was handed to the local notables. Seeking to speed up the transaction, the expedition force would often take a number of the local mandarins as hostage, to be released upon payment of a ransom. It was common practice to plunder both the pawn office and private residences, taking rice, flour, fruit, money, private possessions, weapons, and ammunition. If its demands were not met, the expedition force would burn down the entire village.[60]

Faced with a poor supply system and forced to live off the land, the allied troops planned and executed a program of systematic requisitions, the extent of which followed from the amount of rations provided. The British troops on the Baoding expedition conducted in the fall of 1900 carried with them rations for three weeks. The German, Italian, and French soldiers, on the other hand, were forced to live (at least partially) from the land, and did not pay for what they took.[61]

Indeed, expeditions were often conducted in order to requisition warmer clothing and furs, horses, and mules—undertakings that easily descended into orgies of plundering.[62] Especially endangered were those villages located en route to a further destination and through which a number of different units would pass at regular intervals. The vanguard was followed by the main body of troops, with the medical column bringing up the rear. Even this last body of soldiery was anything but harmless, and there is at least one recorded case of a medical unit requisitioning all the linen it could find, to be employed as bandages. On one occasion, even a large fishing net consecrated to the local divinity was removed from a temple. Folded together, it was put to use as a hammock. As Eugen Wolffhügel, medical officer of the Fourth East Asian Infantry Regiment, noted, "everything that could be put to some use, and was not difficult to transport, was taken during the advance."[63] Villagers were also subject to recruitment for forced labor, primarily to clear paths and maintain water courses. The least of the impositions made on the villagers was the requirement to brew tea for the officers.[64]

Von Waldersee issued explicit orders forbidding the columns returning from Baoding from engaging in any measure of violence against peaceful Chinese (including requisitioning supplies) in the areas along the military communication lines, as these areas were of vital importance for the supply of the allied forces. The spirit of this order stands in complete contradiction to the euphemistic reports from commanders and soldiers to the effect that punitive expeditions represented merely the planned and targeted attack on "Boxer nests." Waldersee's order also implicitly contradicts statements to the effect that the overwhelming mass of the population should be won over by a friendly approach.[65]

In extreme cases, punitive expeditions could quickly assume the character of a massacre if the local commander suspected a settlement of offering resistance or harboring Boxers. After observing an act of resistance on the town of Liangxiang (population 3,000–4,000) thirty kilometers southwest of Peking, a patrol of German officers summoned two sea battalions under the command of General von Hoepfner. Arriving together with a platoon of Bengal Lancers, sappers, and a Maxim gun, the force numbered 1,700.[66] Assuming a position north of Liangxiang, the Bengal Lancers combined with the German dispatch riders to reconnoiter the area and secure the flanks.[67] The capture of the Pagoda Mountain (the focus of the resistance outside the town) provided the allied commander with a good vantage point for his artillery, a move that forced the Chinese defenders to abandon the eastern half of the town. Their retreat was intercepted by the cavalry. Paul von Hoepfner's troops entered the town from three sides, blocking the south gate and cutting off the only retreat for the fleeing Chinese who were penned in by the high walls of the town. Although the situation had never threatened to get out of control or posed any significant threat to the German force, the decision was taken to kill all the fit Chinese of military age (including the unarmed) with the exception of women and children.[68] A number of sources even point to a number of death sentences passed by drumhead courts martial convened following the end of hostilities.[69] The town was burned down to its foundations. It is unclear how many of the inhabitants of Liangxiang died: estimates point to a quarter. The entry for this day in the War Diary of the I Sea Battalion gives the impression of an entirely normal September day.[70]

After a town had been surrounded and stormed by international forces, even defenseless and surrendering Chinese were killed.[71] Witnessing a similar action, a U.S. officer described a different type of behavior, underlining its unusual nature: "There was no longer fight in these men. They were evidently seeking cover and safety, as they permitted the Ninth United States Infantry, upon whose flank they were, and not more than 250 or 300 yards distant at that, to pass them unchallenged by even a single shot. I was proceeding against them with the two companies, under my command when arrested in my movements by the general commanding, who stated that, in his opinion, any further movements against these men would be inhumane, in which opinion I coincide. Still, the American troops are the only troops now operating in China at this particular juncture that would have spared the lives of these men, and I trust they will prove themselves deserving of the clemency shown to them."[72]

The burning down of settlements and the requisition of the harvest in the later summer destroyed entirely the resources available to the population of northern China and resulted in serious levels of homelessness and displacement. The province of Zhili suffered a famine in the winter of 1900–1901. The general situation was exacerbated by the proliferation of gangs, the formation of which was made possible by the breakdown of local authority following the disarming (even killing) of its agents in the course of the allied expeditions. Formed of Chinese soldiers, former Boxers, and peasants, they roamed the vicinity, killing and plundering.[73] Allied deserters formed their own gangs.

Not all the occupying powers shared the German enthusiasm for punitive expeditions. Believing that the Chinese opposition had indeed collapsed, many British and American officers estimated that the individual pockets of Boxers and Chinese imperial troops spread throughout the province did not constitute any real threat.[74] In the view of the British colonel Grierson, many of these expeditions were both superfluous and damaging, as they hampered efforts at reconstruction. "There appears to be no necessity for this expedition, as the country there is perfectly quiet, and it can only seem to disquiet and disturb the population."[75] Nevertheless, British objections to the poor treatment meted out to the Chinese population by the German military were grounded less in humanitarian considerations than in a belief in its counterproductive nature. Such actions hindered the allied troops in their attempts to recruit Chinese auxiliaries, leading to transport problems and a generally high level of insecurity. The main objection raised by the British military leadership was the German tendency to attack villages under British protection.[76]

The American commander, Chaffee, was also of the opinion that the damage done by the allied occupation of northern China could best be remedied by diplomatic means, but only if no further military operations were undertaken. He explicitly forbade American soldiers to set fire to villages and towns. No villages were razed by expeditions with an American presence.[77]

Condemning the conduct of the German expeditions, the American military authorities opened a number of investigations into the manner of their prosecution. The conditions under which the investigations had to be conducted were difficult in the extreme. Not permitted to question the officers of other contingents, or call into question their motives or competence, the investigators had to reconstruct the events by other means. In one such investigation, into the actions of allied troops against an unfortified Chinese village close to Yangcun (itself close to an American camp), a crucial role was played by the interpreter attached to a British unit, whom the Americans persuaded to document his conversations with villagers.

According to these reports, following the plundering of their village by Italian soldiers on 26 October 1900, the settlement was then visited by another and even more excessive attack, probably by a German unit. Taking chickens, mules, donkeys, and whatever household equipment they could find, they fired on villagers who dared to question the legality of their undertakings. Two days later, the village was searched by a troop of Sikhs, followed by an international unit of Germans, French, Italians, and British soldiers, who plundered the village for a third time, also raping a number of women. Unable to find any weapons in the (unfortified) village, the American investigators concluded that it was highly unlikely that the villagers— themselves highly cowed and living in close proximity to an allied military base—had provoked the attacks. In view of the fact that the villagers had long supplied the adjacent camp with foodstuffs at a reasonable price, the Americans rejected the pretext provided by the offending troops, that Chinese profiteering had necessitated the requisitions.[78]

The different approaches to the punitive expeditions adopted by the various allied contingents resulted mainly from political considerations. Accorded extensive discretion in the execution of their orders, the German military was neither given specific instructions nor required to submit any reports regarding its actions. In contrast, acting in the fall of 1900, the Foreign Office instructed the British commander Major General Alfred Gaselee not to participate in any expeditions or perform any operations of any scope without informing Her Majesty's Government. Placing far greater importance on stabilizing the situation in the Yangzi area, the British government managed to rein in its commanders and enforce its primacy in policy making.[79] This does not mean that the British forces in northern China refrained from violence. Following the stagnation of the peace negotiations, Britain provided von Waldersee with encouragement and support in his plans formulated in February 1901, to apply pressure to the recalcitrant Chinese through military operations. Gaselee considered "a somewhat ostentatious mobilization of a large force." He made express reference to the fact that the British forces had not been forbidden to conduct punitive expeditions.[80]

Tensions also existed between the different allied garrisons of the various Chinese towns, which often translated into serious conflicts. November 1900 saw a concentration of incidents involving German troops; the British commander of the town Hexiwu complained to von Waldersee of the poor behavior of members of the German artillery units stationed close to his protectorate, who had committed a number of acts of plunder, causing much damage in the process. German soldiers had exhibited similar indiscipline in Lugouqiao (Marco-Polo Bridge) in the British section of Peking on 14 November, where they threatened and then stole from the locals. Reacting to such complaints, von Waldersee summoned all the German officers to a meeting, where he spoke of such matters in "very grave" terms.[81] In his diary, he referred to German discipline as fundamentally good, adding, however, that it had been corrupted by the influence of other contingents. "They have seen far too much ruthless and coarse behavior, theft, executions etc. and have mixed with far too many bad elements from the other contingents."[82]

Maintaining discipline represented the most serious of problems facing the commanders of the international contingents. Indeed, many generals complained of the deleterious effect of the circumstances on the discipline. Waldersee saw that the nature of the accommodation arrangements prevented close supervision of the ranks, and that the food was too rich when matched by a lack of activity.[83] One of Waldersee's first orders required the commanders of the allied contingents to punish indiscipline among their own ranks with the same rigor as they pursued the Chinese "robbers and Boxers."[84] Quartering the (underemployed) soldiery of various nations in close proximity to each other was not without long-term risk. Waldersee feared that the unity of purpose, which had so far bound the intervention force together, could begin to fissure and break.[85] Only the Chinese stood to profit from such behavior. In his view, the greatest danger was posed by inactivity, especially for the German troops. Coming to China in the hope of fighting a number of glorious battles, they had been disappointed to find the war as good as over by the time they had arrived and reacted with frustration and anger. Neither discipline nor morale could be maintained by regular mopping-up activities or drill. Punitive expeditions thus presented a welcome opportunity to vary an otherwise dull routine and force the Chinese to fight. According to von Waldersee, they represented a necessary safety valve to satisfy the expectations of his troops and soon assumed the character of maneuvers.[86]

The various punitive expeditions performed in the third stage of the war differed in terms of their composition, the practices that they involved, and the extent of the violence meted out in their prosecution. Motivated by the desire not just to punish but also for enrichment, violence was exercised in a selective, unsystematic fashion. The character and scope of each expedition varied according to its specific situation and circumstances. Violence was practiced in the form of contributions and requisitions, plundering, hostage taking, the taking of prisoners, deportation and forced labor, rape, massacres and executions, and the burning and razing of individual buildings and entire settlements. Prisoners' camps were not set up. The nature and level of the competition between the various national contingents exerted a radicalizing effect on the violence practiced.

With the sole exception of the American forces, which had been forbidden to burn down villages, the various methods and forms of violence outlined here were employed by all the allied forces to what represents a comparable extent. Set against this context, imperial Germany played a special role in determining the time and extent of the violent practices, but not the form that they assumed. Although Chinese accounts present a different picture, the punitive expeditions conducted by the German forces in the fall of 1900 and early 1901 were characterized less by their specific brutality than by their frequency, late incidence, and irrelevance to the outcome of the war.

CHAPTER 2

The Herero and Nama War

T HE HERERO RISING in German South-West Africa launched on 12 January 1904 took the German colonial and military administration entirely by surprise. Marking the start of a long series of military engagements between the African population and the colonial power, the revolt developed into a full-scale war in October 1904 with the rising of the Nama and was to end only on 31 May 1907. In his memoirs, Captain Kurd Schwabe recounted a "war [that] raged in our South-Western protectorate for almost three years, fought with a level of passion and acrimony almost unknown in a colonial theater."[1] As Schwabe observed, the level of violence unleashed during the Herero and Nama War was unusual even by contemporary standards.

Origins and Phases

Theodor Leutwein, governor of German South-West Africa, was unable to fathom the rising of the Herero, coming as it did after his assiduous attempts to maintain cordial personal contacts with the regional leaders and his high estimations of success in this respect. Leutwein was unable even to conceive of the possibility that his old ally and loyal friend Samuel Maharero, the supreme Herero chief—whom he had elevated to this position himself—would dare, or even wish, to end the Herero alliance with Germany.[2] Although prepared to countenance a war in the last instance, Leutwein had worked hard to prevent any plans for a concerted war of racial extermination.

Despite its subtropical climate, the sparsely vegetated arid and semiarid environment—water flowed in the rivers only in the wet period, supporting the minimal growth of trees and bushes along their banks—of German South-West Africa made the colony initially highly unattractive for its would-be colonizers when they arrived in 1884. The harsh conditions explain the low population density that they found: an indigenous population of 200,000 inhabited an area one and a half times larger than Germany. This population was dominated by the Herero (in the north), a Bantu grouping. As the supreme chief of the Herero, Samuel Maharero was entitled to pursue Herero interests to any extent acceptable to his German masters. Nevertheless, despite such powers, the local chiefs did not accept his authority in local matters and the true extent of his influence was restricted to the Okahandja-Herero.

Settled in the south of the protectorate, the second large-scale ethnic group—the Nama—were migrants from the Cape Colony who had mixed with the Boers and adopted many of their customs and some of their language. Their "captain" Hendrik Witbooi was Christian. Both Samuel Maharero and Hendrik Witbooi spoke several European languages fluently. Other ethnic groups such as the San (bushmen) and the Damara were small in number and overshadowed by the more numerous Herero and Nama. The nature of the steppe characterizing the terrain and the pattern of rains experienced in the colony permitted extensive animal husbandry but ruled out any cultivation of the land. As a result, both ethnicities subsisted as nomadic pastoralists.[3]

The systematic establishment of a colony of white settlement began with the appointment of Leutwein as governor in 1894. Aiming to establish a working peace, he sought to force the development of the protectorate so as to attract settlers. Leutwein held no illusions as to the effects of colonial rule, himself conceding that "divested of all ideals and talk of humanity, the aim of all colonization lies ultimately in profit."[4] Nevertheless, he was convinced that the native population of his new protectorate would eventually grow accustomed to and accept German rule. Placing heavy yet bearable demands on the native population, the Germans sought to integrate the Africans into the German colonial system as a type of "agricultural civil servant": pastoralists working for the German government. Leutwein acted on the assumption that he possessed sufficient time to realize his policy of change through negotiation. Pursuing a policy of "divide and rule," he maintained friendly relations with the Herero chief Samuel Maharero and the

German South-West Africa: War Zone 1904–1907

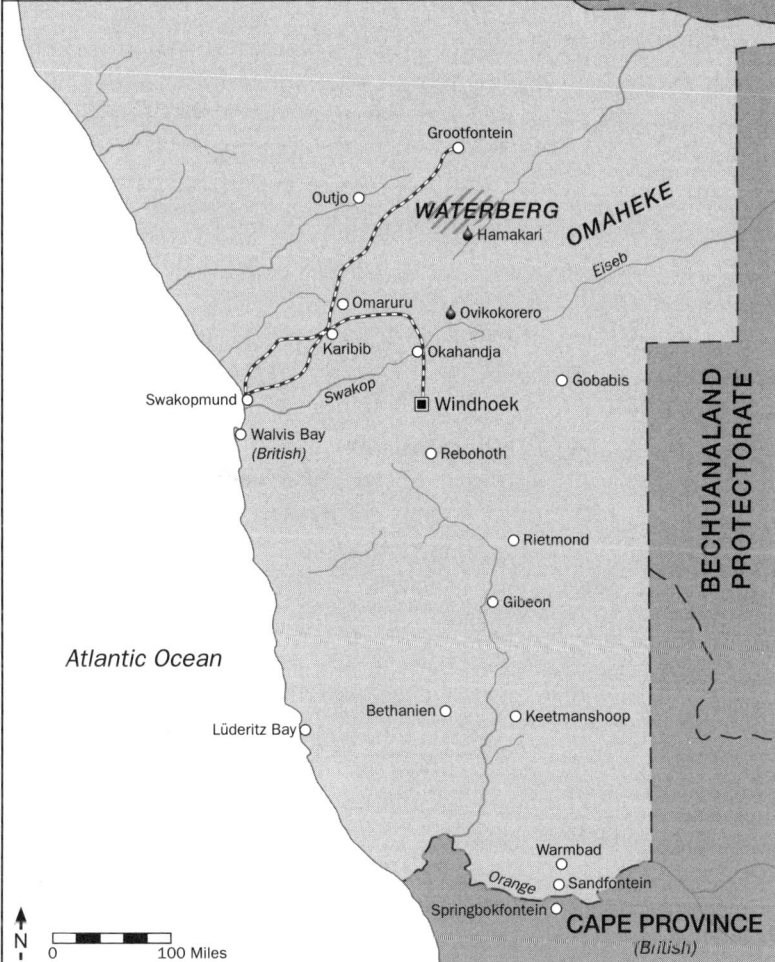

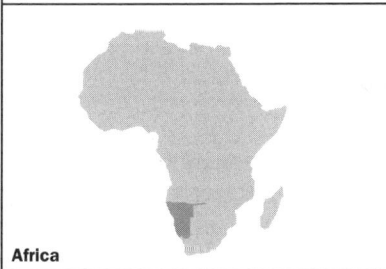

Grootfontein

Outjo

WATERBERG

OMAHEKE

Hamakari

Eiseb

Omaruru

Ovikokorero

Karibib

Okahandja

Swakop

Gobabis

Swakopmund

Windhoek

Walvis Bay
(British)

Rebohoth

BECHUANALAND
PROTECTORATE

Rietmond

Gibeon

Atlantic Ocean

Bethanien

Keetmanshoop

Lüderitz Bay

Warmbad

Orange

Sandfontein

Springbokfontein

CAPE PROVINCE
(British)

N

0   100 Miles

Africa

○   Place

▣   Capital city

🌢   Contested watering hole

━━━   Railroad

──   River

▨   Mountain plateau

Nama "captain" Hendrik Witbooi, but simultaneously sought to take advantage of enmities within Herero and Nama society. The failure of Leutwein's "system" resulted from two factors: his overestimation of the degree to which the decision-making processes within native society could be influenced, and concurrent underestimation of the scope and impact of the socioeconomic changes facing the African population.[5]

The situation of the Herero was exacerbated by a series of further factors. Lacking a stake in the barter economy and having lost 95 percent of their cattle to Rinderpest in 1897, they were forced to sell their labor to the colonists. The new credit ordinance of 1903, issued to protect Africans from the excessive demands of (the majority white) merchants by establishing limitation periods for existing debts, only exacerbated their situation, as creditors began to call in their debts. Already under considerable economic and financial pressure, the African population was incensed by their suffering under what they—and Leutwein—perceived as a system of one-sided colonial justice in which crimes committed by Africans against whites were punished with disproportionately harsh sentences.[6]

Convening a clan meeting in 1903 to discuss their situation, the Herero decided on a revolt against their colonial overlord. Opening hostilities in January 1904 with attacks on the settler farms, Herero forces killed more than a hundred German men, predominantly settlers and soldiers.[7] Acting on the express orders of Samuel Maharero, the Herero warriors did not harm women and children, instead handing them over to the care of missionaries. The Herero strategy also focused on disrupting communications, destroying railroads and telegraph lines and laying siege to fortified or defended settlements in the north of the protectorate. For their part, the German military saw its primary task at this point as the restoration of order.[8]

Hampered by manpower shortages, the German response was restricted to operations in built-up areas. This approach did not prevent a number of considerable defeats. The Protection Force stationed in German South-West Africa in the run-up to the uprising was limited to one staff unit and a field force consisting of four companies, a field battery, a mountain battery, and a unit of police. Although it had a nominal strength of 827, the total force available to Leutwein on 31 December 1903 numbered only 756. Following the uprising, the governor was able to mobilize a further 1,141 reservists, militia men (drawn from the Landwehr and Landsturm) and volunteers.[9] This was supplemented by a landing party of eighty-two sailors from the *Habicht,* a German gunboat dispatched to the region upon the outbreak of the uprising. This was followed by three further units: the 231 men under the command of Alfred von Winkler arrived on 3 February, while the Marine Expedition Corps and the unit led by Hermann Ritter, a total of 741 men, arrived on 9 February.[10] A total of some 2,000 men faced some 8,000 Herero warriors equipped with just over 4,000 rifles. The German force was initially tied down in the south of the protectorate, where Leutwein had been forced to deal first with a revolt of the Bondzelwarts (a Nama group living in the south of the colony).

Initially, both sides suffered an even rate of casualties: in April 1904, German losses amounted to 210, while the Herero had lost 250.[11] The main Herero force was proving to be a formidable enemy and the battles of Ovikokorero (13 March), Onganjira (9 April), and Oviumbo (13 April) saw the deaths of a large number of German officers. Further reinforcements were dispatched from Germany, but suffering from exhaustion and typhus not all the new men could be deployed. Leutwein's negative assessment of the situation was followed by his decision to suspend all large-scale operations and await the arrival of an expeditionary force from the metropole. After the arrival of these fresh men and supplies, the German military presence in her protectorate rose to 4,654 battle-ready soldiers by the end of May.[12] Around the same time, the Herero began to retire with their families and cattle to the Waterberg massif, from where they hoped to open negotiations. Avoiding engagements with the Protection Force, the Herero forces restricted their activities to attacks on smaller German formations. The retreat of the Herero to areas away from the railroads confronted the Germans with a logistical challenge of considerable proportions. Unable to transport supplies by rail, they had to be loaded onto considerably slower ox carts. At the same time, Leutwein drew up plans to bring about a decisive battle at Waterberg. He had resolved to accept a capitulation only after visiting a decisive defeat on the Herero.

During the first phase of the war between January and June 1904, its conduct by the Germans was hampered by the location of decision making over the nature, scope, and dispatch of any reinforcements not in the protectorate, but in Berlin. Lacking any authority to decide on such matters, the Colonial Department (a civilian organization formerly part of the Foreign Ministry but that reported directly to the imperial chancellor) was forced to cede responsibility to the kaiser, who used his military prerogative to issue the necessary orders. Even before the first reinforcements had entered Swakopmund, Wilhelm II entrusted the supreme command of the operation to

Alfred von Schlieffen, chief of the General Staff. The intervention in this matter by the highest institutions of the German state and the importance attached to it by such actors demonstrate the true significance of the events— what had begun as a "local native uprising" was now perceived in Berlin as a full-scale war.

The initial German defeats in early 1904 led to nervousness and impatience within the General Staff. Incredulous that the continuous dispatch of fresh troops and materiel was insufficient to bring swift and decisive victory, critics rounded on Colonel Leutwein, accusing him of lacking the necessary steel; he was replaced as commander in chief of German forces in the protectorate by Lieutenant-General Lothar von Trotha. As a previously neglected letter shows, this decision was made by the kaiser against the will of not only his chancellor but the minister of war, the head of the General Staff, and the director of the Colonial Department in the German Foreign Ministry.[13] The kaiser also ordered that all further military operations were to await the arrival of his new appointment.[14] Leutwein continued in his capacity as governor of German South-West Africa, but given the military nature of all decision making, the appointment of von Trotha reduced it to a merely titular position. Leutwein was eventually dismissed as civil governor in the fall of 1904 and replaced by von Trotha, who occupied both offices in personal union until his own dismissal in November 1905. The Battle of Waterberg in August 1904 marked the radical second phase of the Herero war, which lasted until the cease-fire declared by Germany in December 1905. Despite having broken all Herero resistance, the Germans proceeded to unleash a war of extermination against the Herero. Pursuing them into the Omaheke desert, German forces did not discriminate in the killing of men, women, and children.

The declaration of war in the fall of 1904 by the southern Nama against their German colonial masters transformed the northern Herero uprising to a two-front war.[15] Not only a direct response to the Herero revolt, the Nama rising was motivated by perception of a threat to their own situation. The replacement of Leutwein as civil governor meant that the Nama not only had lost a trusted partner but now saw themselves confronted by settler demands that the German forces arriving in the protectorate finally "deal with the Nama." Speaking to a missionary, nineteen Nama deserters who had fought with the Germans against the Herero spoke in "lurid detail" of plans to "exterminate the Herero."[16] The final push for the revolt was provided by the influence of a native Christian movement hoping to establish an "African Church" independent of German influence.[17]

Attacking German farms after their declaration of war in September 1904, Nama warriors emulated the Herero in the protection that they extended to European women and children. Understanding the nature of German military power, the Nama were careful not to give open battle, but sought to launch an attritional guerilla campaign, a tactic with which they hoped to force the Germans to terms involving improved living conditions. However, not all of the decentralized Nama groups participated in the war. The rising centered around Rietmond and Gibeon, and was only able to mobilize just under 2,000 warriors.[18]

The Nama war unfolded in three phases. Hoping for and pursuing a decisive battle between September and December 1904, the German military commander in the south, Colonel Berthold von Deimling, wrote, "We must not allow the Hottentotts[19] to escape, rather we must encircle and destroy them before they do so."[20] Seeking in December 1904 to force the Witbooi Nama (the largest and most important of the Nama groupings) to give battle in their homeland of Rietmond, the Germans failed to prevent their subsequent escape, but did force them to abandon all their possessions, amounting to some 15,000 head of cattle, domestic equipment, weapons, and ammunition.[21] Despite suffering such grave losses, the Nama were no longer tied to a single area; this increased level of mobility conferred greater military flexibility. A development not missed by von Trotha, he wrote: "As they were no longer in possession of anything which we could take from them, . . . they were resolved to take their operations to extremes."[22]

The capture of Rietmond by German troops marked the beginning of the second phase of the war. Reorganizing their troops into smaller units and thus reverting to their original tactics, the Nama launched a number of individual actions. This new approach proved highly effective against small German formations such as patrols and transport columns, but posed little threat to larger bodies of troops. As one account put it, "Having split up into small bands, [these enemy formations] roamed the country. Marching and resting troops, columns, stations and posts were exposed to constant danger from small groups of the enemy that would suddenly appear [from nowhere]. The situation was best described by the phrase 'enemy present everywhere.'"[23] In his memoirs, Captain Paul von Lettow-Vorbeck wrote of the impossibility of pinning down the enemy with their "tendency to melt away in your hands."[24] The Germans, on the other hand, weighed down by their baggage, remained comparatively immobile. A further logistical difficulty was posed by the necessity to transport not only military equipment, but supplies of water from Lüderitz Bay to Keetmanshoop on cumbrous ox-drawn carts.

The death of the Nama captain Hendrik Witbooi and the dismissal of von Trotha in the fall of 1905 represented a caesura and the beginning of the third phase of the war. The loss of Witbooi, "who had posed the most serious problems for the young colonial power of Germany,"[25] meant that the notoriously fissiparous Nama now lacked the central figure around whom they had been able to unite. The result was that the majority of the Nama groups surrendered. The dismissal of von Trotha, on the other hand, resulted in significant changes to the German conduct of both the war and the ongoing negotiations. Prepared to accept only unconditional surrender and guaranteeing only to spare the lives of those who did so, von Trotha had refused to open negotiations following entreaties by the Nama leader, Jacob Morenga, in early 1905. Offering to lay down his arms and return all his stolen cattle, he demanded in return a guarantee that his followers would keep both their lives and their own cattle. The departure of von Trotha brought with it a more flexible attitude toward negotiations. German commanders also adopted a new strategy, replacing the unsuccessful attempts at concentric encirclement with the deployment of mobile units to conduct a sustained pursuit of the individual Nama groups and thus effect their destruction. The new strategy soon paid off; having lost operative cohesion, the majority of the Nama surrendered.[26] They joined the few survivors of the Herero revolt in prisoner of war camps.

After losing face at the Battle of Waterberg (1904), the German military suffered further loss of prestige during the protracted guerilla campaign conducted by what amounted to only a few hundred Nama. Ending the war required an enormous outlay of men and resources. Of the 14,000 soldiers dispatched to German South-West Africa, some 2,000 died as a result of wounds or illness. The war cost 585 million reichsmarks; combined with the costly policy of naval expansion, it contributed to the ruin of German finances.[27] The lack of reliable population figures makes it difficult to estimate the number of Nama and Herero killed. Estimates give the Herero population as amounting to between 35,000 and 100,000 before the war and between 14,000 and 16,000 in its aftermath. The Nama population is estimated at 20,000 before the war and between 9,000 and 13,000 after the war. As a result, even the most conservative of appraisals put the losses suffered by the Herero and Nama populations either during or in the aftermath of the war at around one third.[28] Population figures for the white settler community, on the other hand, point to an increase between 1907 and 1911 from 7,110 to 13,962 people.[29]

With the population seriously reduced, the structures of Herero and Nama society were entirely destroyed.[30] Once released from prison in April 1908, the native populations were regarded as a mass labor reserve devoid of any rights. The release of African prisoners had been preceded in 1907 by the issue of a series of "native ordinances" expropriating the African population by prohibiting them from engaging in animal husbandry. The ordinances also abrogated their previous formal freedom of movement. Subjecting almost all areas of life to strict legal control, the colonial authorities now had the powers to record the number of Africans currently present in any district at any time. The most important instrument of control was the pass laws, requiring every African over the age of seven to carry an identity card. Movement between districts required a separate passport, the granting of which required prior application. Travelers would then have to register in the area in which they arrived. African workers were also required to maintain a complete record of employment containing all work contracts, signed by their white employer. The pass laws constituted the basis of a labor market designed to maintain a reserve pool of disciplined African labor. In the aftermath of the Herero and Nama War, the German colonial administration forged a society that held no place for the traditional customs and economic practices of its native populations. Nevertheless, as recent research has emphasized, the Herero and Nama activated their family and other social networks to maximize their room for maneuver, forming a political movement that was to grow under the South African rule established during the First World War.

The Battle of Waterberg and the Extermination Proclamations

The replacement of Leutwein by von Trotha as commander of the German forces in German South-West Africa in May 1904 ushered in a new approach to the war. While seeking a decisive battle at the foot of the Waterberg mountain, Leutwein had also sought to integrate the Herero in any postwar settlement, and thus advocated a negotiated peace. As a result, he called for clemency to be exercised toward the African population so as to maintain the long-term economic viability of the German protectorate. Following this plan, he followed African military custom and maintained a close correspondence with the Herero. Leutwein's policy aimed at the conduct of a restricted war so as not to endanger good postwar relations with the Herero and Nama. In so doing, his approach exhibited a certain congruence with Herero and Nama aims and cultural practices in using a conflict to begin negotiations. His successor, Lothar von Trotha (a veteran of the Boxer War and with experience in German East Africa), on the other hand, was known as an advocate of radical military solutions.[31] Invested with absolute powers by the kaiser, he replaced Leutwein's colonial policy with a strategy of annihilation. Nevertheless, the actual differences between the two figures became clear only after the failed battle of Waterberg in the fall of 1904.

Initially, the arrival of von Trotha in the protectorate had little impact on the conduct of the war against the Herero. Although issuing an official declaration of war against the Herero and special military regulations for the conflict during his passage, he continued Leutwein's tactics in preparing for the Battle of Waterberg. One measure that he ordered was the establishment of a prison camp with a capacity of 8,000.[32] Just as those of his predecessor, von Trotha's original plans did not involve the physical extermination of the Herero; rather he sought to encircle and destroy their forces in a decisive battle of annihilation.

Von Trotha assembled his infantry and artillery into six units to be accompanied by two machine gun sections, eight administrative units, and three contingents of native auxiliaries. His force of some 4,000 men with 1,500 rifles, thirty artillery pieces, and twelve machine guns was confronted by a total of some 60,000 Hereros—men, women, and children—of whom 6,000 were armed. The Herero lacked artillery and suffered from shortages of ammunition.[33] The German force received orders to advance on the Herero in a star-shaped formation. However, the difficulties in communication and coordination experienced by the various German units made this maneuver difficult to execute. The signals section stationed on the crest of the Waterberg was not able to coordinate the advancing units.[34]

The ring around the Herero tightened ever more closely until the beginning of August. The reasons for the passivity of the Herero in the face of the advancing enemy remain unclear. Indeed, they did not even make the attempt to cut the German telegraph lines linking the advancing German units. The German patrols were amazed to find that the Herero chief Samuel Maharero had not arranged for any special security measures to safeguard the various camps holding the Herero women, children, and cattle. He did not even take the opportunity to flee to British Bechuanaland when the opportunity arose. The only plausible explanation for such behavior is that

Maharero had expected the Germans to begin negotiations, just as they had done in the 1894 war against Hendrik Witbooi. The difference between that encounter and the situation in 1904 was that the former was commanded by the more conciliatory Leutwein.[35]

Issuing the general order for attack on 4 August, von Trotha made his intentions clear: "I intend to attack the enemy . . . with all sections simultaneously in order to destroy him."[36] Initially, everything proceeded according to plan. However, on the very first day of the offensive, one of the advancing units broke with the battle plan and wheeled off to attack the mission station at Waterberg. Although successfully capturing the station, this action forced the whole Herero force to retreat southward into the Omaheke Desert, where they met with the weakest German unit at the Hamakari watering hole. Not strong enough to engage the advancing Herero, the Germans conceded their position. Having failed to encircle the Herero, the Germans were now unable to prevent their flight into the desert.

Blaming the failure of the encirclement action on the premature action of the individual unit that attacked the mission station, the official account of the battle produced by the General Staff identified the initiative of certain restricted individuals as decisive in the failure of the overall plan.[37] It is highly unlikely that the Herero would have retreated eastward without the unauthorized attack on the mission station from the West. That the Herero were forced to flee into the desert would appear to be the result of not military planning, but the unforeseen course taken by the battle of Waterberg. Even without this "friction," facing a larger enemy force and unable either to coordinate his forces or deploy his artillery, it remains unlikely that von Trotha would have been able to pursue his plan to its successful conclusion.[38]

Other chroniclers of this battle argue that by incorporating the Omaheke desert into his plan as a "natural barrier," von Trotha acted intentionally in stationing his weakest unit to the southeast of the plateau at the Hamakari water hole.[39] Following this line of thought, the escape of the Herero at this very point was intended. The most obvious objection to this argument is the evidence pointing to von Trotha's preparations, not to try to force the Herero into the desert, but to engineer a battle of annihilation culminating in a single "large and visible outcome."[40] He did not intend to bring about a situation in which the Herero would be subject to a slow death through adverse natural conditions.

Whatever the German intention, the Herero force fled past the battlefield into the Omaheke desert. Taking their women and children and a section of their herds, the force abandoned not only all items of value—such as furs, ostrich feathers, and cattle—but also weapons and ammunition. As one member of the General Staff remarked, "the entire national wealth of the Herero was left by the wayside."[41] Following the failure of his original battle plan, von Trotha was forced to develop a new strategy. It was simple: "I will pursue the enemy with all units."[42] In a conventional European battle, the pursuit had been developed to effect the final defeat of an already routed enemy. In this context, it served the function of actually "forcing the enemy to give battle."[43] The Germans were very concerned to prevent the Herero from regrouping or even escaping to the adjacent British Bechuanaland to prepare further action. Seeking to avoid either of these eventualities, Ludwig von Estorff and Berthold von Deimling collected the troops available to them and on 13 August launched a pursuit along the area between the end of the grassland and the start of the desert. Shortly afterward, von Trotha issued two sets of guidelines for successful action. Although stipulating that any "looted cattle" were to be driven to the collection posts wherever possible, absolute priority was to be attached to the "destruction of the enemy."[44] Both sets of guidelines expressly forbade any form of negotiations with the enemy.[45] Even if the strategy of annihilation that von Trotha was eventually to follow was not explicit in his military orders at this stage, it is clear that he did not expect to fight a glorious final battle but rather engage in a series of small skirmishes. One problem posed in conducting the pursuit was the presence of noncombatants (especially unarmed women) among the fleeing force. While the special legal arrangements made for the war in German South-West Africa permitted the German troops to shoot any armed African men on sight, according to the later testimony of one of his officers, von Trotha had expressly forbidden the shooting of women and children.[46] Nevertheless, a number of incidents have been documented in which women and children were shot.[47] Indeed, the often-postulated soldierly "code of honor" regulating dealings with women and children had already been abrogated by Governor Leutwein.

Responding in 1904 to attacks on the German conduct of the war made in Parliament by the SPD leader August Bebel, Leutwein was able to deny the existence of any express orders to kill women and children, but he was forced to concede that such events had taken place. In his report, made to the Colonial Department of the Foreign Ministry, the former governor wrote that "it is only natural after all that has occurred, that our soldiers did not show any leniency [besondere Schonung]. Moreover, it is natural that a superior officer does not order that any such leniency be shown."[48] For Leu-twein, "showing leniency" meant not shooting captive women and children. With only a few exceptions, the practice of differentiating between female and male prisoners had been abandoned in the early phases of the war.

Von Trotha was faced with a mobile opponent spread across an extensive territory and with his own soldiers succumbing to high levels of disease. His second attempt to encircle the Herero on a broad front, launched at the end of August 1904, was also unsuccessful. Nevertheless, he was not unaware of the parlous state in which the Herero found themselves; forced to survive in the Omaheke desert, without sufficient water for the number of men and cattle, many died of exhaustion and thirst. Although his enemy had been ren-dered physically incapable of any further military action,[49] von Trotha re-mained inflexible in his rejection of negotiations with the Herero. Surveying the situation, Ludwig von Estorff saw only the senseless destruction of an entire people. He summarized the flight, pursuit, and death of the Herero succinctly: "Their resistance broken, their number disbanded entirely in the field of sand [the Omaheke desert] . . . , the great majority perished."[50] Von Trotha, on the other hand, justified his conduct with a reference to Napo-leon's humiliation in Russia: "I was confronted by a catastrophe for my men. Had I granted the females access to the few puddles available to me I ran the risk of experiencing my own Beresina."[51]

Learning in September 1904 of Herero attempts to gather on the River Eiseb, he intensified his pursuit so as to "throw [the opponent] back into the sandveld [Omaheke] should he not fight, where thirst and privation will complete his destruction."[52] This statement was the first formulation of a plan to seal the border to the Omaheke and abandon the Herero to a certain death. Accordingly, von Estorff and von Deimling were ordered to prevent the Herero returning from the desert. The conventional differentiation be-tween combatants and noncombatants had become obsolete. The war aims had now refocused on the "absolute destruction" of the enemy.[53] Von Trotha outlined clearly his departure from Leutwein's policy in a number of letters and discussions. "The sealing-off of the eastern border of the colony and pur-suit of a policy of terror against every remaining Herero in the land will continue as long as I remain in the territory. The nation [of the Herero] must perish. If we do not succeed in killing them with guns, then it must be achieved in this fashion."[54] His much-quoted statements to the effect that the war could not be conducted in accordance with the Geneva Convention but in "rivers of blood" and through "blatant terrorism" also date from this period.[55] This assessment of the situation was shared by the chief of the German General Staff, von Schlieffen, who added that "the race war thus unleashed . . . can culminate only in the destruction or final enslavement of one of the two [warring] parties."[56]

The high point of this new and radical policy was reached on 2 October 1904 when the "extermination proclamation" was made to the "Herero people." Captured Herero were issued with translations of the proclamation and released with the task of spreading word of its contents. The proclamation (the authenticity of which is today universally accepted) contains a description of the new situation:[57] "The Herero are no longer German subjects. They have murdered, stolen and cut off the ears and noses and other bodily parts of German soldiers and now out of cowardice refuse to fight. I say to the people: anyone delivering a captain to one of my stations as a prisoner will receive 1,000 Marks. Whoever brings in Samuel Maharero alive will receive 5,000 Marks. The Herero people must leave this land. If they do not, I shall force them to do so by using the Great Gun [artillery]. Within the German border, every Herero, armed or unarmed, with or without cattle, will be shot. I will no longer give shelter to women and children, but will drive them back to their people or have them shot. These are my words to the Herero people."

Although a supplementary order instructed the German soldiers to fire above the heads of women and children, the very act of driving the Herero back into the Omaheke desert guaranteed their deaths. The proclamation served to establish the outlaw status of the Herero. As the Herero had forfeited their subject status through "dishonorable behavior" and "cowardice" and the mutilation of German soldiers, the pecuniary encouragement to hand over their leaders stood in clear contradiction to the threat to shoot all Herero found on German territory. This contradiction can be understood only in terms of the declared aims of the military operation: the disappearance of the Herero at any price through either flight to British territory—which was by this point viewed by the Germans as an acceptable alternative—or death.[58]

Historian Isabel Hull has portrayed von Trotha's missive to be a proclamation ex post facto, arguing that the extermination of the Herero by the German units operating in the Omaheke was already underway. It is true that the move to extermination was first announced in his proclamation, as previously all military decisions had been taken by the commanders on the spot. However, the exact scope of the murders and the precise point at which they began is almost impossible to establish. It is important to note that all decisions were taken by men on the spot down to the section level.

The proclamation was only rescinded a number of weeks later (on 8 December) following orders from Berlin. This move was preceded by a series of arguments summarized and presented to the kaiser by the imperial chancellor. Pointing to the incompatibility of such a policy with the teachings of Christianity and humanity, von Bülow also outlined the damage suffered by Germany's reputation among the "civilized" nations of the world. Such arguments were supported by economic reasons for rescinding the proclamation; German firms in the protectorate were already experiencing difficulty in recruiting sufficient labor. Playing on the kaiser's hostility to all things English, the chancellor pointed out that the adjacent territory of British Bechuanaland would profit from the new personnel no longer working in the German colony.[59]

The order countermanding von Trotha's proclamation specified that all those Herero who could prove their consistent nonbelligerence and had not killed any German soldiers should be granted clemency by being imprisoned. This policy was to be implemented with the cooperation of the Rhineland Missionary Society. From early 1905, the Herero were transported to internment camps. Nevertheless, individual groups were able to make their way to British Bechuanaland, take refuge with the Ovambo in the north, or survive in the bush. German commanders hoped to force the surrender of the Nama in a fashion similar to the Herero with a second "extermination proclamation" issued on 22 April 1905.[60] In contrast to the policy toward the Herero, however, those surrendering voluntarily were to be spared. The only exception was applied to those who had killed whites or issued orders to do so. Such persons were to be given the opportunity to emigrate. The persecution and annihilation of the Herero were to serve as a warning to the Nama; all those not surrendering would suffer a similar fate. The example of the Herero leader Samuel Maharero was also to serve as an example: "hounded like a wild animal, . . . possessing nothing," he was now as "poor as the poorest field Herero." German propaganda now portrayed the Herero as either having died of hunger and thirst in the desert or having been cut down by German horsemen. This campaign was accompanied by a renewed attempt to bribe the Nama into delivering up those "guilty of murder." A price of 5,000 marks was put on the head of Hendrik Witbooi.

Assured of keeping their lives (which would, however, be spent in prison), they were not guaranteed the retention of any property. Although the Germans never threatened the Nama with complete extermination, reference to the fate of the Herero meant that it remained a continuous and unspoken threat. Nevertheless, the Nama proclamation exhibited considerably greater subtlety than that issued to the Herero. While German rule in the north seemed to be guaranteed only through the destruction of the Herero, in the south it seemed to require merely the complete submission of the Nama.

The Nama proclamation was copied and distributed to the German troops, who were instructed to distribute it "among the Hottentotts in every possible manner." Nevertheless, it failed in its aim and did not bring about the complete submission of the Nama people. Wide-spread awareness of the inhumane conditions prevalent in the internment camps acted as a deterrent to voluntary surrender. After a while, the influence of the chancellor also led to the proclamation being rescinded.[61]

Camps and Prisoners

The character of the war in German South-West Africa was established not just by the nature of its conduct but also by the use of internment camps. Developed in Cuba at the turn of the century by the Spanish, such camps first saw widespread use by the British during the South African War. Despite this chronology, it would appear that in setting up these camps, the British drew on their experiences of ruling India rather than learning any lessons from Cuba and the Philippines.[62]

A number of different types of internment camp were established in German South-West Africa. In addition to the "transit camps" *(Sammellager)* run by the Missionary Societies to establish control over disparate groups of displaced and fugitive Herero came the camps established and maintained by the military administration in all the larger settlements of the colony: Okahandja, Omaruru, Karibib, Keetmanshoop, Lüderitz Bay, Swakopmund, and Windhoek. The largest of these camps was at Windhoek. Although the surviving photographs of this camp show a uniform arrangement of round tents, it was separated into a "normal" and a "hospital" area, the latter of which was divided into a number of separate units.[63] The arrangement of huts was surrounded by a "Dornkraal" which was later reinforced with barbed wire. The authorities also permitted the establishment of a number of semiprivate internment camps on farms and railway premises. The communication zone also held a number of smaller camps for prisoners of war, the inmates of which were either set to work or forwarded to larger camps run by the military authorities.[64]

The internment of native warriors and their families in camps was designed to prevent them from fighting against the German colonial authorities. The German administration made no attempt to differentiate between Herero and Nama, nor did it make any exceptions for age or gender. Those taken prisoner and those having surrendered were subject to identical treatment, as were the Nama women and children handed over to the care of the German authorities during the revolt. In contrast to Spanish and British practices, those prisoners not brought into the hospital area could be deployed as forced laborers at any opportunity. Made available to private individuals, firms, farmers, the military, and the railroad companies, they were to make a contribution to establishing the colony as a viable economic concern. First transported to the line command posts, they were then taken to the District Offices, from where they were dispatched to their future place of work. Those benefiting from their labor were to pay fifty pfennigs per day or ten marks per month to the District Offices for each laborer thus "hired."[65]

The first use in a German official document of the term "concentration camp" was made in a telegram from the Imperial Chancellery sent in January 1905.[66] Despite their identical appellation, only limited parallels can be drawn between the concentration camps established in German South-West Africa and the concentration and death camps maintained by the Third Reich.[67] Although expecting, and unperturbed by, the death of the prisoners, the colonial concentration camps did not plan any systematic "extermination through work." The "labor question" had been a topical issue of discussion among government circles, settlers, and missionaries since the beginning of the war. Indeed, much of the vociferous criticism leveled against the camp policy focused on the ensuing labor shortages in which they believed it would result.

The prisoners held in the camps run by the military authorities fell under the authority of the area commanders in the communication zone, who were also responsible for feeding the troops in their area. Despite his best efforts, von Trotha had been unable to transfer the responsibility for these prisoners to the civil authorities. Writing in January 1905, he issued a set of guiding principles for the treatment of prisoners. With priority accorded to the victualing of the troops, the needs of the prisoners were to be provided for only after military requirements had been satisfied.[68] As a result, the accommodation, clothing, feeding, and medical care accorded to them were to be apportioned in accordance with the resources remaining after full provision of the troops had been ensured.[69]

The official daily rations allocated for the prisoners regardless of their state of health began low and were adjusted downward many times. The average daily nutritional intake per head (not taking into account slaughter-house waste) was 56g protein, 32g fat, and 375g carbohydrates, a total of 1,900 calories.[70] Nevertheless, such rations were distributed only when available. This unvaried diet was not adapted to the nutritional habits of the Herero and Nama. As pastoralists, they were accustomed to a varied diet consisting of milk and dairy products (curds and buttermilk, butter, and cheese) supplemented by meat and field fruits. The new diet resulted in a number of illnesses, including scurvy, bronchial catarrh, and chicken pox.[71] This situation was often complicated by the high incidence of pneumonia caused by the provisional nature of the camps which, with their coastal locations, provided little or no protection against the raw sea wind and the damp winter weather. Provision of blankets and clothing was also insufficient. Despite the parlous epidemiological situation, the Medical Office forbade the issue of expensive drugs to prisoners.[72] Even the official medical report recorded that the majority of the ill developed their maladies after a number of months in prison, and even after making an apparently good recovery from exhaustion.[73]

Because female prisoners were given lower rations and subject to higher levels of sexual violence (which resulted in a proliferation of sexually transmitted diseases), the suffering of female prisoners was disproportionately high.[74] The prisoner camp on "Shark Island" off the Luderitz coast was notorious for its poor conditions. The camp was already holding 500 Herero inmates and a large number of Nama in September 1906, and conditions there worsened with the arrival of a further 1,700 prisoners.[75] Missionary reports articulated stringent and repeated criticism of the conditions of internment, adding that the secluded location of the camp had broken the spirit of a number of its prisoners.[76] These conditions led to the death of 1,032 of its 1,795 inmates—a mortality rate of over 57 percent. Of the 245 male survivors, only twenty-five (just over 10 percent) remained fit for work.[77]

Of the 14,019 Africans treated by the German Medical Corps (the majority of whom were prisoners of war) and thus recorded in the Medical Report for German South-West Africa, 21.7 percent died, of whom almost double the number of children died as adults. Moreover, the death rate increased with every year of the war—in 1906 it was almost two and a half times higher than the figures for 1904.[78] Far from exhaustive, these figures cover only those Africans actually treated by the German doctors, and not all those Africans who fell ill actually consulted German medical personnel.

The real number of deaths is likely much higher. Of the 15,000 Herero and 2,000 Nama interned in the prison camps, a total of 7,682 died between October 1904 and March 1907. This amounts to more than 45 percent of the camp population.[79]

The dismissal of von Trotha in 1905 did little to change the conditions prevailing in the prison camps, and the death rates of both the Herero and the Nama remained constant under his replacement as civil governor, Friedrich von Lindequist. Indeed, Lindequist's fantasies of omnipotence even led him to suggest a complete population exchange within German South-West Africa, involving relocating the Nama to the north and the Herero to the south of the protectorate. Such a measure would have resulted in the complete and utter destruction of their culture and history. In 1908, responsibility for all prisoners of war—with the exception of those on Shark Island—was transferred from the military to the civil authorities. Acting two days after this decision, Ludwig von Estorff, the commander of the Protection Force, ordered the relocation of this prison camp to the mainland, much to the chagrin (and against the expressed wishes) of the civil government in Windhoek, who believed that only the island location provided any security against inmate escape.[80]

An alternative to the camp policy presented during the war focused on deportations, which the military hoped would rid itself of the responsibility for holding so many prisoners. It was a policy restricted to the Nama population, and the best-known incident involved the removal of 119 Witbooi warriors from the protectorate in the fall of 1904. Although these men had been provided by the Nama captain Hendrik Witbooi to fight alongside the Protection Force in crushing the Herero rising, they were subsequently interned in Swakopmund. Fearing their flight to the British-held Walvis Bay, the German authorities decided on their deportation to the German colonies Cameroon and Togo. This marked the beginning of a tortuous odyssey—encompassing stations at Togo and Cameroon before eventually returning in 1906 to German South-West Africa—from which only forty-two of the original 116 survived. This did not mark the end of the deportations. Governor von Lindequist continued to toy with the idea of further large-scale measures of resettlement. Proposing the deportation of 300 Witbooi to New Guinea, the Imperial Colonial Office refused on the grounds of cost. Nevertheless, a further ninety-three Witbooi were transported from German South-West Africa to Cameroon, where they were deployed as laborers and their rights were restricted to that of mere existence.[81]

Unlike the wars in China or (as we shall see) in German East Africa, the conflict in German South-West Africa was not characterized by requisitions, contributions, plundering, or the burning and razing of settlements. Instead, the German strategy focused on engineering a single large-scale battle followed by a relentless pursuit of the (even unarmed) enemy by mobile units. Once captured, their African prisoners were then subject to exploitation and neglect in prison camps. Postwar German policy focused on the clearance of the native presence from the colony through death, deportation, or imprisonment. Not just the result of military agency, this represented the wider long-term policy of both the military and civil authorities.

CHAPTER 3

The Maji Maji War

T HE MAJI MAJI UPRISING in the German protectorate of East Africa (July 1905) forced a further deployment of German troops to an African colony. Despite their chronological proximity, it has not yet been possible to establish any link between the wars in German South-West Africa and German East Africa. Moreover, the German military establishment was both unable and apparently unwilling to glean any insight from its experience in South-West Africa that could be applied to this new war. Contemporary military opinion viewed the uprising in German East Africa as an entirely conventional colonial revolt that had to be crushed. Although the Maji Maji War brought a greater number of African deaths and sustained destruction—the effects of which can still be felt in a number of areas today—it remains overshadowed by the events of the war in German South-West Africa.

Origins and Phases

The topography of German East Africa, which was established as a German protectorate in 1885, was characterized by a number of high plateaus, a lake landscape to the West, a coastal environment dominated by mangrove thickets, and wet and dry savanna with its chest-high grasslands. The tropical climate of the area registered considerable variations in temperature, humidity, and rainfall. Its area of 38,500 square miles was almost double that of the German Empire and supported a population of between five and seven million which subsisted principally on the cultivation of corn, sorghum, and cassava. The ethnic composition of the population was highly diverse and included Arabs and Indians. The former predominantly inhabited the coastal area, whereas the black African population was concentrated in the hinterland of the colony.

Following the "Arab rising" (1888–1890) and the Wahehe revolt (1891–1898), the Maji Maji uprising in July 1905 was the third large-scale insurrection in this colony. Centering on the coastal region, the Arab rising predominantly involved conflict between the Arabs—who dominated the caravan and overseas trade of the colony, involving what was known as the "Suaheli system"—and their German masters.[1] The inhabitants of the colony interior involved themselves in the conflict if they chose to show solidarity with the Arab cause.

The resistance to German rule offered by the Wahehe uprising, on the other hand, was restricted to the members of a single black African group.[2] Although confined to a restricted area, this war continued for seven years. In contrast, the Maji Maji revolt united a number of disparate ethnic groupings, and spread across the entire south of the colony. The north of the colony—including the Kilimanjaro region, the main area of German settlement—was not affected by the fighting.

The suppression of the Arab revolt in 1890 and the subsequent consolidation of imperial rule in German South-East Africa was followed by a program of colonial development *(Inwertsetzung)* involving the establishment of a coherent system of administration designed to integrate the black Africans, Arabs, and Indians into colonial society. To this end, the twenty-two districts of the colony (each headed by a German official) were converted into territories headed by *akidas* (predominantly Arabs), who supervised the village chiefs.[3] Lacking effective oversight and thus often corrupt, they constituted the focus of almost constant conflict, resulting in the coining of the term "akida-maladministration," a term that became virtually synonymous for German East Africa.

This administrative reform was accompanied by a raft of measures aimed at the economic development of the colony, the sum of which were to effect radical change to traditional village life. Strict ordinances such as the ban on hunting and dancing were supplemented by the introduction of taxes and levies. Moreover, the conventional instrument of taxation, the hut tax, was replaced by a poll tax demanded in cash. As the majority of Africans existed as subsistence farmers, they were forced to pay off their tax debts with forced labor and were often resettled to the north to do so. Appointed

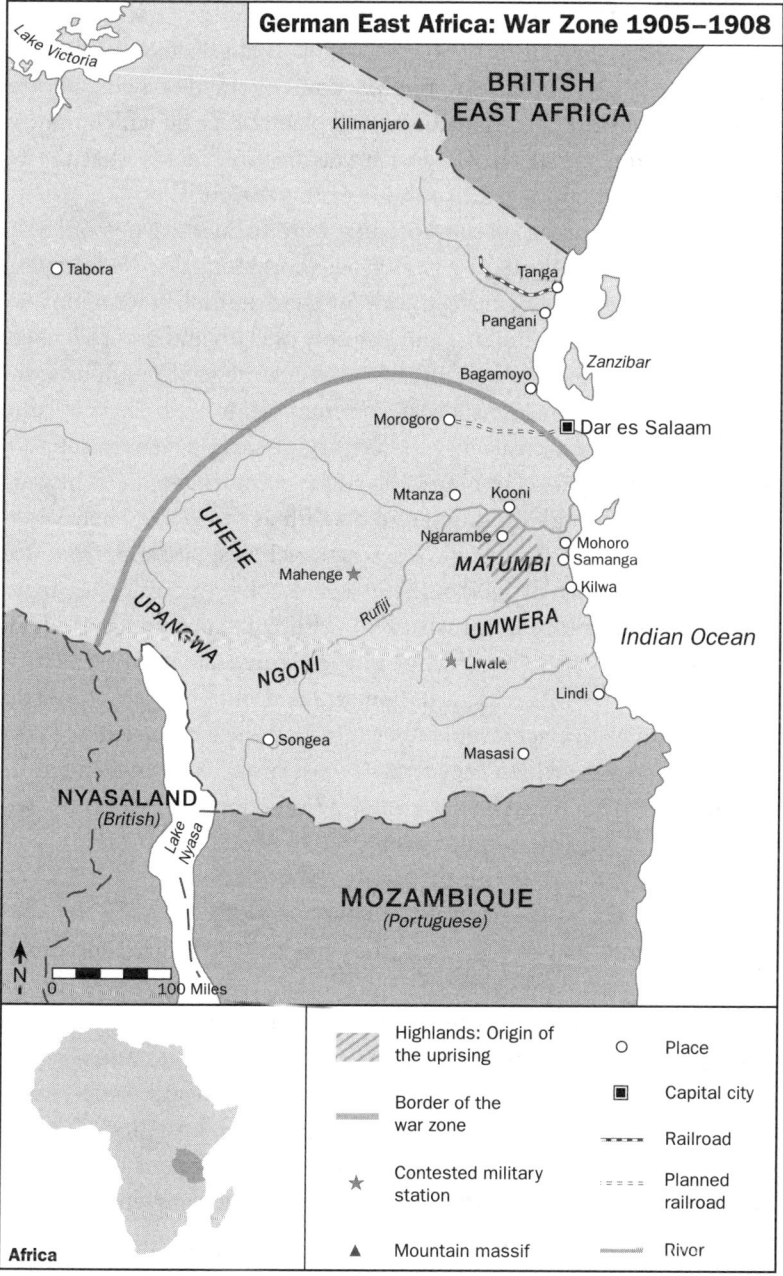

German East Africa: War Zone 1905–1908

Lake Victoria

BRITISH
EAST AFRICA

Kilimanjaro ▲

O Tabora

Tanga
Pangani

Zanzibar

Bagamoyo

Morogoro O Dar es Salaam

Mtanza O   Kooni

Ngarambe O   O Mohoro
    O Samanga
UHEHE
Mahenge ★   MATUMBI   O Kilwa

UPANGWA   Rufiji

NGONI   UMWERA

Indian Ocean

★ Liwale

Lindi O

O Songea

Masasi O

NYASALAND
(British)

Lake Nyasa

MOZAMBIQUE
(Portuguese)

N

0   100 Miles

Africa

	Highlands: Origin of the uprising	O	Place
	Border of the war zone	■	Capital city
★	Contested military station		Railroad
			Planned railroad
▲	Mountain massif		River

in 1901, the recently appointed governor, Gustav Adolf Graf von Götzen, announced a new agricultural policy. This involved selected villages to the south of the protectorate (close to the Matumbi mountains) being allotted a particular area of land known as communal plantations, on which they were to cultivate cotton to pay their taxes. It was no coincidence that the Maji Maji uprising began among the peasants of this region.[4]

The immediate causes of the uprising were located in not only these innovations in colonial rule, but a religious movement that had developed in communities on the western hillside of the Matumbi mountains some months before.[5] Pilgrims drawn from a variety of clans and groups had come to the mountain region of Ngarambe to obtain a range of religious services from the prophet Kinjikitile such as communication with their ancestors, healing from illnesses, ensuring the fertility of their fields, or support in their struggle against the Germans. Placing their faith in a medicine mixed of water, corn, and sorghum (known in Swahili as *Maji*), they believed that taken in combination with specific ritual acts including restraint from sexual intercourse and particular foodstuffs, it would confer a number of benefits including invulnerability to all weapons. Although such conceptions were nothing new in this region, the scope of the claims made by this particular cult and the extent of its dissemination attained unparalleled proportions. Kinjikitile's innovative achievement was to combine a diverse range of traditional ideas so as to widen the attractiveness of the Maji movement. Previously restricted to an exclusive group, he was now able to rally a wider coalition of East Africans behind his ideas, which cut across otherwise significant religious, social, political, and clan divisions.

According to the assessment of the governor von Götzen, a "locally restricted uprising of half-savages [was thus able to grow] into something approaching a national fight against foreign domination."[6] However, although the spread of the Maji enabled the formation of a cross-tribal form of organization, the decision to join its ranks was not always simple. Entrance to the movement entailed inevitable conflict with the German authorities, whereas rejection of its membership invariably incurred the hostility of the Maji movement. Patterns of African resistance or collaboration were thus the product of flexible and complex local alliances that transcended the rigid ethnic framework of the region.[7]

The mass basis of the Maji cult was provided by its pilgrims. The initiation ceremony, at which every clan leader entering the movement was awarded an amulet containing the special Maji medicine, was followed by

parades and drill of a distinctly military nature.[8] This provided an opportunity for clan leaders to meet and talk, and so helped forge an extensive
network of the initiated, the existence of which enabled the uprising to
spread quickly once war had been declared. Authority over this declaration
of war was reserved for the prophet, who told his recruits to maintain calm
and await his order.

The movement was taken entirely unawares by the arrest of Kinjikitile,
on 16 July 1905.[9] Responding to this swift move on the part of the German
authorities, his followers decided to act without delay, beating the war drums
in the Matumbi village of Nandete on 20 July 1905. A small group of insurgents moved on the local communal plantations and in an action amounting
to a declaration of war, began to destroy the cotton crop cultivated under the
hated system of forced labor. Successfully repulsing the forces dispatched by
the akida to pacify the situation, the first battle was fought and won by the
Maji forces at Kibata. The local akida barricaded himself in and on 28 July,
sent for German help from the coastal town of Kilwa. The following days
saw the Maji launch further attacks on other akida and Indian traders, whose
houses they plundered. Establishing an effective communication network
based on a system of messengers known as Hongos, the Maji were able to
organize a large native following, including many former chiefs previously
employed in the administration of the colony.[10]

These actions were followed by further attacks on smaller towns on the
trading routes north of the mountains in the direction of Kilwa. Maji
forces also attacked individual German settlers who, emulating the Indian
traders, fled to the coast. The revolt unleashed its anger on all the visible
representatives of the colonial system: German planters and district administrators, African tax collectors, Arab akida, Indian merchants, and
European missionaries and their supporters.[11] The first German death followed on 30 July 1905. The next day, over a thousand Maji warriors attacked
the coastal town of Samanga, while the Wangindo managed to storm the
military post at Liwale on 13 August after a three-day siege. The entire garrison, led by a noncommissioned officer, was killed in the action. Even
though no further garrisons were defeated during the course of the insurrection, Maji forces continued to threaten the coastal area and the capital Dar es
Salaam.

Initially viewing this violence as an incidence of temporary unrest, the
German administration first began to take the events seriously at the beginning of August 1905. Two weeks after the events in Nandete on 4 August,

the administration hanged the "wizard" blamed for the war—presumably the prophet Kinjikitile. At this point, the German authorities could call on only a modest force with which to respond to the insurrection: 1,701 soldiers of the Protection Force made up of native soldiers or Askaris, 659 policemen, and a naval unit from the cruiser *Bussard*.[12] The three southern districts of Kilwa, Lindi, and Mohoro were protected by only 212 soldiers; indeed, the German military presence in the south of the colony amounted to a total of 588 men of the Protection Force, supplemented by 458 members of the local police force. The reinforcements requested on 15 August (i.e., after the fall of the garrison at Liwale) arrived in German East Africa at the end of September.

Von Götzen's plan involved a holding action to defend the most significant garrisons in the protectorate and reestablish the communications between them. The uprising itself was then to be crushed after the arrival of the reinforcements dispatched by Berlin. Concerned to prevent the spread of the revolt to the north of the territory with its extensive German population, his declared war aim was the "prevention of the further spread of the revolt and the dousing of individual fires."[13] Having received a "free hand" from Berlin to conduct the response, he was not subject to instructions from the General Staff, although he was required to consult with the senior naval officer in Dar es Salaam before deploying the naval contingent. As the revolt was restricted to specific regions, he only declared a state of war in particular districts. The situation of the German troops improved markedly in September after the arrival of the cruisers *Seeadler* and *Thetis,* which secured the coast with their battery and landing parties.

The participation in the Maji Maji War of up to twenty ethnic groups—themselves split into their own clans and subgroups—enables classification of the war in four phases, according to the scope of its impact.[14] The first phase saw the war spread within a month throughout an area highly disparate in terms of both its geography and ethnic composition. This phase saw the uprising reach around two-thirds of its final extent. Lasting from the end of August to the end of September, the second phase saw the rebellion achieve its greatest reach. While the colonial administration remained unsure of its actual range and success, the insurgency had established a firm grip over almost the entire southern half of the territory of what is now modern-day Tanzania. The war area comprised seven districts: Iringa, Kilwa, Lindi, Mahenge, Mohoro, Morogoro, and Songea. This explains the decision taken by the German commander to concentrate on the protection of the life and property of Europeans and "loyal" Africans. Hard-pressed by the Maji forces, the German military controlled a corridor ranging from Liwale and Mahenge to Lake Malawi in the south.

Operating in tight formations of up to 3,000 men,[15] the Maji warriors made use of a firing line and hoped to compensate for the inferiority of their weapons through concentrating their forces in massed attacks on German positions from all sides. Such operations were possible only because of close cooperation and communication between the clan leaders.[16] Despite such intensive preparation and the launch of concentrated attacks, the German forces deployed their machine guns to inflict considerable casualties on the Maji forces. This was compounded by a number of serious defeats such as the abortive and highly costly attack on the German garrison at Mahenge launched on 30 August 1905. Despite this setback, the Maji movement was still capable of registering successes, capturing two mission stations in close proximity of the garrison of Songea some days later.

The nature of the war changed with distance from the center of its outbreak in the south of the protectorate. Assuming the character of a popular revolt in Matumbi and Mahenge, the course assumed by the war in Ungoni was determined by local military leaders. Here, the warriors of the Wangoni abandoned their initial tactics of open warfare and attacks on fortified installations in favor of a guerilla war of ambush and surprise, seeking to land decisive blows on their German opponents while minimizing their own casualties. Despite sharing common aims, the clans operated largely independently of each other and did not establish any form of supraregional collaboration.[17]

Although the fighting spread to encompass an area extending up to Lake Victoria by the end of October 1905, the Maji movement had already passed its peak. The third phase of the war, which lasted until the end of January 1906, saw the Protection Force register a number of victories. Reinforced by detachments of Marine Infantry and a number of newly recruited Askaris, the mixed force of naval units and Protection Force—a combined strength of 3,759 men—succeeded in preventing the war from spreading along the northwestern perimeter of Lake Malawi, the location of a number of German mission stations.[18] Expeditions were dispatched to recover lost territory and a scorched earth policy was operated in the process. The success of these measures by the beginning of 1906 enabled the withdrawal of the Marine Infantry.

Even if this third phase was dominated by a guerilla war, German forces also succeeded in bringing their enemy to give a number of large-scale battles, the outcome of which was to weaken the Maji movement significantly. Of even greater significance, however, was the inability of the insurgents to recruit any more warriors—for example, the plantation workers in the Hinterland of Tanga did not prove receptive to their message. A lengthening war not only made clear the devastating effectiveness of the German tactics but also discredited the claim to invulnerability made by the Maji. In turn, this made it easier for the government to return to their old tactic of *divide et impera,* driving a wedge between individual regions and thus putting down the insurgency province by province.

The insurgency collapsed across the majority of fronts at the beginning of 1906. Indeed, the continuation of resistance in a handful of provinces was due only to the inability on the part of the insurgents to agree on the best method of surrender. Some Maji leaders were handed over by their exhausted and disappointed followers; others were persuaded to surrender by torture. Further of their number were captured by bounty hunters working for the German authorities. Others surrendered voluntarily. Thus the Wangoni commander Mputa Gama was taken prisoner on 10 January, whereas Selemani Mamba (the local leader in Umwera) surrendered voluntarily in the same month. The majority of the Maji leaders and Hongos in Mahenge were either killed or captured by a punitive expedition. Although German forces had succeeded in killing a number of Maji leaders, the majority of the south of the protectorate remained in African hands up to 1906 and still constituted a serious threat to German rule.[19]

The fourth phase of the Maji Maji War lasted from February 1906 to early 1908. Following the recapture by German troops of the Matumbi mountains and the area north of the Rufiji, the only area providing any resistance was the extreme south of the protectorate, where fighting was restricted to a number of isolated conflicts in the Kilwa and Lindi districts. In putting down this resistance, the German forces were no longer confronted by large groups of warriors, but a number of smaller guerilla operations. Although making a number of areas insecure, this campaign did not represent a lasting threat to the restoration of German rule. Ngozingozi, the "last great leader of the rebellion" was shot in May 1908; his successor Mpangire followed him two months later on 18 July. This date marked the final end of the Maji Maji War and the restoration of German rule.

German figures submitted to the Reichstag in August 1907 estimated African losses during the war at 75,000.[20] In contrast, the Tanzanian historian Gilbert Gwassa places the number of African deaths at between 250,000 and 300,000.[21] Such figures—supported by Gwassa's British colleague John Iliffe—correspond to a third of the entire prewar African population of the areas of conflict. Other studies argue that such calculations probably include not only the number of war dead but also those dying from the effects of shortages, hunger, and displacement. A contemporary consensus focuses on a figure of 180,000 victims.[22] German losses are clear: a total of 15 white soldiers, 389 African soldiers and auxiliaries, and 66 bearers died.[23] The demographic impact of the war was not limited to increased morbidity. The near depopulation of the Songea district (registering some 166,000 inhabitants in 1902–1903, these figures fell to no more than 20,000 in the aftermath of the war) cannot be attributed to war deaths alone. The destruction of resources and the resulting mass flight from the land resulted in considerable demographic redistribution within the protectorate.[24]

The postwar policy pursued in German East Africa was very different from the rigid system of colonial rule introduced in German South-West Africa following the end of the Herero and Nama War and manifested in particular in the "native ordinances." Changes in personnel in both Berlin and the colony—the appointment of the economist Bernhard Dernburg as director of the Colonial Department in Berlin and Albrecht von Rechenberg as the governor of German East Africa—resulted in a more constructive and open approach to native participation in the economy. As well as establishing a system of African education, they introduced a laissez-faire economic policy, allowing developments in the protectorate to be determined by market forces.[25]

The new leadership did not see it as its role to champion the interests of white settlers and planters; it sought instead to take responsibility for all the colony's inhabitants. Believing that the grant of widespread economic freedom to the African population not only would bind them into the money economy but in unleashing what they viewed as their inestimable instinct for profit would lead to an economic upturn. This new administration argued that it would be wrong to rely exclusively on punitive measures to force Africans to work: "In East Africa we have access to a far from useless reserve of human labor, although it is spread unevenly across the territory [of the protectorate]. Unfortunately, the most important and (as I would assert) the most serviceable supply of labor, the Herero tribe to the South, has been decimated during the war of the last two years. Given constant care, this tribe should be able to re-establish itself."[26]

Visiting German East Africa in the summer of 1907 in the company of an economic delegation, Dernburg propagated his view that the African population represented the most important asset in the economy of the protectorate. He made clear that colonial economic policy would no longer consist merely in the one-sided promotion of white interests, but would be extended to encompass a concerted and integrated program designed to spread prosperity evenly, thus creating markets for German products. He saw that these aims were not served by the economic activity of settler farms and plantations, as it was restricted to a privileged elite. German colonial policy in German East Africa sought now to put an end to the forced cultivation of export products for the European market and indeed all forms of forced labor. This was to be matched by a return to traditional forms of African production such as the cultivation of oleiferous fruits, rice, peanuts, and cotton. Responding to this program, white settlers argued that state sponsorship of African production would hinder their attempts at labor recruitment, thus rendering the plantation economy less profitable. Nevertheless, Rechenberg succeeded in implementing his administrative reforms in the face of their vehement opposition, addressing in the process the worst excesses of akida-maladministration.

Despite a number of problems, the program for the *"Promotion and Development of the Negro Cultures" (Programm zur Förderung und Entwicklung der Negerkulturen)*[27] proved a countermodel to the policy of extermination or (at least) reduction of the African population as practiced in German South-West Africa. German policy in East Africa ensured the brutal suppression of the insurgent movement, but subsequently sought to establish a regime of cooperation and collaboration in an attempt to create a joint and sustainable future. As such, the immediate postwar settlements to both wars were of a highly diverging character.

Raids

The military response to the Maji Maji uprising concentrated initially on the conduct of a number of expeditions. The Protection Force consisted of African soldiers under the command of Governor von Götzen. The Marine Infantry commanded by Corvette Captain Otto Back assembled in small detachments of between ten and twenty men, often accompanied by African volunteers. Dispatched to conduct operations in the East African bush, they were lightly armed and moved without bearers. Operations were commanded from the gubernatorial office in Dar es Salaam, which, working closely with the naval officer commanding, gathered intelligence from letters and telegrams before establishing the targets for the punitive operations.

The exact route taken by the detachment was decided by its commander. Working closely with the District Offices, he relied heavily on their superior supply of local information.[28]

The initial phase of the conflict also saw naval officers lead these expeditions. On 2 August 1905, immediately after the beginning of the uprising, a detachment of sailors under the command of Lieutenant Hans Paasche was landed in Mohoro Bay from the *Bussard,* from where they proceeded up the Rufiji to the station at Mohoro.[29] Although ordered merely to occupy and to hold their position, Paasche conducted a number of small expeditions within a two-hour radius of the district office.[30] Despite the entirely defensive nature of his orders, he believed that this more aggressive approach would serve to prevent the spread of the rising over a wider area. His inclination to independence of action was favored by the poor nature of the communications with Dar es Salaam, from where orders could arrive with a delay of days or even weeks.

Paasche intended that his troops exercise a "calming"[31] effect on their environment. His soldiers eschewed a planned approach to their missions, usually reacting only to appeals for help from white and black alike, but according especial priority to the protection of mission stations and plantations. For instance, the plantation manager of the *Lindi-Hinterlandgesellschaft Mungwe* requested help from the sailors of the *Bussard* after insurgents set fire to a local village. Villagers often sent emissaries to the troops because they feared for their lives and the security of their provisions. Indeed, the military leadership attached high priority to the "protection of loyal natives,"[32] hoping that acting to secure their lives and livelihoods would engender trust, thereby starving the insurgency of extra troops. Having arrived in a new area, the commander of the expedition was required to make a quick judgment regarding not only the general situation but as to which villages required protection, which village could defend itself, and whether to set up a new position. The troops were also deployed if informed of an impending attack or the location of an enemy position that they could then take by surprise. Although often contradictory, the collation of such intelligence often provided a reliable picture of the main thrust of enemy movements. For their part, insurgent groups often had access to extremely reliable information about the movement of the German expeditions, gathered from their network of scouts and spies.

The expeditions saw the German units move from place to place to hunt "rebels" and ease the plight of their allies. The soldiers were under orders to kill as many insurgents as possible. Although the *Bussard* was able to operate along the coast, the unnavigability of the majority of the inland waterways in the south meant that many target locations could be reached only on foot. Such geographical realities were compounded by the lack of equipment and scouts; as a result, the inland range of operations was extremely restricted. A shortage of bearers and the resulting need to live from the land meant that patrols conducted in areas yielding insufficient provisions often had to be cut short.[33] Moreover, operations were hampered by high levels of illness especially among the German soldiers, reaching up to 50 percent.[34] The sailors were especially prone to disease and could be deployed only as garrison troops. Paasche recognized that the most effective method of combating the insurgents would be the employment of small, fast-moving native units which made a minimum of noise by marching barefoot. The loud and slow-moving European troops made them largely unsuitable for such engagements.[35]

Soldiers in the mobile units were forced to adopt a number of tactics. While attacks on enemy camps were largely conducted as firefights, approaching insurgents were met in formation, with the troops forming ranks for volley fire.[36] When under attack from fortified positions or caught in an ambush, they were to take cover without waiting for the order. Attacked in high grass, they were to fire blindly. The repertoire of action involved in the "hunt for rebels" was equally broad. Suspected rebels were to be shot out of hand, as was anyone observed found running with a gun in their hand. Prisoners taken for questioning were subsequently shot, to avoid burdening the patrol but also to spread fear among the native population. Whole villages were burned down if stolen goods were found. All supplies that could not be plundered were burned. In contrast to this aggressive approach, the leaders of smaller expeditions also conducted negotiations with local chiefs. These often proved successful, and resulted in the voluntary surrender of weapons.

The conditions of surrender were initially established by the individual German commanders. Some foresaw the surrender of weapons; others required that their prisoners pay contributions, perform work, or even provide supplies to the bases in the communications zone and government caravans.[37] Binding rules regulating the surrender were only formulated in November 1905 with Governor von Götzen's "orders to the troop commanders in the insurgent areas." These stipulated that the "ring leaders and magicians" be handed over together with all firearms. Every man surrendering was to pay a fine of three rupees or perform equivalent work for the local government or a local firm. Any large-scale formations or communities surrendering en masse were to provide laborers to perform between three and six months of forced labor as a punishment.[38] Almost all the surviving combatants were subject to sanctions consisting of taxes and forced labor. The conditions of surrender were designed to secure the long-term economic future of the protectorate as a German colony.[39]

Although Paasche's unit suffered only a single fatality while killing 300 Africans,[40] the overall impact of the small mobile units deployed between August and November 1905 was later judged to have been minor and inefficient. "Despite their ability to inflict losses on the insurgents where they encountered them, the detachments of the Protection Force were able to achieve little more than the protection of the life and property of Europeans and loyal natives."[41] This situation was to change at the end of September with the arrival of the Marine Infantry from Germany. Abandoning the defensive tactics hitherto practiced, focusing on limiting the damage suffered to settler property, the reinforcements proceeded to clear the territory of insurgents. One such operation was commanded by Lieutenant Max Engelbrecht. Given a considerable force, he recaptured the railroad to Morogoro. Success in this operation enabled the German forces to penetrate the interior and stabilize the rear areas, thus securing the supply lines.

The arrival of the Marine Infantry in September permitted the organization of larger expeditions. The original mixed units of naval ratings and Protection Force now performed a secondary, supportive role, foraging and requisitioning materiel and supplies. On 21 October 1905, a large-scale offensive was launched under the command of Major Kurt Johannes to reclaim the area of Songea during the course of which a "large number of villages and huts were burned down" and enemy supply camps plundered.[42] The offensive culminated in large-scale battles of encirclement and annihilation, ending in German victories. Control was finally wrested from the natives by the intensification and a more systematic application of patrols, resulting in a scorched earth policy.

Destruction

Seeking to elicit the mood of the naval officers in the colony and gather constructive suggestions for future strategy, the senior naval officer in the African station compiled a "confidential questionnaire" which was distributed to the detachment leaders on 15 November 1905. The responses indicated a widely held belief among the officers that the uprising would spread were it not suppressed with violence. All those questioned rejected an alternative presented in the questionnaire involving "concessions to the natives." It was a matter of consensus that any form of clemency shown to the natives would be interpreted as weakness and would serve only to encourage further, potentially more dangerous uprisings.[43] The respondents referred to the African tactics as "guerilla warfare," involving what they referred to as a "horde of leaderless savages" or a "cowardly and deceitful mob"[44] that concentrated on laying ambush on patrols. Smaller German units patrolling in the bush were seen as vulnerable to attack, while the Africans avoided larger sections. Communications posts and caravans were viewed as particularly vulnerable to attack. The officers indicated how those sections of the population not participating in the insurgency came under considerable pressure from its members. The respondents saw this mixture of forced and voluntary support for the insurgency as conferring a decisive advantage on the guerilla fighters, who were able to evade the German troops and avoid suffering any losses. Indeed, one of their most important tactics was identified as the abandonment of entire villages so as to deny colonial troops success in battle. The detachments gradually grew accustomed to finding deserted villages; those they destroyed—at least according to their reports—were quickly rebuilt.[45] The native population played their part in such tactics, secreting away provisions to covert locations, from where they were distributed among the insurgents. Boundaries between hostile and "peaceful" Africans thus blurred quickly.

The Germans responded to an elusive and well-supplied enemy with a radicalized scorched earth policy, designed to starve the enemy into submission.[46] Captain Curt von Wangenheim, commander of the Morogoro district, summarized the new strategy thus: "Only [the imposition of] hunger and want can effect final submission."[47] The response to the officers' questionnaire not only underlines the level and nature of the violence to which local German commanders were prepared to countenance but most likely obviated the need for orders to achieve such an end. No order has been found specifying the scorched earth policy employed in German East Africa.[48]

The move to a strategy centering on the targeted destruction of all the available resources was completed by the end of 1905 at the latest. Villages and huts were burned down, "not only as a punishment, but to encourage their inhabitants to return and rebuild."[49] The new huts were then also destroyed. Fields were devastated, cattle and foodstuffs sequestered. In addition to foodstuffs, the Germans also plundered valuables and weapons including spears, bows and arrows, and shields as well as war drums and jewelry. Expropriated, these objects were labeled with their place of origin and put on display in Berlin. These tactics not only denied the insurgents the material basis for operations, they also solved German supply problems.[50] As in China, such operations were designed in part to weaken the long-term supply situation of the insurgents and involved such tactics as conducting military operations during the sowing season.

Not always issued with express orders to this effect and usually acting on their own initiative, the troops conducting such actions could usually be sure of at least the acquiescence of their officers. Even the cotton plantations cultivated on the orders of the colonial administration, and themselves representing a cause of the war, were not exempted from the widespread program of destruction. Not only the insurgents but a great number of the loyal clans and Askari serving with the Germans suffered under the effects of the scorched earth policy. Indeed, this suffering was compounded by the need to provide replacement foodstuffs for the losses thus incurred. Some areas of German East Africa even saw the European population suffer from the shortages.[51] Aiming not just at the destruction of tangible assets, the scorched earth policy was part of a concerted attempt to generate a feeling of continuous existential insecurity, referred to as holding the population in a situation of "constant anxiety."[52] To this end, the Germans sought to destroy the supposedly safe areas into which the natives had hoped to retreat. Subject to such a program, the natives' quality of life deteriorated greatly and over the long term affected insurgents and loyalists alike.

The detachments conducting expeditions in German East Africa employed four measures to generate and maintain this climate "of constant anxiety": the taking of prisoners, forced labor, hostage taking, and executions. Those Africans not killed were to be kept in a constant state of fear through maltreatment. Nevertheless, as Paasche knew, such treatment could prove to be counterproductive: "The brutalization of prisoners generates respect amongst the natives whilst hampering their readiness to submit."[53] Interned in small camps near the district offices or military stations, provision for their needs was a local matter, for which no funding was available from Berlin. Indeed, consuming resources intended for the troops, this situation contributed to an unwillingness to take prisoners.

A greater number were subject to corporal punishment. Male prisoners were to expect a minimum punishment of being held in chains: thus manacled, they were often employed as forced laborers. A number of prisoners were still held in chains in the Lindi District Office as late as 1907, when a

Reichstag commission of inquiry visited the German protectorate. One member of the delegation, Judge Richard Kalkhof, wrote in a report that only serious criminals were subject to such treatment; all other felons were chained by a light chain clasped around the neck, by which between six and eight prisoners were chained together in a sufficiently large space. Despite his "initial alarm at this form of treatment" the judge reflected that "in view of the prevailing conditions—the large number of prisoners, the danger of escape and attack, the lack of overseers and the nature of joint work in the open air" such treatment was both "necessary and in no way inhumane."[54]

The "removal of women and children" developed into the "most effective means" by which to force the subjection of the native population and put an end to the uprising.[55] The practice of hostage taking not only led to the detection of hidden villages and supplies but served to reduce the potential reserve of guerilla fighters. One supplementary effect of this policy was to increase the pool of labor available for what the German authorities referred to euphemistically as "the general good" (Allgemeines kulturelles Interesse).[56] Women and children were often temporarily interned in camps under the authority not of the District Office but of the military authorities. Practiced during the Wahehe uprising, such a policy had a long tradition in German East Africa. Those thus interned were released only after their menfolk had surrendered.

Following a declaration of a state of war, hurriedly convened drumhead courts martial were authorized to pass death sentences. Although the process involved the hearing of witnesses and a defense, Paasche felt that these were given little or no credence; in his judgment, the only just sentences were those issued to natives caught red handed.[57] On one day in February 1906, forty-eight Wangoni warriors were executed in the District of Songea. Seeking to increase the deterrent effect of such executions, the authorities took to hanging its prisoners on a high hill, visible for all to see. Such scenes were captured in a number of so-called East African native drawings commissioned by the German ethnologist Karl Weule during an expedition through German East Africa in 1906.[58]

The primary German aim in conducting the Maji Maji War was not the restoration of order, but the desire to punish the insurrectionists and deter any future revolts. Policy makers rejected anything that might amount to an "unsatisfactory peace."[59] The rather broad German definition of punishment combined with their general mistrust of the native population served to legitimate a wide range of punitive measures including the arbitrary and indiscriminate confiscation of foodstuffs. Nevertheless, following the conclusion of hostilities, the colonial administration also granted considerable economic aid to the areas most ravaged by the war, distributing seed and occasionally purchasing the harvest on favorable terms. Nevertheless, such aid was not always forthcoming and rested entirely on the discretion of the local military commander.[60] Indeed, the recipients of such aid were required to pay for the assistance, either in cash or in kind with labor. The colonial administration did not want to give the impression that it was distributing alms to a people with whom it had recently been at war.

The German conduct of the Maji Maji War seriously threatened the long-term viability of the population in the south of German East Africa. Not only were great swathes of the protectorate reduced to a desolate and inhospitable wasteland, the population levels and distribution were subject to considerable long-term disruption. Losing not just the majority of their traditional leaders—as far as they had participated in the uprising—but their villages, harvests, and supplies, the native population faced an extremely uncertain future. The peasantry in particular was forced to accept decisive changes in its living conditions. Put to flight, resettled, or deported, many were forced to begin anew in areas foreign to them. Those remaining on their ancestral homelands were subject to famine conditions which extended across a considerable area.[61] Native mortality levels remained very high even after the end of the war, and a number of those who survived war and hunger later succumbed to a number of epidemics. A drop in births and a high rate of infant mortality seriously affected the long-term viability of the population structure.[62]

The three major colonial wars fought by Germany at the turn of the twentieth century—the Boxer War in 1900–1901, the Herero and Nama War in 1904–1907, and the Maji Maji War in 1905–1908—are characterized by a number of differences. The China war saw a phase of siege warfare and urban conflict followed by a policy of occupation and punitive expeditions. The war in German South-West Africa witnessed a number of set-piece battles followed by a battle of annihilation at Waterberg and an ensuing pursuit. This was followed by the establishment of internment camps and a counterinsurgency campaign conducted by mobile units. The war in German East Africa, on the other hand, was characterized first by a number of skirmishes and battles which were then superseded by expeditions and the scorched earth policy by which the guerilla war was brought to an end.

All three wars witnessed the employment of all conceivable forms of violence against the native population—plundering, requisition, rape, hostage taking, the razing of towns and villages, starvation tactics, shootings, executions, the erection of prison camps—albeit with a different emphasis in each war. German methods in China concentrated on plundering, requisitions, rape, hostage taking, the razing of towns and villages, shootings, and executions. In South-West Africa, they focused on shootings and executions followed by death in camps. German East Africa saw a greater emphasis placed on shootings, hostage taking, the razing of villages, starvation tactics, and forced migration.

Especially striking is the high degree of similarity between the form assumed by the violence unleashed in China and that in German East Africa. However, while the punitive expeditions launched in China tended to culminate in the razing of settlements, the campaign in German East Africa comprised expeditions of a much smaller scale, soon to be replaced by a strategy of scorched earth. The conduct of the war in German South-West Africa confers on it a unique position among the three conflicts: starting as a conventional war of encirclement and pursuit, it culminated in the establishment of internment camps on a large scale. The mobile units developed in the later stages of the war were deployed to put an end to the guerilla war by apprehending and imprisoning the enemy warriors. A combination of conventional warfare and a network of camps resulted in the near-destruction of the two majority ethnic groups, the Herero and the Nama.

The war in German South-West Africa thus assumes a unique position in the sequence of German colonial wars conducted at the turn of the twentieth century not only because of the form it assumed but also because of the extent of the violence meted out in its course. This singular status is demonstrated less by the absolute number of deaths incurred by the insurgent populations than by the proportion of the Herero and Nama exterminated, which amounted to between 30 and 50 percent of the total of the two populations. That this violence was neither initiated nor brought to an end by either the issue or the rescinding of the so-called extermination proclamations indicates merely that the genocidal violence characterizing the war in German South-West Africa emerged entirely independently of any conscious decision for or against a strategy of concerted racial genocide.

The contrasting nature and modality of the German conduct of these three wars and the corresponding exercise of violence in the three colonial settings makes it impossible to explain the descent into genocide experienced in German South-West Africa by reference either to any degree of military intention or to a putative military culture seen to generate recurring modes of behavior in differing contexts. The individual and unrelated decisions taken in each separate context produced a specific form of warfare distinct to each conflict. Any explanation of these differences is to be located in the unique local conditions that the German military experienced in each individual theater of war.

Part II

THE COLONIAL THEATER *of* WAR

CHAPTER 4

The Motivation of White and Native Colonial Soldiers

T HE NATURE of the German colonial possessions, unprofitable and of only minor significance, meant that neither the German military establishment nor the imperial exchequer could countenance the establishment of a standing colonial army or even an officers' training course for service in the colonies. Unlike the situation in the British, French, and Dutch armed forces, there was no arm or service of the German army in which those aspiring to serve in the protectorates were able to gain the relevant training to prepare them for service in a colonial crisis zone. Deploying colonial volunteers drawn from the regular army within a single "Protection Force" (Schutztruppe) established for each protectorate (with the exception of Togo), the operations of these forces were often supported by naval personnel and members of the Marine Infantry. They were also assisted by a number of expeditionary corps—the composition and deployment of which was decided on a case-by-case basis—and contingents of native auxiliaries. The organization of German colonial soldiery[1] was still very much in its infancy at the turn of the twentieth century; indeed it was the succession of colonial wars that gave the decisive impetus for a reform and the creation of a colonial military structure. With the absence of a unitary conception within the German military establishment of the role and duties of colonial military needs, those serving in the colonies acted from a number of differing motivations. Lacking any degree of professionalism, specialism, or a particular esprit de corps, the soldiers dispatched to fight the colonial wars exhibited an extreme level of heterogeneity.

The Protection Force

Following their acquisition by Germany in 1884–1885, the African protectorates were initially policed by a number of military formations: Hermann von Wissmann's force of native mercenaries in German East Africa; François's paramilitary formation in German South-West Africa; and Gravenreuth's police troops in Cameroon. With the character of private armies, these units were not integrated into the formal military structures of imperial Germany.[2] Initially part of the imperial navy, the Protection Forces formed in the colonies after 1891 were established as an independent organization only after 1896. Operating as a third section of the army, the Protection Forces were given the task of "maintaining public order and security in the African Protectorates,"[3] upholding the peace *(Landfrieden)*, and thus guaranteeing the conditions requisite to the economic development of each colony. Although placed under the supreme command of the kaiser, the Protection Forces reported to the chancellor via the Colonial Department of the Foreign Office. All military matters were directed by the Protection Forces High Command, a separate military staff commanded by a senior staff officer and formed in 1897. An imperial decree from May 1907 amalgamated the Colonial Department of the Foreign Ministry and the Protection Force High Command into the Imperial Colonial Office, which reported directly to the chancellor. Although the Foreign Ministry was given authority only in administrative matters, this change was significant in that it placed a military force under the direction of a civilian authority. This situation was exacerbated even further by the fact that this authority was restricted to administrative matters. All long-term strategic and short-term operational matters came under the purview of the general staff.[4]

The "Organizational Regulations for the Imperial Protection Forces in Africa" *(Schutztruppen-Ordnung)* issued in July 1898 established a comprehensive set of regulations for the structure and command of these formations. Supreme local military authority in the protectorates was exercised by the colonial governor, who assumed complete responsibility for military actions and was authorized to deploy and direct the use of force. Operational control of each Protection Force was vested in its military commander, who was granted freedom to shape his response to what he felt to be the dictates of immediate military circumstance. As such, military action was clearly intended be subordinate to political imperatives.[5]

The Protection Forces were composed of a number of volunteers drawn from the armies of the individual German states and the imperial navy, who committed themselves to a number of years of service in the protectorates. The length of service for Cameroon initially amounted to two years; that for German East Africa two and a half years, and service in German South-West Africa amounted to three years, including home leave amounting to four months. Those wishing to extend their term of service could so do by submitting an application shortly before it expired. Applicants were required to demonstrate "good conduct both during and outside service, absolute reliability, exemplary moral conduct, initiative and good military training, especially in field service and weaponry."[6]

As garrisons were primarily stationed in rural settings, recruitment campaigns sought to attract those with practical skills versed in the construction of houses, stations, and roads.[7] The job description of the German "colonial soldier" was therefore not restricted to fighting. The activities of the Protection Force involved both destruction and construction within a wider colonial framework. A commitment made to a Protection Force often represented a more general decision to move to the colonies. An as yet unquantified number of the various Protection Forces later settled in the lands in which they had served.

The white personnel of the Protection Force were supplemented by native auxiliaries. The pay, victualing, and duration of service of these soldiers were regulated by the staff of the Protection Force in individual contracts, the terms of which were subject to gubernatorial confirmation. While the Protection Forces in German East Africa and Cameroon were manned entirely by native forces, in German South-West Africa they were composed overwhelmingly of volunteers from the imperial German navy and army serving together with national servicemen from the metropole. This force was supplemented by a very small native contingent.

The situation in the colony of Qingdao in China was a special case. Subject to the administration of the Imperial Naval Office, civil authority was invested in the senior naval officer commanding, who also acted as commander in chief of the land forces. The Third Sea Battalion of Marine Infantrymen stationed in Qingdao was supplemented by the presence of a Chinese unit established on an experimental basis.

In the absence of a Protection Force or naval unit, the other German overseas possessions—Togo and the South Seas—were controlled entirely by native police units. Such units were also established in Cameroon,

German East Africa, and German South-West Africa. Composed of both whites and natives, the latter were permitted only to fill the ranks. Not enjoying any level of individual autonomy, the local police authorities and Police Corps in German South-West Africa reported to their nearest district office. As the police forces were recruited almost exclusively from a pool of former Protection Force soldiers, the boundaries between the civil police and military Protection Forces remained fluid.[8]

Officers

The organization of the Protection Forces reproduced the conventional hierarchy of the Prussian army: officers, noncommissioned officers (NCOs), and other ranks. The force was administered by a military civil service. Applications for a commission in the Protection Force were open to army officers on active service and holders of a commission in the reserve or Landwehr. Required to establish their fitness for service in the Protection Force, the application criteria focused on professional qualifications and a sound character. Recruiters looked for "a calm, mature character, clear judgment, clear resolution, leadership skills, tact toward superiors, a strong sense of camaraderie, a clean record and a sound financial situation."[9] In reality, however, disgraced officers often viewed colonial service as an easy route to rehabilitation.[10] Moreover, despite the insistence on professional qualifications, applicants were not required to display any profound knowledge of the colonies or hold any skills—such as knowledge of the land or its language—relevant to service overseas. The only colonial-specific training offered to applicants was entirely voluntary in nature.

Service in the colonies was highly lucrative. Those officers and other ranks who served in one of the Protection Forces for an uninterrupted period of more than three years could increase their reckonable service calculations for pension payment by between one-sixth and a maximum of double the basic pension. Indeed, six months of uninterrupted colonial service counted as double that served in an army garrison in the Metropole. Excluded from these calculations were only those years of service that had previously been accepted as wartime service and that were already subject to the double pay calculation. Every officer invalided out of the Protection Force and certified as unfit for duty received a pension corresponding to his length of service and commission and supplemented by an allowance for service in the tropics. Officers who had served a minimum of a full twelve years in the Protection

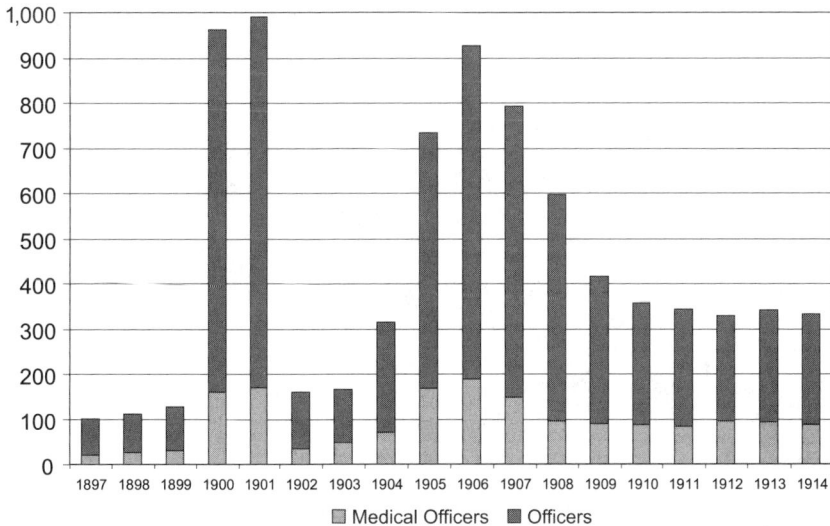

Figure 4.1. Officers in Protection Forces, 1897–1914

Force were entitled to draw their pension without the need to prove their unfitness for service.[11]

Service in the Protection Forces was attractive in terms of career advancement: active service was given consideration in terms of promotion—a fact that encouraged many officers in colonial service to provoke conflicts to an extent impossible in a European military context. Many applicants were attracted by the prospect of adventure or the experience of exotic surroundings, expecting colonial service to consist of an uninterrupted succession of pleasures ranging from hunting big game to exotic native women. The grim reality of service in a remote colonial garrison was a sobering experience for many.

A total of 2,093 officers and 398 medical officers served in the German overseas colonies between 1897 and 1914, including those army volunteers dispatched to China and German South-West Africa.[12] As Figure 4.1 shows, the number of officers employed in the Protection Forces increased erratically with the increasing number of colonial wars, reaching a stable (yet consistently higher) level in 1909.

Tables 4.1–4.3 provide a detailed overview of the number of officers and medical officers deployed in China, German South-West Africa, and German East Africa.[13] In addition to the number of junior and senior ranks and their

Table 4.1. Officers and medical officers deployed in China, 1900–1901.

		Officers		Medical officers	
	Total	No.	%	No.	%
Army	697	577	82.8	120	17.2
Marine infantry	163	153	93.9	10	6.1
Total	860	730	84.9	130	15.1
Aristocratic	274	274	47.5	0	0
Rank to lieut.-col.	751	622	85.2	129	99.2
Rank above lieut.-col.	87	86	14.8	1	0.8
Period of service considered	2 yrs.				
Change to another colony	225	186	25.5	39	30.0
To GSWA	170	141		29	
To GEA	42	37		5	
To Cameroon	13	8		5	

Note: These calculations exclude the Marine Infantry, as they are included in the list of ranks for the Royal Prussian Army and the Thirteenth Royal Wuerttemberg Army Corps in 1900–1901.

Table 4.2. Officers and medical officers deployed in German South-West Africa, 1897–1914.

		Officers		Medical officers	
	Total	No.	%	No.	%
Army	1,013	836	82.5	177	17.5
Aristocratic	269	266	26.3	3	0.2
Rank to lieut.-col.	950	780	93.3	170	96.0
Rank above lieut.-col.	63	56	6.7	7	4.0
Presence 1 yr.	116	94	11.2	22	12.4
Presence 2 yrs.	206	146	17.5	60	33.9
Presence 3 yrs.	261	222	26.6	39	22.0
Presence 6 yrs.	298	266	31.8	32	18.1
Presence 9 yrs.	101	79	9.4	22	12.4
Presence over 9 yrs.	31	29	3.5	2	1.1
Change from/to another colony	242	192	23.0	50	28.2
From China	170	141		29	
From/to GEA	48	35		13	
From/to Cameroon	24	16		8	

Table 4.3. Officers and medical officers deployed in German East Africa, 1897–1914.

	Total	Officers		Medical officers	
		No.	%	No.	%
Army	307	218	71.0	89	29.0
Aristocratic	77	77	25.1	0	0.0
Rank to lieut.-col.	273	187	85.8	86	96.6
Rank above	34	31	14.2	3	3.4
Presence 1 yr.	47	40	18.3	7	7.9
Presence 2 yrs.	35	23	10.6	12	13.5
Presence 3 yrs.	52	43	19.7	9	10.1
Presence 6 yrs.	82	59	27.1	23	25.8
Presence 9 yrs.	42	22	10.1	20	22.5
Presence over 9 yrs.	49	31	14.2	18	20.2
Change from/within a colony	100	77	35.3	23	25.8
From China	42	37		5	
From/to GSWA	48	35		13	
From/to Cameroon	10	5		5	

Note: The presence of an officer in German East Africa was calculated differently, as the term of service amounted to two and a half years rather than the three usual for German South-West Africa.

social origin, the tables also show the duration of service and the number of officers serving in two or three colonial wars.

Around one-third of the officers either serving in the Protection Forces between 1897 and 1914 or volunteering for service in the colonial wars were drawn from the nobility. The great majority of aristocratic volunteers entered the service as subalterns, and very few of those remaining in the colonies for any period reached the rank of major, lieutenant colonel, and colonel. Very few reached any form of generality; the only officer to be made a full general—Paul von Lettow-Vorbeck—required service in the First World War.[14]

Analysis of the time spent by each officer in the colonies reveals two partially overlapping groups. First, there is the group of officers and medical officers who served particularly long periods in the colonies. Second, there are the "changers," that is, participants in more than one colonial war. Examination of the years of service of those officers serving in German

South-West Africa and German East Africa would seem to reveal a high level of fluctuation. Around 60 percent of colonial officers served only a single term in the protectorate (two and a half or three years); 20 percent served for two terms. Only 15 percent of the officers and 20 percent of the medical officers signed up for a period of more than six years. In German East Africa, 25 percent of the officers remained in the protectorate for nine years and longer; the figures for Cameroon and German South-West Africa amount to 21 percent and 13 percent, respectively.

These figures point to the development of a very small yet hard core group of "old hands" within the Protection Forces. Referring to themselves as "old Africans" (sometimes even "very old Africans"), they considered that their training and experience set them apart from callow newcomers and the bureaucrats in Berlin. They were proud of having "proven themselves in the field," and their focus on and glorification of hardness, local knowledge, and a cool head and their disdain for regulations exhibited all the traits of an idealized masculinity typical for a nascent colonial society.[15] The old Africans often displayed a paternalistic attitude to the black population. As Captain Victor Franke put it, "I have grown rather fond of the Hereros. My heart grows heavy when I think of future rulers who have no sympathy for these black scoundrels."[16] Indeed, coming to identify with their new homeland, it was these old Africans such as Franke, Theodor Leutwein, and Ludwig von Estorff who opposed the policy of extermination adopted by von Trotha during the Herero war. They were also influential in shaping the growing view that the black population represented a serious economic resource which should not be risked so lightly.

The extent to which these old Africans in German South-West Africa had "gone native" led newly arrived officers to regard them with suspicion. Uneasy that such a level of adaptation represented the crossing of a cultural Rubicon, they feared that this "kaffirization" could result in a blurring of loyalties and impinge upon the execution of their duty as a German soldier.[17] It was a matter of intense debate as to how much "Africa" a European could assimilate without "going African," especially in German South-West Africa.

In contrast to the "hard core" of German colonial officers who spent long periods in the African colonies, the three tables point to the existence of a further group of officers exhibiting a far greater degree of mobility and flexibility. Participating in a number of colonial wars, and accounting for almost a third of the total personnel, the majority of this group of changers served six or more years in the colonies. Of the 259 of this group, 208 were officers and 51 medical officers. Of the 697 officers recorded as having participated in the Boxer War (including members of the Marine Infantry), 225 were found to have served in Africa; 170 in German South-West Africa, 42 in German East Africa, and 13 in Cameroon. Of the 170 army officers dispatched to German South-West Africa, 135 participated in the Herero and Nama War, and of the 42 sent to German East Africa, 15 participated in the Maji Maji War. The other changers moved during peace time. Forty-eight officers moved between the two African colonies, but not all during a period of conflict. Thirty-two of this number served in the war in German South-West Africa. Only six of the officers (one officer and five medical officers) participated in all three colonial wars. It becomes clear that there was never at any time anything approaching a core number of changers, or indeed anything approaching a "German Foreign Legion" of professional colonial officers who saw service in all the German colonies.

The majority of the officers of the various Protection Forces regarded colonial service as a stepping-stone on the path of professional advancement. Only one-fifth regarded it as a long-term challenge and sought to remain in one of the colonies for any period of time. Active service in the context of a native insurrection was viewed as desirable, as it conferred considerable advantages in the calculation of periods of service. As such, the officers of the Protection Force did not require any specific or special motivation, especially in view of their function within the apparatus of colonial rule. As the executive instrument of colonial rule, itself an inherently violent form of authority, they soon grew accustomed to the associated exercise of violence.

Medical Officers

According to the "Organizational Regulations for the Imperial Protection Forces in Africa," the Protection Force Medical Corps was to be supplemented by volunteers who signed up for a number of years of service.[18] The Naval Medical Corps had been established as an independent organization separate to the army in 1896. Trained in dedicated institutions in Germany (such as the Military Medical Surgical Academy in Berlin), applicants for the army and naval medical services needed to demonstrate a good physical constitution and academic record. Requiring an independent financial position to enable them to finance their studies, the majority of medical officers were drawn almost exclusively (some 99 percent) from the upper middle classes.

The few medical officers active in the Protection Forces deployed in German South-West Africa, German East Africa, and Cameroon ranged in rank from second lieutenant (med.) to colonel (med.).[19] While the number of medical officers serving in German South-West Africa increased to 128 following the dispatch of reinforcements during the course of the war, this figure remained two less than the corresponding figures for the war in China. A total of 398 medical officers were deployed in China and Germany's African colonies between 1897 and 1914.

The nature of colonial service and the shortages of infantry officers meant that medical officers could also see active service, and a number of medical officers were even decorated for their participation in the Herero and Nama War.[20] Nevertheless, the primary task of the colonial medical corps was to provide palliative and curative care for the soldiers under their care. Charged with the prophylactic control of disease, the medical officers also saw themselves as fighting on their very own microbiological front. This task involved a difficult balancing act, as the so-called war hygiene could not be allowed to become an aim in itself. Scientific research of a long-term nature or intricate programs of disease prevention were not permitted to take precedence over the more immediate task of maintaining the fighting strength of the troop. To this end, medical officers were not permitted to make any medical demands that could restrict troop availability.[21]

In performing this function, military medical provision worked within the scope of existing programs of practical troop hygiene and tropical hygiene. The relevant hospital ordinances specified an exact assessment of the danger presented by the climate and geography, the water quality, and the danger of contagion by people, animals, and foodstuffs. As such, the combined duties with which a medical officer was charged established him in a function approaching that of a colonial "spatial sociologist," dedicated to the "prevention of impending labefaction."[22] Medical officers from both the army and navy were required by the local civil administration to provide additional medical services to civil servants and the native personnel of the European settlers and to perform a range of practical scientific duties including conducting "research into the characteristics of native human society and the local fauna."[23] Other duties performed by medical officers included the certification of deaths, autopsies, the maintenance of statistics, and the issuing of reports. Medical officers were also consulted as expert witnesses in investigations of mental health and in all cases of rape, and were accorded a key role in ascertaining the level of criminal responsibility.[24]

If the reasons for and measures necessitated in the medical care of white soldiers were taken as implicit, the need to provide for the native population was subject to clear and explicit justification. The native populations in German East Africa were held to be of considerable significance, both as an economic resource and as a factor in the spread and containment of diseases. One commentator provided a succinct summary of the situation: "On the one hand, the colored represents the most important living property in economic terms and is to be protected with all means available. On the other however, he represents a constant health risk for Europeans. Extremely susceptible to infectious diseases and brought by his habits, into constant contact with Europeans, he represents the perfect agent of their dissemination."[25] Working on the basis of such assumptions, medical officers established clear provisions to regulate European cohabitation and dealings with the native population. This function accorded the medical corps considerable influence in determining questions of colonial ethics.

Service in German East Africa in particular provided the opportunity to work on a number of important scientific issues (such as sleeping sickness and malaria) about which very little was known, and thus make a name in scientific circles. The precondition for assuming a position in the colonies included "reliability and a sufficient level of practical and scientific training."[26] Despite such requirements, however, few medical officers were given sufficient opportunity to prepare themselves for the demands made by the treatment of tropical illness such as malarial fever. No less a person than Robert Koch called for the results of his work on tropical medicine (gathered on a number of research expeditions to locations including German East Africa) to be made available to German colonial doctors. He even offered to provide further training to medical officers at the Royal Institute for Infectious Diseases in Berlin, of which he was head. Moreover, the Hamburg Institute for Maritime and Tropical Diseases established a number of posts for naval and army doctors. Soon afterward, all military and other government-employed doctors were required to attend a course in tropical medicine.[27]

The considerable health risks associated with this scientific work rendered service in tropical locations highly unpopular and necessitated the call up of reservists for colonial service.[28] The life of a medical officer was characterized by medical practice, active service, and scientific research. The motivation of medical officers to participate in a colonial war was thus not restricted to nationalist ardor but could also result from the opportunity that it afforded to gather and interpret the relevant data requisite to cutting-edge scientific research: careerism was just as significant as nationalism.

NCOs and Other Ranks

Aspirants for service as an NCO in the Protection Forces were required to have a minimum of three years of service, one of which was to have been spent in a noncommissioned position.[29] Nevertheless, a sergeant was to enter the Protection Force as a corporal. Promotion was then based on the seniority accrued in the Protection Force. As was the case for the officers, service in the colonies was counted as double that in the regular army for pensionable purposes, as long as it lasted a minimum of six months without interruption. Exempted from this calculation were war years, which were already automatically counted as double.

During the war in German South-West Africa, the various corps headquarters from whose purview the recruits were dispatched began to send NCOs with a criminal record for service in the colonies. This occasioned the commander of the Protection Force to wish in 1904 only for "dependable men and proven NCOs." As a result, the Ministry of War asked the corps headquarters to cater to such wishes as far as the supply of volunteers allowed.[30] Moreover, the supreme command reacted to complaints that the personnel deployed had all been too heavy for the available horses and that in the future, they should not weigh more than 140 pounds. This was qualified with the remark "as far as we have the people."[31]

As was the case with the officers, the generous pay and practices of counting the periods of active service as double service acted as powerful encouragements for the NCOs to serve in the colonies. An added incentive is likely to have been the prospect of decorations and the respect and prestige that such medals conferred in the increasingly militarized society of Wilhelmine Germany. Despite such considerations, however, many NCOS were more likely to have been moved to enlist for colonial service on grounds specific to their station. Imperial Germany provided the members of the lower classes and lower middle classes—from which the members of the NCOs and ranks were predominantly drawn—with very few chances for self-improvement and social mobility. The social misery of the NCOs in the Kaiserreich was particularly notorious. As those NCOs had nothing to lose, service in the colonies offered a real chance to improve their position. The message of one soldier in the Protection Force to the readers of the *Unteroffizier-Zeitung* was, "Life here is much better than that in Germany and I would not swap with anyone back home."[32]

NCOs were also attracted to colonial service by the prospect of the augmented authority that they stood to gain. They saw that the nature of service in a large and undeveloped country would provide them with greater scope for initiative, command, and authority as that which the military constraints of domestic service imposed upon them. The degree of independent decision making accorded to the NCOs in the colonies, serving in considerably smaller garrisons in German South-West Africa and East Africa, was considerably wider than that provided in other wars, and as well as commanding smaller stations, they were permitted to lead detachments or patrols. The level of independence enjoyed by hospital orderlies also grew in proportion to their distance from the district offices and the larger garrisons. This growth in authority was especially attractive to those of poor character. Writing in a circular to the district chiefs in German South-West Africa, composed in 1896, Major Leutwein complained that "the more modest the background" from which the NCOs and ranks were drawn, the more likely they were to abuse their power: "instead of Christian patience and well-considered educative measures, they exhibited coarseness and abruptness."[33] Such observations were confirmed by a diary entry from Victor Franke. Writing of those newly arrived in the German South-West Africa, he averred, "29 April 1902: am not pleased by the [new] chaps—a bad spirit has descended upon our riders. Of course, a consequence of the general social conditions and the declining respect for the army among our own people."[34]

In addition to the usual rewards provided by the military such as pay, food, clothing, status, and a pension, the Protection Force also provided its NCOs with the chance to establish cross-class social contacts. They often took advantage of the chance provided to create new loyalties to a specific officer, a unit, or even a colonial territory. After 1904, the *Unteroffizier-Zeitung* ran a number of adverts encouraging NCOs to settle in the colonies, albeit under the condition that they marry a white woman, and under no circumstances an African woman.[35] Of the 154 NCOs going to German East Africa between 1899 and 1914, nine decided to settle in the protectorate after their term of service.[36]

There are no reliable figures pertaining to the number of NCOs who fought in the three colonial wars. The overwhelming majority of NCOs registered on the muster roll data were born between 1870 and 1885, producing a group in which the eldest and youngest were separated by a generation. One hundred six were drawn from provincial (small-town) Prussia—those from the cities of Berlin or Breslau proved to be the exception. However, no province appears to have dominated as a recruiting ground for these men. The next largest groupings are constituted by Bavaria (eleven) and Saxony (eight) followed by Wurttemberg and Baden. This would explain the confessional distribution of the recruits: 124 NCOs were Lutheran and 30 Roman Catholic.

With the exception of those graduates from NCO training schools and institutes of higher education, all other NCOs had first learned a trade. Fifty-eight of the soldiers had lost their father; 17 had also lost their mother. Only 28 were married; the majority were single. One soldier was accompanied to German East Africa by his wife. The low level of social or familial ties in Germany explains the readiness of these NCOs to enter into colonial service. The majority of NCOs entered the army between the ages of 18 and 20, where they remained for a considerable period of time—the average term of service lying at just under 12 years. This figure is explained by the entitlement for ex-servicemen to join the civil service after 12 years of military service. Only around one-third (59) remained less than 10 years, whereas almost two-thirds (91) spent more than 15 years in the army. The longest period of service amounted to twenty-four years. The average interval between a recruit entering the army and his joining the Protection Force was four years, so that NCOs were between 21 and 25 years of age upon their arrival in the colonies. Remaining an average of 6 years in the Protection Force, 82 (around 54 percent) quit colonial service before this time, in the course of their second period of service. Only 22 served in German East Africa for longer than 10 years.

The overwhelming majority of the NCOs included in these statistics were involved in active service in 1905–1906. Twelve had served in China, two in German South-West Africa, yet only one saw active service in the campaign of 1905. One hundred thirty-two NCOs fell ill over a long period—one every eighty-three days. Far more serious however, was the fact that a total of only twenty-two persons did not contract any form of malady. The risk of illness to which the members of the Protection Force were subject was thus without a doubt much higher than their colleagues serving in Europe. The high number of cases of fever and malaria as well as a whole range of conditions involving the respiratory system and the gastrointestinal tract also added to these figures. Sixty-three NCOs (representing around 40 percent) were invalided out of the Protection Force for German East Africa, of which thirty-nine (over 25 percent) were between 50 and 100 percent disabled. Of the 154 NCOs, thirty-eight (just under 25 percent) died, yet only three were killed as a result of military action during the Maji Maji War. Three other NCOs committed suicide. The overwhelming majority of deaths stemmed from illness and accident.

In such terms, service in the colonies was not entirely desirable from the perspective of the average soldier. The lower ranks ran a much higher risk of death and accident than did their officers. Indeed, their mere presence in the colonial theater represented a risk, where fighting was no prerequisite to dying. Nevertheless, hoping to strike social capital from service in the colonies, noncommissioned volunteers exhibited the tendency to play down or even to ignore the considerable dangers that it involved.

Volunteers

The German troops in China and German South-West Africa were composed entirely of volunteers drawn from all arms and services of the army. Plans drawn up in 1900 to dispatch regular formations to China were rejected by Alfred von Schlieffen, the chief of the General Staff, whose priority was to avoid compromising the ability of the German army to conduct operations in Europe. The public discussion over the need to defend German honor against the uncivilized "Boxer hordes" stimulated a mood of chauvinist revenge within the army (at least according to the official version). Others volunteered out of a thirst for action, hoping to participate in the first military action conducted by Germany since 1871. For such recruits, the events in China merely "woke the yearning for combat in the battle-ready soldiers."[37] Although planners initially intended to grant the newly formed units sufficient time to allow for their consolidation and training, the dramatic turn of events necessitated the abandonment of these plans. As a result, the phase in which the soldiers were to accustom themselves to their new task, their new group, and an alien environment was cut very short. The first units of the expedition corps left Bremerhaven at the end of July 1900, eleven days earlier than planned, and arrived in China in mid-September 1900.

Once arrived in China, the corps was initially subject to wartime rates of pay, in addition to a long service bonus and a reenlistment bonus. The Ministry of War also issued instructions that the expeditionary force held local discretion to grant further allowances. As a result, the soldiers were granted extra cost-of-living allowances which were repeatedly raised. The conditions for acceptance in the East Asian Expeditionary Corps are already known.[38] The minimum physical requirements of each volunteer amounted to a muscular body, a minimum height of 5 feet 4 inches (1.65 meters), fitness for service in the colonies, and good eyesight. Members of the mounted units required a low weight and good riding skills. The volunteers were also required to have high levels of civilian training, ideally in a trade, "as our units are going to be very awkward under foreign conditions." The volunteers were also required to provide proof of good conduct; unmarried status was preferred. Many of the volunteers were taken from the active soldiery, but to the distress of the commission formed in the Ministry of War to oversee the East Asian expedition, a number of soldiers currently under suspension were also dispatched with the force. As one member of the commission noted, "those suspended soldiers volunteering for duty consisted for the most part of a number of failed existences and those for whom life at home had become a little too hot."

A proportion of these so-called China fighters, soon to be referred to under the collective term "East Asians," were reemployed as "Africans" in German South-West Africa, serving as volunteers in the force dispatched to crush the Herero and Nama risings. Nevertheless, the military experiences gathered in China were regarded in German South-West Africa as only second rate. As Captain Franke wrote irritably in his diary: "Some idiotic lieutenant, experienced only in killing a few beggarly Boxers—for which feat they gave him seven medals—is nagging v.E. [von Estorff] incessantly, just so he can gain attention for some operation he wishes to mount."[39] Other assessments also indicate that the volunteers were not satisfied with a monotonous routine and wanted to see some action.

Although the number of officers volunteering for service in German South-West Africa far exceeded the numbers required, the expeditionary force sailed understrength and required reinforcement. This shortage was compounded by deficiencies of personnel in certain key support services and trades—veterinarians, signalers, master tradesmen, gunsmith's assistants, buglers, cooks, cartwrights, joiners, tailors, barbers, and plumbers were all in short supply. The decision was taken as early as May 1904 to accept volunteers from the Landwehr.[40] The Ministry of War also reduced its "requirements of conduct" made of the personnel, so that even those with previous convictions were accepted.[41]

The General Staff, writing in a critical tone in its official publication (the *Generalstabswerk*), noted a number of evils among hurriedly formed volunteer units, which it opined would probably serve to reduce their military value. The pressing need for so many troops meant that the formations lacked the time necessary either to forge anything approaching a coherent esprit de corps or to attain an appropriate level of training. Instead, the reinforcements were hurried off to the colonies in an "unfinished state."[42] In the main, the time accorded to preparations amounted to no more than ten days, in which time the units were to be formed, clothed, equipped, and instructed in the use of firearms, horsemanship, and field service exercises. In contrast to the situation facing applicants for the Protection Force, these volunteers were required only to sign up for a limited period of service in the colonies. Motivated by nationalism and war fever, many simply volunteered to escape the monotony of garrison life and "see some real action." The speed with which the level of volunteering declined (for both China and German South-West Africa) points to the short-lived nature of such a mood.

The Navy

The decision to deploy the imperial navy in the colonial wars was testament not to any particular level of skill in colonial warfare possessed by this institution, but to its high level of mobility. Conducted by the Great Powers as a naval conflict, the Boxer War of 1900–1901 saw the participation of the German navy thanks to the immediate presence of the East Asian cruiser squadron in the Gulf of Zhili and the concurrent speed with which it could be deployed. Similarly, the Protection Force in German South-West Africa was reinforced in January 1904 by the gunboat *Habicht* because it had been anchored in Cape Town and was able to steam to Swakopmund in a relatively short space of time. The intervention of the cruiser *Bussard* in the Maji Maji War of 1905 was conditioned by its fortuitous presence off the coast of German East Africa. The immediate task of the naval landing party deployed in the crisis zone was to hold its position until it could be relieved by reinforcements from Germany. It was not given any offensive tasks. For instance, the landing party deployed in German South-West Africa from the *Habicht* was ordered to secure the railroad communications before being split up into various smaller units to conduct patrols. The arrival of reinforcements led to their withdrawal from the theater of operations.

The changes made to German naval policy within the advent of Wilhelmine Weltpolitik resulted in the establishment and garrisoning of a number of naval stations throughout the world. As such, naval personnel were able to discover and experience the wider world. The move taken around 1900 to reconcentrate the fleet in German home waters, on the other hand, considerably reduced this scope for adventure. German power was now to be projected by gunboats—small, unarmored ships of a low draft and with one or more light, rapid-firing guns—acting as an indication of the level of force that Germany could deploy at short notice. Held ready for immediate action, their commanders were placed under the direct command of the kaiser (orders were issued by the General Staff of the Admiralty) when on active duty, thus enabling their immediate deployment.[43] Although every officer and rating performed a tour of duty in at least one overseas station, the general level of inaction widespread among the officers and men stationed in Kiel and Wilhelmshaven stimulated a corresponding thirst for overseas experiences, albeit not for active service. Involving greater operational independence of action for the officers, such deployments in foreign waters for a minimum of six months brought the added advantage of being counted as double that of home service when calculating the period of time served.[44] Overseas service could also be used as a targeted form of punishment, enabling a commander to rid himself, at least for a short time, of troublesome personnel. One detachment sent to German East Africa included fourteen naval ratings with a criminal record.[45]

According to their own accounts, the ratings and their officers had all joined the navy "to see the world." After 1900, the only outlet for such a desire was to be found in volunteering for colonial service. This would enable them to make "new experiences and [experience] the attractions of the wilderness."[46] Concerns of national prestige also added to the volunteering rates; those asked spoke of the need which they felt to "fly the German flag and teach the restless natives in the young colonies the necessary respect for it."[47] The naval personnel did not shrink from the prospect of land-based combat. As one rating on the *Habicht* reported shortly before its arrival in Swakopmund, "Our spirits rose after hearing that we were to be put ashore."[48]

High spirits did not make up for the fact that they were singularly ill-prepared for conducting land-based military operations. This lack of preparation manifested itself in several ways, the most obvious being the lack of adaptation that they exhibited to the terrain of German South-West Africa.

Originally dressed in a (very smart) gray-white dress uniform, the members of the landing party found that only after being boiled in a mixture of tobacco and coffee did their uniforms adopt the requisite dirty-brown color necessary to afford any level of camouflage.[49] They were inadequately trained for land combat. Receiving what Alfred von Tirpitz described as a "short yet energetic" introduction to land warfare, the remainder of their training was dominated by purely naval exercises such as the operation of a ship and its equipment, rigging drill, and naval gunnery.[50] As a result, the naval personnel dispatched to the colonial crisis zones lacked sufficient experience and training in the use of firearms, marching, or mounted operations. Such deficits had been exposed during the deployment of naval units to quell the Arab rising in German East Africa, where after storming Buschiri's camp in May 1889 the exhausted landing party was unable to set off on the return march.[51]

Further points of criticism raised against the naval ratings included their lack of initiative, their tendency to ignore medical ordinances, their susceptibility to the difficulties and climate of the colonies, and their negligence during guard duty.[52] The poor preparation of the naval personnel for land duty was rooted in their conditions of service; kept under strict ship-discipline, experiences of landing were brief and dedicated to the pleasures of shore leave. Their only land-based experience—a short excursion into the hybrid environments of docks, warehouses, and amusement centers—did nothing to prepare them for more extensive land-based activities. Regarding their primary task of representing and projecting the power of the German Empire on the high seas, once called on to face the demands of prosecuting an infantry campaign against an insurgent population, the naval personnel landed in an alien and hostile environment reacted with shock and underperformance. Thoroughly ill-equipped for such a role mentally, physically, and professionally, the sailors who had volunteered for an overseas adventure found themselves entrusted with a role that they had never foreseen.

The Marine Infantry

The colonial theater also saw the deployment of the Marine Infantry, a maritime infantry force reporting directly to the Imperial Naval Office. Serving as the traditional link between the army and navy, it was a majority volunteer force, consisting of soldiers who had applied to transfer to the navy. The primary duty of this marine land force was to secure and defend the naval facilities at Kiel and Wilhelmshaven in the event of war. Also intended to participate in overseas expeditions and deployed four times before the First World War, the Marine Infantry first saw action in 1897 during the occupation of Qingdao. Divided into three sea battalions, the third battalion was stationed permanently in Qingdao after 1898. The first and second battalions participated in the Boxer War as part of the so-called Naval Expeditionary Corps. The Marine Infantry also saw active service in the wars in German South-West Africa (1904) and German East Africa (1905), forming 125-man companies for the purpose.[53]

A number of the Marine Infantry volunteered for service in the Boxer War of 1900.[54] They were moved to do so (as with their counterparts in the regular army) by national outrage. An additional motive was the desire to help their comrades of the III Sea Battalion stationed in China who had already suffered their first fatalities. The Marine Infantrymen of the III Sea Battalion viewed the operations in the Tianjin and Shandong as the perfect opportunity to escape the often monotonous garrison life in Qingdao.[55]

Many volunteers from the sea battalions were rejected for service in the Boxer War on grounds of unfitness for tropical service. As a result, it was necessary to draw on volunteers (both officers and men) from the Prussian, Bavarian, Wurttemberg, and Saxon army corps.[56] In doing so, the normal physical requirements for service in the sea battalions were not enforced; the only criterion for acceptance was fitness for tropical service.[57] A number of the Marine Infantrymen volunteering for service in German South-West Africa (1904) also exhibited health problems, circumstances leading to the decision to draw on recruits having received only two and a half months of training.[58] In the final reckoning, between a quarter and one-third of every company deployed in this conflict was composed of recruits (a total of fifty-one men) and forty volunteers having signed up for a year of service.[59]

The planners at the Army High Command dividing the companies into platoons and sections often failed to take into account the regional origin of the volunteers and thus the army from which they had been drawn. As a result, the wars in China, German South-West Africa, and German East Africa saw Bavarians serve next to Oldenburgers, Alsatians next to Hanoverians, Wuerttembergers next to Westphalians, and Badeners next to Rhinelanders. Moreover, and in contrast to the practices prevalent in China, the sea battalions deployed to Germany's African colonies were split up. Fighting under the command of units from the Protection Force and the navy, the Marine Infantry had little opportunity for deployment as part of a more homoge-

nous formation and was thus unable to forge any close bonds or group identity. Indeed, the contingent of Marine Infantry dispatched to German South-
West Africa was split up to such an extent that it proved impossible to return
it to anything resembling an operational unit.[60] Fearing the full-scale dissolution of the sea battalions, the Imperial Naval Office requested that they be
returned as soon as possible.[61]

The training of the Marine Infantry was performed in accordance with
the principles set out in the *Infantry Drill Manual,* thus explaining their
greater facility with firearms than with naval personnel.[62] The year 1897 saw
the launch of a practice-based yet ineffective course of training in colonial
service. The only exception to this regime was the members of the III Sea
Battalion in Qingdao, who received additional training on location. Stationed in the Iltis, Bismarck, and Moltke barracks, they underwent a traditional course of military training. None of the three battalions had gathered
any level of experience in Africa, with the result that "the whole work [of the
war in German South-West Africa] rests on the collective experience of . . .
nonexperts."[63]

The lack of qualification for African warfare displayed by the Marine In-
fantry was confirmed by the judgment of their performance by "old Africans."
As Viktor Franke confided to his diary, "The behavior of the sea soldiers
[Marine Infantrymen] is miserable. They slaughter cattle entrusted to them
on the meadow."[64] He also recorded cases of poor nerves among the Marine
Infantry: "Last night, a jumpy sea soldier opened fire at barking dogs; he
deserves a good hiding." Major Kurt von Schleinitz, an officer serving in
German East Africa, pointed out that the men were not even capable of differentiating between African men and women: "Their entire ignorance of the
land and the culture and customs of the natives as well as their language,
their demonstrable inability to recognize women at distance and their realization of such deficiencies renders these people entirely unfit for independent
employment."[65]

The value of the Marine Infantry in land-based colonial wars was as limited as that of the regular naval personnel. Their uniforms also displayed
clear drawbacks for colonial service; their hasty mobilization for the Herero
war meant that they arrived in German South-West Africa with nothing
more than their blue winter uniform. This was highly unfortunate, as only
brown grey, yellow, and grey-green were suitable as colors for the environment in which they were to operate.[66] The inspector of Marine Infantry had
subjected their performance to harsh criticism as early as 1904. "Derring-do

and a ready martial willingness are not enough; we require serious prepa-rations for mobilization on the level displayed by a European Army and Navy." He concluded, "I am unable to state that our Marine Infantry has set out for conflict in South-West Africa well-prepared." His damning judg-ment was in stark contrast to the whitewash presented by Imperial Naval Office: "The troops arrived in the theater well-prepared and in a good frame of mind."[67] The Marine Infantry was originally conceived as a rapid deploy-ment force for operations both in Europe and overseas, from Helgoland to Zanzibar. This vision remained a pipe dream, trained as it was primarily for deployment in Europe. The fact that the infantrymen were only checked for tropical fitness after volunteering for overseas service demonstrates the failure to develop a force prepared for extra-European duties. Displaying similar motives for their volunteering to their army counterparts—indignation at the attack on the German Empire and a hope for action—members of the III Sea Battalion stationed in Qingdao also sought to escape the monotony of their posting.

Chinese Soldiers in Qingdao

Seeking to emulate the Chinese contingent raised by the British in Wei-haiwei in 1899, the German colonial administration established a "Chinese unit," primarily to minimize personnel costs. Viewing the deployment of German soldiers for patrol duty in the protectorate as too expensive, the German government planned to establish a Chinese company to protect and police the concession. It was calculated that the replacement of 120 German soldiers by a native contingent of the same size would bring annual savings of 36,219 marks. Planners also took into account the usual advantages em-ploying native levies: their adaptability to the local climate, their improved physical resistance, and their low demands in terms of accommodation and victuals. Plans were drawn up to raise a company of one hundred infantrymen and twenty dispatch riders officered by a German company commander, two subalterns, and ten NCOs.[68]

Two Chinese agents were commissioned with recruiting healthy Chinese males between the ages of twenty-one and twenty-seven and fit for military service. The monthly wages of eight dollars and a one-off payment of two dollars were so attractive that the 120 men required for the force were mus-tered within only eight days. Sixty percent of the assembled force was drawn from the peasantry, while some 17 and 15 percent were artisans and merchants, respectively.[69] The successful applicants signed up for a three-year term of service and promised to display the "greatest industry and diligence to acquire the skills that a German soldier requires."[70] Although the recruits were trained in accordance with German military practice and required to respond to German as the language of command, the German officers were nevertheless required to learn sufficient Chinese to issue orders to their charges or at least control the Chinese interpreter.

In order to establish a clear differentiation between German and Chinese forces, the German administration placed great emphasis on establishing considerable differences between the two in terms of organization, location, and clothing. Tailored in a mixture of European and Asian style, the Chinese uniforms consisted of a khaki suit, a broad straw hat, and sandals in summer and a corduroy suit with a Manchurian cap and lace-up shoes in winter. As the Chinese army was equipped with state-of-the-art weaponry, the military administration did not emulate the German colonial practice in Africa of issuing its native contingents with substandard arms.[71]

Stationed in Licun, the Chinese company operated in a location where close contacts had not developed between the population and the German troops. Formally placed under the command of the III Sea Battalion, the company commander was given full authority over all matters of discipline and administration. The German administration feared that if integrated too closely in German structures, the Chinese contingent could lose authority in the eyes of the population. Fears that a growing level of self-confidence among the Chinese levies could stimulate conflict between Chinese and German troops were countered by their being subject to the strictest of discipline.[72]

Despite sixteen cases of desertion, eight dismissals, and some deep reservations on the part of the company commander Erich von Falkenhayn, von Falkenhayn nevertheless judged the results of his first term of service (ending in November 1899) to be largely positive. Describing his soldiers as skilled and dogged, he praised their good marching performance—they managed thirty-four kilometers in seven hours—but complained of their often childish nature.[73] He reserved final judgment until he had been granted the opportunity to study their performance in battle.

The first test for the Chinese unit came in June 1900, the result of which can only be classified as a resounding failure. Posted to Jiaozhou to combat the Boxer uprising, the unit all but collapsed through desertion and insubordination. The high level of desertion was conditioned by three factors. Many were unable to cope with the German requirements of cleanliness, organization, and an order; others had only ever considered military service merely on financial grounds; and lastly, Chinese soldiers often had to fear reprisals against their family.[74] Despite such considerations, the German company commander identified the main problem as the "character of the yellow race," accusing his Chinese soldiers of lacking honor but excelling in greed, vindictiveness, and mendacity.[75] As a result, the governor of Qingdao (Paul Jaeschke) decided that the Chinese contingent was unsuitable for military duties, and only to be employed as a police unit. The company remained in nominal existence until being reestablished as a unit of police in September 1901.

The ignoble end of the Chinese unit did not lead to abandonment of the concept.[76] One possible task that could be allotted to such a force was the guarding of the fifty-kilometer special zone surrounding the colony, protection of the railroad line, and clandestine scouting operations. Moreover, it was seen that the continued existence of the unit would accord German NCOs the opportunity to learn more of the Chinese language, customs, and land. This would bring advantages of not only a short-term military but also a long-term personal nature, should they wish to remain in China upon retirement from the army. However, there were no further plans for the "ruthless deployment" of the "less valuable human material of a Chinese unit" in genuine military actions.[77]

Native Contingents in Africa

Fighting in the challenging climates and terrain presented by their African colonies, the Germans were forced to rely on the services of native "middlemen," adapted to both the prevailing conditions and the behavior of the insurgents. With the ordinary German soldier unable to read or navigate the local environment, the German military increasingly relied on the "eyes, ears and touch" of their African scouts.[78] In addition to their scouting role, the "auxiliary peoples" *(Hilfsvölker)* also performed valuable service in intelligence duties, conducting search parties and guarding prisoners. Africans were also deployed in battle. Whether they were to operate independently or under German command and the manner in which they were to be armed were decisions made according to the circumstances of the action.

Africans had been employed as soldiers as early as three years after the colonization of German South-West Africa. Nevertheless, with Africans representing only a minority of the fighting troop, the Protection Force remained overwhelmingly white. Herero and Nama served in a range of auxiliary functions such as ox drivers, herdsmen, servants, and washerwomen.[79] A contract signed with the Witbooi Nama in 1894 required them to perform military service in a unit commanded by a German lieutenant who issued commands via an interpreter. Under wartime conditions, the soldiers wore the uniform of the Protection Force supplemented by a white hat—important inasmuch as they were not part of the Protection Force. So marked, however, they were transformed into clearly identifiable agents of the colonial authority. In July 1895, the government moved to acquire further native levies, signing a contract with the Rehobother Baster who were to provide first forty men for military training in the Protection Force, to be followed by a further twenty every subsequent year.[80] Acting as reservists to be called up in the case of war, they were given further refresher training every year; once trained, the Baster were liable for military service for the next twelve years. Those Baster distinguishing themselves in battle were to be promoted; the families of those killed were entitled to a pension. Both the Witbooi-Nama and between seventy and eighty Baster fought in the Herero war. Deployed in various companies, they were issued with a longarm, a belt, an ammunition pouch, and forty rounds. As a uniform, they wore a broad-brimmed hat and cockade, which resembled an earlier version of the uniform worn by the Protection Force.

Lacking white personnel, the Protection Force in German East Africa was forced to make more extensive use of African troops, who made up the core of the forces deployed. The German military had long relied on African auxiliaries to police the protectorate, importing Zulus from Mozambique or Sudanese troops from Egypt in the 1880s, the latter of which came with Wissmann. Valued as much for their teetotalism as for their military training (acquired while serving the British), the Protection Force hoped to ensure their reliability with generous pay. Once the British colonial authorities had banned the recruitment of Sudanese troops from their sphere of influence, the German authorities set about enlisting "native Askaris" in the various regions of German East Africa, often drawn from groups living on the colonial periphery so as to circumvent any problems of loyalty. In view of the high level of ethnic diversity displayed by the protectorate, this policy allowed the German colonial authorities to address the otherwise fundamental problem of native loyalty in such a sensitive area of African collaboration. Although all regular soldiers serving in German East Africa were equipped with an identical uniform, there was a clear hierarchy, also expressed in terms of pay, the apex of which was occupied by the experienced Sudanese, followed by the Zulus and then the Askaris. The punishments meted out to the black members of the Protection Force included beatings, wage docking, arrest, working in a chain gang, and posting to the punishment company in Dar es Salaam. Rewards included commendations on parade, cash bonuses, and promotions.[81]

In the early years of the German Protection Force, Africans were able to rise from the ranks to take a commission. Although the "Organizational Regulations for the Imperial Protection Force in German East Africa" from 1891 established the automatic seniority of Germans over the African soldiers of the same rank, relations between German officers, NCOs, and civil servants and colored officers were not characterized by any degree of subordination on racial lines.[82] Only after a number of problems in military routine—arising from the need for white soldiers to take orders from black officers—were the routes of promotion for black soldiers capped. Security fears and accusations of neglecting their weaponry moved commanders to deny the Askari access to and training on the most up-to-date weaponry such as the M/98 rifle or machine guns.[83]

Black soldiers in German East Africa were often viewed as incapable of understanding and applying the central tenets and practices of military training, to which they were said to attach no value. In the eyes of the German military, they also lacked the characteristics of autonomy and self-discipline that were seen as required by a marksman. Nevertheless, the author of the *Field Service Manual for German East Africa* did claim that the Africans were imbued with a certain sense of "discipline" and subordination, rooted in the despotic rule of the clan chiefs.[84] Seeking to exploit this alleged African devotion to authority, German officers were encouraged to maintain the strictest of discipline so as to maintain their loyalty. The "myth of the devoted Askari" loyalty propagated by the accounts of the First World War hero Paul von Lettow-Vorbeck masked incidences in which the Askari troops offered passive support to insurgents.[85]

The regular troops available to the military authorities in German East Africa were supplemented by an indeterminate number of "irregulars" or Rugaruga warriors, who were recruited to meet the needs of individual conflicts and campaigns launched against a particular clan or within a clearly demarcated area. The Rugaruga represented a supraethnic group defined by their status as highly effective mercenaries. Despite this clear-cut status, the German military applied the term "Rugaruga" to any temporary native members of the Protection Force, irrespective of their ethnicity. Not all mercenaries, other Africans joined with the Germans for a whole range of reasons. Revenge, clan politics, and hopes of enrichment constituted merely a few cases within the diffuse motivation for joining with the Germans. As a result, the local level of the war could develop into a "battle within a battle"[86] involving a complicated interplay of cooperation, collaboration, and treachery with rapidly changing constellations of enemy and ally.

Some battles were conducted entirely by black soldiers, Askari and Rugaruga. These were marked out in appearance by their wearing of symbols unmistakable from a distance—such as forage caps typical to the region, special Khaki symbols, or small German pennants. After completing specific tasks, they were paid in kind by German officers with captured women or cattle.[87] This followed the native custom of sharing the spoils of war as a method of showing appreciation. Although the officers were aware of the necessity of working to prevent unnecessary destruction, unpermitted raids, and cruelty, such events were also organized in order "to take account of the feelings of these primitive peoples in apportioning the spoils."[88] Such short-term and geographically limited cooperation provided the Germans with a valuable opportunity to justify their own inhuman practices with reference to "African traditions." Indeed, the special motivation of the Rugaruga soldiers transformed them into a preferred partner: "Good marksmen, [they] lie in wait at watering holes day and night; they conduct an inexorable pursuit of the fleeing rebels to their most secret, outlying hiding places. Then plunder, burning and the destruction of fields. Chivying on a large scale. This is no job for Europeans: too slow, unfamiliar with the land and far too humane."[89]

With its practice in German South-West Africa of integrating black African soldiers into particular white units, or even integrating whole black units into the Protection Force (as in German East Africa and Cameroon), the German military attempted to retain the monopoly of knowledge and command in white hands and also, wherever possible, maintain a clear policy of racial segregation in the Protection Force. Nevertheless, wartime conditions rendered a clear delimitation between German and African combatants almost entirely impossible. A strict bipolarity between "whites" and "blacks" existed only in the contemporary literature on colonial warfare, a dichotomy not reflected by reality.

A final consideration is the extreme degree to which the German naval personnel, Marine Infantrymen, army volunteers, members of the Protection Force, mercenaries, native contingents, and the Rugaruga were mixed together to create a number of entirely "hybridized" forces. China saw combat groups consisting of naval personnel, Marine Infantrymen, and army volunteers. Members of the Protection Force, the imperial navy, Marine Infantrymen, army volunteers, and "native contingents" fought together in German South-West Africa, while the Maji Maji War in German East Africa was conducted by a Protection Force consisting of black soldiers supplemented by a number of naval personnel, Marine Infantrymen, and native auxiliaries. Although the officer corps of the Protection Forces deployed in the African colonies consisted of a very small yet hard core group, only a third of the officers at the most were deployed in both China and one of the two African colonies. Only a very small number participated in all three of the major colonial wars conducted by Germany and examined in this study. The three wars under consideration were thus prosecuted by a heterogeneous collection of individuals who did not think and act as a uniform bloc.

The composition of the troops fighting the wars in China and Africa also reflected the initially haphazard and purposeless response to the conflicts on the part of the military planners in Berlin, an approached exhibited by all the institutions involved including the High Command of the Protection Forces, the Imperial Naval Office, the General Staff of the Admiralty, the Army General Staff, the Ministry of War, the imperial chancellor, and the kaiser himself. Not the product of long discussions and planning, the military operations were the product of a rapid reaction to pressing political and military pressures. In consequence, the great majority of the soldiers deployed in these colonial operations were badly prepared for the conditions and environment with which they were confronted upon arrival. The pressure of events often led to a drastic reduction in the amount of time originally intended for training and preparation. Especially affected by such poor preparation were the Marine Infantry recruits dispatched to German South-West Africa and who arrived in the protectorate after only two months of service. Rates of volunteering for service in the wars in China and German South-West Africa show that the level of enthusiasm lasted only a very short time and was limited to the period immediately after the outbreak of war. Its almost immediate ebbing resulted in increasing personnel shortages with every further month of the war's duration. As a result, the physical fitness and moral integrity of the white soldiers recruited to prosecute the war decreased. The only common characteristic shared by the army volunteers, naval personnel, and Marine Infantrymen was their complete lack of a group identity, military professionalism, or martial ethic.

The mixed forces dispatched to the colonial theaters fought for a number of different reasons. Finding themselves on the spot upon the outbreak of war, the members of the Protection Force were merely doing a job for which they had previously volunteered, even if its demands had suddenly increased. While the native members of the Protection Forces fought for reasons entirely pecuniary in nature, the members of the "native contingent" fighting in German South-West Africa were forced into fighting a war not of their choosing. The native auxiliaries deployed sporadically and with a regional concentration regarded their participation in a German war as an opportunity to settle old scores with their traditional enemies and took the juncture to prosecute a number of private wars within a war. In this way, an originally colonial war was transformed into an interethnic conflict often assuming exceptionally violent proportions. In contrast to the Protection Force, the German volunteers from the regular army had willingly signed up for a special overseas mission. They regarded it as both a personal challenge and their national duty to defend the interests of the German Empire in China or German South-West Africa. Representing a change to their military routine, the war presented a welcome opportunity to experience active service. The naval personnel participating in the conflict, on the other hand, found themselves thrown into a war at extremely short notice. Although interested in gathering new overseas experiences, they had no experience of land-based combat and were highly unused to leaving their ships for anything but a very short period. Although the Marine Infantry was expressly intended for service in the colonies, with the exception of the III Sea Battalion (stationed in China), its members were entirely unprepared when the eventuality arose.

Our understanding of the individual motives of the German participants in the colonial wars examined here can be refined beyond consideration of the unit in which they served. A number of profiles can serve as examples: the aristocratic Protection Force officer seeking to advance his career by a spell in the colonies; the paternalist Protection Force officer seeking to "teach the natives a lesson" but without exterminating them; the criminal Protection Force officer pushed off to the colonies by his superiors; the middle-class medical officer who had dedicated his life to war and medicine; the socially disaffected Protection Force officer hoping for a better post; the brutal NCO who, having escaped the restrictive morality of Wilhelmine Germany, now sought to lord it over natives; the convinced (or even fanatical) volunteer ready to die for a just cause; the courageous naval rating hoping to experience adventure in the wilderness; the breezy Marine Infantryman, unable to differentiate between African men and women; his comrade, bored by the monotony of garrison life in Qingdao; the Chinese mercenary fighting for money yet struggling with questions of loyalty; the black professional who joined the Protection Force to support a family; the native auxiliary fighting to gain a share in the booty.

A wide range of both affective and cognitive explanations can be advanced to explain the readiness to fight and employ extreme violence displayed by the German soldiers deployed in the colonial wars: a thirst for adventure, a readiness to fight, national defense, booty, pay, social advancement, a flight from a threatened existence, the search for rehabilitation, scientific interest, careerism, and a quest for revenge. This was compounded in many cases by the romantic association of fighting and love and fear and nervousness about new and volatile situations. The variety of different motivations outlined in this chapter provides an explanation for the diverse modes of behavior exhibited in the colonial theater by the members of various units. For instance, it becomes clear why inactive volunteer troops in China posed a considerable threat to internal discipline and why the "Chinese soldiers" could only be deployed with minimal success in what represented a sideshow. An appreciation of these diverse motivations sheds light on the particular brutality exhibited by German naval personnel and Marine Infantrymen during the early stages of the war in German South-West Africa. An explanation for such behavior is not to be found in a particular and specifically German will to extermination as claimed by a number of scholars, but the complete inexperience and ignorance of colonial warfare on the part of the soldiers involved. An appreciation of such diverging motivations enables us to grasp the reasons for the considerable differences exhibited between the South-West African Protection Force and the German soldiers dispatched to reinforce them. Such awareness also makes clear just why the native troops employed in the war could proceed with the same level of brutality as their white counterparts.

Consideration of the heterogeneity of the soldiers deployed in the German colonial wars and the group-specific dispositions of individual military units combined with an appreciation of the variety of reasons for going to war demonstrate that the causes of the individual acts of violence perpetrated in the colonies were similarly diverse. However, a complete explanation of the actions of the soldiers and their conduct of the wars in China and Africa—including the form and extent of violence perpetrated—requires further analysis of a range of factors beyond the subjective individual will of those conducting them. This requires understanding the collective nature of the shared experience and socialization experienced by the white colonial soldiers in imperial Germany. This requires an examination of the official directives and guidelines regulating the conduct of warfare in general and colonial warfare in particular, as well as an assessment of the ideological topography of the German Empire itself.

CHAPTER 5

Training and Weaponry

T HE GERMAN army and navy equipped their soldiers with both the weaponry for fighting modern
wars and the training with which to conduct them. Military training encompassed a broad field of knowledge and skills including technical instruction, weaponry, exhaustive tactical instruction, general legal theory, and the
rules governing war and a soldier's conduct in it. Nevertheless, the great
majority of the soldiers employed in the various colonial theaters examined
in this study were not given any specific training in or preparation for the
conditions specific to colonial warfare and the weaponry involved. Servicemen were, however, able to adapt their training (which focused primarily
on deployment in a European theater) to the new settings in which they
found themselves, through independent study of widely available books and
articles. This reading enabled them to develop rudimentary skills requisite to
colonial warfare, thus enabling them to adopt a pragmatic approach to the
local conditions that they found upon arrival.

Arms

A contemporary small-arms training manual defined weapons as an instrument of military violence designed to increase the scope and impact of the
destruction visited upon the enemy.[1] All varieties of weapons take as their
targets buildings, defensive fortifications, and first and foremost the human
body, which is to be killed, wounded, or at the very least put out of action.
Soldiers of all ranks were armed with a modern rifle or carbine and a melee

weapon of bladed or blunt variety. These personal arms were supplemented by machine guns and artillery.

In the period between their establishment in 1891 and the outbreak of the First World War, the soldiers of the Protection Forces *(Schutztruppe)* were equipped with a standard Mauser infantry rifle, which was subject to three upgrades within this period. A breech-loading rifle, the Mauser had superseded the breech-loading needle gun which had been the standard longarm of the Prussian army until the mid-nineteenth century. The upgrade proved to be a success, outperforming its predecessor significantly in terms of speed, accuracy, and range. The new technology produced an almost threefold increase in the initial speed of the round from 300 to 860 meters per second within only a few decades. The range of the rifle increased from 800 to almost 1,800 meters within the same period.[2] Such improvements in firepower altered not just the distance at which violence could be inflicted but also its extent. This was borne out by the rapid increase in enemy casualty figures during the wars of German unification in 1870–1871.

The first model of infantry rifle, the M/71, an 11 mm single-shot, breech-loading rifle with a cylinder breechblock, exhibited considerable drawbacks. Discharging lead rounds with a heavily smoking propellant, it was easy to locate the soldier firing the weapon. In addition, the rifle exhibited the tendency to pull to the right. As a remedy, the M/88, a repeater rifle with a central magazine, was developed and first sold in 1888. The simple lead ammunition was replaced with fully cased rounds of a smaller caliber to address the problems of imprecision and wavering or tumbling projectiles. Of a smaller caliber and thus lighter, the rifle generated considerably less smoke than its lead-firing predecessors. These developments were supplemented by a true innovation of the Mauser weapons factory at the turn of the century in the shape of the 8 mm M/98, an improved form of which was eventually to see service as the standard-issue rifle used by the German army in the First World War. This repeater rifle accommodated five rounds in its integrated box magazine. According to the Gunnery Field Manual, the nickel-copper-plated steel-cased rounds could inflict serious injuries on "living targets."[3]

That such claims were not always borne out in practice was shown by the testimony of the naval lieutenant Hans Paasche. Speaking of his service in the Maji Maji War, he wrote, "The first black which I had in my sights fell only after my third shot. I obviously hit him each time, as there were three bullet wounds on his body."[4] Such different levels of effectiveness—both exceptionally serious and conspicuously light injuries—were characteristic for encased, nondeformable rounds, as the lead core did not inflict a uniform pattern of impact wound. The degree of the injury suffered by the victim depended on the level of resistance encountered by the projectile. The smaller the caliber of the bullet, the less was the likelihood of its hitting a vital area. Moreover, small-caliber ammunition produced only low primary wound pain. Military surgeons noted that wounds suffered at extremely close range produced very fine entry and exit wounds of a small radius which healed surprisingly quickly and easily. This also applied to serious injuries to both the lungs and the liver. The clean penetration of these projectiles brought many to regard them as more humane than their predecessors, thus bringing into conflict the requirements of weaponry, military surgery, and ethics.[5]

The "benign character of the wounds caused by the humane small-caliber rounds" celebrated in the small-arms and weapons training manuals were often advanced as important constituents of the much-trumpeted "humane warfare"[6] being waged in the colonies. Nevertheless, as one army surgeon complained, there was "inflationary abuse of the term 'humane bullet.'"[7] The military justification for the use of this type of ammunition, with its highly unpredictable physical effects on its targets, had already been the subject of intense diplomatic discussion, a discourse that eventually culminated in the banning of the so-called dum-dum bullet by the Hague Convention of 1899—despite British opposition. Equipped with the M/71, the German naval ratings stationed in East Asia waited impatiently for the new M/98 with which their counterparts in the army had already been issued.[8] Their chagrin could only have been heightened by knowledge that the partially modernized Chinese army was equipped with state-of-the-art weaponry. The Boxers supplemented these modern weapons with the more traditional lance, sword, saber, and knives.

The German Protection Forces in Africa were equipped with the latest M/98 from 1904. Their African opponents retained their traditional weapons such as the battle axe and blowpipe, but primarily used older models of rifle such as the M/71 or M/88, some of which were muzzle-loading. This resulted in a lower level of accuracy among the African troops. Some of the reports of frequent mutilation suffered by the German troops could have been caused by the extensive use of this older weaponry.[9]

The decisive advantage held by the colonial troops was possession of the machine gun, a weapon subject to considerable experimentation for a number of decades. First coming into widespread use in the American Civil

War, the machine gun was characterized by a combination of the targeted concentration of a great number of rounds and its mobility. The machine gun was first introduced in the Prussian-German army in 1900, in a number of forms and from a number of different manufacturers. Highly inaccurate because of a tendency to pull to the side, the Swedish Nordenfelt machine gun proved to be vastly inferior to the American-manufactured Maxim. Both fired some 600 rounds per minute, and made use of conventional infantry ammunition (although not that compatible with the M/71 or M/88). The turn of the twentieth century saw the introduction in the Protection Force of the Berlin-produced machine gun MG01.

The myth of the machine gun was born in 1898 after its use by the British army to put down the Mahdi uprising at Omdurman 1898.[10] The German equivalent to the Battle of Omdurman took place at the East African mission at Mahenge in 1905. Taking refuge in the station amid the mountainous terrain of Upogoro, Captain Theodor von Hassel defended his position with a force of ten Europeans, 250 Askaris (with women and children), 1,000 Kiwanga warriors, and 1,000 villagers. His force was equipped with two machine guns. Clearing a clear field of fire and setting up distance markers, Hassel demonstrated the effectiveness of the new weapon by his successful defense of his post against repeated waves of attack by a force of some 8,000 African warriors, which took serious casualties.[11] Although a number of individual warriors managed to reach the perimeter, they were unable to exploit their advantage in numbers to take the station. As one report put it, "their force of numbers was broken by the presence of two machine guns and the steady nerves of their operators."[12] The defenders of Mahenge came within a hair's breadth of defeat as a result of their extreme shortage of ammunition. Nevertheless, it would be wrong to regard the outcome as a triumph of technology, decided as it was by failure on the part of the attacking force to coordinate its various waves of assault.

Lacking sufficient supplies, neither the imperial German navy nor the German Expeditionary Corps was equipped with machine guns in the course of their expedition to China. Nevertheless, the campaign saw the deployment of the weapon by other allied forces. The German East Asian Occupation Brigade was only later equipped with a few machine guns. The Protection Force in German South East Africa had already taken delivery of nine 8 mm Maxim guns; on the eve of war in German South-West Africa, the Protection Force was equipped with only five nonmobile machine guns. Receiving two machine guns from the gunboat *Habicht*—one had been delivered from Cameroon, and the other came with a Marine expeditionary force—six further machine guns arrived at the beginning of March 1904. With these reinforcements, the force was able to build a horse-drawn machine gun unit with four machine guns. This was later supplemented by a further such unit. Both saw service in the Battle of Waterberg.[13]

The *Prussian-German Infantry Drill Book* identified the role of the machine gun as providing infantry support by directing "considerable fire" to the decisive positions during both attack and defense.[14] The machine gun was initially regarded purely as an auxiliary weapon; the *Instruction Manual for the Machine Gun Section* from 1906 informed its readers that "machine guns are not intended to replace either the infantry or the artillery."[15] In the main, these weapons were set up in such a fashion as to enable direction of their fire over the heads of their own forces. Any reduction of the distance between their own troops and the enemy required the machine gun section to cease firing so as to avoid hitting its own side. In Africa, machine gun sections could provide covering fire even in the thickest of bush, environments that ruled out the deployment of artillery. Although machine guns had to be dismantled for transport, they could be reassembled quickly. The real disadvantage of this new weapon was the need to provide its operators with specialist training. The problems of range (the machine gun troops had to be in close proximity to the enemy) and maintaining sufficient levels of ammunition were also factors limiting their deployment.

Infantry units operating in a colonial theater were also provided with artillery support. The task of the artillery was to provide support to the infantry firing line and draw enemy fire. The campaign in China witnessed only a single deployment of heavy naval artillery, during the storming of the Dagu forts. As in Africa, the artillery campaign was dominated by the deployment of light mobile field guns. The limited nature, if not total absence, of enemy artillery meant that the performance of the German artillery did not play a decisive role. Such an advantage was balanced by logistical problems, including the supply of ammunition and the transport of the heavy iron weaponry. The preferred method of transport—stripping the guns to their component parts and entrusting them to horses or mules—ruled out the deployment of larger artillery pieces with barrels of over one meter in length. Although able to draw a maximum of 120 kilograms each, the horses were unable to sustain such loads for long periods and the mounted artillery was unable to accompany the infantry at all times. An alternative was provided by mobile guns on limber wheels. Lighter and more mobile mountain artillery proved its worth in the Chinese campaign, as the conditions in the uplands west of Peking ruled out the deployment of other types of artillery.[16]

Contemporary military thinking established that the main task of the artillery in colonial warfare was the demoralization of the enemy, using the "Great Gun," to spread fear and shock among the African populations.[17] Speaking in his so-called Extermination Proclamation to the Hereros, issued in October 1904, von Trotha made explicit reference to the power of our "long barrels": "The Herero people must leave this land. If they do not, I shall force them to do so by using the Great Gun [artillery]." Despite this threat, the German force made hardly any use of its artillery against the fleeing Herero. In the Boxer campaign, captured enemy guns and flags were regarded as victory trophies, indicating that the value of such weapons was measured not just according to their destructive force. The mere presence of the artillery, even when silent, was often enough to instill fear in the enemy.

The use of machine guns and artillery did little to alter the traditional realities of an infantryman's life of close combat and the bayonet charge in which every attack culminated. These hard facts were reflected in the standard issue to every infantryman, gunner, and trooper active in a colonial theater of a melee weapon of some nature. The highly polished metal out of which these sidearms were fashioned united the members of all ranks in a shared risk. As von Waldersee put it, "the clear and sunny conditions prevalent in China meant that all reflective metal surfaces bring the disadvantage of making the troops visible from long range."[18] This also applied to the officers' scabbards. Once fixed onto their rifles, the bayonets, twenty-five centimeters in length and serrated on one edge, transformed the firearm into a stabbing weapon.[19] The cavalry also fought the majority of its engagements with a (bladed) melee weapon, because of the nature of its deployment—in constant movement and presented with the chests of enemy infantry at a convenient thrusting height.

The Chinese campaign saw the deployment of only one battalion of cavalry, subsequently reduced to four squadrons; difficulties in procuring enough horses meant that no further mounted units were deployed.[20] Equipped with a Carbine 98, a short firearm easy to handle on horseback, troopers also carried a sabre and a lance. Field Marshal von Waldersee criticized the use of the standard cavalry sabre, arguing (correctly) that although effective when thrust, it did not function well as a blade. The lance also failed to perform according to expectations. The winter conditions prevalent during the Boxer

War transformed the Chinese padded dress into an impenetrably protective layer almost resembling a suit of armor, in which the lance stuck fast, thereby preventing any injury to its wearer. The wide sleeves of the Chinese attire provided protection to the hands of its wearers, enabling them to seize the oncoming lance by its pennant and thus blunt any cavalry attack. Learning from the conditions in China, von Waldersee pleaded for the German lances not only to be equipped with a sharper point (either through simple sharpening or provision with a leaf-shaped tip) but to be shortened, thus transferring the center of gravity rearward.[21] The description of the Chinese technique for dealing with cavalry charges is telling—soldiers did not wear the wide-armed garments that gave the horsemen such trouble; as such we can conclude that the cavalry must have been deployed against civilians. This conclusion is confirmed by the statement of one soldier, according to which "all the Chinese"—that is, regardless of their combat status—were to be struck down or impaled so as to save ammunition.[22] The cavalry was not deployed in any of the African campaigns, although a similar function was performed by mounted infantry in German South-West Africa. Officers, medical officers, and civil servants were accorded precedence in the dispensation of riding lessons.[23] The climate of German East Africa precluded the use of either horses or mules, explaining the complete absence of any mounted troops.

The colonial wars provided the ideal circumstances and environment in which to test new weapons, the practice of which was undertaken on a large scale. The arms carried by the German forces in the three colonial theaters were largely similar although not identical, and exhibited a significant degree of innovation in the short period. While the naval forces dispatched to China still carried the standard M/71 rifle, the forces deployed in German South-West Africa and German East Africa were equipped with the newer, smoke-reduced M/98, with its longer range and allegedly more humane characteristics. The differences in the two rifles influenced both the nature of the killing and the number of enemy dead. Despite such advances, the decisive change was effected by the deployment of machine guns, which were also considerably easier to transport than the less mobile artillery. While the expeditionary force to China was forced to borrow machine guns from its allies, the German forces in both African campaigns were issued with their own machine guns from the outset.

The successful deployment of weapons in all three campaigns was subject to two conditions. First, destruction of the enemy in standard situations such as firefights, sieges, defenses, and set-piece battles was possible only if the commander succeeded in deploying his firepower on the enemy directly and quickly. In situations of surprise such as an ambush, this necessity often proved impossible to execute. Moreover, the possession of superior military technology was no guarantee of success—the poor performance of the artillery and machine gun sections in the Battle of Waterberg meant that they exerted no influence on the outcome of the engagement. Second, the reliable function of these modern weapons depended on their correct transportation, regular maintenance, and specified operation. Not all sections of the colonial armies were trained sufficiently for their duties, and officers and noncommissioned officers (NCOs) received instruction in the deployment of machine guns only shortly before being shipped out. The Marine Infantry also required remedial target practice before departing for German South-West Africa in 1904. The field companies in German South-West Africa required special training to deal with the small, proximate, and numerous targets with which they were confronted.[24] Indeed, although possession of superior weaponry gave the German soldiers a high level of confidence, such feelings of superiority could be counterproductive. Not just a tool of war, the weapons could also act to influence tactics—their presence, absence, and state of repair dictated the nature of the operations that could be performed.

Any consideration of the influence of the increased killing potential of these new weapons on the actual incidence of extreme violence in the colonial wars is and remains essentially speculative. However, one line of thought could focus profitably on the attitude toward killing displayed by the soldiers equipped with modern weaponry. The deployment of machine guns, for instance, involved a destructive potential so high that its operator could no longer register the death and destruction that he meted out. As the act of killing was transformed into a mechanical process, death was robbed of its face. By comparison, the use of the archaic sword and lance created a more intense experience of killing—the sucking and grating noise of the sword thrust, the streams of blood, and the cries of agony—which many found difficult to bear. Nevertheless, the shared sensory experience could also serve to create and strengthen a feeling of community and belonging among those killing. Direct violence meted out with weapons was only one part of the imperial repertoire of violence in the colonial theaters; mass shootings and artillery bombardments were accompanied by the specter of their threat in order to facilitate plunder, requisitions, rape, and imprisonment. This was also supplemented by forms of violence entirely independent of weapons such as the use of fire to burn houses, settlements, and crops.

A further factor influencing the conduct of colonial wars and related to weaponry was the use of horses. Deployed in both China and German South-West Africa, their use was not just restricted to the transport of machine guns and artillery. The Chinese campaign even saw their use as an independent force in both the set-piece battles and the subsequent pursuit. In South-West Africa, mounted troops provided the Protection Force with a high level of mobility, enabling a considerable extension in the range of military control. Indeed, instruction in the breeding, care, and transport of horses should have been accorded just as much attention in training as the maintenance of the weaponry. The German military came to appreciate uses and value of mounted troops in a colonial context only during the wars themselves.

Training and Instruction

Colonies and colonial warfare provided only a footnote to the course of training for officers, NCOs, and other ranks in the army and the navy alike. The elite naval academy in Kiel and its military equivalent—the Prussian Academy of War in Berlin—at which above all staff officers were trained, similarly ignored the characteristics and demands of what was to prove an important theater of operations. Taught by civilian and military instructors, the students of both institutions received a traditional military education. Naval cadets followed a curriculum focusing on technical-nautical training, with the doctrine of naval warfare and its history receiving much less attention.[25] Similarly, the treatment of colonial warfare in Berlin was conspicuous by its absence. The only change came in 1907–1908 with the introduction not of colonial warfare, but instruction in equestrianism. Nevertheless, both academies touched on the existence of the German colonies with the teaching of geography and history, both taught by civilian instructors.[26]

A similar situation was to be found in the naval school at Mürwik as well as the army colleges and the numerous NCO training centers. Courses in colonial geography provided a short overview of China, German East Africa, and German South-West Africa. A lecture script from 1905 in geography made the laconic comment that the southern territories of German East Africa were prone to periodic incursions and uprisings. Nevertheless, descriptive instruction in physical and cultural geography and demography imparted specific conceptions as to the reasons behind holding colonies. German South-West Africa was described as a colony of settlement, with instruction focusing on the settler society at Windhoek which was said to be of decisive importance for the colony. German possession of East Africa, on the other hand, where settlement played only a secondary role, was described as a philanthropic undertaking, intended to increase native African prosperity and purchasing power.[27] After the conclusion of the colonial wars, the courses of history provided at these institutions included short units focusing on the Boxer uprising and the war in South-West Africa. However, the lesson scripts only ever include short bullet points imparting only the most basic information. The lessons given by civilian instructors ignored the military specifics of colonial warfare entirely.

Officers applying for a posting to the Protection Force (regardless of the conflict) were given the opportunity to prepare for their tasks at the civilian-run Institute for Oriental Languages attached to the Friedrich-Wilhelms University in Berlin. Established in 1887 and modeled on British practice, the institute organized lectures and seminars designed to prepare its participants for general colonial service. Providing specialist training for interpreters set to work for the Diplomatic Corps, the institute increasingly came to focus on the provision of language training, which was eventually accorded priority. Teaching was provided in English, Chinese for use in Qingdao, Arabic and Swahili for use in German East Africa, and Herero, Nama, and Ovambo (German South-West Africa). In 1900, during the Boxer War, a Chinese course for fourteen officers was added to the curriculum, twelve of whom were sent to the institute by the military cabinet; two were sent by the naval cabinet.[28] In addition to its language courses, the institute also provided instruction in the applied geography and economics of Africa and Asia, as well as courses covering its tropical crops and more generalized courses in tropical hygiene or geography, astronomy, and orientation. A number of these courses were instructed by military officers who had returned from the colonies.

An aspiring colonial officer would usually attend the Berlin Institute for Oriental Languages for two semesters. In an attempt to adapt to the needs of the various Protection Forces, the total duration of studies at the institute was not subject to any regulation. A total of 130 officers were registered as students at the institute from the winter semester of 1892–1893 to the end of the summer semester of 1903.[29] While some of the participants attended on a voluntary basis, others did so on the orders of the General Staff or the Imperial Colonial Office. The High Command of the Protection Force sent two of its officers to the institute every year, thus ensuring that at least a small proportion of its officers were in possession of rudimentary linguistic training and basic knowledge of the colonies in which they were to serve. Over time, the Institute for Oriental Languages developed into a forum of exchange between aspiring civil servants and active soldiers. Although well attended by professional soldiers and providing a forum for professional military exchange, the Berlin-based institute remained a civilian organization and did not focus on the specifics of colonial warfare.

Only the Marine Infantry received any form of practical training specifically tailored to the demands of colonial warfare. The program of instruction in colonial warfare was drawn up in 1897 by the commander of the II Sea Battalion, acting on the suggestion of the inspector of Marine Infantry.[30] The plan foresaw the provision of weekly instruction for NCOs by officers trained at the Berlin Institute in general questions pertaining to operations in a colonial theater. This program was to be supplemented by an ambitious project to equip all sea battalions with a library of literature focusing on the colonies. Lastly came the order to train combat, marching, and drill under "African conditions"—although, of course, these conditions were impossible to simulate in Germany. This program was to be complemented by a course of practical training provided for all ranks held over two afternoons. The course focused on the construction of fortified positions, temporary fortifications, bridges, rafts, dams, huts, and camps as well as the techniques to overcome natural and artificial obstacles and for the destruction of houses. The special program was rounded off with applied gymnastics and instruction for NCOs in laying down rapid gunfire. These exercises were followed by simulations of tactical marching in thick scrub, attacks on African fortifications (bomas), river crossings, and the storming of palisades and timber fortifications.

It remains unclear whether this course was ever taken by members of the Marine Infantry. Despite these provisions, the available sources give no indication of the actual extent and intensity of the exercises in colonial warfare practiced by the Marine Infantry. Indeed, the only evidence that these exercises took place at all is provided by contemporary descriptions from members of the sea battalions.[31] Despite such references, official records of exercises do not make any mention of the special colonial exercises. Maneuvers retained a clear focus on the defense of coastal positions and towns as well as the boarding of ships and defense against landing ships. Whatever plans may have existed to introduce even a limited focus on the specific demands of colonial warfare, such intentions did not always manifest themselves in the training of the Marine Infantry.

Service Regulations and the Battle of Annihilation

The actions of soldiers and sailors in battle situations were regulated by the service regulations issued by the imperial army and navy, above all the *Field Service Regulations* issued in 1900, a cross-service manual for intelligence and security. Members of the army were also bound by the stipulations of the 1889 *Infantry Drill Manual,* which was revised in 1906. A separate *Infantry Drill Manual* covered the navy.[32] Revised in 1907, it echoed the army regulations in its decisive passages. In order to enable soldiers to cope with a range of offensive and defensive situations, these were to be "practiced in peacetime until achieving complete confidence through the learning and application of simple forms."[33]

The tactical battlefield concept favored by the imperial service regulations focused on the encirclement and destruction of the enemy in a single battle. Drawing their inspiration from ancient warfare, the principles outlined in such a doctrine represented a modern equivalent of Hannibal's successful attack on the flank and rear of enemy formations so as to force a quick and decisive outcome. This precept was given succinct expression by the *Infantry Drill Manual* from 1889: "The superiority in firepower decisive to success is best effected by means of encirclement."[34] In keeping with this doctrine, Colonel Theodor Leutwein wrote of the necessity for "comprehensive attack from all sides, always with the aim of dispensing a knockout blow."[35]

Closely associated with the demands of a war of encirclement and annihilation was the subsequent phase of pursuit.[36] The appeal that neither fatigue nor tiredness was to prevent a successful follow-up of initial success was manifested in an order of unbending hardness toward the German troops that "whatever collapses will be left on the wayside."[37] The pursuit was traditionally performed by the cavalry, and designed to "culminate wherever possible in the complete dissolution of the enemy force." Moreover, "such a pursuit has to be unremitting, involving the full number of the cavalry and performed without consideration for the men, even to the extent of exhaustion by day and continued action by night."[38] The artillery should also be involved in the pursuit, "even at the risk of both man and horse" in order to break the "main points of enemy resistance" quickly.[39] This doctrine reached its apotheosis in the great plan by the chief of the Imperial General Staff, Alfred von Schlieffen developed to enable the German Empire to fight a successful two-front war. Completed in 1905, the plan foresaw an attack on France by a strong right flank, with a simultaneous holding action being fought in Russia. Despite its ingenuity, the Schlieffen Plan remained "a highly risky adventure,"[40] the perils of which have been extensively demonstrated.

The authors of the *Service Regulations* wrote to address the demands presented by a symmetrical European war. However, the realities of colonial warfare and the poor communications that they involved rendered the doctrine of encirclement and destruction only partially viable. As a result, this type of warfare often ended in a disaster such as that suffered at the Battle of Waterberg in August 1904. This situation was compounded by the universality of the tactic of encirclement, which was also often employed successfully by the African forces. A pamphlet issued to German soldiers immediately before being shipped out and titled *Practical Experiences in South-West Africa* included the instruction that if subject to surprise attack, soldiers of the Protection Force should take action to prevent encirclement.[41]

The conditions experienced by the German soldiers in each colony often ruled out the possibility of conducting a pursuit. Nimble and familiar with the local territory, African fighters were able to disappear into retreats unknown to the German troops. This situation was compounded by the weakening during the initial phases of action of the men and horses originally intended to conduct the pursuit and who were now in no position to do so. Such a situation could have grave consequences for not only the lives of individual soldiers but the existence of whole units. As a result, it became standard practice in German East Africa to conduct the pursuit exclusively with African auxiliary contingents. The pursuit was of vital psychological importance to the colonial troops: a successful rout and an unsuccessful pursuit amounted to a lost victory from which the enemy would live to regroup and fight another day. The conditions of colonial warfare also led its protagonists to question the guiding principles established in the *Service Regulations.* The revised *Infantry Drill Manual,* published in 1889, updated military practice to incorporate the lessons drawn from the use of the new breech-loading rifle during the Wars of German Unification and the resulting changes in battlefield tactics. Supplanting the traditional attack as a column with an advancing line,[42] strategists replaced the traditional horizontal command structure with a system of "mission tactics." Thus instead of a detailed set of instructions stipulating the movements of whole units, a battle now consisted of a number of separate engagements. Conferring individual officers a considerable degree of independence in deciding how to realize their objectives, the change also resulted in the development of a system of volley fire that provided individual soldiers with a degree of security.

Although this new system intended the direction of operations by officers, the realities of colonial warfare served to extend the scope for action of individual soldiers. Following service in German South-West Africa, Captain Maximilian Bayer wrote in 1909 that the campaign required both officers and other ranks to exhibit a "greater degree of independence" than their training provided. Volley fire delivered by soldiers in dressed ranks remained the exception throughout the colonial wars fought by the various German Protection Forces. The reality was that individual soldiers were left to pick their own targets, which, being fast moving and fleeting in nature, required immediate action. This was unfortunate for the careful reader of the small-arms ordinances, which ruled out such a tactical approach—and which had not been covered in training.[43] Commanders in the South-West African war soon established two soldiers as the smallest unit capable of independent action, one of whom picked the targets (and provided an estimate of their range) for his partner to fire upon.[44] Such circumstances rendered mission tactics in their conventional form obsolete. Not only the level of initiative displayed by officers but also that among the other ranks had now become decisive to success.

A greater degree of independence was also required of NCOs and rank-and-file soldiers in a number of situations away from the battlefield. A range of decisions regarding the life and death of the local population were made in the absence of officers, and for which specific orders or even general directives were not issued. This matter was highlighted in the pamphlet *Practical Experiences from South-West Africa:* "The incalculability of the environment and the insecure nature of communications in South-West Africa means that when issuing instructions to units spread over a large area, such instructions tend to take the form not of direct orders, but directives. Establishing the objective to be achieved, the methods to be used in their execution are left to the discretion of those pursuing them."[45]

The colonial wars were often small or guerilla wars. A form not unknown to nineteenth-century Europe, such conflicts include the risings in the

Vendée (1793–1795), Tirol (1809), and Spain (1809–1813). Although defining the "small war" as one conducted by a national population against a force of occupation, Carl von Clausewitz maintained that the occupier would be ejected only if such a tactics were pursued in conjunction with a conventional campaign conducted by a standing army.[46]

With its propensity to assume a political-revolutionary character, the small war remained an object of continued suspicion to the Prussian-German military. Recognized at the most as the accompaniment to a conventional or large war, it was accorded only a single section in the canonical *Field Manual for Tactical Instruction in His Majesty's Military Academies*, in which it was listed as one variety of "combat under special conditions."[47] According to the *Field Manual*, small wars were conducted only if an invading army could not be beaten on the open field or if the physical nature of terrain—such as a mountainous region—ruled out the possibility of large-scale warfare. Such a war was characterized by a high level of mobility, the sudden appearance and disappearance of the enemy, cooperation with scouts and trusted auxiliaries, cunning, and audacity. The political reservations of the military about such a war culminated in warnings that a small war could easily provoke reprisals: this would rouse popular passions and could produce atrocities. Nevertheless, the *Manual* conceded that "the sum of minor successes could result in significant damage to or even endangerment of the lines of communications."[48]

In contrast to a large-scale conventional war, the small war could not be decided by a single, decisive engagement; instead, exhaustion would prove to be decisive. Of the two basic forms of warfare, a strategy of annihilation and attrition, the latter remained severely neglected by the German General Staff. Even the planners of the next naval war focused on delivering a knockout blow in a single decisive engagement, despite the fact that naval warfare had traditionally relied on conducting campaigns of attrition.

Viewed as a special form of the small war, colonial warfare was not incorporated in the official *Service Regulations;* the restricted applicability of this publication to the unfamiliar conditions was soon demonstrated by practical experience. The conduct of the three German colonial wars did not entirely follow the tactical precepts and principles outlined in a document developed for a European conflict. The soldiers involved in the campaigns also had access to alternative sources of information about war in the colonies, of which they made use, clearly taking up a number of different guiding ideas.

International Colonial Warfare

In contrast to the situation presented in Great Britain and France, the German military establishment made no move to consolidate the available knowledge regarding colonial warfare and present it in a practical manual. Rather, the available military knowledge pertaining to colonial warfare remained in fragmented form scattered across a variety of sources. Despite this situation, officers (and to a lesser extent, NCOs and the other ranks) had access to an additional, semiofficial supplementary source of knowledge in the form of pamphlets and essay-length treatment of colonial warfare.

Responding to the events of the "Arab Rising" in East Africa (1889–1890), the *Militär-wochenblatt* (the premier German military journal of semiofficial character) began with the publication of a number of articles and essays dealing with the German conduct of the wars in Africa.[49] Authored by travel writers or army officers (often the writers were both), the contributions focused on the course of the war in question or the provision descriptions of the country depending on the interest of the author or the perceived interest of the readership. This information was not restricted to officers and at least one of the contributions—that penned by a member of the Protection Force, Hermann von Wissmann—was reprinted in summary form in the *Unteroffizier-Zeitung*, a publication aimed at a readership of NCOs, and incorporated into the planning process for the Marine Infantry exercises.[50] Further evidence for the familiarity with colonial warfare in military circles was the amateur dramatics program of an NCO training school in Neubreisach (Alsace). Celebrating the kaiser's birthday, the festivities included two productions with a colonial theme, dealing with Qingdao (1901) and South-West Africa (1907).[51] The culture of military remembrance also focused on the dead of these wars, and a memorial for the NCOs who died in the various colonial campaigns was unveiled in the town of Jülich in 1910 to mark the fiftieth anniversary of the NCO school there.

The first definitive account of the conditions and tactics experienced during the African campaigns—Carl Peters' *Schriftlein für Afrikareisende*—was published in 1892. Widely held to be the archetype of the ruthless colonialist, Peters believed that the "Africans" lacked any form of courage. Wont to stampede into battle like a herd of cattle, he depicted them as whipped on at best by their own clamoring. Lacking any respect for the norms and standards of civilized warfare, Peters characterized their behavior as brutal, bestial, and indifferent to the suffering of others.[52] In view of this litany of barbarism, Peters pleaded for the adoption of an offensive approach. Europeans should be mindful to retain the initiative: "The best method of demonstrating that we do not fear our opponent is to attack him." Attack was advanced as the easiest and most advantageous form of campaigning in Africa, as the attacker always enjoyed the better morale. To this end, Peters recommended psychological tactics such as the use of drums, flags, rockets, flares, or even just employment of chants such as "March, March, Hurrah!" He even concluded that "African" conditions made the small war the choicest form of warfare.

A similar argument was advanced in a lecture given to the *Militärische Gesellschaft* in Berlin a year later by the army officer Georg Maercker. Focusing on the conduct of the war in East Africa, it was subsequently reprinted in the *Militär-Wochenblatt*. This was followed soon after by the publication by Hermann von Wissmann (at that time still governor of German East Africa) of *Advice for Preparing for Service in the German Protectorates*, consisting of a number of articles that had already appeared in the *Militär-Wochenblatt* in 1894. Like Peters and Maercker, von Wissmann also advocated the primacy of attack and the application of "ruthless methods," justified above all by the striking brutality of the "African" conduct of war.[53] He argued for a conventional battle with which to administer a knockout blow. Should the enemy manage to escape or even evade such an engagement, the occupying force was to concentrate on a ruthless pursuit. Moreover, given the propensity of the enemy to retreat into impenetrable and difficult terrain, the occupier was to make use of the methods of destruction and pillage, even wiping out entire villages. At the same time, von Wissmann eschewed the precepts of a putative "African" way in warfare which (allegedly) involved the refusal to take prisoners. Instead of killing the recalcitrant population, the Germans should first safeguard the lives of all noncombatants before burning down their village. Auxiliary troops were to be instructed not to kill women, children, or unarmed men, rather to take them prisoner. Nevertheless, a strategy of conciliation designed to enable the insurgents to end hostilities while saving face was permissible only in the absence of grounds for punishment or if the commander had reason to believe that a violent response would result in heavy casualties among his own men.

Addressing the *Geographische Gesellschaft* in June 1897, Colonel Lothar von Trotha covered a number of geographical points—geological conditions, soil type, and natural features—and their influence on the military campaign. He dealt only briefly with the "African methods of warfare":

"I learned everything I needed to know of the African methods of warfare after an encounter with a pole driven into the center of a road, thus impeding the progress of my platoon. Impaled on the apex of this pole was a freshly severed human head; its eyes were open, directing at myself a reproachful glance as though I were his murderer. I hope only that one of my Askaris accorded him final rest."[54]

More detailed reflections on colonial warfare in South-West Africa from the governor Theodor Leutwein were published in the *Militär-Wochenblatt* in 1898. In contrast to the accounts provided by Peters and von Wissmann, Leutwein was seriously interested in establishing what he saw as the features of warfare common to both Africa and Europe.[55] After a series of descriptions of combat with both the Herero and the Nama, he argued that every day the war continued weakened the German imperial position; following this estimation, a protracted war amounted to at least a minor victory for the Africans. Consequently, every soldier should be required to double as a diplomat so as to establish ties with and promote collaboration among the indigenous population. In reaching this position, he was consciously following the direction indicated by von Wissmann in his deliberations on the grounds for seeking to defuse difficult situations.[56]

Leutwein hoped to use his address to promote his long-term goal: a comprehensive program of colonialism aimed predominantly at improving economic cooperation with the African colonial subjects. However, despite such a close focus on colonial warfare and the nature of its conduct, he ignored what amounted to a number of decisive questions such as the treatment of women, children, and prisoners; the practice of requisitioning and destruction; and the maintenance of military superiority in the open field. Instead, he concentrated on the successful prosecution of military engagements with the purpose of preventing a guerilla war.

There is no evidence of any form of direct contacts between German, British, and French officers publishing on the topic of colonial warfare. Nevertheless, it is clear that the individual authors did consider related events in which their nation was not involved, actively incorporating the literature of the other authors into their accounts. Writing in the third edition of his book on small wars, the British officer Callwell made repeated reference to the German wars in South-West Africa.[57] For his part, von Wissmann saw Great Britain as exemplary, and despite considering their writings on the subject self-serving, recommended that the German military planners incorporate the insights gained from British accounts into their operations.[58]

Shorter English-language works on colonial warfare had already been translated into German.[59] Both the main library of the Imperial Naval Academy in Kiel and the Library of the Royal Prussian Great General Staff in Berlin held not only a copy of every German-language publication on the subject but also a selection of British and French literature.[60] The libraries also maintained subscriptions to the most important military periodicals the *Army and Navy Gazette* and *La France Militaire*. In 1897, British and French manuals were consulted in drawing up the new special program of training for deployment in the colonies; as the British Royal Marines had never served in the colonies, the French Marines were taken as role models to be emulated.[61] The first German drill manuals for colonial operations were drawn up after the campaigns in China, South-West Africa, and East Africa in 1908. In addition, the High Command of the Protection Forces ordered the military attaché in Paris to conduct a review of French regulations on training for overseas service.[62]

Of all the publications on the subject, Callwell's book was widely viewed as the best summary of warfare in a colonial theater: instead of making recommendations, it provided descriptions of each individual engagement from which the reader could draw lessons. Written by a veteran of the South African War, it was taken as being entirely authentic. In addition to this international standard (translated into French, but not German, soon after publication),[63] the insights gained into colonial warfare were principally disseminated in compendia, publications similar to manuals. One such example was the *Soldier's Pocket-Book for Field Service*, written by Garnet Wolseley, the commander in chief of the British army.[64] Acquiring a semiofficial status, a number of privately printed publications—especially those focusing on the conflict on the northwest frontier[65]—included summaries of these two texts.

Callwell was convinced that a guerilla war could be put down only through inflicting serious material and nonmaterial damage. He wrote, "The enemy must not only be beaten. He must be beaten thoroughly." He continued, "If the enemy cannot be touched in his patriotism or his honor, he can be touched through his pocket." He was quite explicit that such a campaign could be brutal, writing that "the war assumes an aspect which may shock the humanitarian."[66] Callwell was clear in his distinction between wars in Europe and those in the colonies. In his estimation, such campaigns could be won in Europe by simple reprisals against the villages acting as the source of the uprising. The stock example to which he and most British writers referred to support this conclusion was that of the guerilla war in the Vendée.[67] He maintained the necessity of rigorous measures and conducting reprisals in Africa or Asia, by contrast, against all the villages in the area.[68]

Wolseley came to a similar conclusion, arguing in his (much reprinted) *The Soldier's Pocket-Book* that in a war against an uncivilized nation, "Your first objective should be the capture of whatever they prize most, and the destruction or deprivation of which will probably bring the war most rapidly to a conclusion. Thus the capture of their cattle and the destruction of their crops, and of the grain stored in their kraals or villages, in depriving them of food is most efficacious."[69]

Nevertheless, Wolseley warned against burning down houses and villages of no military value, as these were quick and easy to rebuild. Moreover, he reasoned, such action served only to anger the local population without inflicting any real damage. Of far greater value and efficacy was an attack on enemy territory shortly before the harvest; if it caused considerable losses, such a measure could prove to have a considerable long-term effect. The seizure of cattle could also exercise a persuasive effect on a recalcitrant tribe.[70]

According to Wolseley, conventional European strategic expertise was of as limited a value to the conduct of a colonial war as was company drill. His solution was to adopt the enemy tactics, adapted as they were to local conditions. "Savages" would be surprised by rapid speed at which the Europeans now moved and would react with demoralization. As a result, the occupying force should be careful to observe the fighting tactics of the enemy and remain aware of their most widely used weapons of surprise, deceit, and treachery: "Always distrust eastern and savage nations in war; allow no assurances on their part to cause you to relax your precautions in the least."[71]

Colonial warfare had been a topic of discussion in France since its conquest of Algeria. Following the insight gained in 1840 that he was fighting against not an army but a whole population, General Thomas Robert Bugeaud deployed mobile columns (their first use in colonial theater) which made systematic use of plunder and destruction as part of so-called raids.[72] Publishing his insights in book form, his account not only defended the actions ordered by General Aimable Pélissier, in which more than 500 Arabs (including women and children) were suffocated in caves in June 1845, but also suggested the routine use of such tactics.

Despite such an initial position, the experience of the successful invasions in Africa, Indo-China, and Madagascar in the 1880s led the Third

Republic to adopt an increasing level of tactical flexibility, associated with the generals Joseph-Simon Gallieni and Louis Hubert Lyautey, all of whom published their recommendations in book form.[73] According to Gallieni, a colonial army should not just conquer, but actively colonize the territory, working to extend the exploitation of agricultural resources. In doing so, the army was to convince the subjected populations that cooperation with the imperial power would serve their own prosperity. Despite such a new approach to soldiering, these methods remained paired with more traditional methods.

In 1894, at the same time as the Herero war, Gallieni introduced the tactic of "progressive occupation" designed to force the pace of the occupation of Madagascar. This involved a system of patrols between outposts to extend French control over an area. Addressing soldiers charged with putting down a rising in the southwest, his book sought to remind them of the situation: "Remember that the operation is one of pacification—we are not conducting a war of extermination. Avoid both fraternization and unnecessary destruction."[74] Learning from his service in Indo-China with Gallieni, Lyautey's conduct of the 1903 Moroccan campaign saw the use of both French and native troops. Employing tactics similar to those tested in Madagascar, with patrols roving between forward bases, this approach was also supplemented by raids.

This range of approaches to colonial warfare did not have any impact on the countless manuals for African warfare compiled by a number of officers, often acting on the instructions of the Ministry of War.[75] One French compendium focusing on colonial warfare adopted the approach currently prevalent in Germany and Britain and which followed Carl Peters and Hermann von Wissmann in arguing that "a victory alone is not sufficient. The destruction of property and possessions is vital—cruel and barbaric, but absolutely necessary."[76] Far from the "stopgap" or "special solution," as identified by Erick J. Mann, the destructive methods employed by the German Protection Force to quell the Arab rising in German East Africa were universal instruments of colonial warfare.[77]

All the colonial powers were united in their conviction as to the best approach to dealing with foreign cultures during war: Africans and Asians only understood the language of violence. At the worst, clemency of any sort would be misconstrued as weakness; at the best, it would only provoke further resistance.[78] All agreed that wounded soldiers should never be left to the mercies of the native forces, as they were sure to be tortured. The nature of the putative "African methods of warfare," taken as being "inherently cruel,"[79] was taken as a universal legitimation for atrocities.

Military Law

The members of the army, navy and Protection Forces engaged in the various German colonial wars fought at the turn of the twentieth century were all bound by the prescriptions of German military law. Based on the provisions of the Disciplinary Offences Ordinance for the German army (published October 1872), the Military Penal Code of the same year, and the Military Tribunals Ordinance (1898), it also regulated the conduct of naval personnel. In addition, members of the Protection Force were also expressly subject to a version of the Articles of War for the army published in 1872 and extended in 1902.[80] Breaches of military order and service regulations not covered by military justice were subject to disciplinary punishment. Officers, NCOs, and ordinary soldiers could be censured by the mechanisms of a simple, formal, and severe charge. Members of the other ranks could also be subject to special fatigue duties such as guard duty.[81] Punishments handed down on the basis of the Military Penal Code, on the other hand, required (with only a few exceptions) a prior trial.[82] Courts-martial were regulated by the prescriptions of the Military Tribunals Ordinance.[83]

The formal process of court-based proceedings opened against soldiers in the colonies was subject to early additional regulation by a number of supplementary prescriptions. The commander of the François force in German South-West Africa (which operated independently of the German army) was commissioned in 1889 to institute court-martial proceedings against infringements of the Military Penal Code. Two regulations were established as part of this process. If the accused was a European, proceedings were to follow the prescriptions of the Military Tribunals Ordinance from 1845, as far as local conditions and the events in question would allow. The trial of "natives" was to take into account "tribal custom" in both the process itself and the verdict to be reached. Those found guilty of offences committed against the support units were to be tried in accordance with the customs of war, whereas members of "civilized nations" were to be dealt with in accordance with the conventions traditionally governing war in their nation.[84]

The year 1896 saw the issue of a "Prescription Pertaining to Tribunals involving Military Personnel of the Imperial Protection Forces"[85] outlining the various jurisdictions and levels of court in the protectorates. Military jurisdiction was exercised by the court of the High Command of the Protection Force, the Gubernatorial Court, and the divisional court (section 2). The court of the High Command of the Protection Force consisted of the German imperial chancellor as the court president, who claimed principal jurisdiction over all members of the Protection Force and a council equipped with judicial powers to act as an auditor (section 3). The Gubernatorial Court was made up of the colony governor or state governor *(Landeshauptmann)* as court president and an auditor (section 4). A divisional court could be formed by every division nominated by the responsible colony governor or state governor. Each court was presided over by a commanding officer as court president and an officer leading the investigation. The divisional court held only lower jurisdiction over the members of the division and any military personnel transferred to it. If a number of such divisions were united in the same area under a single command, the most senior officer would assume the presidency of the court (section 5).

All military personnel were subject to a court-martial or drumhead court-martial (section 8). The composition of the judges' bench depended on the rank of the accused. An officer could be tried by a senior company commander and two lieutenants; an NCO could be tried by a senior company commander acting as chairman, two officers, and two NCOs; a corporal or private was to be tried by a senior company commander as chairman, two officers, and two corporals or privates.

This prescription clearly specified that the military courts, naval courts, and those of the Protection Force were to cooperate in terms of both investigations and the provision of jurors for courts-martial, drumhead courts-martial, and courts of inquiry (section 12). The enforcement of prison sentences of up to a year was to be arranged for locally, whereas sentences of a longer duration were to be served in Germany. Moreover, in accordance with section 180 of the Military Tribunals Ordinance, the sentences were to be handed down in correspondence with the legal prescriptions binding the army.[86] Between January 1904 and June 1905, fifty-seven convicts were shipped from German South-West Africa to Germany to serve a prison sentence.[87]

Following the issue of the Military Tribunals Ordinance of 1898, detailed prescriptions drafted specifically for application to the Protection Force were announced in 1900.[88] The Military Tribunals Ordinance and its supplementary provisions for the colonies established an extremely clear and well-defined legal procedure for the prosecution of military personnel. Disciplinary law and military penal law were to provide the basis for the maintenance of troop discipline and regulate the relations and communication between officers and men. Misconduct punished by disciplinary measures included a breach of military authority in the form of insubordination, disobedience, insulting or threatening behavior, physical assault, mutiny, resistance, dereliction of duty, and drunkenness (both on and off duty). A court-martial, on the other hand, was convened only if the referent power of a soldier's superior was threatened or had already been lost. Military routine in the colonies and life during the war were characterized by harsh punishments for comparably minor breaches of duty and discipline among officers and ranks alike.

Following the loss of the legal documents pertaining to the Protection Force or the navy in the colonies, the only evidence for court proceedings convened in German South-West Africa is provided by the Medical Report and occasional articles in the *Unteroffizier-Zeitung*. According to the Medical Report, the period between January 1904 and March 1907 saw 474 recorded infringements of penal law confirmed by a court-martial resulting in a prison sentence. Discounting nine of the cases in which the offenses were committed by individuals either not belonging to the Protection Force or outside the protectorate, or were not proven, this leaves 465 felonies.[89] The offenses of deserting a cattle post and negligent homicide with a service weapon were both punished by a prison sentence of one and a half years. A case of lying to a superior and insult was punished with two years.[90] The maintenance of discipline through the imposition of strict punishments was viewed as a matter of particular importance, as the colonial troops did not represent a well-defined unit and a number of the volunteer soldiers were viewed as being of dubious character. The necessity of maintaining absolute military obedience *(Manneszucht)* was stressed repeatedly, both before and during operations in the colonial theater.[91]

The interministerial and military commission dispatched to German South-West Africa to evaluate the conduct of the war often criticized the harsh punishments meted out by the military justice system. Identifying the minimum sentences stipulated by the laws of war as being too high, it was seen that judges were unable to take into account the individual nature of each case. Instead, the commission suggested a review, with the aim of reducing the minimum sentences but retaining the maximum level of punishment. Seeking to reduce the number of court proceedings held in the field, moreover, the conduct of which was seen as especially time consuming in the far-flung colonial theaters, the commission recommended extending the range of military offenses that could be subject to military discipline. The proposal thus envisaged an expansion in both the jurisdiction of disciplinary action and the number of punishments meted out under its aegis.[92]

Military penal law not only was applied to matters of internal conduct, but through the laws of war, it also encompassed "punishable actions conducted in the field" and thus external matters. In accordance with sections 9 and 11, this also applied to military action undertaken in the absence of a formal declaration of war, as was the case in China or German East Africa. The pertinent authorities were obliged to prosecute all crimes against property or the person or "crimes or offences against morality." The officers called to judge a case were obliged to open proceedings "regardless of any application on the part of an injured party or person entitled to make such an application" (section 127). Crimes involving assault and rape were to be dealt with in accordance with the relevant prescriptions contained in the Imperial Penal Code.[93] Criminal law also applied expressly to prisoners of war, who were to be informed of this fact. The laws of war (sections 128, 129, and 133) also made clear that acts of plundering or looting would be punished by a custodial sentence of up to three years or demotion to the lowest form of private. If the act involved assault or resulted in grievous bodily harm, a punishment of up to ten years in prison would be applied. Should the action result in the death of the person attacked, a capital sentence could be handed down.

A brief yet precise summary of these penal norms regulating relations with the civil population and property in war was provided by article 17 of the laws of war.[94] The provisions of this article were read out slowly and clearly in the presence of every soldier and sailor and were subject to further explanation before the recruit swore his oath of service. The *Field Manual for Instruction in Military Service* also focused on the provisions of article 17.[95] The annual repetition of the articles of war in every company, squadron, and battery allows the assumption that officers and soldiers were entirely conversant with the legal boundary between permissible and impermissible violence.

While the German military hierarchy exhibited particular strictness in its punishment of offenses committed by German troops against each other, crimes perpetrated against the civilian populations of China and Africa were not subject to any level of consistent investigation or forceful sanction. In cases in which imperial officers tolerated, covered up, or even ordered an infringement of the law, they had themselves committed an indictable offense under section 147 of the Military Penal Code, which set out the responsibilities of supervision and reporting demanded of a superior officer: "Those culpably failing in the duties of supervising their subordinates or deliberately failing to report or punish penal offences committed by their subordinates will be punished with a sentence of up to six months' imprisonment. Officers can be dismissed."[96]

Although the provisions of international law regulating the humane conduct of war established at the First Hague Peace Conference of 1899 were not applicable during the Boxer and African wars, the very presence in China of a number of international contingents resulted in the de facto enforcement of number of different national military laws, such as the British *Manual of Military Law*, the French *Nouveaux codes français et lois usuelles civiles et militaires*, and the American *Articles of War*.[97] Although the various national legal codes all agreed in forbidding excesses against the civilian population, these same codes also established the possibility that such prohibitions could be suspended in extreme situations. As the French regulations stipulated, "in exceptional situations, the protection of the expedition sometimes requires deviation from military law."[98]

The conduct of the war in China demonstrated the existence of a tacit agreement between the imperial powers by which the Military Penal Codes were to be applied selectively and restrictively when considering crimes committed against the Chinese. Only in exceptional cases were officers and soldiers of the multinational force to be held accountable for violations of the rules governing European wars. American penal documents reveal a surprisingly high number of courts-martial; closer examination reveals, however, that the majority of these cases pertained to violence committed against American or allied troops.[99] The records reveal only one American conviction for rape.[100] It is certain, however, that many more crimes were committed. On the German side, the only recorded trial was that a Bavarian infantryman court-martialed in November 1900 for plundering; he was demoted to private second class and given a prison sentence of six months.[101] The records would seem to indicate that incidents of plundering were subject to increased prosecution from the fall of 1900, soon after Great Britain and the United States had established a functioning system for recovering illegally acquired goods.[102] Negative reports in the German, British, American, and French press as well as the publication of negative soldiers' letters in newspapers could also have influenced the increase in the number of courts-martial. Despite this change in policy, the convictions handed down were insufficient to exert anything approaching a deterrent effect and bring a change in the behavior of the troops toward Chinese lives and property. The punishments do demonstrate the existence of particular standards of behavior which were intended to be maintained, but give no indication of the actual extent of the criminal offences committed. The internal discipline of the troops fighting in the colonial theaters was to be maintained under all circumstances, yet conduct toward the native populations was not subject to such strict standards of regulation. The intention was to exercise controlled, disciplined violence in a manner that never threatened colonial rule. This situation was exacerbated in German East Africa, where (according to a German officer) the presence of African auxiliary troops made it difficult to punish a white soldier. Such actions—so he maintained— would lead to a loss of respect for the particular individual and thus all white soldiers.[103] Following this logic, one can interpret colonial wars as a cycle of punishment and violence. The rebellious population should be punished severely for its resistance—itself a challenge to the "civilized" world— whereas the soldiers administering this punishment were to remain largely unpunished for any excesses committed during their dealings with the native populations. Despite this considerable level of freedom, the soldiers remained subject to strict internal discipline which itself resulted in considerable frustration. This in turn was channeled into violence toward the insurgent population.

In addition to the jurisdiction of the Military Penal Code and the Military Tribunals Ordinance, the wars in China and German South-West Africa were also subject to special legal arrangements. The actions of German soldiers deployed to quell the Boxer War were regulated by the Imperial Ordinance for Judicature in the Army in Times of War and the Exceptional Courts-Martial of Foreign Nationals and the Exercise of Jurisdiction over Prisoners of War issued in December 1899. The general ordinance was designed to provide the military with penal directives supplementing the existing legal ordinances so as to create a Martial Penal Law applicable to civilians in the Chinese areas to be occupied.[104] As was the case in Europe, this ordinance now authorized "foreign nationals found guilty of treacherous actions directed against German or allied troops to be dealt with according to the previous customs of war and without a prior process, should they be found repeating their actions" (section 18).[105] The "foreign nationals" referred to in this ordinance were civilians. A court-marital investigation to establish their status as combatants was not foreseen.

This ordinance was not applied in German South-West Africa or German East Africa, as they were already under German administration. Nevertheless, South-West Africa was also subjected to a special legal ordinance; a number of binding legal prescriptions regulating the conduct of the Protection Force were issued to the troops in May 1904 by Lieutenant General Lothar von Trotha during their passage to Africa. Referring explicitly to them as constituting laws of war,[106] von Trotha employed formulations that were based very closely on the Imperial Ordinance from 1899. According to these regulations, every commanding officer was authorized to shoot all "colored natives caught red handed in the execution of treacherous activities injurious to German troops, for example all armed rebels found to be pursuing activities of warlike intent. This is to be performed without prior court proceedings and in accordance with the traditional customs of war" (section 7a). All other Africans taken prisoner "by German military personnel on suspicion of having committed penal offences" were to be condemned by special courts-martial (section 7b).

Von Trotha's ordinance equated "colored natives" in South-West Africa with those civilian "foreign nationals" dealt with in the Imperial Ordinance from 1899, thus only paraphrasing the legal situation existent prior to the Herero and Nama War. In this respect, the rules for the prosecution of the war as established by von Trotha's "laws of war" were thus not—as sometimes asserted[107]—aiming at a specifically cruel war of racial extermination, nor can they be advanced as evidence of a targeted eliminationist policy developed in early 1904. Nevertheless, von Trotha's laws of war did considerably extend the scope for the use of armed force. One factor contributing to this outcome was his order that "the men are to be instructed that independent execution of any sentences against coloreds will be prosecuted in accordance with the generally applicable prescriptions concerning assault, manslaughter and murder and will be punished severely. The use of armed violence outside the scope of an engagement is permissible only for the purposes of self-defense and the prevention of attempted escapes" (8). On the one hand, the use of "armed violence" both for self-defense and for the "prevention of escape attempts" accorded the men considerable leeway for action. At the same time, however, it is unmistakable that the threat of severe punishment sought to rule out any acts of arbitrary violence.

Military penal law clearly provided German soldiers in German South-West Africa with considerable guidance in calibrating their behavior. A state constituted by law, imperial Germany practiced positive law, defining crimes and offenses to such an extent as to rule out any source of uncertainty.

All events, even such extreme circumstances as war, were regulated by not just the nonbinding international law but also positive (and thus binding) Military penal law. Nevertheless, the situation was far from clear-cut. The clear legal prescriptions established to prevent arbitrary action were widely regarded as a *quantité négligeable*. Disregarding the extensive battery of legislation regulating their behavior, many soldiers believed themselves to be virtually immune from punishment.

Far from representing an innovation, the argument for establishing the special legal status of colonial warfare had been advanced by General Julius von Hartmann in an article from 1879. Having established a reputation for placing the demands of warfare over those of humanity, Hartmann offered a simple justification for this stance: terrorism in war was a principle of military necessity.[108] He has often been advanced as the key figure demonstrating a line of continuity in German military thinking stretching from imperial Germany to the Second World War, and his statements have been used to establish the German military establishment as consistent and convinced purveyors of an inherent and ingrained military doctrine of pronounced and deliberate brutality.[109] However, advocates of such a theory fail to recognize that colonial military activity had long been established by all nations as a special branch of warfare to be pursued in a fashion, and with methods, that differed clearly from European warfare. Moreover, this process had been completed before Germany ever came to acquire colonies itself.[110] Learning from the examples of the Turkish massacre of the Bulgarians, the Russian atrocities in Central Asia, the brutal French conduct of their war in Algeria, and the suppression of an uprising in India by the British, Hartmann concluded that military necessity was apt to manifest itself in a number of different forms and "must be made dependent not only on the behavior but also the level of the culture of the nation, tribes or parties against which the war was to be waged."[111] Expressed in other words, the "necessities of war" could become much more pressing when confronted with an alien culture. An unremitting course of action was also necessary after the war had been concluded. As he wrote, "it is exactly at the point at which a modern state comes into hostile contact with peoples and tribal communities drawn from a lower culture, or even one in terminal decline, that the rape [of this grouping] achieved during the action of war must be maintained."[112]

German military penal law was not best suited to application in a colonial theater. Conceived for application in occupied European territories, it was designed to suppress any civil resistance before such resistance had a chance to develop. Its application to an area of open insurgence was thus not entirely practicable. Moreover, the prescriptions and directives of international law were not always taken into consideration while drawing it up. Although apparently adding substance to the theory of the continuity of brutality in any putative German way of warfare,[113] closer examination reveals a situation in which law was subject to tacit and systematic avoidance. It was in no way necessary to use the argument of the necessities of war as a justification for avoiding a legal situation that did not permit the application of brutal means. Both infringements of international law and crimes under military penal law could become legitimate actions through the mere fact of their having been committed in a colonial war. The patterns of behavior necessary for this end were at least reinforced or amplified through the summons by the Supreme Military Commander to "show no quarter." The best formula to characterize the behavior and conduct of the German troops in colonial wars would be "the replacement of legality with legitimacy."

Neither the armament nor the training of the German soldiers was in any way adapted to the needs of warfare in a colonial theater. Not trained for the exigencies of colonial warfare and the strategies best suited to their prosecution, the German servicemen conducting the wars in China and Africa were not even properly trained to handle the weapons with which they had been issued. The troops were not deployed following anything approaching a practicable plan of attack, and the battle plans designed for use in a European theater were hardly applicable to the conditions prevalent in Africa or China. The level of independence demanded of troops in colonial wars was not planned for, nor was it something for which the soldiers had been trained. Nevertheless, the soldiers did have access to publications providing rudimentary instruction in a number of basic rules applicable to colonial warfare. The near-identical nature of the information and doctrines disseminated among the colonial forces of all nations ensured that colonial wars were all conducted according to a different set of rules from those applying in Europe. All actions were deemed permissible as long as they served the primary aim of the campaign: the pacification of a territory through the suppression of an insurrection. Such a situation and doctrine established an unlimited leeway for, and unlimited opportunity to make, local, individual, decisions.

Despite these considerations, the level of discretion open to German soldiers remained limited by the existence of the clearly established regulations of military law. In particular, the application of extreme violence toward the life and property of the civilian population remained subject to punishment. Although effecting a massive reduction in the rights of the respective civilian populations, the special legal regulations issued for China and German South-West Africa did not tolerate any form of genocidal conduct on the part of German soldiers. The punishment of misconduct was in no way suspended during the three major colonial wars fought by the German Empire, and the requirements of German military law were repeatedly made clear to all the soldiers involved in the campaigns. In essence, the German soldiers were not permitted de jure to do as they pleased; rather, they were subject to specific standards of conduct. Nevertheless, the German military apparatus did give its tacit approval to the practice of only issuing exemplary punishments to those found guilty of applying military violence to the civilian population. The roots of this consensus are to be located in the ideological superstructure of imperial Germany itself.

CHAPTER 6

Ideology and Passage to War

T HE MILITARY FORCES fighting the colonial wars of the early twentieth century were influenced by an imperialist understanding of the world typical for their time. Characterized as it was by a "triumph of ideologies," the Wilhelmine outlook promised a "stabilizing view of the world; a satisfying explanation of an ever-more complex environment promising orientation, security and guidance."[1] Contemporary ideas of nationalism, racism, and social Darwinism transformed the preexisting pejorative views of non-European subject races such as the Chinese and Africans into almost tangible conceptions of the "enemy." Although the mere existence of these radicalized images did not dictate or even license violent actions, they did act to reduce inhibitions to this end. The long passage to the theater of war not only gave colonial soldiers the opportunity for weapons training and tactical instruction, it also provided the scope to develop existing prejudices and rehearse arguments for a whole range of actions. Some soldiers may have even taken the opportunity to consider the legal implications of these projections.

Conceptions of the Enemy

The image circulating among the German troops of the Chinese and African "other" was based on the ready supply of stereotypical "knowledge" in imperial Germany. Aware of China and Africa since the sixteenth century, the German popular consciousness had developed a conception of the Chinese and African "character"—both negative and positive—formed by the current political trends and ideologies. The formation of such views was dependent on the level of knowledge, degree of education, and political standpoint of the holder. However, although the view held of China or Africa says more about the person holding them than the actual object of consideration, there were a range of dominant conceptions, which can be considered as transcending class and political stripe.

Celebrated by the enlightened humanism of the eighteenth century as a center of philosophy and learning free of the negative and restraining influence of religion or feudalism, this conception of China was replaced in Europe around 1830 by a hierarchy of cultures and races. Coupled with this concept was the idea of progress, which many interpreted as being embodied by the military and technical advantage enjoyed by the white races. Taken to prove the idea of the dominance of the Western world, the purveyors of this ideology accorded the white race a universal civilizing mission.

These conceptions of China and Africa informed numerous publications on the subject. In contrast to the status of Africa, Latin America, and the South Sea Islands, China was accorded a special place in this new racial hierarchy. Initially, Europe had viewed China as an "old race of culture" (alte Kulturrasse). Then the European conception of China shifted: European opinion judged that the ancient Chinese civilization, long an equal to its European counterpart, had failed to keep step with the modern, progressive West. Its now perceived inferiority was in turn associated with racially determined character traits. The "slitty eyes" of the Chinese were now viewed not merely as a physical characteristic, but an outward manifestation of an inner character marked by wiliness, perfidy, and deceit. The "wily Chinaman" had a squalid and dirty appearance. Contemporary literature rarely established individual Chinese characters, concentrating rather on variations on the familiar stock characterization of "the Chinaman."[2]

The German image of the "black peoples" predated the history of German colonization in Africa, yet the military actions that this involved contributed to the spread and amplification of such preexisting conceptions. Before Germany acquired its colonial empire, the German image of Africa was dominated by the positive image of the "noble savage" propagated by Enlightenment writers such as Jean Jacques Rousseau. Despite the considerable changes in opinion registered within the course of the nineteenth century, these currents retained a certain level of influence. Accorded a number of negative attributes, "blacks" were now taken to be ugly, apish, incompetent, ignorant, uneducated, lazy, cruel, lacking in pity, cannibalistic, childish, irresponsible, base, bestial, impulsive, and driven by their passionate nature.[3] Considered as the slave of their drives, instincts, and immediate needs, German opinion came to believe that black Africans were incapable of harnessing and managing nature.

Such demeaning stereotyping served to establish a popular consensus focusing on the inherent inferiority of Africans; this, in turn, served to legitimate a paternalistic style of colonial leadership. Characterized by the maxim "hard but fair," such an ideology pervaded a number of colonial guides such as *Advice for Preparing for Service in the German Protectorates* written by Hermann von Wissmann, a veteran of German East Africa. Portraying the African race as still in the stage of childhood, this approach established a conception of Africans as only partially human. Although they commanded pity, their shortcomings of character and mental faculty meant that they were only partially educable.[4] The brochure *Practical Experiences from German South-West Africa*, circulated among the German troops during their passage to Africa, advanced a similar opinion: "When dealing with a native, it is decisive that he is not accorded equal status with a white [man] or dealt with as a mature member of human society. Such considerations produce a patriarchal relationship and the white [man's] duty to raise the morally weaker native. This must not be realized with hard, cruel treatment resulting in his exploitation; success is the result of constant work performed in [an atmosphere of] mutual trust. For the German soldier and above all, the officer, the treatment of the natives represents the most difficult, yet the greatest and most rewarding of cultural duties [*Kulturaufgabe*]."[5]

While the advocates of a patriarchal style of leadership accorded the Africans a range of positive character traits (thus succeeding in establishing their suitability for employment in a range of subordinate positions), a number of pan-German racist colonial apologists regarded the Africans not as children but rather animals or beasts. The image constructed was one of a violent, barbarous, and mentally inferior "native," a member of an incapable and ultimately nonviable primitive race to be accorded no more than a helot existence in the service of the "white race." Others went even further to forecast their complete demise, an alternative that implicitly included the extermination of the African peoples.[6] Such stereotypes were also to be found in the works of contemporary ethnologists, cultural anthropologists, geographers, and doctors seeking to establish the biological cultural and mental superiority of the white race.

Entering an alliance with an ethnocentric, biologicist, and aggressive nationalism, the clear order propagated by nineteenth-century racial theorists established the nation as a community defined by race. Within such clear-cut taxonomies, belonging and exclusion were established not through a process of mutable political decisions, but as the result of inherent and immutable characteristics. This process of rigid group demarcation was accompanied by a radical xenophobia, in which all and every foreign element was viewed as a potential danger for the respective in-group.[7] Social-Darwinist conceptions of a "struggle for life" and "living space" facilitated the establishment of a connection between a belief in the doctrine of progress and natural selection and race war. The inevitable outcome of this struggle would be the decline (and even destruction) of the so-called inferior races (to which Africans belonged) and the conquest and exploitation of the groups such as the Chinese, whose prior trajectory of development had equipped them with the basic skills of survival. Not only constitutive to the construction of systems of white supremacy, such hierarchical conceptions also served an exculpatory function, enabling its proponents to distract from the contradictions and ambivalence that such claims engendered.

The position of the Asian peoples in the middle of the racial hierarchy—not entirely incapable, but devoid of true culture—led to their demonization as a threat to Western civilization. Paired with an increase in economic and military power (manifested in the Japanese-Chinese war of 1894), this new way of thinking stoked fears that the Asian world could acquire a significance far greater than its cultural capacity warranted.[8] A rallying cry with a wide social resonance, the perception of the danger emanating from East Asia was far greater than the actual sum of the exports and investment from the region. The public debate over this horror scenario was conducted with contributions coming from not only diplomats, economists, and missionaries but also military authors: Colonel Maximilian Yorck von Wartenburg—a member of the East Asian Expeditionary Corps and thus a participant in the Boxer War—ended his *Outline of World History,* first published in 1897, with a final conflict between the Pacific and Atlantic worlds.[9]

Such xenophobia and racism were easily exploited for military and political ends, especially from the right-wing, government-critical Alldeutscher Verband (founded in 1891), which sought to establish not only the evil nature of the enemy but the necessity of taking military action against him.[10] The German colonial wars were not preceded by any sustained form of wide-scale indoctrination, and the soldiers involved in prosecuting the war were not subject to any continuous program of propaganda during the course of their training. Nevertheless, playing on the preexisting prejudice latent in Wilhelmine society, the military did move to mobilize a range of emotions.

Responding to the outrage provoked in German and international public opinion at the Boxer actions, the kaiser sought to defend German honor in a number of speeches. Addressing the soldiers embarking at Wilhelmshaven on 2 July 1900, he called on them to exact "exemplary punishment and revenge," as "the German flag has been insulted and the German Empire mocked." Closing his speech, he told the departing audience "I send you forth to avenge this injustice."[11] Speaking to a gathering in Bavaria on the following day, he called for the application of the "severest of methods." In a further intervention—the so-called sea sermon of 29 July 1900, he said, "How much we have to ask of God in the name of our brothers now going to war. They should be strong of arm, to punish the assassin. They are an armored fist entering a situation of depravity; they will fight our holy cause with sword in hand."

The high point of this round of speeches was the address given on 27 July 1900 to the troops departing for East Asia from Bremerhaven. There are two forms of what became known as the "Hun speech": a sanitized version edited for press consumption by Chancellor von Bülow, and a number of uncensored, largely consistent shorthand accounts made by journalists. Despite von Bülow's entreaties to the contrary, the members of the press were so shocked by the tone of the speech that they decided to publish the uncensored version. The controversial passage read thus: "Should you meet the enemy, he is to be struck down! Show no quarter! Take no prisoners! Those falling into your hand are at your mercy! Just as the name of King Etzel still reverberates in myth, so shall the name of Germany thunder throughout China for a thousand years, that no Chinese will ever dare [even] to look askance at a German again!"[12] Von Bülow's sanitized version put other words into the mouth of the kaiser: "You know your enemy to be a cunning, courageous, well-armed and barbarous opponent. You should also know that you will receive no quarter upon engagement; prisoners will not be taken. Conduct yourself in battle in such a way that for a thousand years no Chinaman will ever dare [even] to look askance at a German again!"[13]

Von Bülow's version of the "Hun speech" not only lacked the word "Hun" but through insertion of the second person plural *(euch)* now permitted an entirely contrary interpretation: that it was the German troops, not the Chinese, who could hope for no mercy. These simple amendments gave the speech an entirely opposite meaning to that originally intended. With its evocation of both the Hun invasion of Christendom led by King Etzel in the fifth century and the "Mongol hordes" threatening Latin Christendom in the twelfth and thirteenth centuries, Wilhelm's speech had a double meaning. Placing on the one hand the Huns as a martial example to be emulated, he called on the German soldiers to be as equally ruthless in conduct. On the other hand, his speech sought to associate the Chinese with the "Mongolian racial type and habitus," something not yet firmly established in Western perception, and thus identify a new "Hun horde" to be neutered. Not only had the kaiser called on his soldiers to conduct the war in a fashion entirely at variance with international law, his command to "give no quarter" represented a direct violation of the Second Hague Convention. Article 23 of the latter states, "In addition to the prohibitions provided by special Conventions, it is especially forbidden . . . (d) to declare that no quarter will be given." Even if the provisions of the Hague Convention were expressly restricted to the "civilized nations" (from which China was excluded), the behavior implied in the royal summon represented a clear contravention of German military law.

The kaiser's speeches and above all his "Hun speech" were not without effect. The diaries and letters of the participants in the expeditions show that his words came to the attention of many beyond the immediate circle of listeners. Moreover, the oft-repeated injunction to proceed against their opponents with the "severest of methods" made a deep and lasting impression.[14] The kaiser's appeal for the employment of a heightened level of violence and inhumane methods had a signal effect. As one officer put it, "as was to be expected, the speech had a powerful impact, as it meant war."[15] A volunteer in the first East Asian Infantry Regiment made clear that in speaking his unforgettable words, the voice of the kaiser had become "highly roused and forceful."[16] The address triggered considerable enthusiasm among the soldiers, and a great number of units went to war with these words ringing in their ears. The railroad cars transporting further battalions and equipment to Bremerhaven were daubed with the motto "Show no quarter" (Pardon wird nicht gegeben). Outliving its immediate context, this maxim became popular among soldiers of the Herero war three years later in German South-West Africa. A sailor wrote in his diary, "It is out of the question to show mercy toward such bestial fellows; our motto was and remains 'Show no quarter.'"[17]

The "Hun speech" laid out to the German soldiers in no uncertain terms the manner in which they were to fight for Germany's cause. Despite such clarity, the impact of the kaiser's oratory was not restricted to its immediate audience, but was disseminated through other, more subtle, channels: soldiers' songs. Indeed, the subtlety of such channels probably explains the fact that their purpose has long gone unnoticed.

Soldiers' Songs

The profound impact of the kaiser's words to his troops is demonstrated by a song composed to mark the dispatch of the East Asian Expeditionary Corps. Given a positive reception (at least according to its civilian composer) by the officers and men of one of the transports leaving Bremerhaven, it later served as instruction material for troops bound for China.[18]

> ### The latest China Song: *Pardon wird nicht gegeben*[19]
> *Dedicated to our courageous China troops*
> BY A. BRANDHORST, OLDENBURG
> Melody: Was blasen die Trompeten
>
> [1] If I do remember rightly, our own Graf v. Waldersee
> Has always enjoyed a drop of China's finest-tasting tea.
> Now given the chance to drink from the source;
> He'll give the Chinese a good hiding while he's there of course!—
> Italy, France, Japan, Russia and America—
> Welcome his choice with a hearty hurrica!
> Let's hope old Waldersee soon strikes John Bull dumb
> And hangs a muzzle on the stupid ole son.
>
> [2] For those our brave boys already in the yellow lan'
> I will pay a visit to Etzhorn and seek out old Jan Hullmann:
> "Ole Hullmann" I will say,
> Can't you give us a little grog for our lads across the way,
> Cans and Cigars are all very fine
> But better a few hectoliters of wine?
> If I know ole Hullmann, he won't decline,
> lest I go elsewhere.
> If each of our boys get a few ales
> Then we'll soon be spitting on the old Chinaman's pigtails.

[3] And if you stay a while in China, never mind where you are,
Please mind to teach those pigtailed yellow men more than just how to
play the flute!
The whole yellow clan—beat 'em to mush and mash,
Even if they call for quarter and even Wei—ei—wei![20]
Be sure to think of those our comrades
Whose hero's blood now honors China's land!
Avenge your brave comrades, do your duty brave,
Quarter you'll none be given, so Quarter give ye not!

[4] Prayers from our Emperor and people will carry you on your way,
You brave China troops!
So show those foreign troops who will join you on your task,
That we Germans fear God and God alone.
Think always of those wise words, which our Emperor spoke to you,
Filled with Holy vengeance for the dishonor done to us.
Avenge your comrades, do your duty,
Quarter you'll none be given, so Quarter give ye not!

[5] Doing your duty in far China,
You'll want surely for naught!
Shedding your blood for our brothers,
Will be met with our heartfelt quittance,
With God for justice and the Emperor
Unfurl the banner,
We shall tend to the tears of your loved-ones!

The rhyming couplets of the five verses of this song seek to deliver separate messages. Beginning with the image of the tea-drinking commander of
the international Expeditionary Corps von Waldersee, the first verse opens
in restrained fashion. The bridge from the field marshal to China is clear,
effected via tea. The second and third verses arrange for Germany's rivals
Italy, France, Russia, Japan, and America to acclaim von Waldersee's choice
as commander in chief, while the subsequent couplet is aimed at Great
Britain. Represented by John Bull, he is to be silenced with a muzzle.

The second verse changes scene, and the text gathers momentum. As the
verse celebrates "our brave boys" in China, they are portrayed as requiring
stronger stimulants than tea. After receiving donations of wine, beer, and
cigars, they need only a dose of grog before the campaign can become a full-

scale binge. Responsibility for transforming the celebration into unrestrained carousal—a level of identity missing in the description of the unspecified "others"—was accorded to the alcohol wholesaler J. Hullmann mentioned three times, once as a friend. The "gallons of spirits" delivered by this firm are the focus of the couplet of the second verse. Combined with the beer to produce full-scale revelry, all inhibitions have been successfully lowered to enable the men to "spit disgustingly on the Chinaman's pigtails."

The third and central verse formulates the unmistakable command to teach the "pig-tailed" Chinese more than just "how to play the flute." They are to be beaten to "mush and mash." Hence the motto "Beat 'em hard" even if they, or the "whole yellow clan," call for "quarter" and cry "Wei—ei—wei." While the cry of pain alludes to the British colony on Weihaiwei, the twice repeated "quarter" refers unmistakably to Wilhelm's "Hun speech." The song gives two reasons for the German duty to treat the Chinese violently: firstly to avenge the "hero's blood" of the fallen comrades, and secondly as a measure of self-preservation. The last verse clearly commits the soldiers neither to give nor to hope for quarter.

The fourth verse not only legitimized the use of violence through reference to the kaiser and nation but in its use of prayer transcends the scope of the campaign, to glorify the military undertaking as a religious obligation. Once again incorporating Germany's international competitors, the text now seeks to distance itself from them. The foreign troops are to be given an unmistakable demonstration of the fact that Germans fear "God alone" and nothing else on this earth. The following verses combine this religiously sanctioned defense of national honor with the motive of revenge outlined in verse three through reference to the "Hun speech." This marks the culmination of the verse and states the guiding principle of the whole song. This part of the song is expressed almost as a chorus, and the listener is reminded that quarter is neither to be given nor expected.

Assuming the form of a summary, the fifth verse seeks to establish the link between service in China and defense of the home front. "Duty" is to be done both at home and abroad. While the brave defend their kaiser and his law with their "blood," others make only a mental or financial contribution from their "heart" and from their property. Beginning as a first-person singular speculation on the thoughts of von Waldersee, the third verse of the song moves into a first personal plural instruction to Germans at home to comfort the relatives of those soldiers who fell in combat, referred to now in the second person plural. In a more formulaic yet transcendental form of address, those soldiers now "with God" remain, despite their death, somehow connected to the "we" of Wilhelmine Germany.

Not content to evoke prejudice and negative conceptions of the enemy, this song seeks actively to stir up and disseminate such notions and sentiments through a continual sharpening of the pejorative meaning of the selected metaphors. Starting in the realm of the banal—pigtailed, flute-playing purveyors of tea—the stereotypical depiction of the Chinese works its way up to a denunciation of the "whole yellow clan" as cruel, double-dealing, cowardly, and despicable Chinamen deserving only of a swift death. At the same time, it opens up a front against not only China, but the whole international expedition in general, and against the British in particular. The last question raised is that of the violence to be perpetrated against the Chinese—strike hard even against the helpless, wailing, and calling for mercy. The task in hand justifies all actions. This text was intended to reduce all inhibitions and scruples of the soldiers embarking for the war in China. It was set to the well-known melody of *Was blasen die Trompeten,* and so soldiers were able to concentrate fully on the text of *Pardon wird nicht gegeben* (or other such songs) and thus absorb its message.[21]

Any consideration of soldiers' songs needs to differentiate between songs written by and for the soldiers, private regimental songs, and those adapted from folk songs. However, as the introduction to the soldiers' song book outlined, such songs all had one common aim: to engender strength and confidence, forge a group spirit, and promote discipline. Such considerations were grounded in the assumption that singing represented a ritual with a far greater capability than any other to create and strengthen group ties. War songs fulfill an entirely different function, seeking as they do to distract their singers from deep-seated fears of death and injury. They are also able to give expression to suppressed desires and hopes. The song enables its singer to integrate himself within a male-bonding group of temporary duration, aiding his flight from the reality of war and expressing his yearning for a civilian life.[22] The list of negative characteristics attributed to "the enemy" serves to give shape to this otherwise nebulous category. The songs also serve to provide a snapshot of the immediate life of the soldier, encompassing his farewell from home, homesickness, readiness to fight, courage, comradeship, illness, injuries, and death, as well as life in the field and particular battles. A number of different songs were available for each situation of war.

That composed for the troops departing to China, *"Pardon wird nicht gegeben,"* was no exception. Speaking of the sendoff of the sea battalions in

a Reichstag speech given in July 1900, the SPD deputy August Bebel referred to songs and poems, "the contents of which [did not] have an edi-
fying or morally improving effect on the troops" but rather served to incite
and agitate them.[23] On the other hand, the soldiers' songbooks contained
no descriptions of violence as explicit as that offered in *"Pardon wird nicht
gegeben."* Exhibiting greater restraint, these songs restricted themselves to a
short justification of the war, a derogatory depiction of the enemy, and a vague
threat of reprisals.

Thus far, the sources have failed to yield similar songs from the initial
phase of the war in German South-West Africa and used as a medium of
instruction for the troops. Those songs found to have been sung in the two
African wars were composed either by the Protection Force before 1904 or
by colonial apologists after the event. In accordance with this periodization,
the songs represent a one-sided celebration of the adventurous nature of
colonial warfare: life in the field, marches in the bush or steppe, mounted
patrols, and camp fire romanticism. The enemy was not dealt with in any
way, and any appearance he makes is sporadic and fleeting.[24]

The soldiers dispatched to the colonial campaigns were influenced by the
negative conceptions of the Chinese and Africans current in contemporary
German society. The songs that they sang provided the opportunity—in
the absence of any systematic and intensive form of indoctrination—both to
give form to a specific conception of the enemy and to celebrate extreme
violence. Set to music, such messages incited singers to acts that were forbidden by the more sober program of military instruction. The songs provided unofficial license to extensive excesses of violence against those begging
"for quarter." More than at any other time, such songs were sung on the long
passage to the colonial theater.

The Passage to War

The long sea passages to the various colonies served as the bonding process
for the newly raised units, the heterogeneous nature of which did not favor
the formation of strong group identities. Beginning in the port of Bremerhaven, which had been transformed into a colorful tent-town for the purpose, the whole affair of seeing off the various contingents dispatched to the
Boxer War adopted the character of a popular festival.[25] Those steaming for
Africa usually departed from Hamburg or Cuxhaven using the steamers of
the Woermann line, the Hamburg-America line, the North German Lloyd

line, and the German East Africa line. Some of the troops heading for German East Africa were even dispatched from French or Italian Mediterranean ports.

Conditions were difficult on the transport ships. Almost entirely cut off from the outside world, life on board afforded little freedom of movement and forced its passengers to endure almost unbearably high temperatures. Despite such difficulties, however, the state of health of the soldiers on board the *Palatia* (making for German South-West Africa) remained good for the duration of the passage. Although a number succumbed to seasickness in the early stages of the journey and a number of gastrointestinal infections broke out, the records do not show any febrile illnesses or serious external injuries. There were no deaths. Six cases of venereal disease were recorded, despite appropriate medical checks being performed at the muster point. These cases had been developed in the run up to embarkation. Seeking to prevent any further cases of venereal disease, the troops did not receive any leave upon arrival in Las Palmas.

Advancing at a sedate 12.5 knots, the passage to China took between five and six weeks; that to German South-West and German East Africa between four and five. With time stretching, boredom was a constant threat to discipline and the number of arrests rose quickly. The officers reacted by ordering drill and gymnastics. The exact daily routine consisted of exercises to maintain physical fitness. Target practice and weapons training were conducted without ammunition to save space.[26] The onboard program included lectures focusing on the articles of war, the laws of war, the gunnery field manual, marching, combat, camp and outpost duty, and the applied geography of the land of destination. The soldiers were also given instruction in tropical hygiene and sanitation. The Sunday sermons provided a certain level of variety from the daily routine. After a few personal words of introduction, the commander read verbatim from a collection of sermons edited by the Imperial Naval Office. Further entertainment was provided by the newly formed battalion band and a memorial celebration to mark the anniversary of the Battle of Gravelotte, during the Franco German war of 1870–1871. Swimming in the sea was very popular; deck games involving all officers and ranks marching at the double and accompanied by the band probably met with less enthusiasm. If horses were kept on board, the confines of space required attention to both their care and exercise. With two horses cared for by one groom, the daily routine required feeding, watering, and cleaning many times a day. The 21 officers, 12 medical officers, 10 civil servants, 402

Table 6.1. Daily regime on board the *Gertrud Woermann*.

Time	Activity	Time	Activity
4:15	First post	12:45	Lunch served
4:30	Water rations	2:15–3:45	Horse exercise (fifth group)
4:45–5:30	Food and water for the horses	3:45	Assembly for coffee
5:30	Coffee first group	4:00	Coffee served
5:45	Coffee second group	4:30–5:00	Instruction
6:00–7:30	Horse exercise (first group)	5:15–5:45	Swimming
7:30–9:00	Horse exercise (second group)	5:45	Evening meal
9:00	Sick bay duty	6:00	Dinner, address for the warrant officers
9:00–10:30	Horse exercise (third group)	6:45	Address to NCOs
10:30–11:45	Horse exercise (fourth group)	7:00	Food and water for the horses
11:15–12:30	Food and water for the horses	9:00	Hay for the horses
12:30	Assembly for lunch		

men, and an unrecorded number of horses traveling to German South-West Africa on board the *Gertrud Woermann* in August were subject to the daily regime shown in Table 6.1.[27]

Designed to maintain the physical fitness of both man and animal, the tightly packed program of activities sought to deliver its participants to their destination in a prime state of healthy readiness despite the cramped conditions that they experienced. The monotonous onboard routine also whetted the appetite for battle and had the potential to reinforce fears that they would arrive in the theater only to find that the war had already been won.

The immediate concern of those on board was to pass the time. One method to this end was to record daily observations in a diary, especially experiences of foreign peoples. Conversation presented a further method by which to evade the leaden boredom. Topics of discussion included hopes, expectations, and conceptions of the enemy. In this way, the opponent was already present in symbolic form during the passage. For instance, anti-Chinese jokes were rife during the passage to China. One transport to German South-West Africa saw the men tease the horses with a "negro doll." "He, he, Herero etc. The animals bit hard."[28] The picture of the bestial, cruel enemy carefully built up over the course of the passage was confirmed on location: supposed scenarios of threat and preexisting conceptions of the enemy had now been vindicated. One statement from a bombardier in the East Asian Expeditionary Corps demonstrates how soldiers consciously utilized such images to amplify their own aggression or deal with their own fear. "Buying into the tales of 'atrocities' and 'terrible events' told by our comrades, we allowed ourselves to be overtaken by a warlike mood and we took to sleeping with a bare blade and loaded carbine."[29]

Lasting several weeks, the passage to the colonial theater represents much more than a slow journey to a far distant place. Serving as a journey of initiation, the soldiers were subject to a process of both mental and physical preparation for the engagement with a hitherto unknown enemy. Acting as a real alternative to the home that the soldiers had recently departed, the ship became a floating enclave governed by its own rules. Despite the strongly regimented daily routine to which they were subject, the soldiers were led into a realm of fantasy in which they were able to anticipate life in the colony upon which they were advancing. Living in one heterotopia (the ship), the soldiers prepared themselves for a further, equally heterotopic environment—the colony. With its rites, rituals, and training and its dependence on the caprice of the ocean, the sea passage provided a much greater imaginative space than would other forms of transport such as a train. As Foucault identified, "[When considering] the nature of a ship's environment . . . [we see that it is] the largest imaginative arsenal in the world. A rocking space, a place without place; self-perpetuating and self-contained; subject entirely to the infinite nature of the sea."[30]

The white soldiers and officers deployed in the three great German colonial wars were influenced by a diffuse conglomeration of nationalist-racist ideas. Such racist nationalism was, however, never part of any official state doctrine and was never implemented as the official policy of imperial Germany. Moreover, the prevalent colonial racism made clear differentiation between China and Africa, according the Chinese a higher place on the hierarchy of racial worth. Such a differentiation between inferior groupings had a clear impact on colonial policy, yet was also abrogated within the atmosphere of acute military necessity presented by the war with China and manifested in the kaiser's instructions to proceed ruthlessly and break existing military law. Representing a neat summary of the Wilhelmine Zeitgeist, his instructions to "give no quarter" both confirmed and reinforced his soldiers in their mood. His message, rendered as rhyming couplets, echoed into his African wars.

Exhibiting different motivations for their participation in the colonial wars, the soldiers conducting them were united only by the metropolitan ideological "baggage" that they took with them. Their weapons, rudimentary yet unsuitable training for a colonial conflict, cursory familiarity with military regulations and racialist ideology united this otherwise disparate group of individuals behind a belief in the superiority and just nature of the German "cause" so that they were thus prepared to unleash extreme violence in its defense. Although united by such ideological considerations, these common traits were not sufficient to engender a unitary or predictable form of warfare or even violence. The patterns of this nature that eventually emerged were the result of the combination of nationalism, racism, and fanatical war fever in interaction with the local conditions and contexts presented by the colonial theaters of war, above all the respective environments, the opponents that they found, and the impact of disease and injury.

CHAPTER 7

Environment and Enemy

E VERY SYSTEM of colonial rule operated in the nineteenth and early twentieth centuries was presented with the complex challenge of both maintaining order and initiating the economic development of an unexplored area with restricted personnel resources and a poor infrastructure. Military domination of the area required exact knowledge of not only the topography of the colony and the resources available but the habits and fighting practices of the native population. As a result, military cartographers and ethnographers were required to produce maps of the colony of a quality sufficient to facilitate its administration, planning, and thus control. Punitive expeditions were the conventional means by which to secure colonial rule. Characterized by the arbitrary and indiscriminate use of violence, they were used as instruments of punishment and subjugation. The character of the colonial theater of war was thus determined by not only the behavior of the native opponent but also the physical conditions presented by the colony, the perceptions of these conditions on the part of the soldiers, and their understanding of the projected development of the area in which they operated.

Military Cartography and Ethnography

Participants in this colonial learning process included not just the colonial administration but also the colonial military establishment, both of which were constantly engaged in the gathering and processing of a considerable body of knowledge, all with the aim of improving military performance in the next war. Officers were required to gather new insights from both their own sketches and notes and the data collected by others. This knowledge was then filtered into a form of instruction that was intended to support the decision-making process. Such tools to this end included military maps, ethnographic tables, and further descriptions. The complexities of colonial soldiering thus render unsustainable the distinction, made by John Noyes, between a military establishment interested solely in acquiring and maintaining an omnipresent authority on the one hand and the knowledge-gathering missionaries and scientists on the other.[1]

"Culturalizing tasks" *(Kulturaufgaben)* were not solely the preserve of the Protection Force; the imperial navy also maintained a range of services focusing on geodesy mapping the coastline of each protectorate. Producing a number of maps of lakes and estuaries, charting depths, reefs, and currents, the maritime geodesic research performed in Qingdao also involved astronomy, meteorology, triangulation, topography, and hydrography.[2] Although primarily motivated by military considerations, such maritime-based research was also made available to the merchant navy.

Despite these activities, there were no reliable maps of the northern Chinese provinces of Zhilli or Shanxi to which the German expeditionary force was dispatched in 1900. Although military surveyors accompanied the expeditionary corps, the sheer size of the area that they were expected to cover and the short time available to them forced them to restrict the scope of their activities. Not all the units deployed in the region had personnel skilled in sketching and were unable to gather the information required. As a result, it was often necessary to dispatch officers to gain a general impression of the landscape in which the troops were to operate and establish the reliability of the existing cartographical material.

Seeking to gather rough-and-ready information for immediate use, the German military authorities drew up "German-Chinese questionnaires" to gather information from Chinese population on matters relevant to the supply and movement of the troops.[3] The British military was much more advanced in this respect and always ensured that it had established precise information regarding the nature of the land in which an expedition was to be conducted before it was launched. It also maintained a field press that provided an information sheet outlining the number and locations of suitable sites for encampments, information regarding distances, the nature and quality of the roads, the location of the rivers, the presence of bridges, and the size and composition of the enemy forces.[4] The German units profited from this information when conducting joint expeditions with British forces.

Those conducting the German colonial wars in Africa lacked reliable specialist maps providing an overview of the territory in which they were operating. During the Bondelzwart uprising of 1903 in German South-West Africa, the colonial veteran Curt von François remarked in the *Militärwochenblatt* (the semiofficial publication of the German General Staff) on the extremely meager level of knowledge of the extreme south of the colony.[5] The maps available to them dated from 1890–1893 (scale 1:600.000); even that from 1879 (scale 1:742.000) was still in use. No official maps existed with information regarding altitude, the course of the rivers, the nature of the watering holes, or the land cover to the degree of accuracy necessary to enable the planning and evaluation of military operations. The areas away from the major routes were entirely blank.

Reacting to this problem, the Protection Force High Command and the *Reichsmarineant* commissioned the Colonial Graphical Institute in Berlin to draft a war map of German South-West Africa on the scale 1:800.000. The map was produced in eight sections, and five copies of the page covering Windhoek were presented to the High Command at the end of January 1904. The whole map was sent to the protectorate by the beginning of March 1904, two months after the outbreak of the conflict.[6] Even if the claims made by the *Handbuch der neuzeitlichen Wehrwissenschaften* in 1936—that the only map available to the German military in German South-West Africa had been a scale map of 1:1.000.000, supplemented by a number of sketches with the distance between watering holes—were untrue, the cartographical material available to the Protection Force was unfit for purpose.[7]

One of the first to recognize the significance of scientific research conducted by officers and civil servants was the founder of the German East Africa Protection Force, Hermann von Wissmann. In his colonial handbook *Advice in Preparation for Service in the Colonies* published in 1895, he argued that the primary duty of colonial officers and administrators was "opening up the unknown continent."[8] Officers should set about amassing new insights from both their own sketches and notes and the data collected by others. Especial significance was to be accorded to geographical-cartographic research with the aim of giving structure to the colonial space, thus making it "comprehensible." The route surveys conducted in preparation for such cartographic undertakings were performed not just by a few specialists but also by a number of laymen, including Protection Force

Officers, who gathered information during the course of patrols and exercises. These records were collected by the District Officer and forwarded to the government, where an Office for Ordinance Surveys integrated them into an exact map. The Colonial Department of the German Foreign Office in Berlin also collected and transmitted such data to the Colonial Cartographic Institute at the publishing house *Dietrich Reimer* from which it commissioned a number of maps of the colonies.[9]

The Colonial Department viewed sketches and maps of unknown areas produced by colonial officers as the natural by-product of official journeys and as such, public property. Nevertheless, not all officers shared this estimation. A notable incident involved Lothar von Trotha, who only agreed to surrender his notes and sketches following the intervention of the kaiser.[10] This episode shows the significance attached to such maps. Exceeding their intrinsic cartographic value, their possession indicated the extent of influence claimed by their owners. Even the army General Staff, whose power in German East Africa was limited, ordered maps of the colony so as to exert its authority.[11]

Seeking to provide training for officers in simple trigonometry, the respective Bureaus for Ordinance Survey devised courses in the theory and practice of topography and trained sketching assistants. Similar courses were provided at the Institute for Oriental Languages in Berlin. Although the German government took pains to coordinate the efforts in this direction, issuing regular instructions that the colonial and military administrations work together in the use of existing resources to generate cartographic material, the military and civilian institutes nonetheless maintained a certain rivalry in this area.[12]

Not just a manifestation of conventional institutional jealousies, this friction was explained by the diverging ideas regarding the approach to and value of maps and mapmaking held by the military and civilian establishments. Army officers such as Ludwig von Estorff often complained of the lack of topographic details provided by "civilian" maps and thus their unsuitability for military purposes.[13] Military expectations of the maps provided thus did not restrict themselves to the exact reproduction of the topography but also information regarding the length and quality of paths, the quality and quantity of water resources, and the nature of the grazing land for horses, oxen, and the slaughter cattle accompanying them. In China and German South-West Africa, distances were usually marked in riding hours; maps of German East Africa, on the other hand, indicated marching time. The failure to produce anything approaching a uniform cartographic approach to colonization shows the lack of any colonial forethought or planned approach to imperialism on the part of its German agents.

Specialized military maps contained more detailed information. One such example was that of German East Africa (1:100.000) included in the Military Orientation Manual for German East Africa published in 1911—after the Maji Maji War. Spread across nine pages, the map marked the positions of the districts of Dar es Salaam, Bagamoyo, Sadani, Pangani, Banderu, Tanga, Wilhelmstal, Morogoro, and Mohoro. As well as listing the locations of stations and villages, it indicated whether these locations provided "plentiful sources of water," "little water," or "no water" during the dry season. Similar information was provided regarding the supply situation (for 300 people) graded as "plentiful supplies," "few supplies," or "no supplies." The marching times indicated corresponded to the amount of time required for a military caravan with bearers. Arrows indicated the flow of a river and possible crossing points; paths were indicated as "accessible only for carts," "cleared path," "narrow path," and "negro path." The maps also marked the course of railroads and the presence of railroad stations and mission stations.[14] The addition of such explanations, symbols, and legends transformed maps into visualized reports.

The German military was forced to prosecute all of the three colonial wars examined in this study based on imprecise, incomplete, and unreliable cartographic material and provisional sketches. The differing levels to which the areas had been "cultivated" were also reflected in the quality of the maps. Those depicting China and German East Africa located settlements, villages, and towns with water and food. The campaign in German South-West Africa, on the other hand, focused on securing the water supply and the transport of horses, slaughter cattle, and oxen in order to guarantee troop supplies. The difference between the two situations—a scarcity of resources in German South-West Africa and sufficient (or even abundant) supplies in China and German East Africa—exercised an impact both on the appearance of the military cartographical material and the conduct of the war. Military maps of the German colonies were not reliable depictions of the prevailing geographical conditions; they were designed as a guide to maneuvering in hostile terrain with the minimum of loss. German colonial knowledge was always military knowledge of little or no value to other agents or interests.

In addition to the topographical and geographical knowledge required to conduct the wars, colonial soldiers also needed an understanding of the native population of each colonial environment. It was necessary to investigate their attitudes to life, their behavior, the arms available to them, and their chosen method of fighting. All this ethnographic information remained highly subjective and reflective of colonial priorities and perceptions. Focusing on the levels of collaboration exhibited by each ethnic grouping, both military and civilian instances were assiduous in their attempts to gather and share information pertinent to this end. Inspections of the districts by the District Chiefs and military commanders also served to expand the colonists' knowledge in this regard.

In China, the disadvantages of policing the area with native troops were weighed against their putative strengths, seen to include frugality, hardness, and bodily strength. Recent newcomers to the region, the German military was not in possession of any reliable familiarity with the Chinese population in provinces other than Shandong and was unable to draw up any form of native military hierarchy. Only on the outbreak of the war did the General Staff arrange for the creation of a number of hastily produced orientation manuals.[15] As such, recruitment for military tasks was restricted to Shandong Province or at least among applicants whose parents and close relatives lived east of a specific line in the province.[16] Failing to attract sufficient levies, the recruiting agencies sought to circumvent these tight regulations and often instructed their charges to give false information.

In contrast to the ethnic homogeneity of the Chinese population, German South-West Africa was inhabited by five main ethnic groups, of which only two, the Herero and the Nama, had a history of rebelliousness. Defeated and almost entirely wiped out during the eponymous conflict, these two groupings no longer posed a threat to German authority, and the colonial authorities saw little point in undertaking any classification of the ethnic situation in the colony. Nevertheless, during his time as governor, Leutwein had made a number of efforts to obtain reliable information regarding the ethnic composition of the colony, the state of native armaments, local networks, and their disposal to collaboration. An evaluation of the character and readiness of various ethnicities for colonial collaboration had already been undertaken in 1895 within the framework of the native recruitment drive for service in the Protection Force. In addition to the Herero and Nama, the Rehobother Baster were included in this survey as a mixed ethnicity. The officers of the Protection Force maintained that a colony of white settlement must maintain stringent standards: "The country should be developed into a true 'colony' and not just remain a sphere of interest in which we—as in East Africa and Cameroon—seek nothing more than trading partners."[17]

The discussion occasioned among the four district military commanders by Leutwein's move to recruit natives for the Protection Force sheds light on German colonial conceptions of ethnicity. Attributing each grouping a range of putative characteristics, the administration constructed a racial hierarchy of value. Viewed as militarily useless and unsuitable as allies, the Herero were placed at the bottom of this "league table" of military worth. The large size of this allegedly inferior grouping was perceived as a hindrance to the development of German South-West Africa as early as 1895.[18] Lieutenant Otto Eggers from Okahandja was explicit in his criticism: "All those familiar with the land are of the view that colonization is impossible without teaching those impudent Hereros a lesson they are not likely to forget."[19]

The Witbooi-Nama assumed an intermediate position in this racial hierarchy, seen as not the best fighters, but much more reliable than the Herero. Leutwein's favorable assessment of the Witbooi resulted from the peace treaty concluded with Hendrik Witbooi in 1894. Initially rejected by the General Staff as far too liberal in its terms, Leutwein could save it only with considerable effort. The most favored of the possible allies were the Rehobother Baster, former Witbooi who had assimilated more strongly within the colonial system. Communication with the Baster, as a Dutch-speaking grouping, was far easier. Bearing the closest resemblance among native groupings to the white population in terms of both appearance and culture, they were accorded characteristics thought to be "German." Linked to the Herero and the Nama by similar customs, mores, ancestry, lifestyle, and kin, the Rehobother Baster functioned as the link between the colonial and native populations.

The German system used in South-West Africa was by no means unique and followed British practices in India. Classifying the so-called martial races resident in its territories, the British military adapted its recruiting practices to the resulting "insights," concentrating its efforts on North-Western Punjab, whose residents it believed to be especially serviceable thanks to their "Aryan" heritage. The criteria used to assess the various ethnicities in the British Empire involved both positive traits such as intelligence, leadership, and individuality and negative characteristics such as stupidity and carelessness; establishing checks and balances on native worth served to maintain European confidence in their own superiority. The "martial qualities" ascribed to a particular group usually stood in direct relation to the number of volunteers that they produced.[20] The conception of the martial race, according to which specific ethnicities were in possession of special military skills, was based on an ethnic ranking established to meet the needs and wishes of the colonial power. The ethnic hierarchy established in German South-West Africa was just as much a colonial construct.

In German East Africa, the civil and military personnel of the District Offices and military stations exchanged information regarding the level of native collaboration. The actors of these informal networks maintained their own language and terminology to refer to each ethnic grouping. Only after the end of the Maji Maji War was the ethnographic information collected for German East Africa subject to systemization.[21] According to the Orientation Manual, the colony was inhabited by the members of a total of 168 different ethnicities, including not only Africans but Arabs, Washirazi, Indians, Chinese, and Goans. As the ethnic composition of the protectorate was far too complex to be represented on a map, the basic information for the twenty-two districts was simply collated and presented in tabular form, thus enabling the most important facts to be comprehended at a glance. This treatment included eight subpoints: first, the name of the tribe, location, and size of the settlement; second, the number of arms-bearing men; third, the numbers of muzzle-loading and other weapons; fourth, their history of military engagement—including their methods of fighting; fifth, their response to German rule, the influence of the administration, and the tribal structure; sixth, their language and the spread of Swahili; seventh, the nature of their dwellings and defenses; eighth, their habits and diet, the size of their cattle herd, and the nature of the donkeys that they bred.

The Wahehes, for instance, were reported to be some 25,000 strong. Five thousand were recorded as bearing arms, including 800 muzzle-loaders and a number of thrusting and throwing spears. Having killed all the members of a German expedition dispatched in 1891, they were also recorded as having perpetrated a number of raids in 1892–1893. Although a punitive expedition led by the governor Friedrich von Schele overran the stronghold of the Wahehe chief Mkwawa, he fled and launched a long guerilla war, which ended following his surrender as late as 1899. Despite this victory, the Germans continued to regard the Wahehe as a restive enemy, and a formation of the Protection Force was stationed permanently close to their area of influence, where it remained in a constant state of readiness.

The *Military Orientation Manual,* something approaching a colonial handbook, was much more than an almanac. Together with a range of geographical and ethnographical information, the authors incorporated an understanding of recent military history to estimate the readiness of each ethnicity to collaborate with the German colonial administration. The long data tables that it contained amounted to nothing less than a comprehensive friend–foe categorization. Despite taking an analytic approach, the inflexible nature of the manual—the section on the Wahehe focused on their attitude during the 1890s while ignoring their pro-German stance during the Maji Maji War—reduced its practical value. The British published a translation of the *Orientierungsheft*, which appeared under the title *A Handbook of German East Africa*. Designed to assist the British in the administration of their newly acquired mandate, the ethnic assessments were subject to a process of reevaluation; the British hoped new patterns of collaboration could emerge.[22]

Military ethnographers classified the population of a colony according to the interests of the colonizers. Unable to rest on ethnic considerations, the hierarchy produced for China exercised almost no influence on the course taken by the Boxer War, which was conducted far from Shandong Province. In Africa, by contrast, the activities of the military ethnographers produced a great deal of war-relevant data. Two decisive differences between the African colonies become immediately clear. First, the greater ethnic variety of German East Africa enabled a much more flexible and variegated constellation of alliances than in German South-West Africa, with its lower level of ethnic diversity. Second, the military commanders in German South-West Africa used the findings of the ethnographic study to underline the nature of German South-West Africa as a "true colony" of white settlement, thus establishing a central role for the Protection Force. This reveals the depth of attachment to the ideal of colonization in military circles.

Punitive Expeditions as an Instrument of Rule

Military stations and the punitive expedition were the two instruments used to enforce colonial authority. Like the medieval castle, the larger military stations dominated the landscape as monuments of colonial authority—and were designed to compensate for the lack of personnel. The colonial military establishment viewed all forms of unrest and insurrection as testament to its own absence and insufficient recourse to violence.[23] "Presenting themselves at the station" was a ritual of subordination often involved as a condition of submission for unruly natives. While the military station represented the fixed point of military power (and also a safe retreat for the white population during times of trouble), punitive expeditions were seen as a flexible method with which to enforce imperial authority.

Punitive expeditions represented the special form of expeditions that had themselves developed from caravan and research tourism. The quasi-military character of such undertakings had already been recognized as early as 1969 by Dorothy Middleton, who wrote that they were "designed to overcome resistance, whether from the terrain or from its inhabitants and to come back with a trophy."[24] Whereas research expeditions focused on collection and discovery, thereby making a contribution to the scientific understanding of the areas in which they were conducted, in their imperial context, an "expedition" was intended to maintain or reassert colonial authority over a subjugated area. Between 1885 and 1886, agents of the German East African Company crossed great swathes of East African territory in a number of expeditions aiming to open up the land and extend the area of "sovereignty" of the company. A great deal of the insights gained in the course of these expeditions, which were often conducted by young army officers seeking adventure, were used in the foundation process of the new German Protection Forces.[25] Curt von François, Hermann von Wissmann, and Carl Peters—all later significant figures in German colonial history rose to prominence as leaders of exploratory expeditions.[26]

Although ostensibly dedicated to exploration, the hostility of the terrain and the native population meant that expeditions usually involved the application of some form of violence. As a result, their evolution into punitive expeditions meant that the latter were characterized less by the nature of the weapons and equipment carried as the purpose for which they were launched: "In some respects, expeditions resemble a colonial war. The boundaries between these types of martial undertaking are generally fluid and are often crossed. A further factor blurring the difference is the need, arising from political considerations, to name such undertakings which resemble a war in composition, scope and aim with the more harmless-sounding appellation 'expedition.'"[27]

Punitive expeditions represented a specific form of colonial expedition and an integral part of colonial rule. They were either led by the Commanding Officer of a military station himself or sent on his orders to "comb through" his area of responsibility in order to enforce a specific order or exact punishment for a range of offenses. In launching a punitive expedition, the German military sought to realize a particular "instructive effect": the populace of the area in question was to feel the effects of the punitive expedition long after its departure. Word of its course was to spread fear and subservience. Thus the punitive expedition sought to maximize the long-term German reach even in areas in which it had no physical presence. The attractiveness of this "economy of violence"[28] increased with the decline in the number of methods with which the colonial power sought to enforce its authority. Whatever the immediate effects of such a violent approach, its long-term impact was often limited to the duration of its practice. Despite ushering in a period of peace and order, the native population of German East Africa viewed such cycles of violence as they would an uncontrollable natural disaster with no relevance for their future conduct:[29] "Africa cannot be pacified by governing from a station, and perhaps dispatching a few Police patrols to administer the occasional punishment. No: it is necessary to work in a preventative manner so as to ensure that the population shrinks from unrest. The Negroes forget quickly; punished today, they recover from their shock tomorrow, the day after the troops leave. They are soon taken by the thought: 'the heavens are wide and the Tsar is far!' It is necessary to demonstrate that this Tsar can come any day."[30]

Compounding this situation was the recourse to violence for personal reasons, including enrichment and prestige. Responding to a spate of native violence from 1903, the government countered calls for a punitive expedition with the standard economic arguments focusing on mild treatment of the native population as the only route to increasing native productivity and tax revenues. Any action that would decrease the size of the population and its cattle stocks could only damage the areas affected and undermine future prosperity. Issuing the first of two circulars, addressed to all District Offices and their subsidiaries, military stations, and officers' posts, the administration divided the colonial military space into areas proximate to a station and those far from such an outpost. "Peaceful areas of rule" were taken as not those districts in which the native population lived in general peace, but areas in which the government was able to maintain order without fear of large-scale uprisings. Seeking to reduce the exercise of armed violence in the immediate area of the District Offices and military stations, the authorities in these "peaceful areas" were instructed to issue punishments on an individual basis. Collective reprisals were to be reserved for wartime.[31]

These rules were not intended to be applied outside the "peaceful areas of rule," where relatively nonviolent solutions were always to be pursued. Punitive expeditions and other forms of punishment were only ever to be performed as a measure of last resort. Issues of no importance such as "negro talk about not accepting legal authority or ignoring a station order etc." were not to be taken as the cause for violent action. The revenue authorities were instructed not to allow tax collection disputes to develop into unrest, and tax collectors were to make recourse to their arms only in exceptional cases. The heads of the colonial administrations were to instruct their subordinates "to exhaust all the possibilities presented to resolve all questions using much more troublesome and less prestigious peaceful means before recourse to more convenient intervention with the superior European weaponry." The circular closed with an appeal to the colonial sense of duty: "As the conqueror of the territory of an inferior race, we have the duty to allow the natives—not inherently evil, but uncultivated and often led astray and ignorant of our aims and intentions—to accustom themselves to our rule."[32]

A second circular from the Colonial Department of the Foreign Ministry to the governor revoked the previous differentiation between the "peaceful areas" and the other districts in order to redress the impression that incidents far removed from the center of power required less urgent an intervention than more proximate disruptions.[33] The new provision now extended the validity of the conditions for military intervention in the "peaceful areas of rule" to the whole of the district. The circular made the renewed attempt to convince the civil and military District Officers and commanders that it was more commendable to make an individualized and preventative response to unrest, targeted at the ringleaders of violence, rather than responding with the less discriminating tool of overwhelming military force. To this end, the circular provided a number of examples deemed worthy of emulation, including an episode on the Makonde [sic] Plateau[34] in which Captain Kurt Johannes cooperated with the District Officer Carl Ewerbeck to defuse a potentially serious situation without the use of violence and thus establish long-term calm.

Seeking to encourage greater circumspection, the Colonial Department raised the possibility of awarding medals and other awards for the peaceful resolution of unrest. Correspondingly, it decided to restrict the award of campaign medals for military action in German East Africa to a very low number of cases in which the officer involved was able to demonstrate convincingly the "complete necessity" of deploying troops in a fashion exceeding the scope of a police action. Moreover, the commander was required to demonstrate that the violence had resulted from the nature of the immediate circumstances, including troop losses.[35] This reveals that the German colonial authorities were not unaware of the potentially damaging consequences of excessive violence to good relations within their protectorate and took (albeit limited) steps to keep it within certain bounds.

The extent to which the contents of these ordinances were actually comprehended and followed is not clear. Theodor Leutwein's annotations on his copy of these ordinances indicate his suspicion that unlike his colleagues in German East Africa, the administrators in his charge were not inclined to employ an unnecessary level of violence. He believed that simple police actions would suffice to maintain order in the Nama and Herero areas. As the Colonial Department was well aware, only the Ovambo lands were not in the hands of either the police or the Protection Force. The ordinances applied only to the handful of officers stationed in the north of the Ovambo country, nominally a part of the Herero lands.[36] This optimistic assessment of the situation was made only six months before the outbreak of the Herero war.

The distance from the military stations mentioned in the two ordinances served to shape military perceptions of local conditions. Those natives living in close proximity to the stations were viewed as being friendly. Those resisting imperial rule were seen as living somewhat further, yet still within reach of the station. Those living beyond the reach of the station were viewed almost as part of the wilderness and were described as being shy and frightened.[37] Despite this differentiation, the distance or proximity of the native population was of little significance for the level of violence unleashed by the German forces. Villages in close proximity to a military station were not only easy to control but often subject to attacks from the Protection Force. It was such a circumstance that led the government in Dar es Salaam to place them under particular protection. Areas further afield enjoyed a certain level of "natural security" from such attacks. Constrained, as they were, by the availability of bearers and provisions (i.e., political social and economic factors) as well as climatic and topographic conditions, reactions to events in the form of a punitive expedition were often subject to serious delay.

The violence exercised by a punitive expedition was not solely external, and non-German members of the expedition could also experience its impact. Punitive expeditions in German East Africa were not composed entirely of military personnel, but took with them a wide variety of native auxiliaries, their families, and other assorted camp followers. Swollen further by the taking of prisoners en route, these additions increased the scope for physical and sexual punishments and executions. Black women (and their children) were particularly frequent victims of physical but above all sexual violence. Their lives cheap, there was no restriction on their treatment, up to and including death.[38]

Characterized by the arbitrary and indiscriminate use of violence, punitive expeditions were used as instruments of punishment and subjugation. Every form of violence was permitted in all directions, toward its members and nonmembers alike. The government and Colonial Department being unable to exert their influence throughout the region, their regular initiatives to reduce this level of violence had little effect. With no effective method of sanction, the only course open to officials was to appeal to the better nature of the participants. Although military law expressly forbade the exercise of violence against civilians, the expeditions were in practice governed by a tacit set of informal rules agreed between the commander and its members. With the level and nature of violence arising from situative considerations, the legal footing of such undertakings remained unclear.

The Absence of "Restraining Factors of a Civilized Nature"

Punitive expeditions also often involved conventional set-piece engagements or even battles. The German campaign in China included the assault and capture of fortified villages. In contrast, the war in South-West Africa was initially conducted as a number of assaults on positions prepared by the Herero in Onganjira, Oviumbo, and Ovikokorero. Indeed, the fortifications constructed to defend these positions even attracted considerable German praise.[39] The war in German East Africa, on the other hand, was characterized by a number of frontal engagements. Taking advantage of the natural cover provided by the grasslands, the enemy was able to launch a number of surprise attacks.[40] Engagements not conducted in open country but involving the storming of fortified residential areas were always followed by considerable disorder. The German approach to a defended position involved a three-phase assault. First came the bombardment from artillery and machine guns stationed on any areas of high ground designed to reduce the fortifications and prepare the town for an assault. All Chinese towns of any size were surrounded by a wall; villages were arranged in a defensive position with houses constructed to form a ring, often joined by a wall so as to encircle the village center. The few access points were easy to seal and could be defended by only a handful of soldiers.

The bombardment was followed by the storming of the town at bayonet point, which the villagers often sought to flee. The layout of Chinese settlements prevented any such flight, however, and the civilians were placed at the mercy of the incoming troops. Although street-fighting was rare in the China campaign, the matting fence surrounding Chinese houses transformed them into a mini-fortress. In view of the Chinese practice of posting marksmen on the roofs of the houses, the Germans were forced to capture the town house by house, a task at which they soon became highly accomplished.

The third phase of the assault involved actions not foreseen by the army manuals or ordinances: a wave of plundering, rape, killing, and the taking of prisoners as was unleashed in Peking. The last act of violence involved the burning of houses and entire settlements. Fires were set only following express orders so as not to endanger the lives of those soldiers searching for weapons, ammunition, or supplies.[41] Intended not merely as a punishment, such actions were also designed as a visible and long-term demonstration of the power of the conquerors. Colonial rule was marked by pillars of smoke, wind-borne ash, and burnt stumps. As one participant observed, a burning village was both impressively apocalyptic and bizarre in the illumination that it provided.[42] Writing to his king from China, the Saxon major Kurt von Schönberg noted that "after almost 26 years of peace, this is no heroic beginning for the practical use of my professional skills."[43]

Once this excess had been completed, violence soon reassumed its apparently regulated forms: courts martial were followed by executions. Killing was now dignified by a perfunctory exercise in military justice. Often, the most simple of techniques were applied to save ammunition. Adapting to local custom (or so the official justification), the German force in China executed its prisoners by beheading.[44] In Africa, hangings were carried out on high hills, so as to spread a clear and visible message.[45] The German force in China was never intended to maintain any prison camps. The explanation for this remains a matter of speculation: perhaps it was a response to the kaiser's injunction to "take no prisoners." Economic considerations also militated against the establishment of prison camps on any large scale, as the large Chinese population presented a ready pool of conscript labor. Seeking to return to normality as soon as possible, the allied commanders did not wish to take any measures that would prevent the Chinese population from returning to work.

The nature of this type of warfare required a population on which to visit the wrath of the conqueror such as the inhabited towns and villages found at the outset of the Boxer and Maji Maji wars. Not passive victims of this violence, the Chinese population sought to evade its impact by maintaining a close intelligence network and measures of camouflage and negotiation. Responding in a pragmatic fashion, the local reaction took advantage of family ties and long experience in suffering the arrival of a violent expeditionary force:

there was no form of regional coordination.[46] The communicative response to the occupying armies eschewed open rejection, concentrating instead on evasion and obfuscation.

The German forces only encountered a guerilla war in Africa. Although launched as a conventional conflict, the Herero war eventually descended into a hit-and-run campaign following the German fiasco at the Waterberg. The adoption of such tactics by the Herero and especially the Nama was facilitated by their predominantly nomadic patterns of living and their decision to hand over their women and children to the care of the German authorities. The native society of German East Africa was more sedentary, but its members had little difficulty in leaving their dwellings and building up new temporary accommodation. In such a way, the movement of whole villages also enabled a guerilla war. Posting lookouts, they were always aware of oncoming troops and were able to flee in time.[47]

The ad hoc response by the German military to the guerilla warfare launched in German South-West Africa involved operations by mobile units in open country maintained by a number of fixed supply depots. This strategy was perfected in the Nama war, with small mounted units moving from post to post, where they rested, to be relieved by a waiting force. Such a campaign required not only horses but sufficient personnel with equestrian training. This enabled the German commanders to maintain an uninterrupted pursuit performed by constantly fresh and well-supplied troops. Worn down in a relentless campaign of attrition, the exhausted insurgents were easily captured and incarcerated.

The concentration camps established in German South-West Africa represented the establishment of "a space within a space." "Concentration camps" in a dual sense, they "concentrated" the exhausted and desperate Africans in a single area of control, while at the same time, exercising "concentrated" rule.[48] Largely left to their own devices, the Herero and Nama were taken out only to perform forced labor on farms or the railroad so as to shape the colony according to the wishes of their colonial masters. The building of such camps was made possible by the presence of a sufficient number of German soldiers to capture and guard the prisoners.

The response to the guerilla campaign launched in German East Africa involved a program of destruction and sequestration encompassing fields, cattle, and food reserves. The systematic destruction of the resources on which the native population depended produced a lasting period of existential insecurity throughout the protectorate. This undertaking was facilitated by hostage taking (focusing on women and children) as a method of both forcing villagers to reveal hidden supplies and reducing the supply of guerilla fighters. Requiring little complex planning, cheap to implement, and requiring no special skills, this plan could be implemented by native auxiliaries. The only point crucial to the undertaking was the necessity not to destroy one's own supplies. The absence in German East Africa of conditions conducive to the maintenance of concentration camps—vast spaces, a low population density, plans for colonization, and the ready availability of personnel—meant that they were never given serious consideration. Because the German military did not develop any plans to concentrate the whole of the insurgent population in one area, the only prisons constructed were smaller establishments designed to incarcerate women and children for only a short duration. The provisory nature of such establishments was reflected in the war budget for the colony, which unlike that for German South-West Africa made no provision for prisoners.[49]

Conditioned not just by the approach of the local population to warfare, the differences between these two strategies also reflected the personnel and financial resources available to the German military and their adaptation to the perception and evaluation of different colonial geographies. In this sense, China did not represent a "classical" colonial environment. The Chinese provinces of Zhili (150,000 km^2 in area and with a population of 19.5 million) and Shandong (a population of 25 million spread over 145,000 km^2) presented a considerable challenge in terms of policing for the international expeditionary corps of some 90,000 soldiers.[50] The local population lived in a large number of fortified towns and a large capital city. A road network existed, but the lack of a railroad system meant that the long distances had to be covered by horse and pony wagons. Every movement was hindered by a "number of rivers," only a few of which were served by a "calamitous bridge." The mountains were transected by "neglected paths" over a number of passes. The paths leading to settlements often incorporated the most uncomfortable and narrow of passes.[51] This necessitated the deployment of pioneer units as a vanguard to clear the path. Although water and provisions were available in large supply, they did not accord to the eating and hygiene habits of the troops. Nevertheless, the prevalence of such conditions characteristic for a colonial environment detracts in no way from the ability of the soldiers to differentiate between "culture" and "nature."

German South-West Africa, on the other hand, comprised an area of 835,000 km^2 with a native population of some 200,000. A force of 785 soldiers was available for its control. This produced a ratio of 0.24 inhabitants per 1 km² and 0.94 soldiers per 1,000 km². The ratio of control amounted to four soldiers per 1,000 inhabitants. The wide spaces of subtropical German South-West Africa provided only a few points of cultural reference for the European. As the general staff publication remarked, the nomadic lives of the natives meant that the existence of settlements with massive buildings remained very much the exception.[52] As a result, German forces rarely encountered either fortified points or any agricultural facilities such as villages, fields, stalls, or stores: "We are supposed to reach a place by the name of Otjikuoko by 5 May. . . . Those unfamiliar with the country probably expected huts and palms, clean fences, and wells. . . . Looking around, I was unable to recognize anything even resembling a settlement; trees and bushes, but where was the settlement?"[53]

According to the official history of the war, all areas of the protectorate were characterized by the same "barren uniformity of landscape." Even the monotonously identical form of the mountains brought no relief. Nothing made it more difficult for the European—accustomed as he was to the rich nature of his homeland—to orient himself in the colony than this singular, torpid uniformity. As a result, the main problem besetting the soldiers in German South-West Africa was complete disorientation. This was compounded by an experience that was unknown in either China or German East Africa: that of depopulation. Confronted by an apparently infinite expanse, the soldier found no culture, resources, or people. As Captain Kurd Schwabe wrote, "in its cultural barrenness" without road, path, or water, large swathes of this territory resembled "a desert."[54] In such an environment, locating the enemy was regarded as perhaps the biggest of the challenges facing the German forces: "A small tribe can disappear entirely within this area. If [we] are to fight or punish them and they do not want to be found, then the hunt for them is one of the most difficult tasks. Orientation in this depopulated area is never certain and every point of the compass indicates an enemy."[55]

Although the contemporary understanding of the conflict in both German South-West Africa and German East Africa was that of a "people of culture" (Kulturvolk) against a "primitive people" (Naturvolk), the German military went even further. Failing to find any evidence of native culture, the German forces came to believe that the native population lacked any form of culture whatsoever. The problems presented in the conduct of the war seemed to stem from the necessity to overcome nature: "An interesting facet of conducting a war in this land with the constantly light sky and the dry ground is that movement is unopposed by any restraining factors of a civilized nature [*hemmende Kulturschranke*]. The need to overcome the difficulties presented by the wild nature of the country requires our full concentration and physical resources. Having wrestled with wild nature, we can take heart in our confrontation with the natives who, with their familiarity with the land, are opponents to be reckoned with."[56]

The "restraining factors of a civilized nature" to which Curt von François referred included houses and buildings, but also fields and other recognizable "cultural" achievements. Leading a nomadic existence in mobile huts, the fighters melted into the apparently never-ending hinterland, where they could survive for long periods. Such realities ruled out any form of "destruction of culture" through which the German forces could exert pressure on the insurgents. The idea that the real opponent was nature itself was used by von François, in his coverage of the war in German South-West Africa for the *Militär-Wochenblatt*. Writing in 1905, he provided an elaborate defense of the slow progress of the German forces and their apparent inability to rout the Nama: "No one would be happier to repeat the successes of 1870–71 than our Protection Force. Nevertheless, such a swift victory is impossible in a country such as German South-West Africa, where our opponents seek their strength in concealment and movement and our chief enemy is the power of nature."[57]

"Rich in nature" yet "devoid of culture," the colony in German South-West Africa presented considerable problems to the German military in terms of supply. Lacking in almost every necessity for the troops, it is no coincidence that von Trotha's military ordinance from May 1904 proscribed the "arbitrary removal of supplies etc. intended for the troops" which would be "punished with the most serious of sanctions."[58] The complete absence of fields and stores of food in German South-West Africa necessitated the formation of a massive and personnel-intensive system of victualing. Cattle could be herded with the expeditions, but themselves requiring food, they represented a serious burden. As a result, prisoners were viewed as superfluous competitors for food. "We were relieved when we had one less black mouth to feed, as our supplies ran very low," wrote the sailor Auer in his diary.[59] The supply situation became even more critical immediately after the Herero defeat at Waterberg and especially during the pursuit in the desert. This was compounded by poor communications and the practice of splitting up the force, bringing considerable logistical difficulties to the victualing columns.[60]

Requiring water and grazing for the horses and cattle transported on their expeditions, the Germans felt unable to emulate the tactics of resource destruction adopted by the Herero and Nama. This tactic was employed only by the natives familiar with the land. A manual remarked, "Experience shows that the grass fires on the South-West African steppe are not as dangerous as one would think as the grass is low and thin. However, the resulting destruction of the pasture means that fires should be avoided wherever possible."[61] Although a number of Herero and Nama huts were destroyed, a systematic strategy of destruction was not pursued in German South-West Africa, as the damage inflicted on the native population by such a strategy would have far outweighed the negative consequences for the German military.

Seeking to deny the insurrectionists access to food and water, German forces herded cattle together and placed them under guard; they also occupied the watering holes. These measures were accompanied by the establishment of German supply stations.[62] The military operations conducted in German South-West Africa were executed in the "colonial space" constructed in the perception of the actors operating in it. Not an independent or immutable variable, this space was the product of the interaction of geographical conditions with social dynamics and imported preconceptions. The colony was occupied and organized according to military requirements. The program of colonial development begun during the war was continued in peacetime: seeking to improve the postwar German position, the Protection Force High Command forced the pace of railroad construction, so as to improve mobilization times, troop supply, and remounting. They also embarked on reforms of the administration, the communications zone, and the medical and veterinary services. In so doing, they hoped to "culturalize" what they viewed as an almost uncivilized area. In the hope to improve their dominance of the protectorate, this program was motivated by the conception of German South-West Africa as a colony of white settlement and the activities undertaken were designed to realize this as speedily as possible.[63]

Not restricting the scope of its task to the restoration of order, the military sought to prepare the land for German colonization. With their recently acquired familiarity with the country, resistance to the prevailing conditions, and their personal characteristics, the colonial soldiers were viewed as the ideal colonizers. As one commentator remarked, "These chaps would make excellent settlers."[64] The supplementary budget of 1906, necessitated by the war in German South-West Africa, intended to use the money put aside for the return of the German soldiers to the metropole as a "settlement grant."[65]

Surveying the scene, the official publication of the General Staff saw that "the Herero have failed to do so [cultivate the land]—chivvied from one watering hole to the next, he finished as an aboulic victim of his own country."[66] Long having ceased to be a demonstration of military superiority, the war had now become the instrument with which to implement a new political, economic, social, and cultural settlement. The significance accorded to the colony by the German military increased the significance of the war.

The justification advanced by the General Staff for this program of settlement—only those subjugating nature have a right to the land—was redolent of the German geographer Friedrich Ratzel (whose theories later inspired the *Lebensraum* program of the Third Reich).[67] Such an argument for the settlement of "uncultivated" land had a long intellectual currency, and was used by English settlers as a justification for their expansion in North America. Believed by some to have been proposed by John Locke (this question is currently a matter of heated debate), this so-called agriculturalist argument was expounded to its fullest extent (and gained popular currency) by the Swiss jurist, Emer de Vattel, in his *Droit des gens* (1758). Arguing that those peoples who "to avoid labour, chuse [*sic*] to live only by hunting, and their flocks" pursued an "idle mode of life, usurp more extensive territories than . . . they would have occasion for, and have therefore no reason to complain, if other nations, more industrious, and too closely confined, come to take possession of a part of those lands."[68]

German East Africa presented an entirely different situation. Of 995,000 km² in area and populated by some 7 million natives, the colony was policed by 1,701 soldiers. Thus with a population density of 7.04 persons per km² and 2.4 soldiers per 1,000 km², every 1,000 natives were kept in order by 0.34 soldiers. German East Africa also presented clearly perceptible features of culture that the Europeans could use as a source of orientation: the villages, fields, stalls, and stores developed by the native population. The German colonial administration attempted to use these "cultural" units, which they very much perceived as such, for their own purposes. Unable to transport regular supplies to the interior of the colony, they were forced to live off the land.[69]

The high mobility of the African opponent and the low number of slow-moving German soldiers (always accompanied by a large baggage train) forced the Protection Force to rely on the service of African auxiliaries to conduct the pursuit. As German East Africa was not intended as a settler colony (only the peaceful mountainous area in the north of the colony had a German population) and amid a plentiful supply situation, German commanders felt no qualms in implementing a scorched earth policy. As Major Kurt von Schleinitz noted in 1907, "while under European conditions, the pursuit of an enemy aims at his complete destruction, the aim in this context is to take his property (cattle, supplies) and to raze villages and fields."[70]

The violence exercised within the scope of the three colonial wars was not the direct result of any German "will to destruction" latent in its military structures. The key factors conditioning the escalation of violence in all three theaters were the perceived and actual realities presented by the colonial environment and its population. The soldiers deployed in German South-West Africa were confronted with an expansive country with restricted resources in which the native population was always viewed as a competitor for the scarce resources. Vexed by the few "uncultured" inhabitants, their primary aims focused less on fighting the enemy than on dominating the environment with which they were presented. An exaggerated interpretation could involve classification of the resulting genocide as an attempt to transform an apparently underpopulated area into an uninhabited area in order to facilitate its "cultivation" by settlers.[71] In contrast, the more visible presence of the native population in German East-Africa and its usability for German ends meant that while genocide would have been possible, the outcome would have been counterproductive from a German perspective. This situation presented the possibility of restoring rule by material destruction—with deadly consequences for both the African population and the environment. The situation in China—ready availability of people and resources—meant that plundering and destruction did not affect allied access to resources. This and the temporary presence of German forces meant that they were never confronted with the consequences of their actions: concerned only with their concession in Shandong, the majority of German troops were returned home post haste. The events in colonial theaters of war were not determined solely by military doctrine and racist ideology. The events in German South-West Africa always remained an exception, the results of German adaptation to local conditions conditioned by their wider aims and long-term plans for the colony.

CHAPTER 8

Diseases and Injuries

INJURY, DISEASE, AND DEATH are integral
features of war. Soldiers fighting in early twentieth-
century colonial wars were at risk from not only enemy operations but also
the expanse of the territory in which they were fighting and the (for them)
entirely unfamiliar health problems presented by such an environment. The
beating sun and biting cold were just as dangerous as an unvaried diet and
water shortages. Although risks could be minimized by adherence to clear-
cut medical directives, they remained ever-present. One particular and constant source of infection for the healthy colonial soldier identified by German
medical officers was the "diseased native." In response to the perceived
threats, the military medicinal discourse concentrated on the standard topics
of hygiene, tropical fitness, and the adaption of white soldiers to the conditions of each colony. The nature and extent of the injuries and illnesses suffered varied between each colony and within the campaigns fought in them,
thus exercising a different impact on their conduct.

The Army Medical Corps

The various colonial wars fought by the German Empire presented its military corps with a whole range of new tasks. An army fighting under tropical
and subtropical conditions needed medical care and supplies. The ill and
injured troops also needed accommodation, transport, and care, all of which
required a highly efficient support organization. Seeking to hold up the "advance and establishment of the enemies of soldiers' health"[1] required the

cleansing of the communication zone. Wartime epidemics such as typhus were to be contained and combatted primarily through improved hygiene and a campaign of vaccinations.

Reporting to the military commander of each colony, the military medical service developed its own forms of organization. The Boxer War saw the deployment of medical units from both the navy and the army. In addition to a medical company and a reserve depot, a navy hospital ship was deployed for the first time. Four large hospitals were established in Tianjin, supplemented by two in Peking (including one hospital staffed by naval personnel) and a smaller hospital in Baoding. Six field hospitals constituted the mobile medical provision for the fighting troops. This was supplemented by six smaller stations established along the communication routes, and a hospital in Yangchuan administered by the German Red Cross. The latter institution was unique among the German military hospitals in that it also offered care to the Chinese.[2] The medical units accompanying the East Asian Expeditionary Corps provided a capacity to treat a total of 2,000 persons. Nevertheless, no more than between 1,200 and 1,300 patients were actually treated at any one time.[3]

The organization of the Medical Corps in German South-West Africa was regulated by the Imperial Medical Ordinance issued in July 1904.[4] Following the declaration of war, a corps medical officer replaced the previous chief physician of the Protection Force as the head of the newly created Medical Office. Assisted by the personnel and equipment of the naval expeditionary corps, he now assumed command of what had previously operated as an autonomous unit. Before the war, German South-West Africa had been equipped with fifteen large medical stations, with a capacity to treat only the 772 members of the Protection Force. The deployment of thousands of soldiers during the Herero and Nama War moved the authorities to establish additional facilities in the communication zone.[5]

The medical establishment in German East Africa was headed by the government medical department. Run by the chief physician of the Protection Force, this office was combined with that of chief government physician, and its holder acted as the lead for the entire medical system. Following the outbreak of war, a ship's surgeon was seconded to the office of the naval commanding officer to advise him on medical matters. Both naval and army physicians were deployed in the Maji Maji War, and shared responsibility for the provision of medical care to the various units now operating in the protectorate. There were no military hospitals in German East Africa;

military and civilian personnel were treated together in the "government hospitals," the largest of which were located in Dar es Salaam and Tanga. The military stations located outside the towns were all equipped with an infirmary for Europeans and smaller clinics for the natives, both staffed by a medical officer and an orderly. The equipment accorded to these stations was restricted to what could fit in a canvas medical bag.

The practical duties accorded to the medical service varied greatly between each colony. The extensive nature of the medical organization established to serve the expeditionary corps in China and the limited demands placed on it meant that the wounded and ill were processed quickly and easily. Nevertheless, according to the reports of the Bavarian medical officer Eugen Wolffhügel, the poor communications between the battlefield and the dressing stations led to difficulties in processing greater demand.[6] However, with the war concluded before the arrival of the expeditionary corps, its soldiers had little to do and the medical officers were accorded considerable opportunity to gather experience in matters of troop hygiene and medical tactics.

In contrast, the situation in German South-West Africa presented the German Medical Corps with considerable difficulties. With the encircling enemy rendering the provision of battlefield medical services in the rear lines all but impossible, medical officers were forced to establish dressing stations in the front line; wherever possible, under the cover of natural features. As a result, the wounded could be transported away from the battlefield only after the enemy had withdrawn and covering units had been brought up. By the fall of 1904, the dispersal of the soldiers into smaller units led to the abandonment of the original aim of establishing constant medical provision through the presence of medical companies and field hospitals. "The exceptionally difficult conditions of transport dictated leaving everything behind which did not appear to be absolutely vital. It was often a matter of the greatest difficulty to establish the field hospitals punctually at the locations at which a battle was expected."[7] It was exactly at this point that the exertions of the troops conducting the pursuit in the desert led to a considerable increase in the number of typhus cases. Medical provision could be guaranteed only where the system of communications was well organized and ran smoothly. Failing in their endeavors to establish such a system during the Maji Maji War, the troops operating in German East Africa were forced to rely on their own resources. As a result, medical officers remained with the fighting and marching soldiers, a development that often had a negative effect on their performance and that prevented the wounded from receiving treatment in adequate facilities. This new arrangement also saw the assumption by medical officers of command responsibilities.

Despite the differences of organization between the medical services established during the three theaters, they all exhibited one common feature: the laboratories set up to supplement the hospitals. Employed not to provide immediate medical care for the ill and wounded, instead they served a primarily prophylactic and diagnostic function and thus constituted the institutional link between the provision of medical services and the performance of scientific medical research. The East Asian Expeditionary Corps was equipped with a number of laboratories for the dedicated investigation and study of hygiene issues, bacteriology, and pathology.[8] Comparable facilities were also available in German South-West Africa, although the bacteriological investigations initially had to be conducted in a small military hospital in Swakopmund. Two medical officers trained as bacteriologists—Hugo Bofinger and Otto Nägele—were dispatched to the protectorate at the end of January 1905, and a new laboratory was set up in immediate proximity to the prisoner of war camp on Shark Island in April. This was followed by an Institute of Chemistry in February 1906. The chemical-bacteriological facilities at Dar es Salaam and Tanga (German East Africa) were much less sophisticated.[9]

The duties accorded to the chemistry laboratories in China and Africa included the investigation of foodstuffs and stimulants as well as quantitative analyses of water.[10] They also conducted tests on devices for the heating and purification of water and investigations in the field of forensic, technical, and pharmaceutical chemistry.[11] The bacteriological institutes performed blood, urine, and feces tests in order to diagnose pathogens such as malaria parasites, plague, typhus, tuberculosis, and recurring spirrlia. These institutions were also responsible for testing the vaginal secretions of the prostitutes working in licensed brothels. The work of the laboratories in German South-West Africa was not restricted to conducting tests on the German soldiers stationed in the protectorate. Nevertheless, the Medical Reports made only passing reference to the inclusion of African prisoners as test subjects. Both pathology institutes and military hospitals performed a number of autopsies. Hugo Bofinger stated that "numerous autopsies" were a matter of course.[12] In 1906, 778 autopsies were performed in the camp in Windhoek alone.[13] Some of these procedures were witnessed by prisoners, who saw how "e.g. a heart was removed from the body, placed in spirits and sent away."[14] In fact, bodies and body parts were used for research purposes beyond, as well as within, Africa: a number were transported to Germany under the same conditions as accorded to the fallen German soldiers. These transports also included the bodies of Herero and Nama children. The medical department of the Prussian Ministry of War arranged for a number of brains taken from the corpses of Herero and Ovambo tribesmen to be sent to the Anatomical Institute in Berlin. Their relatives were often informed of the death only after the alleged burial.[15]

One typical duty performed by doctors of the Medical Corps was the collection and dispatch to Berlin of a number of skulls taken from native corpses. Despite such widespread practices, the government of the protectorate replied upon inquiry that they had not removed or gathered any skulls from the Herero. Internally, it was stated that "were it to become known that we removed skulls during an autopsy [this would] strengthen native unwillingness and fear of the military hospitals."[16] The German authorities knew that they would never obtain permission from Africans to undertake such a procedure.

Mirroring the situation characteristic of those involved in the administration and policing of the German overseas empire, the German colonial medical profession was divided between those who, regarding them as a valuable source of labor, argued that the African population should be handled with care and those who championed their extermination as the best policy of colonial administration. An essay discussing the medical services provided during the war in German South-West Africa quoted two doctors representative of the extreme racist position.[17] A counterexample was provided by Otto Nägele, who circulated a number of suggestions as to how the health of the Africans could best be subject to long-term improvement. In doing so, he made clear that the illness and death of many Africans in the war were caused above all by the substandard accommodation in the military hospitals, and he criticized the state of medical provision: "Employment as a doctor in the native hospital [is] the most dispiriting of tasks that one can imagine."[18] The rejection of Nägele's proposals by the government of German South-West Africa was noteworthy: as nothing had been undertaken for the medical care of the African population, such an ambitious project of hospital building could not be started without drawing attention to its previous absence. Such a course of action would represent lurching from one extreme to the other.[19]

All three German colonial wars saw the German Medical Corps develop a sophisticated scientific medical division dedicated to performing a range of tasks that far exceeded the primary provision of medical treatment. Providing what was viewed as objective scientific data regarding colonial warfare in a tropical and subtropical environment, their much-vaunted objectivity did not prevent them from viewing the Herero as the progenitors of the typhus epidemic of 1904. This judgment gave apparent credence and concrete political support to the racist conceptions and prejudice already rife in German society in general and among colonial soldiers in particular. Despite such similarities, however, the demands made of the military medical services in each war varied considerably: while services in China were significantly undercapacity, those in German South-West Africa were overstretched. The system in German East Africa suffered from the double function of care and command, which its doctors were expected to perform.

"Fit for Colonial Service" and Acclimatization

Both the members of the Protection Forces and other white colonial soldiers required robust health for overseas service. Although subtropical areas were commonly viewed as more tolerable than tropical areas because of their low humidity, both climates posed considerable risks for Europeans. In view of these special health risks, and in order to ensure that they would stand up to the mental and physical demands placed on them, all potential colonial soldiers were examined for their fitness for service in a tropical environment.[20]

A binding set of rules for establishing tropical fitness were established for the examinations. Basing his analysis on the corresponding articles of the Protection Force Ordinance, Lieutenant (med.) Emil Steudel, a veteran of German East Africa and head of the Protection Forces medical department in the Imperial Colonial Office, emphasized the dangers posed by tropical conditions to various human organ systems, which he listed as the heart, nerves, blood vessels, digestive tract, joints and muscles, the middle ear and ear drum, and the exterior auditory canal and the sexual organs.[21] A nervous disposition, a weak digestive system, or even a tendency to rheumatoid arthritis could be better diagnosed through taking a thorough case history than from a physical examination. The diagnosis of a nervous disposition, on the other hand, would be best established not just by inquiry as to the family history, but from close observation for any indications of an unbalanced nature.[22] Those who reacted sensitively to minor events were as unsuitable for tropical service as noticeably nervous applicants. Nevertheless, he maintained that a certain level of eagerness for action (yet without any signs of nervousness) was desirable.[23] Regular consumption of alcohol, tobacco, or other narcotics or a susceptibility to chronic, especially rheumatic, illnesses was to be established as a criterion of unfitness.

The final consideration of a physical examination was accorded to the general state of health. Signs of premature aging and obesity both sufficed as grounds for immediate rejection. The heart was to be examined with considerable care and the physician was instructed to be sensitive to even moderate deviations such as an extended or irregular heartbeat. A further aspect requiring special attention was the circulatory system; applicants with varicose veins were to be rejected, as they would be susceptible to a range of complaints, especially during the wet period. Conditions resulting in immediate rejection included tuberculosis and kidney and bladder complaints. Moreover, the search for venereal disease (VD) assumed top priority, and those in an acute stage were ruled out for any form of colonial service. Any recent syphilis infection should have been contracted a minimum of two years prior to service in the colonies. Further conditions rendering their sufferers unfit for colonial service included a propensity to boils and eczema as well as a tendency to excessive sweating, especially sweaty feet. Further reasons for rejection included refraction complaints of the eyes and chronic ear complaints.

Despite their existence, such precise criteria determining fitness for service in a tropical environment were not always enforced, and acute manpower shortages led to a number of obese recruits being dispatched to German South-West Africa. Even when observed, the selection criteria could not always prevent the situation in which service in a climate "unfavorable to Europeans"[24] led to soldiers' being exposed to extreme and health-threatening conditions. Direct sunlight, increased ground temperatures, a uniformly high air temperature, and high levels of humidity resulted in high levels of bodily atony.[25] With every movement perceived as a great effort and accompanied by consistently high levels of sweating, those forced to operate in such an environment found it to be not only highly uncomfortable but even life-threatening.

While fitness for tropical service could be ascertained only in Germany, the (equally important) question of acclimatization was one that could be addressed only on location in the colony. One of the central problems facing those selected for service in a tropical or subtropical climate was their ability to perform under extreme circumstances, an important example being a route march. Thus while a German infantryman marching under European conditions could cover up to fifty kilometers per day while carrying between twenty-six and twenty-seven kilograms of equipment, unburdened and marching in an African setting, this distance was reduced to between thirty and forty kilometers per day at best. As a result, white troops serving in a tropical location carried only the most essential of objects with them: their weapon and ammunition, an aluminum water bottle, iron rations, quinine tablets against malaria (when in German East Africa), bandages, and tobacco. Native bearers were employed to carry the rest of the equipment. This increased the size of military formations while reducing their level of mobility. In response to these and other demands, medical officers were forced to develop the new subdiscipline of "tropical marching hygiene" to provide commanders with guidance in the planning of troop movements to incorporate rests, sleep, taking on fluids, eating, and dressing.[26]

The decisive medical question concerning both the settlement of the colonies and the establishment of a colonial army was the extent to which Europeans were able to acclimatize to the prevailing conditions without suffering any deleterious effects to their health and constitution. There were a number of very different answers to this question. While one section of medical opinion insisted that the climate increased susceptibility to tropical illnesses, others assumed that it was not the climatic conditions but the level of infectious diseases found in tropical climes that was responsible for the greater incidence of illness among European populations in the tropics.[27] The latter school of thought was even of the opinion that Europeans could thrive in the colonies following a rigorous regime of private and public hygiene, whereas the former opined that long-term survival was possible only following a mixing of the races.[28] Tacking to and fro between these two poles of opinion were the practitioners of tropical medicine, whose task it was to "guard against known agents of contagion and make our people stronger and more resistant."[29] To this end, its practitioners conducted a number of investigations of plant and animal pathogens, the air humidity, and in particular the nature of the soil and its products, the water quality, the danger of infection from man and beast, and the living habits of the respective native population.

During the Boxer War, rumors circulated among the soldiers of an environment "full of germs dangerous to Europeans."[30] This evaluation was even shared by the medical officers of the expedition, who saw that the soil itself contributed to the development of illness. The Chinese were said to have no idea of "what we call hygiene."[31] German observers concluded that practices such as the disposal of effluent and feces, the provision of good drinking water, and domestic or general cleanliness were unknown to the Chinese. The effluent was simply poured onto the street, and animal and human feces were collected and stored in shallow holes in the ground covered with tiles. Left to dry, this was later refashioned by hand into agricultural fertilizer. Such practices resulted in the development of a soil strata consisting of rubble, waste, and excrement in which all nature of bacteria developed and spread. This "contaminated" layer of earth had a deleterious effect on human health as soon as it was disturbed and spread to plates or cutlery. Bacteria also filtered into the drinking water. The soil of the land acted as a breeding ground for dysentery and typhus, and as a result was more dangerous than the climate. The lack of Chinese hygiene, both in fact and as a cultural construct, was viewed by the German military as a ticking time-bomb which could explode at any moment. Von Waldersee refused to delay the withdrawal of his troops in 1901 for a number of reasons, including his expectation of imminent epidemics.[32]

The experience of the colonial wars covered in this study moved health questions into the central focus of everyday military life, and colonial soldiers were bombarded with a whole raft of special instructions pertaining to the maintenance of good health. This involved a number of leaflets, brochures, books, and oral instructions focusing on the basic question of healthy living: personal hygiene, questions of clothing, correct washing practices for plates, the boiling and filtration of water, nutrition, mosquito nets, and sexual behavior. In contrast to the lack of innovation in colonial tactics, this area saw the development of a number of new rules of conduct adapted to service in the colonial theater. Despite a raft of preventative measures—including the (in practice often lax) attempt to dispatch only those servicemen deemed fit for colonial service, a number of diseases eventually developed and exercised a decisive influence on the conduct of the three wars.

Nerves, Alcohol, and Morphine

One question to which contemporary tropical medicine accorded considerable attention was what its practitioners described as the increased "excitability of the nervous system" in a colonial setting. In addition to an increased emotional imbalance, which itself could lead to a "tropical frenzy," such a state also involved a number of physical complaints involving stomach and intestinal trouble, heart failure, sleeplessness, profuse sweating, and states of anxiety and debility. The contributory factors to such a state were recognized as heat, alcohol, and a range of infectious diseases including malaria, typhus, and dysentery.[33] Writing of "illnesses of the nervous system," the Medical Report for German South-West Africa subsumed a whole range of different and contrasting complaints under this heading including mental illness, falling sickness, the affliction of individual nerve tracts, meningitis, brain disease, concussion and concussion of the spinal cord, spinal complaints, inflammation of the hip, nervous debilities, and hysterics. A total of 447 separate diagnoses of "nervous illnesses" were recorded in the report together with 192 entries outlining their side effects and complications. Despite such meticulousness, those drawing up the Medical Reports were not able to record every such case, as the illnesses were often first diagnosed or even developed upon a soldier's return to the metropole.

Records for German South-West Africa indicate that a total of 52 officers, 11 medical officers, 46 senior administrators, and 338 noncommissioned officers (NCOs) and other ranks were recorded as suffering from nervous complaints. Mental illness was regarded as the most extreme form of nervous illness. This included not only psychoses in the narrower sense but also extreme mental disturbances. A total of forty-four such cases were recorded; inclusion of the psychoses increases the total to 104. Although apparently low, this rate exceeded that normally exhibited by the German army by almost three times. Those investigating the twenty-seven suicides and four attempted suicides registered for German South-West Africa suspected that at least a proportion of them were to be explained by an abnormal state of mind.[34]

The Medical Reports submitted by the doctors of the East Asian Expeditionary Corps were far less differentiated than those for German South-West Africa. Referring to a situation in which 153 persons were diagnosed as suffering from "illnesses of the nervous system," as one doctor commented, many presented neurasthenic complaints—some in consequence of an infectious disease from which they had recovered, others through the influence of a new and unfamiliar environment. Two deaths were recorded as resulting from paretic mental debility and meningitis. Express reference was made to the fact that ninety-six of those suffering from various nervous complaints had remained fit for duty.[35] In German East Africa, only three cases of an "illness of the individual nerve tract" were recorded, all of which responded fully to the treatment administered.[36]

A certain proportion of the nervous illnesses diagnosed amounted to a simple state of exhaustion resulting from constant tiredness and exertion and triggered by even minor alcohol consumption, the presentation of a simple mental task, heat, a minor illness, or some other cause. The majority of such cases were, however, caused by the new and unfamiliar environment in which the soldiers were forced to operate and which significantly altered the European standards that they applied to warfare in general and the perception of danger in particular. As the Medical Reports indicated, newly arrived soldiers could easily display panic reactions especially when deployed alone and at night: "The unfamiliar nature of their environment and the experiences [to which they are subject] combined with an active imagination—resulting in imprecise judgment through uncertain and insecure observation and even delusions—and fears, often produces injudicious and impulsive actions, even [proving to be] of momentous consequence."[37]

These "consequences" included shots fired at an imaginary enemy, discharged by excitable and anxious sentries and patrols, especially at nighttime. Such reactions were also recorded during the Boxer War. The range of new and foreign impressions combined with a latent fear of an overestimated enemy often resulted in indiscriminate firing and a number of deaths and wounds from friendly fire.[38] Entirely unprepared through either experience or training for the situations with which they were suddenly presented and seized by the fear of making mistakes, this mechanism ran out of control among the colonial soldiers. It is hardly possible to assess which actions merely constituted a reaction to unusual circumstances and those indicative of a pathological act. Reacting to the unusually high number of deaths and wounds resulting from such actions in China and German South-West Africa, the Marine Infantry Headquarters in Kiel sought an explanation in the soldiers' extreme carelessness in handling their firearms.[39]

Both the cause and the symptom of heightened nervous tension were the consumption of alcohol and morphine. The Medical Report for German South-West Africa registered thirty cases of alcohol poisoning during the war years. The majority of such cases were minor and only six involved chronic alcoholism. Nevertheless, as the report conceded, those cases actually subject to investigation did not provide a complete picture of the situation.[40] In reality, only a fraction of the cases of alcohol poisoning were actually diagnosed and treated.

The colonial theater afforded sufficient other causes for excessive drinking in addition to the problem of constant stress. Excessive heat and the resulting thirst, the impossibility of escaping the sun, and the monotony of colonial life all played their part. As a number of diary entries make clear, every opportunity was welcomed to drink alcohol, which was available in plentiful supply.[41] Indeed, spirits were regarded as necessary to cushion the harder side of soldiering and maintain a certain (positive) form of life: "Is not the camaraderie, our gladful perseverance in this remote position—with its lack of relief and paucity of pleasure—the main thing for us?" Those at home were told that every bottle of wine or spirits sent was a contribution to the health and stamina of the troops.[42]

The advisability of alcohol consumption on active service was discussed by the German military not only in general terms but also in terms of the health implications of alcohol consumption in the tropics. Proponents of total abstinence (including a number of colonial doctors such as Philatheles Kuhn) argued that the interests of the army would be best served by a total ban on drinking when on colonial service.[43] All the conventional arguments against alcohol consumption were reinforced by reference to the conditions of a tropical environment. Moreover, the beers brewed for colonial consumption were stronger, so as to lengthen their storage life. As a result, a number of cases of heart failure, tropical frenzy, and anxiety are to be explained by increased alcohol consumption. This was often compounded by chronic gastritis, liver swelling, and chronic nephritis. As tropical conditions reduce the human resistance to alcohol, those imbibing could suffer adverse consequences from even moderate consumption. The military temperance movement argued that the consumption of alcohol not only reduced resistance to a number of mental and physical complaints but also influenced the subsequent course taken by these illnesses.

Those arguing for a strict ban on the consumption of alcohol did not gain the support of the commanders of the various Protection Forces. Writing in the *Münchner Medizinische Wochenschrift*, Captain (med.) Eugen Wolffhügel (battalion medical officer to the Fourth East-Asian Infantry Regiment deployed in the Boxer War) maintained that "all those having once learnt the benefit of alcohol consumption in the field would protest at any move to forbid entirely the enjoyment of alcohol in this context."[44] The Medical Report for German South-West Africa advanced a wide range of arguments against a total ban on the consumption of alcohol.[45] Alcohol appeared to be necessary in order to maintain morale, thus enabling the troop to endure the monotony, austerity, stress, and difficulties of colonial soldiering. Moreover, the report presented its warming and sedative effects and its use to improve the taste of bad water as clear arguments in favor of its consumption. Alcohol was also used as a food supplement during times of food shortage. In addition to such positive arguments, opponents of abstinence were convinced that subject to a ban, the soldiers would merely act to procure alcohol through illicit channels. For the men, it was not merely a pleasure but a necessity. However, the Protection Force High Command still warned against the effects of excessive consumption: drinking during hot periods could result in heat stroke, sweltering, and raving madness with the potential of delirium.[46] As a result, it was deemed necessary that alcohol not be consumed in large quantities either during episodes of extreme heat or immediately before going into action.

Although alcohol was included in the soldiers' rations, the amount actually consumed by the soldiers on colonial duty depended on the attitude of the respective force commander. As he did not issue any written orders to this effect, his decision was transmitted orally. This enabled the Protection Forces to place only informal orders for the amounts of drink they required and the archival record contains no corresponding indication of the quantities either dispatched or consumed.

According to a questionnaire conducted by the military administration among officers and soldiers deployed in German South-West Africa, Governor Leutwein issued only water to his troops during the Naukluft War (1894) and that against the eastern Herero (1896). This policy was amended successively during the course of the war, although no record was made of the quantity and frequency of alcohol issue. In July 1901, Leutwein set the monthly ration to a liter of rum or one and a half kilograms of fruit juice issued in equal quantities. Immediately before the Battle of Waterberg, von Trotha increased this allowance to two liters of rum per month. This amount was increased further in 1905 to almost three liters of alcohol per month. After 1908, taking drinks of a lower alcohol content would enable a soldier to drink up to almost 6.5 liters per month.[47]

Reflecting as they do merely the official extent of the alcohol ration, we can assume that the level of private purchases of alcohol increased by a similar measure: the actual level of alcohol consumption remains at best a matter of speculation. We can assume that the Protection Force commanders increased alcohol rations to the troops shortly before making increased demands on their military performance. Whether the consumption of alcohol served to reduce inhibitions and contributed to the spiral of violence is not a question to which the available sources can provide any level of insight.

In contrast to the clear regulation of alcohol consumption, the approach to the use of morphine was much less clear. A laconic entry in the Medical Report for German South-West Africa ran that there were no cases of morphine or gas poisoning in the campaign.[48] None of the Medical Reports for the African conflicts provide any clear information on a subject that was obviously subject to a considerable taboo. Nevertheless, it was an open secret among soldiers that a number of senior officers were addicted to morphine. Captain Victor Franke confessed to his diary, "2 May 1902: continue to be relieved that although my nerves are shot to pieces, I remain seated in critical moments. 11 April 1903: haven't had such a good night's sleep for a long time. Probably the result of a treble dose of morphine muraticum."[49]

Another famous figure to make regular use of the soothing drug was Hermann von Wissmann, hero of the "Arab revolt" in German East Africa and later *Reichskommissar* of the protectorate. The "needs" of such addicted officers were probably served in injection form by medical officers who held a ready supply of morphine for the wounded and ill. It was common practice to sedate soldiers suffering from heat-induced delirium or poorly healing wounds.[50] Familiar as they were with the "difficult days of African life," many medical officers displayed understanding for those addicts who "carrying the load of responsibility of a Wissmann and struck by fever struggled in vain through a dark, muggy, twelve-hour tropical night . . . for a [few moments] of sleep."[51]

Drug use was common among the black soldiers serving in the Protection Force in German East Africa, although religious grounds meant that opium rather than morphine was the drug of choice. The problems for military discipline arising from such drug consumption were made clear in one of the phrases included in the *Military Swahili Phrase Book for German East Africa*: "I forbid the smoking of opium!"[52] Nevertheless, it is questionable whether the opium consumption of black soldiers serving in the Protection Force was either investigated or prosecuted. The sources yield even less information regarding the opium problem than they do about the morphine consumption of the German officers.

Nervous conditions and alcohol and drug abuse undoubtedly featured in the military life of the German colonies, yet the sources available do not permit a reliable quantification of the problem. The figures regarding substance abuse and nervous illnesses given by the Medical Reports compiled for the three wars are too low to enable any conclusions to be drawn regarding their impact on the conduct of the war and the German propensity for violence. The effects of other health problems on the conduct of the war can be subject to far better estimation.

Typhus in German South-West Africa

Typhus was a constant companion during the various European and extra-European military campaigns conducted in the nineteenth century, ranging from the wars of German unification (1866 and 1870–1871) to the South African War (1889–1901) and the British wars in Africa.[53] European doctors had established exact crisis plans designed to restrict the spread of the disease, involving early recognition and a strict regime of quarantine. This was to be followed by the destruction of the pathogen and the exclusion of all forms of its carrier. Those suffering from the disease were not to be touched, especially not their gastrointestinal system. The program was completed by vaccination against the "invisible enemy": the typhus bacilli. Despite the plan's long existence, the conditions in German South-West Africa severely hampered its implementation: "The land itself provides nothing which one can use to restrict the spread of the epidemic; our actions cannot be measured against peace-time or European standards. Everything out there is different to that at home; even the use of familiar names rarely refers to familiar phenomena."[54]

Despite such difficulties, a range of prophylactic measures were announced, both in China and in German South-West Africa. Thus the order was given to drink and wash only in boiled water. Indeed, this order was considered to be so essential that it was incorporated in the Medical Ordinance for German South-West Africa: "It is strictly forbidden to drink unboiled water. The use of a filter is to be viewed as a duty [of every soldier] and should be used only to clean cloudy water; the water must then be boiled. Wherever possible, washing water should also be boiled. Typhus prevention is the primary task of all health measures. The troops are to be instructed in these tasks; officers and medical officers are to ensure that the provisions are maintained."[55]

The medical ordinance also stipulated that the location of all watering holes and storage facilities suspected of carrying typhus were to be made public. All military facilities were to develop a system for the daily disposal of feces and ensure daily disinfection of the field latrines. Moreover, those rooms in which a typhus infection had become known were to be disinfected and the clothes of all sufferers were to be burned. After September 1904, typhus immunization was to be administered wherever possible to the troops present in the protectorate and its regular (white) population; those troops leaving for Africa after early 1905 were to be inoculated, at least on a voluntary basis.[56] The voluntary nature of this program followed official assessment of the vaccinations as unsafe.

The provisions of the ordinance brought little practical advantage; although addressed by a raft of hygiene measures, many sources of infection remained. The most serious problem was the impossibility of maintaining the cleanliness of watering holes, the majority of which were used by man and beast alike. Water filters and mobile water purifying units soon became entirely clogged up by the muddy water. These problems were compounded by the effects of an overworked medical transport system. Sick beds were even mounted on the same ox carts used to transport foodstuffs. The much-stressed need to boil water presented the soldiers with considerable difficulty. Not only was the laying of fire forbidden for those on long patrols; it was not always possible to provide the cooking implements necessary for the task.[57]

The outbreak of two typhus epidemics in German South-West Africa in 1904, one in summer and one in the fall, were both caused by the same pathogen but produced very different symptoms. That besetting the eastern unit early in the year produced a number of serious illnesses, many of which developed in resemblance to an acute cerebrospinal meningitis. Those suffering in the epidemic of the fall presented only a weakened version of such symptoms, yet often contracted scurvy or illnesses similar to dysentery, the symptoms of which also included anomalies of the heart-rhythm and circulation, producing a number of deaths from thrombosis.[58] Both epidemics coincided exactly with the two phases in which the course of the war underwent a phase of serious radicalization.

The presence of naval personnel in the eastern unit hit by the epidemic of early 1904 enables us to reconstruct the course taken by the disease in both the Marine Infantry and the soldiers of the Protection Force. After a number of initial cases, the first death from typhus was registered on 11 April.[59] This was soon followed by further fatalities. The eastern unit returned to its designated quarantine station (the watering hole at Otjihaenena) following the first cases of typhus, where it was broken up and its fit members—around a third of its original force—were posted to positions behind the front line. All current plans for an offensive, including the planned encirclement of the Herero, had to be postponed into the distant future. Following hard on the heels of these developments was the change in command from Leutwein to von Trotha.

While the number of typhus infections began to fall during the period in which von Trotha hurried on the preparations for the Battle of Waterberg, the rate of infection increased sporadically between September and November 1904. This coincided with the stressful period for the undersupplied German soldiers involved in the pursuit of the Herero in the Omaheke desert. The strains to which the German forces were subject often resulted in the breakup of a number of the larger formations into a number of disparate units. One of this number, under the command of Captain Otto Klein, advanced on the watering hole at Orlogsende only for his unit to dissolve entirely. A number of individual soldiers were transported back to Kalkfontein under the greatest of difficulty.[60]

November 1904 saw the typhus epidemic reach its peak. The increasing incidence of scurvy affected the majority of undernourished soldiers of von Estorff's and Mühlenfel's units, exhausted by long periods in the field. In contrast, von Deimling's unit, although affected to equal measure by typhus, presented only a few cases of scurvy. This is to be explained by the shorter time that they had spent in the field.[61] The breakdown of the system of German lines and all form of systematic medical provision meant that the ill and undernourished German soldiers saw what had begun as a conventional pursuit develop into a naked fight for survival—both in their perception and in reality.

Responding to the critical situation, the medical officers on the spot implemented immediate measures in an attempt to contain the spread of the disease. A discussion between medical officers began while the war was still underway as to the source and nature of the infection. The general consensus centered on failures in hygiene. A much-discussed doctoral dissertation published by the naval medical officer Ernst Kaerger in 1905 focused on the existence of a certain disposition to this illness, constituted by the influences of poor nutrition, specific weather conditions, gastric problems, the exertion involved in marching and fighting, the unfavorable hydrological conditions present in the protectorate, and the impurities of soil resulting from the long presence of troops in a single area. The latter factor was said to enable the transmission of the typhus epidemic through flies and dust.[62] The emphasis on the role of dust, flies, blankets, and hands in the transmission of the disease also found support among the authors of the Naval Medical Report. One question of intense discussion was the role played by the water and its quality. While Kaerger ascribed great significance to the role played by impure water, the Naval Medical Report referred to the slow increase in the number of cases and concluded that impure water could not have been the cause of the typhus.[63]

A completely different and highly controversial explanation for the typhus epidemic was advanced in 1905 by Emil Steudel, a medical officer in the service of the Imperial Colonial Office. Addressing an audience at the Colonial Congress, he provided a highly detailed reconstruction of the march route taken by the naval expeditionary corps which subsequently succumbed to the epidemic. Landing in Swakopmund on 9 February, the troop then embarked on a march to the eastern border of the protectorate. Coming into contact with a group of Herero on the return route, eighty-seven members of the 300-strong group suddenly fell ill at the end of April. Steudel followed this narrative with a controversial analysis: the drinking water taken from the springs at Onjatu must have been infected with the typhus pathogen. As the eastern Herero had used the very same watering holes, it was far from improbable that the soldiers had acquired the infection from the spring.[64] Steudel proceeded to assemble a chain of evidence, which he maintained proved the guilt of the Herero for the outbreak of the epidemic. Such assertions, underpinned with medical "facts," represent a widespread consensus shared by a number of medical officers, soldiers, and the colonially interested. The "theory of Herero guilt" provided not only a neat explanation for the genesis of the infectious disease but also a further justification for the employment of excessive violence against the Herero and the Nama. Such a belief was only contradicted by publication in 1920 of the second part of the Medical Report for German South-West Africa. In contradicting this theory so vehemently, the report's publication underlined the extent to which the theory had achieved acceptance.

As part of the debate on current colonial policy and the search for the causes of the epidemic, the Protection Forces High Command (which survived the loss of the colonies and continued until 1920) sought to defend the German colonial record amid a much-changed political atmosphere: "Placing the events of 1904 in their context, it becomes clear that the agent of the subsequent typhus epidemic was most likely not carried dormant by the soldiers of the Protection Force from a third location or transmitted by the native rebels, but that the germs were endemic in the colony. As a result, we need focus only on the causes of its epidemic transmission."[65]

The conception of Herero responsibility for the typhus epidemic reinforced the widespread conception that although the "most valuable living property in economic terms," they also represented a "permanent risk" to

European health.[66] Thus health concerns provided an extra justification for the extreme violence meted out to the native population. Nevertheless, as the example of VD shows, levels of troop illness could not be solved entirely through the exercise of violence against the native population.

Venereal Disease

For medical officers, sexually transmitted disease was an unavoidable component of all warfare: "The high incidence of venereal disease during the campaign provides no surprise to those accustomed to the history of the old Protection Force and with any experience of war. Experience has shown that war and venereal disease have a long and close history of association."[67] Nevertheless, the number of cases of sexually transmitted diseases registered among the German troops in the second half of the war in German South-West Africa was almost as high as the figures for the East-Asian Expeditionary Force and the occupation brigade and almost six times as high as the figures for the Prussian army as a whole.[68] Broken down into various strains of VD, consideration of all the colonial wars produces a similar picture, with the number of gonorrhea infections exceeding those of chancre and syphilis.

The majority of cases of VD registered among the naval units deployed in China were located in Peking. The highest number of new cases was recorded in January 1901, following from infections contracted in the weeks immediately after Christmas. The East Asian Expeditionary Corps, in contrast, registered a successive increase in such infections between July 1900 and March 1901. The Medical Report for East Asia explains this development with the "increasing familiarity among the troops with the Chinese establishments."[69]

The most common sites of infection among the German troops in German South-West Africa were the various stations in the communication zone. Although the difference in infection exhibited between the field troops (1,770 infections) and those in the communication zone (1,559 cases) remained relatively low, the rate of infection among the fighting troops (53.4 percent) was almost double that of their comrades in the communication zone (22.7 percent).[70] The authors of the Medical Report sought an explanation for this situation in the restricted opportunities for sexual intercourse presented to the frontline troops and the resulting lack of discrimination in their choice of sexual partner. The greater opportunities for such relations available to all other troops, on the other hand, enabled them to exercise greater care in their choosing healthy female partners.

In German East Africa, the reports maintained that the sexually transmitted diseases contracted by the naval units were found almost exclusively among the detachments stationed in larger settlements. The list was headed by the units in Muansa, where the twelve recorded cases represented a third of the total unit. The statistical danger of infection was also higher in locations on caravan routes in which a large number of prostitutes plied their trade.[71] The reasons for the high number of cases of VD were clear. For the German colonial soldiers, subject to a system of rigorous organization, unprotected sexual intercourse with native women was a regular feature of life. This was compounded by high levels of infection with VD among the native female population. Contraception was not widely practiced and in the absence of official pressure or a campaign of education to this end, the efforts of medical officers to contain the spread of VD remained necessarily ineffective. Drastic suggestions to this end were made by Major (med.) Karl Herhold, who demanded not only that the men be housed exclusively in barracks and subject to a curfew after six or seven o'clock in the evening, but that those failing to report an infection or contracting an infection, even after receiving express and repeated instructions to the contrary, be subject to stiff penalties.[72] Such a level of regimentation remained unrealistic, as the military administration feared that the threat of punishment would result only in the widespread concealment of infections and a deterioration of the existing situation.

A further factor conditioning the spread of sexually transmitted disease in German South-West Africa was the incidence of rape and sexual assault committed against the female population of the internment camps set up during the course of the war. The Medical Reports established a clear correlation between the camps, their rising population and the increasing number of infections.[73] A further document drafted in 1907 recorded that a daily average of sixty riders were examined for signs of VD.[74]

Sexually transmitted diseases involved a much longer period of treatment and recuperation compared with that for other conditions. Those patients requiring up to eight weeks of medical care were generally returned to Germany. In 1907, 165 patients were returned to the metropole for such treatment, a figure representing 31 percent of total patient transports. Soldiers suffering complicated cases of VD were invalided out of service and could claim a pension. Whatever the outcome, in addition to reducing the fighting power of the German colonial fighting force, the incidence of sexually trans-mitted disease burdened the exchequer with additional costs involved in the dispatch of replacements and the provision of medical care and wel-fare support. This explains the considerable interest exhibited in govern-ment and military circles in reducing the incidence and spread of such infections.

The military medical authorities in German South-West Africa formu-lated a three-step plan to prevent the spread of VD during the Herero and Nama War. Following the establishment of a comprehensive system of health provision and education, the authorities launched a campaign to pro-mote the use of personal prophylaxis and other forms of prevention among the soldiers. This was followed by the examination of female Africans for symptoms of illness. Those found to be infected were to be separated from the soldiers. In addition to oral instructions, a range of information leaflets regarding contraceptive practices were displayed in the mess halls as standard. These campaigns registered little success. Preventative treatment from each naval surgeon and campaigns of information from the ship's commander had long represented standard practice in the navy since 1891.[75] Before landing, all naval personnel were issued a "health package" containing Vaseline, soap, and a gauze swab containing an alcoholic solution packed in waterproof paper. Records for the Chinese campaign show that at least the Marine Infantry were provided with such a package.

By the end of 1904, official cognizance of the increased incidence of VD during the war against the Herero and the Nama led to the launch of a strict program to combat its spread. Prompted by an order from the Medical Of-fice, a preventative campaign was launched, comprising a number of mea-sures including washing with a sublimate solution tested by the navy and a ureteric injection of a 1 percent luncar caustic solution. In addition, the troops were presented with large quantities of condoms and disinfectants to be ap-plied after intercourse.[76] However, not all of the products provided protec-tion against the complete range of sexually transmitted diseases to which the soldiers were exposed, and those providing more comprehensive protection were available in only small quantities. The situation in German East Africa was much worse, where products for prevention and treatment were in short supply.[77]

Native women suffering from VD were subject to measures of a far more serious nature, the extent of which was initially restricted to local brothel-based prostitutes, who were examined by government or military medical officers. In the larger Chinese cities, military officials attempted to concentrate sex workers in the registered brothels, and hired Chinese detectives to hunt down those providing unofficial services.[78] Prostitutes found to be carriers of sexually transmitted diseases, or even suspected of such, were separated wherever possible. In Baoding, a Franco-German clinic provided a capacity of up to twelve women, who were treated by the doctors of the nation responsible for transferring them to the clinic.[79] Despite such an intricate system of treatment and control, it soon proved very difficult to find any healthy prostitutes. Faced with such a situation and shrinking from forced prostitution, of which there are no documented cases, the military authorities saw no choice other than to provide warnings of the situation and perform examinations every fourteen days.[80] The medical committee in Peking reached the conclusion that without taking the—impossible—step of controlling every prostitute, the measures to be taken against the spread of sexually transmitted diseases could never be fully effective.[81]

In German South-West Africa, the military authorities established brothels at every significant point in the communication zone. These establishments included a number of white Boer and German prostitutes; the Medical Report for German South-West Africa claimed that the women were subjected to regular health checks.[82] Nevertheless, the existence of such institutions could not entirely prevent the incidence of sexual relations between German soldiers and the so-called free black women. Reacting to this situation, the military authorities included infected black women in obligatory health checks. Those testing positive for VD were interned in the native hospitals of the concentration camps. In January 1906, the hospital in Windhoek was extended by the addition of twenty round huts, each with a capacity for five such women.[83] It was also general practice to test prisoners (including males) every fourteen days for sexually transmitted diseases; those testing positive were separated. Imprecise and subject to considerable variation, the official figures for the number of VD sufferers incarcerated in Windhoek—both prisoners of war and native women—ranged between 350 (mid-1906) and 800 (1905–1906). The majority of sufferers were women; all were transferred to the natives' hospital.[84]

As the Medical Report for German South-West Africa documents, one insight gained by medical officers was the "natives represent an exceptionally important factor for the health of the white military and civil population."[85] The military establishment was haunted by the fear that the transmission of ill health could seriously compromise the military efficiency of the troops, and result in the loss of the colony. Such fears were even used by von Trotha in his attempt to justify the issue of his so-called proclamation of destruction, arguing that the already weakened military should not be allowed to be infected by "ill Herero women."[86] The illnesses of the native population were widely viewed as constituting a "natural front" and as such, posed a particular danger to the white population. The Herero and Nama prisoners, weakened by the long years of war and in a "poor physical state,"[87] were viewed as either ill or the carriers of illness and were to be incarcerated indefinitely. The nature of the danger posed to German soldiers by the women infected with VD meant that they too were subject to incarceration. They were interned in quarantine, and these areas were marked off by an additional Dornkraal.

Originally established for prisoners of war, the camp hospitals were now used to segregate the native women infected with a range of sexually transmitted diseases. In short: illness led to incarceration in the same pitiful conditions as those of the rebels. Originally intended to separate ill and healthy prisoners, black and white, such forms of segregation ultimately proved impossible to enforce. As the Medical Report stated, "Their [the prisoners'] segregation not only served the purpose of military control, but was necessitated above all by reasons of health: the need to keep them from coming into contact with military and civil personnel and thus prevent the transmission of disease. As a result, entry to the prison camps was forbidden. This requirement could hardly be maintained, as it was necessary to take prisoners from the Kraal to perform acts of work outside."[88]

The report omitted the significant detail that guards, thorns, barbed wire, and the admonitions of their commanding officers did not prevent the German soldiers from entering the prison camps to assault their female inmates.[89] The women were unable to protect themselves; the men involved were not punished.

The project to intern women in order to stop the spread of sexually transmitted diseases eventually proved a failure. Abandoned in 1906, its suspension was not the result of humanitarian concern. Although missionaries protested against the illegality of the practice, no attention was accorded to the humiliation of the women involved, despite the efforts of local elders to explain how difficult it was for them to subject themselves to intimate examination by a white man.[90] This view was not shared by the Medical Corps; Captain (med.) Schelle countered this point: "Native women are not characterized by any particular level of shame."[91] The program was ended for the simple reason of its failure in view of the sheer size and fluctuating numbers of the nomadic native population.

With the "native's hospitals" unable to handle and treat the large number of VD cases among the native population following the end of the war, the government sought coercive alternatives. One such alternative was the methods of Major (med.) Hans Weindel. Accorded responsibility for treating infected women in Grootfontein during the Herero and Nama War, he marked them with a large earring made of zinc wiring, which was riveted and removed only after their convalescence. It was thought that these earrings, easily identifiable in the dark, would not be removed without authority if to do so were to be subject to considerable sanction.[92] A similar procedure was considered in 1908 for women who, although infected with a sexually transmitted disease, were prevented by hospital overcrowding from receiving in-patient care. Nevertheless, medical officers active in the colony began to accept that the spread of VD was not to be halted by excluding native women, but required their active participation within a wider scheme of prevention. As a result, the medical officers began to disseminate information regarding sexual prophylactics among the native population.[93]

The soldiers responsible for interning women in the prison camps set up during the Herero and Nama War—where they were registered, isolated, and in all probability raped—were able to choose whether to pursue intercourse with the women and whether to take contraceptive precautions. The rape of the Herero and Nama women transformed these locations from prisoner of war camps (a classification that many historians revised only recently) to locations of violence directed specifically against nominally free women. With the abandonment in 1906 of the policy of coercion, the camps functioned purely as prisoner of war camps. The round huts previously used to intern the infected women were now used to quarter those suffering from pox and scurvy. The attempt to solve the VD problem with coercive means had failed.

Numbers and Conclusions

The contributions to the campaign by both the army and the navy medical services are recorded in the Medical Reports produced by each service for every war.[94] These publications document the overwhelming attention accorded by the medical officers to firearms injuries sustained as a result of both enemy action and accident. This was followed by the care accorded to sufferers of gastric conditions as well as a range of illnesses typical to a colonial theater such as typhus, dysentery, malaria, heatstroke, VD, foot sores, bruises, and sprains.

In the aftermath of the Boxer War, the German military medical authorities referred to the state of health exhibited by the East-Asian Expeditionary Corps as "fair." In 1900–1901, the medical services attached to the force of 18,360 registered the treatment of 19,583 persons, of whom half were confined to the hospital.[95] Some 20 percent of those hospitalized had suffered mechanical injuries (a figure including gunshot wounds); a similar figure was recorded for those suffering from complaints of the digestive system. Fourteen percent presented problems with their respiratory organs and VD, respectively, while the figures for those treated for dysentery and typhus stood at 6 and 3 percent, respectively.[96] Of the 201 deaths registered by the expeditionary corps (itself representing only 1.1 percent of the German troop strength), 133 were the victims of disease, of whom seventy had died from typhus. Three fatalities were the result of suicide; sixty-five had fallen victim to "accident," a euphemism also covering those killed in action.[97] Six hundred eighty-nine persons had been recorded as invalids by September 1904, representing 3.8 percent of the total strength of the force. The 3,690-strong naval expeditionary corps deployed in the conflict registered 117 deaths (3.2 percent), of which fifty-two (1.4 percent) followed from an infectious disease.[98] Eighty-eight men (2.5 percent) were invalided out of the service. While the I and II Sea Battalions, the Field Battery, and the Pioneer Company recorded only a handful of wounded, those naval personnel participating in the Seymour expedition and the III Sea Battalion from Qingdao registered a considerably higher level of dead, wounded, and invalidity.[99]

Of the 17,856 soldiers dispatched to German South-West Africa between January 1904 and March 1907, 1,613 died. Eighty-eight of those deaths had resulted from combat or accidents. This figure is dwarfed by the 725 fatalities caused by illness.[100] The loss of 450 men in the course of the typhus epidemic—which reached its high point in December 1904—is to be compared against a total number of 8,195 soldiers deployed in the conflict at this point. The year 1904 alone saw the death of 1,038 men. Four hundred twelve died of illness, the majority from typhus, while the rest died in action, from wounds, or through accidents or were recorded as missing. By 1908, 7,831 men were rendered invalid, over 90 percent of whom were classed as unfit for active and tropical service; only some 10 percent were rendered unfit for active service.[101]

The 839 men of the naval expeditionary corps dispatched to German South-West Africa and active between January 1904 and April 1905 registered a total of 866 cases of illness, of which almost a third involved typhus, enteritis, and malaria.[102] Of the ninety-two fatalities (11 percent of the total strength of the force), forty-seven (5.6 per cent) died in battle and forty-two from illness (5 per cent). Thirty-nine of these deaths were from typhus. One hundred thirty soldiers were returned to Germany for treatment, of whom thirty-two (4.8 percent) were accorded invalid status.[103] Compared with the situation in German South-West Africa, the medical services in German East Africa were faced with a higher rate of illness. The short period between August 1905 and April 1906 saw the 402-strong naval expeditionary corps dispatched to the protectorate present a surprising 512 cases of illness, representing a rate of 127.4 percent. Four hundred seventy-eight patients achieved a full recovery and returned to service. Three hundred twenty-one cases were caused by an infection: 287 of malaria and seventeen of dysentery. Nine soldiers died in battle, one suffered an accident, and seven died of illness—three cases of malaria, three cases of dysentery, and one of pyohemia.[104] In contrast to such detailed records for the German troops, the information regarding the East African Protection Force and other black soldiers is sparse.

Analysis of the Medical Reports compiled for the German colonial wars show that with the total number of internal infections exceeding the number of war wounds, the threat posed to the German colonial soldiers by illness (primarily gastric infections, abdominal typhus, and dysentery) was greater than that posed by the enemy (see Table 8.1). As one anonymous commentator put it, "Almost worse than enemy bullets are the typhus, malaria and scurvy [currently] decimating the rows of German soldiers"[105] In China and German South-West Africa, the ratio between deaths from enemy action and deaths from illness reached 1:1. Far from anomalous, this situation was reproduced across a range of colonial conflicts conducted by Germany's colonial competitors; indeed, some conflicts even witnessed more deaths from illness than enemy action.[106] Such figures would seem to indicate that the German medical service was working at an exceptionally high level of efficiency.

In statistical terms, the number of cases of illness presented to this hardworking service exceeded the nominal troop strengths, with many soldiers requiring repeated treatment. An indication of the serious nature of the illnesses suffered by the German soldiers was the length of the average period of medical care that they required. Long periods of convalescence, spent in the war zone, in Germany, and during the Chinese campaign, in Japan, also

Table 8.1. Illnesses and injuries in the three German colonial wars.

	East Asia		GSWA		GEA
	Exped. corps	Navy and Mar. Infantry	Exped. corps	Naval exped. corps	Naval exped. corps
Period	July 1900–June 1901	October 1900–September 1901	January 1904–March 1907	January 1904–October 1905	August 1905–April 1906
Troop strength*	18,360	3,690	17,856	839	402
No. of illnesses	19,583	4,288	47,426	866	512
In-patient treatment	8,171				
Average length of treatment (days)		27.3	25.6	27.1	10.3
Deaths	201	117	1,613	92	9
From illness	133	52	725	45	7
Accidents and battle casualties	65		888	47	2
Suicide	3		27		
Illnesses					
Injuries	3,434	135	1,961	66	17
Gastrointestinal	3,523	895	5,429	245	71
Coronary illnesses	2,590	215	4,552	30	5
Respiratory problems	2,590	215	1,351	19	12
VD	2,573	413	3,329	58	29
Dysentery	1,028	229	1,919	4	17
Typhus	564	319	4,709	229	
Malaria	81	36	1,512	104	287
Scurvy	15		893	5	
TB	18		29		
Invalided from service	689**	88	7,381***	38	2****

Source: Compiled from the Military Medical Reports.

* Average of the nominal strengths; ** to 9/30/1904; *** to 9/30/1908; **** only NCOs.

necessitated the dispatch of a high number of replacements. Many of those returned to the metropole for medical attention were later accorded varying degrees of invalidity support. The colonial wars were expensive therefore not only in their conduct but also in terms of their subsequent costs.

The close analysis of the Medical Reports presented here reveals the varied nature of the impact of illness and disease on the various military units deployed in the three colonial conflicts and in turn the course and conduct of each war. This permits a number of conclusions. The naval expeditionary corps deployed in each campaign suffered the greatest loss through illness and casualties throughout the three colonial wars. Death resulted from disease and enemy action in equal measure. The explanation for the relatively high level of casualties and illness is to be found in the nature of training and equipment accorded to the naval personnel, which failed to prepare them for the specific demands of land warfare. Reaching the war zone ahead of the main body of troops meant that their arrival came at a time in which a functioning medical infrastructure was still under construction.

The great difficulties presented by the environment of German South-West Africa also explain the high rates of death and illness that this conflict produced. Indeed, this war generated a death rate eight times that of German losses in the Boxer War and rates of illness that are almost double that of the Chinese campaign. Half of all deaths suffered in German South-West Africa were the result of infectious diseases, while in China the figure is a quarter. Moreover, the high rates of mortality in the Herero and Nama War cannot be explained by reference to its long duration: 1,038 soldiers had died from various diseases during the first year of the war alone. This finding would indicate that the military medical service—at least in German South-West Africa—was not characterized by particular efficiency.

In contrast, despite the conspicuously high levels of illness presented by the German servicemen deployed in the Maji Maji War, the corresponding death rates remained extremely low. Malaria was the dominant tropical disease in German East Africa and China, and could be prevented by the use of quinine and the destruction of the breeding grounds of anopheles. Nevertheless, the repeated incidence of fever necessitated repeated treatment.

Analysis of the illnesses and injuries suffered by the German armed forces within the scope of the three major German colonial wars conducted at the beginning of the twentieth century reveals a number of common characteristics: the use of military medicine for scientific ends; the use of repeated programs of health instruction to maintain the fighting potential of the troops; problems with alcohol and morphine abuse and nervous conditions; and finally, the greater prevalence of disease-related fatalities in comparison with battlefield death. Contrasting with such convergences, the war in German South-West Africa assumes an exceptional position within this analysis following the collapse of the military medical service during the course of 1904–1905. The actual and relative level of illness and the mortality rate of the German soldiers in this theater resulted from the spread of typhus. As this disease put whole units out of action, it was often impossible to organize replacements. The excessive demands placed on the soldiers combined with the apparently ceaseless depletion of both their number and the medical personnel served to generate a pervading sense of menace. Such experiences strengthened racial interpretations of war, which sought to place the guilt for the typhus epidemic squarely at the door of the Herero.

The influence of illness on the conduct of the war in German South-West Africa was not restricted to that suffered by its German participants—at least during the Nama campaign. The illnesses suffered by the native population also became a part of the conduct of the war. The diagnosis of VD was used to justify the internment of so-called free African women amid conditions as abject and lethal as those endured by the prisoners of war. For both sides in the Herero and Nama War, disease and illness exercised a central influence on the outcome and experience of the war.

CHAPTER 9

Reaction from the
Foreign Powers

THE COURSE assumed by German military action in her colonial possessions was also influenced by the reaction of the major powers. The international discussion of warfare and especially colonial warfare concentrated to a great extent on the conception of civilization and the "civilizing mission" of the Great Powers. Wars fought against foreign cultures in tropical colonies were not viewed as part of the exchanges within the civilized world, but were rather conceived of as part of a wider struggle between civilization and barbarity. Colonial expansion brought the agents of "civilization" into contact with an uncivilized—and by extension cruel—enemy, to be defeated at all costs. The methods chosen with which to conduct this struggle were accorded no specific importance. This disregard for ethical principles eventually led to the advancement of a justification for extreme brutality. Ensuring quick victory and thus reducing the extent of bloodshed, this course of action was cast as the most humane. The colonizing powers developed a dichotomous (and self-serving) pattern of thinking: civilization versus violence; humanity versus brutality; culture versus nature; modernity versus backwardness; conventional war versus irregular war. Dealing in such categories, the colonial powers contrasted their own "progressive" constructive violence with the "primitive" and purely destructive violence of their colonial opponents. That the German conduct of their major colonial wars should be viewed as merely part of a wider framework of action is demonstrated by the international reception of and comment on German conduct in the Boxer War and both African wars by the British, French, and American military. Similarly, the German evaluation of the South African War confirms the joint nature of the European approach to colonial warfare. Diverging opinions within this international discourse developed only after the First World War had encouraged new perspectives on violence.

The Boxer War as an International Military Display

The Boxer War accorded its participants the unique opportunity to observe the martial performance of the other belligerent nations, enabling comparison with their own military establishment. The military value of each army was measured by the efficiency of its structure, organization, equipment, arms, and impact. Of further interest in the contemporary assessments of each army were the relations between officers and the ranks and the nature of relations within the officer corps and the units themselves. In establishing an unofficial military league table, the military observers of the various nations hoped to reach conclusions regarding the international competitiveness of their own armies. Each military establishment was haunted by the constant fear of a loss of prestige. On the positive side, they hoped to use the war as a learning experience from which to draw lessons and improve their own performance. Firsthand observation of their current allies also enabled them to evaluate potential future enemies. Such insights were gleaned from simple observation of military routine but also from the deployment of liaison officers.[1]

Colonel J. M. Grierson, the author of a considerable number of British reports focusing on the military capabilities of other nations, also made detailed written observations of the German units involved in crushing the Boxer revolt. The central theme of his reports centered on the inexperience of the German troops in colonial campaigns. Indeed, it seemed that they relied on British officers as their chief source of information on warfare in a foreign environment and to whom they often turned for advice. "The Germans are always asking questions and making notes, and our transport, our commissariat, our equipment, our system of recruiting and training native troops, and in general our methods of warfare are of great and constant interest to German officers."[2] Speaking of the troops themselves, he reported that they demonstrated an exceptionally high level of training and morale, which was, however, unable to compensate for inexperience and youth. Few of the German soldiers were over the age of twenty-two, and the majority of them had never before ventured out of the provinces of their birth. Moreover, having never learned how to protect their health and having little to learn from their non-commissioned officers or officers, many succumbed to illness.

Grierson also observed conspicuous levels of indiscipline. "There seems to be no idea of quietness after 'lights out' among them, indeed lights do not go out and singing in beery tones continues frequently late into the night, even at Army Headquarters."[3] Sentries were nervous and exhibited a proclivity to open fire every time they heard or saw something move, be they cats, dogs, or people. Soldiers of the British army would come before a drum-head court-martial for such behavior. German troops were also very keen on plundering, an activity to which they referred as "requisitioning," and handled the local population with extreme cruelty. Grierson located the reason for this behavior in their inexperience. After thirty years of peace since Sedan, the army was now eager to "taste its own share of blood." The army High Command even ordered expeditions as a pretext for action: "Most Chinamen are 'Boxers,' and villages are shelled, 'stormed' and then fined and subject to requisitioning on the most slender grounds. I can quite appreciate and understand the motive, but from a military-political point of view I cannot approve the action."[4]

Grierson credited the German soldiers with a good marching order, yet criticized the officers for riding off together and leaving their men to catch up on foot. Nevertheless, the good marching discipline and military drill exhibited by the German troops led him to revise his initial judgment that such hastily assembled units would be unable to reach any level of internal cohesion. He decided that the common experience of the long journey to China was the vital ingredient in forming their integrated esprit de corps.

Grierson asserted that the discipline of the German soldiers exhibited during exercises remained unmatched among the allies. While the American units exhibited a high level of physical fitness, their drill was found to be wanting. However, Grierson continued in his criticisms, identifying considerable organizational shortcomings in the German units. Transport carts collapsed, and a number of the horses were both too young and insufficiently trained. He concluded that the high levels of illness exhibited by German soldiers were rooted in poor nutrition: the soldiers consumed too little meat, and too much bread and vegetables. The German depot system was highly inefficient and provisions were not distributed regularly.

Despite a greater natural interest in Japan and Great Britain with whom they were confronted in the Pacific theater, American observers also maintained a close interest in the German Marine Infantry, which arrived in

Peking at the end of August 1900.[5] It was noticed on the American side that lacking in tents, German quartermasters were forced to rely on quartering their men with the local population. There were sufficient Chinese houses for this purpose, but such close contact with the native population exposed the billeted troops to a far higher risk of infection. Officers rode out in advance of the main body of the German force, marking out the houses for their men and animals. Although not mentioned explicitly in the American reports, this meant that of all the nations in the international force, it was the German military with which the Chinese civil population made the closest of contacts and from whom they necessarily had the most to fear in terms of losses of life and property.

The American reports also singled out the excellent quality of German marching order. German officers were described as typically well mannered, smart, clean, polite, and assiduous. Many spoke a number of languages. Nevertheless, there were a number of complaints in Tianjin pertaining to their highly inconsiderate and markedly crude behavior. Discipline in the ranks had been excellent in Peking, and they demonstrated respect toward foreign officers. The German soldier appeared to be obedient toward his superior, who maintained discipline at all times. This contrasted, however, with the widespread and illegal habit among the ranks of requisitioning, which together with other criminal offenses remained unpunished.

The British and American reports concurred in their assessment that the German troops displayed a marked "hardness" in their dealings with the Chinese population. "Hard" was merely a euphemism for "ruthless," "cruel," or "brutal." British reports of the cases of plunder and rape committed by members of the French and Italian units were set into context by the remarks that such actions had been committed by all the nations involved in the international expeditionary corps.[6] The observers found it impossible to ascertain which nation had been the most violent, and no clear criteria existed with which to rank the excesses of the nations involved. Such evaluations rested on hearsay, official reports, and anecdote. Highly subjective in nature, such sources reflected the personal leanings of the individual involved and often sought to excuse, hide, or emphasize and single out certain patterns of behavior. While reflecting on the cruelty of other nations, the observers consistently ignored its recipients, the Chinese. One noteworthy exception was presented by the diary of the Punjabi infantryman Gadhadar Singh which describes the atrocities allegedly committed against the Chinese population in striking detail. Identifying clear parallels between China and India, this provides evidence of an awareness of the common Asian bonds uniting the Chinese and Indians.[7]

Indeed, far from reflecting a clear appraisal of the situation presented, the reports of the various intervention powers were based on prejudices developed before arrival in China and which drew on specific preconceptions and national stereotypes. Arnold von Lequis, an officer in a German pioneer battalion, regarded "the English" as "reserved [and] closest to us in our attitudes thanks to our common Germanic ancestry." The Sikhs were described as a "proud warrior caste [who] performed their service with precision." His view of "the French" was far less positive; he regarded them as "superficial" in nature and whose units, despite displaying a "pronounced adroitness," were acutely lacking in discipline. Moreover, he ascribed to them a "coarse attitude towards the Chinese [and a] pronounced carnality."[8]

American military observers regarded their British counterparts as "experienced campaigners," and in every way exemplary. One practice advanced as evidence of their greater experience was their use of troop positions and markings to give symbolic expression to their capture of occupied territory and to delimit it against the territories of other nations. The British were always very quick to hoist flags on buildings, vehicles, and other objects. They were also supremely skilled at finding provisions and valuables,[9] and they admired the facility of a number of British officers in a range of native languages. The observers were also impressed by the respectful tone of communication between British officers and Muslim troops, who themselves drank no alcohol and cared well for their weapons, horses, and equipment. In contrast, the Americans harbored little love for the Russian contingent; this is made clear in an American's remark that the Russians never passed on exact information or ever presented themselves for closer inspection.[10]

The British drew up a "sympathy league table" reflecting their attitude to the various foreign military contingents, resembling closely those drawn up in the colonies to rank the local ethnicities in order of preference. Topped by the German and American contingent, the list was followed by the French, Austrians, and Italians; the Russians came last. Grierson viewed the French units as backward in terms of their demeanor, appearance, efficiency, and discipline. Their problems with drill manifested themselves in the field, where they were unable to maintain formation.[11] The Italians, so he opined, were the worst of the European troops and the dirtiest that he had ever seen. Entirely lacking in discipline, their presence was accompanied by a constant stream of complaints about plundering and other crimes. He was unable to proffer a judgment on their fighting prowess, but knew that the Germans held a low opinion of them in this respect.[12] While the Italians were widely viewed as the pariahs of the international military force, the Russians—not considered as real Europeans—were met with palpable mistrust. For the Americans and British, the real discovery of the Boxer War was the Japanese. Described in American reports as "a most valuable ally and a most formidable enemy,"[13] many of the characteristics identified in the reports— steely combatants with indifference for the lives of their own soldiers— would be echoed by observers sent to the Russo-Japanese War four years later. European military observers in the Boxer War were struck by the incomprehension of Japanese military commanders of the need to limit casualties.[14]

Despite the influence of prejudice and stereotype already noted, the observers also recorded a number of experiences that contradicted conventional modes of Western European or North American understanding. For instance, while reflecting on typical "Russian cruelty," a British officer was unable to find any confirmation of his beliefs in his dealings with Russian troops.[15] An American military journal even went as far as to focus on the levels of solidarity and fraternization exhibited between soldiers of the "irreconcilable enemies" France and Germany.[16] A French infantryman wrote in his diary, "Who of us would have believed a year ago that we would eat at the same table with the Germans and even raise our glasses together?" In the same breath, he pointed out that this situation was exceptional: "something approaching friendship began to develop between the Germans and French."[17] The new, positive experiences were not able to break down traditional stereotypes. Rather the soldiers saw that the common threat to Western civilization posed by the Boxers and the special nature of the war in East Asia created extraordinary circumstances.

Ludwig von Estorff and the South African War

The South African War (1899–1902)[18] and war in German South-West Africa displayed some striking parallels, and German colonial officers were keen to observe the conduct and course of the South African War, so as to learn lessons applicable to their own profession. Both conflicts were conducted a considerable distance from the imperial metropole, in areas with an almost identical climate and topology. The British and German forces dispatched to fight the two wars were poorly organized and were confronted by considerable problems of a technical and logistical nature. The 460,000 British soldiers dispatched to South Africa faced a Boer force of 35,000.[19] Both wars descended into a guerilla insurgency and in both cases the imperial forces employed concentration camps. The British interned predominantly women and children: over 26,000 prisoners died in approximately eighty camps.

Despite such similarities, the two conflicts differed in one important regard: the South African War saw white troops pitted against white troops, both of which were equipped with machine guns, artillery, and other modern weaponry. Both warring parties were convinced of the "superiority of the white race," for which reason the British decided against the deployment of Indian troops. Nevertheless, both sides made limited use of African auxiliaries, whom they employed not just as scouts or messengers but also as fighting troops. Both sides ignored established ethical standards in the treatment of the African populations. Racial considerations manifested themselves clearly in the different treatment meted out to white and black prisoners of war. Moreover, African refugees were held apart from their white counterparts, where they suffered even worse conditions and higher death rates—up to 14,000 died.[20] Whereas the suffering of the Boer civilians in British camps (under military administration until November 1901) provoked considerable outcry among the British public, the conditions in the "black" camps was hardly registered—a fact that is sometimes overlooked.[21] The South African War was "a conflict scored by its African context, thinly disguised as a crisis solely affecting Europeans."[22]

Some 300 to 400 war reporters covered the events of the Boer War, including such illustrious figures as Winston Churchill, Arthur Conan Doyle, Edgar Wallace, and Rudyard Kipling. The high level of media interest was matched by an indeterminate number of war observers, the majority of whom were professional army officers; their numbers included the German officer Ludwig von Estorff. After serving in the South-West African Protection Force in 1894, he was posted in 1899 to the General Staff in Berlin, from where he was seconded to observe the proceedings in South Africa. Securing a posting as German military attaché to South Africa upon the outbreak of the war, he sought out Horatio Kitchener in the British military headquarters in Pretoria in 1901 to request permission to travel to the front as an observer. Despite permission being granted, he did not witness a single battle throughout the course of the war. Nevertheless, extensive travel with British columns in search of Boer forces gave him a valuable insight into the conduct of guerilla warfare, an experience that he recorded in two books, one published during the conflict and another decades later.[23]

Writing in his first book (published in 1901), von Estorff referred to the guerilla war, despite the successes that it could bring, as "a feeble form of warfare, at variance with the true nature of war."[24] He conceded that guerilla tactics could not exercise a "decisive influence" on the further course of the war, and that the continuous and replenishable "supply of English soldiers and materiel"[25] meant it was doomed to failure. Masking the British scorched earth policy of destroying farms, property, and livestock with this euphemism, he failed to mention the British concentration camps and their treatment of prisoners of war.

Only his memoirs included any reference to his visit to a concentration camp, made together with the German consul general von Lindequist (later to become governor of German South-West Africa). The wives and children of Boer farmers kept prisoner in these camps were housed in tents. Accustomed as they were to the extensive freedoms afforded by country life, they suffered by day from the restrictions placed on their movement. Denied fuel for any fires, they were unable to keep warm at night. Given such conditions, the devastating levels of illness that resulted should have come as no surprise.[26] He differentiated clearly between strategic cruelty that contributed to victory and superfluous cruelty. In his judgment, the cruelty toward and neglect of women and children were just as futile as they were abominable.[27] The destruction of Boer farms, on the other hand, met with his approval. He averred that despite the "considerable successes of the Boer guerilla tactics . . . the cause of the Boers" was doomed even though "many of their fighters had developed into excellent soldiers." He predicted "one more year of resistance before the whole thing was finished."[28]

We can be sure that von Estorff had seen the concentration camps. Whether he recommended emulating such tactics in German South-West Africa (in either reports or informal consultations) cannot be established. Neither the German General Staff nor military authors displayed any interest in the camps or the treatment meted out to their inmates, and they confined themselves instead to purely tactical discussions of a number of issues arising from the strongly defensive Boer tactics. These tactics had demonstrated the near-inability of the British troops to proceed unprotected across open territory while subject to the murderous bombardment of modern weaponry. The General Staff concluded that such campaigns required more careful use of natural cover, greater caution when introducing supporting troops, and the avoidance of senseless mass attacks on well-defended positions.[29]

Seeking to learn the lessons of the South African War, in 1903 the German General Staff focused carefully on improving the tactics of attack. The measures designed to effect this—increasing troop mobility, establishing techniques to storm fortified positions, and the creation of a strong artillery corps—were general changes not specific to the needs of colonial warfare.[30] The General Staff looked to apply the "lessons" learned from both the South African and the Russo-Japanese wars (both conducted in an extra-European theater) to European warfare. The guerilla tactics that had incurred von Estorff's disdain were not accorded any attention. The sources reveal a general consensus among the military hierarchy that the guerilla techniques of the colonial theater could not be transferred to Europe, and much literature was generated to make this point. One example of this output was the article written by the army officer Colmar von der Goltz for the *Deutsche Revue*. Focusing on the South African War, he wrote that conditions prevalent in what he termed the "Western theater" prevented the application of the guerilla tactics of disrupting the lines of communication and unsettling the troops deployed in the rear lines. Such tactics required vast, open, unsettled areas affording plenty of areas in which a guerilla force could retreat. Moreover, he also argued such tactics could only be employed against an immobile opponent.[31] Nevertheless, he did concede that guerilla tactics could "prove efficacious in wars in Germany's eastern territories, should they become of long duration."[32] In doing so, he was in effect referring to wars—as in a colonial war—in which the conventional rules of European warfare could possibly require modification.

The German analysis of the South African War does not appear to have exercised any impact on the doctrines of German colonial warfare. It did not result in any alteration to the training of the Protection Forces, nor did it lead to the introduction of any new military doctrines or practices. Despite considerable sympathy for the Boers and their cause, German military planners regarded the tactics that they had adopted as both inappropriate and cumbersome and entirely devoid of significance for the future. It would seem that they shared the conclusions reached by von Estorff: that sustained military investment would defeat any insurgency.

British Information Networks and Military Reports

For the British, whose colonial possessions shared a long common border with the German protectorates of South-West Africa and East Africa, the major German colonial wars in Africa began not with the Herero rising of 1904, but with the uprising of the Bondelzwarts in the fall of 1903. "The campaign in South-West Africa from 25th October, 1903 to 8th February, 1907, involved 295 actions, of which 88 were against the Hereros and 207 against the Hottentots."[33] This special periodization followed by the British resulted from the immediate proximity of the Bondelzwart uprising to South Africa and the threat that it posed to ethnic peace in the four self-governing colonies. The contingencies of the local situation engendered an ambivalent response from the Colonial Office and the War Office to the Herero and Nama War. On the one hand, the British government had a clear interest in a swift end to the uprising and hoped that the German government would soon regain control of the situation. On the other, however, they did not dare to provide direct support to the Germans for fear of provoking the African populations of their own colonies. Ultimately, the British response was guided by fears that the unrest in German South-West Africa could spread uncontrollably. While in 1904 the British government refused permission for the German government to land troops in Walvis Bay, the Nama rising conditioned a rethink of policy and the Colonial Office granted the German government free passage to transport military supplies through the Cape Colony.

In contrast to the situation in German South-West Africa, Great Britain was prepared to accord her colonial rival far greater technical and logistical assistance in East Africa, where the fighting was conducted on the border with Mozambique. Not only permitting the use of the Uganda Railroad to transport the Marine Infantry to Muansa, Great Britain also opened the British-Portuguese Zambezi-Shire route. The Germans were also given unrestricted access to the British telegraph lines from Cape Town to Lake Njassa and Bismarckburg, Langenburg, and Songea.[34]

The British government, above all the War Office, Foreign Office, and Colonial Office, required reliable information about the war in German South-West Africa. Generally well informed about the situation in the German sphere of influence, the three ministries pooled information and cooperated closely in defining their response. As a result, it is impossible to differentiate between "military" and "civil" intelligence gathered. Rather, the methods of information collection obtained their specific character through the agents of their collection and origin, whether metropolitan or regional.

At the outset of the Nama rising in the fall of 1903, the British Imperial General Staff appointed Captain Henry C. Lowther to collate and evaluate all intelligence pertaining to the disturbance before forwarding it to the War Office.[35] Copies were sent to the Foreign Office and the Colonial Office. The British military attaché in Berlin also compiled reports from study of the German newspapers and information from contacts with German army officers, which he sent directly to the Foreign Office.[36] This gave the British an insight into the topics exercising German military circles as well as a range of firsthand information and evaluations. He also forwarded information from the Imperial General Staff in London to the British Embassy in Berlin.

In contrast to the members of the metropolitan network, who were not in a position to develop a firsthand understanding of the situation in German South-West Africa, the regional administration in Cape Town exploited their proximity to events to gather useful information. Among the "men on the spot" were Viscount Alfred Milner, high commissioner, as well as those staffing a number of offices such as the Native Department, the general officers commanding, and the acting resident commissioners. The most significant of those able to gather firsthand information was John Cleverly, head of the Office of the Residence Magistrate in Walvis Bay.[37] Also involved in the process of information gathering was the Admiralty, which questioned the captains of merchant ships who had tied up in the enclave and had come into contact with refugees fleeing the fighting.[38]

The British also had informants in German South-West Africa. Civilians in the employ of the British Secret Service (referred to as SS men) had traveled through the territory since early 1904. Gathering their information from contacts at the "stores" established at every settlement,[39] they recorded opinions and rumors canvassed from the white and native populations alike. One such report revealed, "The feeling here and in fact all through the country, is very bitter against the Governor."[40] One common mission with which these SS men were entrusted was the close observation of the activities of the Boers in South-West Africa, whom the British authorities suspected and feared might use the crisis as a cover to smuggle arms to the Transvaal. Fearing a further Boer rising in South Africa, British officials were eager to keep abreast of even the lowest scale of Boer activities.

Military intelligence fell under the purview of the War Office, which dealt with individual contacts operating directly in the German military units. Recruited on the basis of their linguistic skills, the plural identities that they held (many held a range of nationalities) facilitated their work and the movement between European and non-European groups that it entailed. One such contact was Friedrich Freiherr von Nettelbladt. Of Swedish extraction, he had been attached to a German section since early 1904. Starting with von Estorff's unit, he switched to the group under the command of von Heyde before transferring to the main section. In the spring and summer of 1904, he composed a number of reports outlining German troop movements immediately before the battle of Waterberg. A new report from 11–12 August gave a sober summary of the poor standard of German communications which had enabled the Herero to destroy weakened German units.[41]

The German military knew the identities of these spies: as one Boer communiqué put it, "the SS men were too curious."[42] Even if the Secret Service men were unable to learn the specifics of German plans in South-West Africa, their close observations enabled them to gather detailed information regarding all the steps taken by the German forces in the region, which they forwarded to the War Office. In March 1905, the Army Council of the War Office appointed a British officer as official attaché to the German force in German South-West Africa. Explaining the move with reference to the size of the German force and the proposed duration of its operations, an official Foreign Office request to this end was granted by the German government.[43] Colonel Frederic J. A. Trench (Royal Garrison Artillery) was selected for the duty, yet it was unclear where he should take up his post. The matter was settled by von Trotha, commander of the Protection Force, who invited him to his operational headquarters as an official observer.[44] He reported to the War Office minister and the permanent undersecretary at the Foreign Office, and copies of his reports were also sent to the Colonial Office and the general officer commanding, Cape Colony. In contrast to the more general communiqués from Berlin and the local details provided in the reports from the Secret Service men, Trench provided not only information on German military operations but also translations of general orders and a range of technical detail concerning the arms, field telegraph, medical services, field hospitals, and the water sterilization units used by the Germans.

All the reports, regardless of their origin, sought to provide precise and highly detailed information on the strength and equipment of German units and their deployment. The written reports were often accompanied by hand-sketches, maps, and statistics. Nevertheless, despite his position as the official British military observer, even Colonel Trench experienced considerable difficulty in obtaining "hard facts," noting, "It is exceedingly difficult to get at the exact numbers actually present in the command. First, exact returns of numbers do not seem to be rendered to the Headquarter staff, but to go only to the administrative office in Windhoek. Secondly this question of numbers seems to be that it is regarded as strictly confidential and one which cannot possibly concern me."[45]

Highly anxious to gather reliable intelligence regarding the Herero and Nama War (1904–1907), the British developed a complex intercontinental intelligence network integrating both civilian and military agencies. A clear division of responsibility was laid out. Taking charge of questions involving borders and issues of international law, the Foreign Office dealt with matters such as the appearance of a group of refugees in the Cape Colony, Betschuanaland, or Walvis Bay. For its part, the War Office restricted itself to purely military matters. This involved producing summaries of the intelligence gathered through various channels which were issued as a confidential military report, produced every two years from 1906.[46] This process also involved scouring specialist journals such as the *Deutsche Kolonialblatt,* and the *Deutsche Kolonialzeitung* as well as standard works of German colonial history. The authors of the reports also consulted French publications and American documents.[47] The War Office compiled two military reports focusing on German East Africa in 1902 and 1905.[48] In the absence of any intelligence networks (or at least of any evidence of their existence) focusing on this area, it would seem that such reports were compiled on the basis of secondary literature alone.

The reports on both African colonies followed an almost identical structure. Beginning with a general description of the protectorate, it established the history and geography of the region, providing an outline of its borders and physical features, vegetation, zoology, climate, and population. This was followed by a chapter focusing on the towns, ports, and stations in the area. A chapter on communications was divided into a number of subsections examining the railway network, roads, telegraph system, postal system, and waterways. The resources of the area (farming, livestock, minerals, and transport) were subsumed within a single further chapter. Only after establishing this background did the report move to an account of the military situation, examining the state of the Protection Force and its activities. The reports concluded with a so-called ethnographic chapter considering the administration and civil government of the colony. The report also contained an appendix with various tables: the districts and their populations, plantations and trading firms, the distribution of military resources for the year, an extensive street directory, and a diagram of the telegraphic system. The report for German South-West Africa even contained a list of all watering holes and of all rifles registered in the colony.[49]

These sizeable compendia—while the report for German East Africa for 1905 was made up of seventy-three pages, that for German South-West Africa from 1906 ran to 208 pages with an appendix—represented a comprehensive source of information for the respective colonies. As well as an attempt to determine precise figures, the authors of the report also estimated the combat readiness and morale of the troops in German South-West Africa and East Africa.[50] The reports were taken as preliminary in nature; the foreword to the report on German East Africa requested its readers to play their part in filling any possible gaps. Anybody capable of adding information had to contact the War Office. This was signed by Major General J. M. Grierson, who had served in China in 1900–1901 and had composed the reports regarding the other contingents. Although edited and published by the War Office, the reports did not deal with the German conduct of the war. Indeed, the conduct, strategy, and tactics of the colonial wars were given no more than a passing mention. The account of von Trotha's handling of the battle at Waterberg (involving a concentric advance of multiple units around the plateau to corner and destroy the Herero) was concise in the extreme: "This culminated in an action on the 11th and 12th August; but also the Germans were to some extent successful, they failed to crush the enemy as they had hoped to be able to do, and the rebels, in spite of severe losses, managed to slip away, principally in a south-easterly direction. The operations now resolved themselves into purely guerrilla warfare, the difficulties of which were much increased by the nature of the country."[51] Criticism of the conduct of the action remained brief: "The measures for the repression of the rebellion adopted by this officer were harsh."[52]

The reports on German East Africa followed a similar approach. The report for 1905 (a war year) made only passing mention of the employment of European troops to put down a mutiny. An appendix added subsequently contained the supplementary remark that the situation in January 1906 was so calm that reinforcements ordered from Germany had already returned to the metropole. The British military did not share the gubernatorial analysis of the causes of the uprising, which focused on the size of the land, insufficient controls, dissatisfaction with the introduction of civilization, and a desire to conserve traditional ways of life. Instead, the British analysis advanced the introduction of taxes, forced labor, the nature of the plantation system, and the uprising in German South-West Africa as the decisive causes of the uprising.[53]

The British reports on the two colonies did not seek to document the course taken by the war or the methods used in its conduct or to draw any lessons from such matters; rather they represented a compendium of facts and dates from all areas of colonial life. Nevertheless, their purpose was not just to provide background information. The detailed figures and estimations of the performance of the German troops and considerations regarding the relationship between the native populations and their colonial masters reveal the actual purpose of the reports, designed to provide the basic information necessary to plan a German-British war. The breakdown of negotiations for a German alliance (1901) and the conclusion of the *Entente cordiale* with France (1904) transformed Germany into the most likely opponent in a war conducted in either Europe or a colonial theater; British military strategists now required detailed information to draw up the requisite plans. The Intelligence Department of the War Office had been preparing for this eventuality since 1896–1897.[54]

Largely ignoring the existence of the German colonial empire in its strategic calculations, British military planning focused on the territory of the German Empire. Indeed, regarding them as merely sentimental in value, the authors of a draft plan from 1905 concluded that seizure of the colonies in a general war would represent nothing more than a blow to German prestige. Nevertheless, German East Africa was accorded a special role in British strategy. Sandwiched between Britain's eastern and Central African possessions, the Colonial Office hoped that its annexation would eliminate the strategic threat posed to British holdings resulting from German possession of the area and tidy up the piecemeal nature of the map of Africa.[55] A plan to invade German East Africa using South African and Indian troops had been drawn up as early as 1897.[56] British military planners assumed that the German colonies would be cut off from the motherland in the event of a European war. Barely large enough to face down the African population and lacking in permanent defenses, the small German garrison would (so they believed) be easily overcome. They assumed that German East Africa and German South-West Africa would be easy to invade. The only German colonial garrison taken seriously was that of the German protectorate of Qingdao in China, not least because of the presence of a German fleet.[57]

Viewed against the background of the alliance policy conditioned by the *Entente cordiale*, the British military reports on the German colonies represent just one aspect of a more comprehensive process of political-military planning. The only importance attached to German South-West and East Africa and Qingdao was the need to account for their existence in the case of general war. To this end, the military reports represented a framework analysis of the conditions that would present themselves following a British attack. They did not outline what was considered politically correct or immoral in any colonial war.

Military Journals and the German Colonial Administration

The German colonial wars were not only the subject of confidential military reports but also the focus of discussion in a number of international military journals. An informed reader in London would have had access to a clear and detailed discussion of the events of the war. Within the media market, the *Times* was venerated as almost infallible in its reporting.[58] The most significant British military journal was the weekly publication *The Army and Navy Gazette*. It debated wars, technical innovations, and the arms programs of all the Great Powers.

With a principal focus on other areas, the gazette did not maintain a correspondent either in Cape Town (South Africa) or in Nairobi (British East Africa). Its coverage of the Herero and Nama War in German South-West Africa was limited to a very few articles, while the Maji Maji War in German East Africa was ignored entirely. Its authors drew their information solely from German military and civilian newspapers—above all the *Militär-Wochenblatt* and the *Kölnische Zeitung*. Its articles covering the conflict in South-West Africa were short, and contained no detailed information regarding the nature and strength of the German forces deployed or their armament. The articles restricted themselves to a terse summary of and commentary on the latest situation.[59] They even betrayed a certain level of *Schadenfreude* that the German military were now being given cause to regret their know-it-all attitude displayed during the Boer War: "The Germans are finding out that Africa campaigning is not quite so easy as they seemed to think when we were engaged with the Boers."[60] Despite such mirth, the authors were clear that a German defeat would involve a loss of prestige not just for Germany but also for Great Britain and Portugal, as the other colonial powers in the region.[61]

The American coverage of the war, as exemplified by the *United States Army and Navy Journal* (Washington, D.C.) was even more restrained. Restricting its coverage to a mere two articles (one long article published in May 1904 and a far briefer contribution in June 1905), it made clear that it found neither Africa nor Germany to be of any great importance.[62] American military publications exhibited a greater interest in the Russo-Japanese War (1904–1905) because of its strategic location.

French interest in the war (as exemplified by the premier military journal *La France Militaire*), on the other hand, was far greater. Although France feared that the insurgency could spread to the French colonies, the true reason for such interest was rooted in a national obsession with all German military engagements. Still smarting from the humiliation of 1871, the French nation in general and its military establishment in particular followed every such campaign as an indicator of German general military strength and war-readiness. Despite such an interest, however, *La France Militaire* did not send any reporters to the theater, preferring to obtain all of its information from such German military periodicals as the *Militär-Wochenblatt*, the *Deutsches Offizierblatt*, or the *Neuen Militärischen Blättern*. They also made recourse to the coverage of a number of daily newspapers, including the *Strassburger Post, Kölnische Zeitung, Deutsche Zeitung, Berliner Tageblatt, Berliner Lokal-Anzeiger*, and *Vorwärts*. Indeed, the level of the daily information provided to the readers of *La France Militaire* regarding the Herero war in 1904 was such that it enables a subsequent reconstruction of the course of the colonial war. Reinforcements, illness, losses, costs, and even the medical services provided in the theater as well as the parliamentary debates on the war and the issue of the so-called second extermination proclamation (April 1905) were included in the coverage. These articles were supplemented by publication of the telegrams from the German High Command and a number of occasional soldiers' letters.[63] Despite such interest, however, fresh developments in international relations and increased Franco-German tensions after 1904 led to a reduction in the coverage accorded to the Nama war after 1905. The Maji Maji War in German East Africa was given some attention, but the focus accorded to German military policy concentrated on the naval race and the first Morocco crisis.

Led by the nature of their own national interests and the particular interests of their readership, the military journals of Britain and France (as the leading colonial powers) and the United States displayed an idiosyncratic interest in German colonial policy. Focusing on the war in German South-West Africa, they largely ignored the rising in German East Africa. The interest in this otherwise obscure area of German colonial possession was engendered by the spectacular defeat in 1904 of a Western military garrison by what amounted to a handful of Herero warriors and the death of a number of (white) officers. Focusing on the strategic-tactical incompetence of the German military, the publications were quick to highlight the latent threat posed to colonial rule as a whole by the defeat and death of a large body of well-equipped white soldiers. The violence suffered by the civilian population and the number of deaths that it involved were not a topic of interest. At the same time, the international military press exhibited a clear interest in the military technology that the Germans deployed. In an article written in 1904, the *Army and Navy Gazette* ignored the current pursuit of native troops in the sandveld, choosing instead to focus on the tactical employment of machine guns and the formation of a machine gun section.[64] Reports of the Nama war focused exclusively on technical improvements such as the increasing use of wireless telegraphy.

The coverage of the war in German South-West Africa in the French military periodical *La France Militaire* became increasingly cool and sharp in tone throughout 1904. Indeed, it had remarked as early as January that the Herero uprising "reveals an extraordinary lack of foresight on the part of the local authorities and the colonial administration."[65] This was followed some five months later, by clear condemnation of German procedure: "As this short overview once again demonstrates, after their failure to foresee the uprising of the Hereros, the German authorities responded with a number of small measures [*système des petits paquets*], thus allowing the revolt to grow in strength."[66] In October 1904, *La France Militaire* reported that "the Herero revolt is far from being subdued as the [German] government announced a number of weeks ago."[67] The start of the Nama war was followed by sheer horror: "The marginalization of the Chief of the Hottentott tribe, formerly allied with the Germans, represents an exceptionally unfortunate event."[68] This was then followed by a remarkable conclusion: "The extent of this revolt in German South-West Africa provides further proof of the overwhelming need to deal forcibly with the natives in the colonies, in order to prevent further dangerous adventures."[69]

Apart from such trenchant conclusions (perceptions shared by the specialist periodical *Revue des troupes coloniales*),[70] *La France Militaire* made two observations. First, not only was the reaction of the German units stationed in German South-West Africa identified as being far too slow and overtentative, it was depicted as the wrong approach entirely. Second, both uprisings were said to have been provoked by the unjust nature of the German colonial administration, which in turn had demonstrated incompetence in its being taken by surprise. The French publications made two further serious accusations against the Germans: inefficiency and weakness. Decried as a *"système des petits paquets,"* this criticism was echoed by the British press, who wrote, "They had entirely failed to crush the rebellion."[71] The view was unanimous: the uprising should have been put down with massive force before it had a chance to develop.

Franco-British criticism of the German handling of the revolt was not dampened by the replacement of Leutwein by von Trotha. The large-scale Battle of Waterberg (August 1904) was depicted as a tactical fiasco predated by a litany of errors. This view was also shared by the British colonel Charles Edward Callwell, author of the standard textbook on colonial warfare. In its third edition (published in 1906), he sought the explanation for the German failure to encircle the enemy in the technical-organizational problems that they faced. These problems resulted in the Germans acting too slowly, enabling the Herero to break through the ring: "They withdrew, it is true, into a district of sand-veld where they appear to have suffered severely."[72] According to Callwell, the German unit should have advanced more quickly and started a concentrated attack both to win the war of nerves and to implement a concentrated pursuit, thus sparing the troops "long marches in a difficult country," the effect of which was eventually to reduce their fighting potential.

Although the international military journals held back from criticizing von Trotha, the British and French civilian press did not. Nevertheless, von Trotha's appointment as civil governor of German South-West Africa in the fall of 1904 provided the *Times* with the opportunity to draw a positive comparison between Leutwein's *divide et impera* approach and von Trotha's strategy of annihilation. According to this judgment, it was undeniable that Leutwein's strategy was "infinitely preferable to the policy of extermination which in one form or another is being so recklessly urged in this country."[73] The French newspaper *Le Temps* also made an association between the resistance offered by the Nama and Leutwein's dismissal, later pointing out that von Trotha's successes could be classed only as minor as "he succeeded in dispersing, but not subduing, the natives."[74] Subsequent publication in August 1905 of excerpts from the Herero proclamation provoked withering criticism: German honor forbade that a man with such a barbaric mindset should be given command of a German military force.[75]

The second fundamental criticism leveled at the German colonial administration by the international military press focused on its incompetence and injustice, both of which were identified as the original cause of the uprising in both German protectorates. Echoing the criticism of *La France Militaire,* the British *Army and Navy Gazette* found what it regarded as further proof of the incompetence of the German authorities, manifested in the fact of their complete lack of preparedness for the revolt.[76] Moreover, the

Military Report on German East Africa established that the German colonial administration had not been able to secure the loyalty of their African subjects. "The hatred of the natives for the Germans has always been reported by non-German visitors to the protectorate as being very pronounced. The present rising bears this out."[77] It went as far as to contend that every colonial administration that provoked its subject population would eventually suffer a similar fate.

This was also the tenor of criticism advanced in an article published in the *United States Army and Navy Journal*.[78] Locating the causes of the uprising in the nature of the German administrative system, the author accused it of placing an unnecessary burden on the native population. Germany now faced a hard test of both its colonial system and its organizational capabilities. The German troops had, so the author contended, achieved very little and faced great difficulties, suffering high losses. Indeed, this very fact was advanced as an encouragement to African resistance. Germany was in danger of being drawn into "an expeditionary war of the most trying character." For the *Army and Navy Journal*, the Herero war was taken as an instructive example from which the United States should learn: these lessons were to be applied in the continuing wars in Cuba and the Philippines. The best example of a successful colonial policy was given by the British Empire, from which (according to the authors) the United States could learn a great deal: "If there is any lesson for us in the limited experience of Germany in colonial enterprise it is a warning to heed, rather than an example to follow. But in the splendid fabric of the British Empire we shall find the safest and shortest path to the beneficent achievement to which we have set ourselves in the Far East."[79]

The administrative incompetence displayed by the Germans in managing their colonies was a matter of contemporary discussion long before the flood of government "colored books" issued on the subject after the First World War. In assessing the German military response to the uprising, contemporary critics focused exclusively on the efficiency of the German response. In German South-West Africa, it was seen that a sizeable German army had been unable to deal with a few hundred insurgent Nama; conditions in the colony were taken as a potential source of instability for adjacent South Africa. Disparaging remarks over the German conduct of the war put imperial Germany under considerable pressure to act quickly and decisively in quelling the rising. German conduct in her East African colony, on the other hand, was characterized by a far greater level of poise, which enabled the administration to return to the status quo ante with little effort. This explains why the other colonial powers exhibited little interest in German conduct of this war. They viewed Germany's primary task in her colonies as the maintenance of order; the methods employed to this end were of no importance. The international daily press was careful to distance itself from von Trotha's policy of extermination, but there was no moral outrage. Only during the campaign conducted to justify stripping Germany of her colonies after the First World War did the other colonial powers begin to exploit the propaganda potential of German incompetence and the excesses of imperial rule exhibited during the conduct of her colonial wars.

The Battle of the Colored Books

The First World War in Africa ended on 25 November 1918, two weeks after the cease-fire in Europe, with the capitulation of Major General Paul von Lettow-Vorbeck and the last 1,300 soldiers of the German Protection Force in German East Africa. The majority of the other German colonial troops had surrendered considerably earlier. The Protection Force stationed in German South-West Africa had surrendered on 9 July 1915 and in Cameroon on 18 February 1916. The small garrison at Qingdao had already been captured by Japanese forces on 7 November 1914. According to the terms of the Treaty of Versailles (signed on 28 June 1919), Germany was required to cede her former colonial protectorates, which became mandates of the newly established League of Nations. The majority of German East Africa was placed under British administration; the remainder was awarded to Portugal. Ruanda and Urundi were awarded to Belgium. The majority of Cameroon went to France, with Britain receiving the rest. Togo was divided between Britain and France. German South-West Africa was mandated to the South African Union and thus Great Britain. Japan received Qingdao. Samoa was awarded to New Zealand; the other Pacific areas including New Guinea were awarded to Australia. The dismemberment of the German colonial empire meant the dissolution of the Imperial Colonial Office and remaining duties were transferred to the newly created Colonial Department in the Ministry for Reconstruction (Kolonial-Zentralverwaltung in the Reichsministerium für Wiederaufbau).

The division of Germany's colonial possessions among the colonial powers (with Great Britain receiving the lion's share) was accompanied by a large scale propaganda campaign initiated by the Imperial Colonial Office as early as 1917. Issuing a number of pamphlets dealing with the fate of German colonial prisoners from German East Africa, Cameroon, and Togo held by the Belgians and French, it condemned the circumstances of their capture, the conditions in which they were held, and the conduct of the English and French troops under British command.[80] At the same time, the Imperial Colonial Office attacked the French and British for seeking to "eradicate the entire German presence on the West African coast."[81] The condition and future of the African population were not raised.

The situation changed in 1918 with the growth in significance of the colonial question in foreign policy. Published in August 1918, the British blue book dealing with the treatment of Africans in German South-West Africa and entitled *Report on the Natives of South-West Africa*[82] met with a considerable response in Germany. Perceiving a threat to their interests, the Hanseatic cities led the response. Writing to the imperial chancellor on behalf of the Senate Commission for Imperial and Foreign Affairs in September 1918, Martin Donandt, president of the Bremen Senate, called for an official rebuttal. He suggested the compilation of reports focusing on English brutality, not a difficult task, as "the history of the English world empire . . . was written with so much blood."[83] The imperial government had already commissioned a government white book in response to the British blue book. Marking the high point of the dispute between Germany and Great Britain over colonies, *The Treatment of Native and Other Populations in the Colonial Possessions of Germany and England* was published in 1919 and reprinted in the same year in German translation.[84]

The German Imperial Chancellery and Colonial Office were convinced that British policy aimed the full annexation of the German colonies to be achieved by deception and slander. The logical conclusion of British arguments was that only they, with their army of liberal and humane colonial administrators, possessed the necessary experience and skill to administer the colonies correctly. The propaganda offensive sought to depict Britain as the only worthy alternative to Germany, while convincing the world of their its moral motives for seeking to annex the German colonies. In essence, moral indignation was designed to mask otherwise naked political and economic interests. For their part, the Germans denied all accusations of atrocities, contesting that their treatment of the colonial population was no worse than that meted out by the British. Moreover, they pointed to what they saw as a pronouncedly philanthropic colonial policy and the efforts taken toward economic stimulus.[85] This was the tenor of countless memoirs and pamphlets. Heinrich Schnee, a former governor of German East Africa, coined the emotive phrase "the lie of German colonial guilt" *(koloniale Schuldlüge)* which provided the title for a dossier summarizing the arguments of German colonial apologists.[86]

A historiographical consensus has established British motives as entirely opportunistic in seeking to expand the British Empire. The British prime minister, Arthur Balfour, used a number of parliamentary speeches to emphasize that Germany had forfeited its right to rule. Indeed, pre-empting criticism of British knowledge of and inaction during the German excesses in German South-West Africa, the blue books claimed that with the colony sealed to the outside world, the events there had gone almost unreported. Had it been aware of such actions, the British government would, so the book claimed, have acted accordingly.[87] In view of the extensive intelligence network run by the British, these claims were highly dubious. In publishing its blue book, the government sought to serve political, not humanitarian, motives. The reevaluation of this issue and its instrumentalization for imperial ends is demonstrated by the publication in 1920 by the British Admiralty of the *Handbook of German East Africa,* which sought to provide a justification of British policy in the former German colony.[88] In assessing the general situation in former German East Africa (largely understood as the readiness or otherwise of the native population to collaborate with their new imperial masters), the Admiralty handbook made considerable recourse to the *Military Orientation Manual* of 1911 focusing on German East Africa, from which it reprinted whole passages. The authors of the manual concluded that the colony had first been pacified in 1905 following the crushing of the rising of the same year. However, despite the large number of tribes, the German colonial administration had been unable to find any trustworthy partners. Indeed, even the most bitter of rivalries between clans and other groups had been cast aside in the common fight against Germany. For the authors, the German inability to find any collaborators within the colony indicated the resounding failure of their colonial policy.

In contrast, the British assessment of the German conduct of the war was far from negative. German troops had gathered their colonial experience through a number of punitive expeditions. The first German expeditions had focused on either fortified settlements or the hiding places of women and children. They also searched for and destroyed stores of food, cattle, and water. Seeking to inflict the highest possible losses on the enemy, they soon found this tactic to be difficult, requiring as it did the operation of mobile units capable of operating independently of the German lines. In the end, the Germans were required to resort to tricks to provoke battle, such as dressing their Askaris as bearers. An expedition often ended with the starvation of the enemy fighters, although women and children were treated humanely: "The military authorities seem, at least in later wars, to have practiced the removal and feeding of the women and children when these could be found, while they accepted famine as their ally against the men."[89]

The Admiralty publication was a neutral documentation of German colonial policy and her conduct of the war. Having accepted the League of Nations mandate to administer the colonies, Great Britain was now forced to devise a strategy for their administration. Placed in a unique situation, British policy makers sought to draw on not only British colonial experience but also that gathered by the Germans. British rejection of German methods was based not on moral grounds, but on considerations of their efficacy. Nevertheless, the competition for the moral high ground between Germany and Britain saw a shift in British colonial policy, which focused now on practical ethics. Cheered on by the national press, British and German diplomats now found themselves using the rhetoric of civilization, humanity, and morality,[90] terms and concepts previously absent from military reports.

Although conceding that atrocities had been committed in the colonies, the German white book sought to portray the death of civilians at the hands of German troops as intrinsic to their civilizing mission. Barbarity was portrayed as the vanguard of civilization, and featuring in the conduct of all colonial powers, the Germans insisted that it amounted to a general phenomenon.[91] In contrast, the British use of the concept of civilization in its blue book underwent something of a reinterpretation. Previously seen as the defense of international law (as in the suppression of the Boxer rebellion), it was now used to mean the humane treatment of all people, regardless of their race. Chapter 15 described how in 1905, the German settler commissioner Paul Rohrbach denounced the extermination of the Herero because "in the blind fury of von Trotha" not only people were killed but also their cattle.[92] Rohrbach never indicted any level of sympathy for the Herero killed in this action. Maltreatment of the native population was now portrayed by the British as not only uneconomical and damaging in the long run but also a factor of considerable immorality. The German white book replied that the methods of British colonial rule were in no way different from those employed by Germany: "coming from such an accuser, every accusation is morally nullified in advance."[93] Indeed, had not the British contravened the

Congo Act in extending the First World War to Africa? What was more immoral: the maltreatment of the native population or conducting an illegal war against whites?

Each compiling long lists of the atrocities perpetrated by the "other," both nations sought to establish the depravity of their colonial competitor. While the British blue book concentrated on eyewitness reports, the German white book presented a number of published speeches and other sources of written evidence. Both concentrated on the conduct of the war and the treatment of prisoners, women, children, and civilians. The German publication paid much attention to the British conduct of the South African War as an example of pronounced brutality meted out to women and children who were forced first to witness the destruction of their farms before being interned. Such measures (as the German authors claimed) were aimed at undermining the morale of the Boer fighters. The most serious allegation made against the British was that their aggression was also directed toward whites, as demonstrated by that British "colony in Europe": Ireland—where the excesses committed were far worse than those perpetrated in South Africa.[94]

Initially not involved in the German propaganda offensive, the military historical section of the German General Staff issued an (undated) memorandum regarding the "material destruction and treatment of the native populations inflicted by English troops in the Boer War 1899–1902."[95] The Germans advanced the fact of the British campaign against the (white) Boers to defuse charges of German atrocities in Europe during the First World War. Examples were provided and given the titles such as "The Butchering of Cattle," "The Treatment of Prisoners," "The Treatment of Natives," "English Warfare: General," "English Warfare: Comparison with German," "Concentration Camps: General," "Sanitary Conditions," "Mortality in the Concentration Camps," "Mortality in the German Prison Camps," "The Destruction of Supplies," "The Destruction of Houses," etc.[96] Crimes that enjoyed widespread acceptance at the time they were committed were now the subject of moral outrage with which to condemn the "others."

Conducted in and influenced by the context of the immediate postwar situation, the war of the colored books itself served to transform the terms of the discourse on colonial warfare. Previously absent from the international colonial discussion, depictions of extreme violence in colonial wars were now a key weapon in what had become a morally charged debate. The clear restriction of the term "civilization" to international law and thus specifically to white nations had traditionally prevented any discussion of the means selected to pursue wars in the colonies. Colonial warfare could have culminated in massacres or genocide without being subject to any consistent level of criticism in military circles.

The First World War altered this situation, resulting in an extension of the concept of humanity and its application to the native population of the colonies. Actions committed in war that would previously have passed unmentioned now required justification. International interest in the German engagements in China and Africa received a further impetus as many assumed that their study could reveal important information regarding the fighting capacity of the German army. While France observed all German military developments with routine and close preoccupation, British interest in the conflicts in German South-West Africa and German East Africa was rooted in their geographical proximity to her own colonial holdings.

The international military reports on the German colonial wars sought to locate German action within their international context. Not concerned with criticizing the German violence against the civilian population, military interest focused on the German failure to suppress the rising in German South-West Africa. Leveled by such close rivals, these criticisms could only have been taken as an insult to the German military establishment to which it would be forced to respond. The greater interest exhibited by the international military observers in the conflict in German South-West Africa contrasts clearly with the reduced interest in the Chinese campaign and the general indifference displayed toward German conduct of the Maji Maji War. Transforming it into a pivotal conflict for the reputation of the German military, the intensity and quality of this foreign commentary served both to underline and to increase its significance.

CHAPTER 10

Parliament and the Military Press

T HE CONDUCT by the German military of their colonial wars was affected by not only international discussions but the domestic national discourse. Although unable to take any decisions regarding a declaration of war, the German Reichstag represented the whole range of German domestic political opinion on the colonial wars and exercised considerable influence on both the troop strength sent to these conflicts and the duration of their conduct. This control was exercised via their rights of budgetary control. Despite having no formal powers to control the nature of their conduct, the Reichstag debates did focus on the violence unleashed within the three colonial wars, and thus discussed what amounted to national standards for colonial warfare. The discussions of the topic in the military press and literature, on the other hand, ignored questions of the violence meted out to the Chinese or African population, or rather viewed it as a matter of course. Using the example of German South-West Africa, the military press developed the concept of a multifunctional colonial soldier, able to work in a constructive or destructive manner as required.

Indemnity and German East Africa

The conduct of the wars in the colonies depended on parliamentary grants. Parliament was summoned by the kaiser working in consultation with the Bundesrat. A hybrid system, the German Empire combined a constitutional structure with elements of bureaucratic authoritarianism. This meant that although the parties were incorporated in the political process, their formal powers were considerably limited.[1] The German Parliament reflected a wide range of opinion, ranging from the Conservative Party, the German Conservatives, the German Empire Party (Deutsche Reichspartei), and the anti-Semitic German Social Party on the right; to the Catholic Centre Party, liberal People's Party, the Liberal Union, the German People's Party, and the National Liberals in the political center; to the Social Democratic Party on the left.

Relying on the liberal bloc for his parliamentary majority, Chancellor von Bülow depended on the support of these parties for his—constitutionally dubious—methods of financing military engagements with an "indemnity," a constitutional instrument designed to maintain the special status of the German military within the imperial constitutional settlement. With article 69 of the imperial constitution stipulating annual parliamentary approval of the government budget, this requirement had proven impossible to enforce in practice, so the executive took to presenting supplementary budgets or records of extrabudgetary expenditure for subsequent parliamentary approval.[2] If the Reichstag was not in session upon the outbreak of a war, the instrument of an indemnity was employed to bypass the need for parliamentary approval of the necessary expenditure. The deployment of German troops in all three colonial wars was effected therefore in an entirely unconstitutional fashion.

Until 1904, the Center Party was widely viewed as a reliable source of parliamentary support for German colonial policy, and its support was instrumental in securing parliamentary assent (granted in November 1900) for the 152,770,000 marks required to finance the Chinese expedition.[3] These monies included expenditure for the administration of the imperial army (119,800,000 marks), the administration of the imperial navy (28,857,000 marks), post and telegraph costs (3,800,000 marks), pensions and benefits (243,000 marks), and the costs of striking a campaign medal (70,000 marks).[4] A further sum of 40,000,000 marks was voted for the war in December 1901.[5] Under the terms of the "Boxer Protocol," China was to foot the bill for the majority of the costs incurred.

The parliamentary grants for German South-West Africa were similarly forthcoming, and in 1904, Parliament sanctioned 73,580,250 marks of extra expenditure to fund the suppression of the Herero and Nama uprisings.[6] Even the Social Democrats were willing to cooperate, abstaining during the vote in January 1904 on the first reading of the supplementary budget.

Nevertheless, during subsequent debates, the parties all demanded that in the future they be consulted in advance of, or at least during, decisions involving considerable financial expenditure, especially overseas expeditions. They sought to use their budgetary rights to influence the purpose, scope, and execution of such measures.

Following the first news of the uprising in German East Africa in August 1905, it was initially unclear as to whether the government would be able to assemble a parliamentary majority for an indemnity grant. In view of the unfavorable "particularly sensitive political mood in the Reichstag regarding overbudgetary spending on foreign policy activities,"[7] the government seemed to have spent too much political capital in this area. Fearful of provoking further parliamentary attack, the executive—the Office of Marine Affairs, the Office of Colonial Affairs, the Office of Justice, the Imperial Treasury, and the Imperial Office of the Interior—were reluctant to launch a war without prior parliamentary consultation. Such a course would have provoked parliamentary uproar and endangered not only any supplementary budget for intervention in German East Africa but the current taxation proposals and thus the entire imperial budget. For his part, however, the chancellor was just as afraid of recalling Parliament, fearing that the deputies would take the opportunity to force a discussion of the war in German South-West Africa and the associated policy of railroad construction in the colony.[8] The financing and the possible dimensions of the war in German East Africa had become tied up with maneuvers in domestic policy.

There was no question of dispatching any number of regular troops to German East Africa. Hamstrung by a lack of funds, such a move would also contravene the provisions of the Protection Force regulations, which foresaw the establishment and maintenance of a white force only for German South-West Africa. Any alteration to the law would require the approval of the Bundesrat and the Reichstag. In such a situation, the government decided to dispatch a contingent of Marine Infantry to Dar es Salaam. The costs involved in executing this measure were not high, and the Reichsmarineamt indicated that the operation could be conducted from its existing muster rolls, if the personnel were replaced from other unspecified sources and the naval budget was not subject to increased burden.[9] As a result, recourse to a supplementary budget became inevitable. With the estimated cost of the military response running at 200,000 marks—a low figure in comparison to other colonial expenses—the executive assumed that they could avoid the need to summon Parliament. In the end, the gamble paid off. Although the costs of the war in German East Africa eventually amounted to 1,998,500 marks and the parliamentary budgetary committee subjected the government action to overt criticism—observing that it was "striking" that the navy budget would actually have covered the dispatch of an expeditionary corps—the government secured a majority for its indemnity in the vote of 1906.[10] The Marine Infantry dispatched to German East Africa was accounted as "an extrabudgetary" section of the occupation forces in German East Africa.[11] As a result, all naval units in German East Africa were commanded by the naval officer in Dar es Salaam and not the governor.

Despite this government success, parliamentary support for the war began to crumble. In 1906, a majority of Social Democrats and Center Party deputies rejected the supplementary budget presented to Parliament to ensure the continuation of the war in German South-West Africa. Taking advantage of the affront, von Bülow used the vote to dissolve Parliament and call what became known as the "Hottentott election."[12] Campaigning on the subject of the colonial war, the chancellor succeeded in securing a Conservative–National Liberal majority, which acted without delay to grant the monies required for the continuation of the Nama war. Enjoying a parliamentary majority for at least one further parliamentary session, the government took heart from the public rejection of an antiwar Parliament.

Parliamentary Debates

Concerning, as they did, the first wars conducted by the young German state, the parliamentary debates of the colonial wars occasioned some of the strongest verbal exchanges between the executive and the legislature ever witnessed in the Reichstag. This situation was compounded by procedural considerations. Passed only after three readings, supplementary budgets afforded considerable scope for the venting of frustrations. While the debates over the Boxer War and the Herero and Nama War were characterized by verve and passion, those over the Maji Maji War were shorter and far less acrimonious.[13] All the relevant matters of principle had been exhaustively discussed in the debate of the previous wars. Moreover, the conduct of the war by a majority black Protection Force meant that it involved neither great cost nor German lives.

Focusing on a number of topics, the debates discussed the justification for the war and Germany's wider colonial policy, the causes of the war, its cost and the methods of its prosecution, the relationship of the German soldiers to the native population, and the extent of and restrictions imposed upon the application of military violence. The reactions to and interpretations of the war by each party and their concomitant demands were conditioned less by the issues involved in the actual war in hand than by their attitudes toward wider government policy and their interpretation of the imperial constitution in general. Each party took advantage of the opportunity to position itself on a matter of fundamental national importance, thereby hoping for greater attention from the wide press coverage accorded to the debate. As a result, both the support offered to the government in defense of the military conduct of the war provided by the Conservative parties and the vituperative Socialist attacks constituted no surprise.

The high point of the first day of the Reichstag debate over the China campaign (19 November) came with a lengthy speech over several hours from the Social Democrat leader August Bebel. Summarizing the SPD position, he decried the German campaign as a "retaliatory action of a barbarity unprecedented in the last decades."[14] He characterized the kaiser's speech from 27 July 1900 as a blemish on German honor which was bound to have the most serious of consequences: the words "give no quarter" amounted to a summons, indeed an order, to adopt the most brutal approach to the war. As a result, the war in China had assumed the character of a wild animal hunt. The mere sighting of a uniformed Chinese led the wearer to be hunted down like game.

Responding to Bebel's tirade, the minister of war, Heinrich von Goßler, defended the conduct of the troops. Refuting accusations of unregulated and arbitrary action, he conceded the incidence of atrocities, but indicated that such or similar acts always brought punishment. Responding to the charges of incitement, he argued that far from representing a summons, the words of the kaiser actually sought to warn the departing German troops of the expected practices and behavior of the Chinese: "When the supreme war lord sees his troops for the last time before dispatching them . . . and warns them of the situation and conditions which they can expect to meet, is such behavior not entirely human, indeed indicative of the highest humanity?"[15]

Von Goßler then sought to tone down the comparison to the Hun: the peoples of Europe had united not to emulate the Huns, but to restore law and justice to East Asia. This gambit established the battle lines for the subsequent debate. Speaking for the Left Liberals, Eugen Richter supported Bebel and demanded that the kaiser consult with his ministers before making programmatic speeches. Richter was convinced that the "mass executions [in

China] were the direct result of the phrase 'give no quarter.'"[16] Speaking for the Center Party, Philipp Lieber maintained a circumspect stance, speaking only of "those sharp words spoken to our departing warriors."[17] Indeed, he went on to provide support for the foreign policy vision of the kaiser: Germany had now become a key international player, whose participation and voice were vital to world affairs. Ernst Bassermann of the National Liberals defended any possible excesses with reference to the atrocities perpetrated by the Boxers; such an enemy would not respond to kid-gloved methods. He called for "conduct of the war free of all sentimentality," yet wherever possible, within the bounds of humanity.[18] The Conservative deputy Albert von Levetzow, on the other hand, rejected the course of barbarity: it was not in the nature of our "good-natured and well-disciplined compatriots to lay a single finger on the women and children and other peaceable inhabitants of an enemy country."[19] Moreover, looking around in the Reichstag, he could not see a single Hun—"nor can I among our German soldiers." Any excesses were exceptions which were to be prosecuted. He regarded the discipline and restraint exercised by the German troops as exemplary.

The essential features of this argument were repeated in the parliamentary discussion of the Herero and Nama War. If the Social Democrats had exercised restraint in January 1904, they sharpened the tone of their comments as the details of the German conduct of the war in German South-West Africa became known. Speaking during the debate of the second supplementary budget in mid-March, August Bebel read out letters from two soldiers commenting on the brutalization of the war and the end of the practice of taking prisoners.[20] He made repeated calls on the government to ensure that the extra-European wars pursued by the German Empire were conducted according to the tenets of humanity.[21] As in the previous debates, the Social Democratic position was countered by that of other parties, who found it inadvisable to display "too great a degree of humanity toward the blood-thirsty beasts in human form."[22]

The news of Lieutenant General von Trotha's second "extermination proclamations" occasioned significant conflict in the Reichstag. In von Trotha's threatening the insurgents with extermination should they not surrender immediately, a price had been placed their heads. The Social Democrat Georg Ledebour criticized strongly the incentive given by this proclamation to assassins. Making clear that he considered such a course to "contradict our entire conception of humanity in war, even in those conducted against natives,"[23] he demanded the immediate dismissal of the military commander in German South-West Africa: "If the colonial adminis-tration is serious in keeping its word, it is inconceivable that a man contravening so flagrantly not only German military standards, but the orders issued by the German government, can remain at his post."[24]

The Center Party politician Matthias Erzberger counseled restraint, seeking to give von Trotha the opportunity to explain his actions: "The good general may well have been moved to do so by the most noble of mo-tives."[25] Moreover, Erzberger justified the conduct of the war by identifying important differences between wars conducted between "civilized nations" and those between blacks and whites. He added, "There are currently no greater criminals in [German] South-West Africa than those against whom such a proclamation has been issued."[26] He concluded his general defense of the Protection Force: "I can only sum up with the words: I have always believed that the leveling by members of this house of serious accusations against soldiers, officers and their commanders must be answered by a counter-attack by other members."[27] Erzberger continued to defend the German conduct of the war in December 1905,[28] despite his opposition to the plans outlined by the German military to build a railroad in German South-West Africa.

The debate saw the first parliamentary intervention by an officer from the Protection Force. Speaking on the matter of the water shortage and diffi-culties of transport within German South-West Africa, Colonel Berthold von Deimling defended his commander in chief by reference to atrocities committed against German soldiers by the Nama: "And we should use kid glove measures against such a barbarous and perfidious enemy? . . . Mercy shown to the natives is an atrocity against our own people."[29] Changing tack, the colonel advanced new arguments in his second parliamentary address, in which he sought to justify continuation of the war with reference to its significance for the further development of the German army. The war, he said, presented a unique opportunity for young men to gain valuable experi-ence.[30] Deimling's third and last parliamentary address, given only a few days after his appointment as the new commander of the Protection Force for German South-West-Africa, caused an uproar. As he reacted to Erz-berger's proposal to abandon the southern part of the colony, the strength of his reply not only revealed his powerful antiparliamentary sentiments in the emphasis that he gave to imperial authority over parliamentary budget rights but culminated in the words, "Gentlemen, must I present to the house a few corpses of those who starved to death . . . before you grant the necessary monies for the railroad?"[31] Remembered in parliamentary history as the "starved corpses" quote, this rhetorical move was to prove counterproductive; the railway was rejected with the votes of the Center Party proving decisive.

The parliamentary debates on the war in the colonies rehearsed the whole range of stock arguments developed in Western colonialist thought: brutality is generic to war; wars against "wild peoples" provoke base instincts; the brutality and low level of cultural development among the colonial peoples justified, indeed required, a violent response; and Africans and Europeans could not be judged by the same standards. Indeed, despite the traditional judgment that Europe displayed a "higher level of civilization" than Africa, the latter verdict was also applied to China; its long cultural history was balanced by the religious fanaticism, barbarity, and uncivilized nature *(Unkultur)* of its people. Did not history teach that violence must be met with violence? China's history was characterized by wars, dynastic instability, revolutions, and atrocities. Indeed, the current conflict was said to be tame compared with the Taiping war with its sea of blood and tears, murder and plundering.[32]

Such arguments were countered by assertion of the universality of cultural values *(kulturelle Werte)* and their applicability to all nations, whatever their level of cultural development.[33] Faced with a barbaric enemy, the German soldier should not stoop to his level; to do so served only to debase German culture. The Social Democrats in Parliament saw that after their return to Europe, the military and civilian colonial personnel would "infect European society with their [acquired] bestiality,"[34] possibly serving to increase the acceptance of violence as part of the domestic political culture. This description of the interdependence of colonial rule and German domestic policy was an innovation in the traditional Social Democratic understanding of colonialism, previously interpreted as a one-sided attack on the native colonized population.

The Reichstag debates of the conduct of the colonial wars and the extent of the violence practiced within them were dominated by deeply rooted partisan conceptions of the nation and the Wilhelmine political settlement. Equating national policy with military policy, Conservative nationalists understood their role as providing automatic fiscal support for the demands of the military establishment. They regarded any form of criticism of the German conduct of the war in China and Africa as tantamount to slander, equating criticism of the military establishment with criticism of the nation

as a whole. Within this constellation, it was the *revelation* of German misconduct, not its incidence, that served to dishonor the army and the nation.

For their part, aware of the nationalist hothouse atmosphere of Wilhelmine
Germany, the internationalist Social Democrats restricted their criticism of
colonial policy to the parliamentary arena and declined to organize public
protests on any great scale. This strategy was not uncontroversial within the
party, and drew considerable criticism from Rosa Luxemburg, arguing that
it gave the impression that the Social Democrats paid far too much respect
to both official and unofficial chauvinism. For their part, the Conservatives
accused Bebel and his party of a lack of patriotism and "fouling one's own
nest."[35] The criticism leveled against the Social Democrats during the "Hottentott election" from those in the Bülow bloc and their equation of "Socialist" and "barbarous native" established all colonial critics as deeply unpatriotic.[36] Having developed into a mass movement, nationalism (itself not
unattractive to Social Democratic voters) had become a considerable problem
for the Social Democratic movement.

Divided as they were on a number of questions, the parties in the Reichstag were united by their understanding of military law as an unequivocal set
of standards forming clear boundaries for the application of violence. The
parliamentary Right insisted that German soldiers abided by the provisions
of the military code, any deviation from which would be punished according
to its statutes. For its part, the Left recognized that although a number of
crimes committed in the Boxer War had been subject to the sanction of military law,[37] it doubted whether the number of punishments meted out reflected the true extent of the violence and crimes perpetrated by the German
military force. It made repeated reference to the fact that the mere existence
of military law and a number of cases tried according to its precepts were
insufficient as proof of its effectiveness. They demanded that all the cases of
killings of the defenseless and those surrendering as well as the incidence of
plunder, theft, and rape be tried by courts martial.

The "Hun Letter" Proceedings

Seeking to demonstrate the inhumanity in the German conduct of the war
in China, Social Democratic Reichstag deputies made repeated reference to
a number of so-called Hun letters.[38] Referring to forty-seven letters written
by soldiers deployed in the Boxer War and published in the Social Democratic newspaper *Vorwärts* between August 1900 and January 1901, their

sobriquet drew on Wilhelm's Bremerhaven address, later dubbed the "Hun speech."[39] Containing passages describing episodes of especial brutality toward prisoners and civilians and written in highly explicit language, the majority of the letters were printed in anonymous form. As a source, the *Vorwärts* editors often gave the names of conservative regional newspapers in which the letters had originally been published. It remains impossible to determine whether the publication of the letters represented the individual wishes of their authors or of their recipients and is equally impossible to establish their reasons for doing so.

In seeking to resolve the question as to their authenticity and despite a number of discrepancies in detail, comparison of these letters with descriptions of the battles in diaries and officers' memoirs reveals a distinct level of congruence.[40] According to the twenty letters, it was common practice to murder civilians; seventeen letters mentioned the killing of prisoners of war in the form of mass executions, twelve letters mention plundering, and five refer to the maltreatment of Chinese civilians. One letter also portrayed rape as a common occurrence. Six letters corroborate each other in reporting a mass execution that probably took place in Peking at the end of August and was corroborated by the travel writer Rudolf Zabel. An event reported in eight separate letters involved a massacre committed in the town of Liangxiang on 11 September 1900.

Rejecting the accusations leveled in the letters, von Bülow's government spoke of lies and forgeries. One rumor circulating in the government and in newspapers even maintained the existence in Zürich of a "factory for Hun letters" that produced these "falsifications."[41] Addressing the Reichstag in November 1900, the minister of war, von Goßler, left his listeners in no doubt that the acts of barbarism described in the Hun letters were in any way consistent "with our statutes and prescriptions. Should the contents of these letters prove to be accurate, then such people are to be proceeded against with courts martial. I should like to draw your attention to the fact that the events here described involve plundering and killings: crimes for which the Military Penal Code prescribes a capital punishment."[42]

Rejecting the repeated demands made by the minister of war to reveal the identity of the letters' authors and in seeking to protect his sources, August Bebel maintained, "I have no reason to do so."[43] The passages of the letters from which he had quoted had all been published in the press and as such were available to the state prosecutor. Indeed, as he criticized, were they to prove untrue, the allegations raised in the letters and repeated in a series of newspaper articles represented the most "bloody defamation" of the army.[44]

Speaking in a parliamentary statement made in February 1901, the minister of war informed the Reichstag that only a very few offenses had been recorded in China for which the soldiers responsible had been punished severely. Referencing three cases, he provided the details of two. One case involved a soldier found guilty of shooting another soldier; the second involved the murder of a Chinese man. The second case saw the soldier in question being tried for murder because he had been unable to prove that he had been attacked.[45] For the minister of war, examination of the three cases had proven that the soldier had acted alone. He did not submit any trial documents. Instead, he began to collect witness statements to the contrary, and in March 1901, announced his intention to launch legal proceedings against the claims made in the Hun letters.[46]

Making good his promise, the minister worked together with the commander of the East Asian Expeditionary Corps to pursue criminal proceedings against the editors of the Social Democratic newspapers in Stuttgart, Frankfurt am Main, Halle, and Berlin in which the Hun letters had been published. An undertaking neglected by previous scholars of imperial Germany, these prosecutions were initially tried by regional courts.[47] Seeking to prevent the opening of the main proceedings, the defense counsel for the editors prosecuted in Berlin placed a number of motions to take evidence from the war reporters who had witnessed the events described in the letters and to present the original letters. He also called on the court to summon the editors of the conservative press organs who had originally published the letters. In addition to this strategy, the counsel for the defense made clear that in its denunciation of "Hunnish war practices," the editors of the *Vorwärts* did not seek to impugn every member of the East Asian Expeditionary Corps.[48] He also called on the court to compel the minister of war to surrender the documents pertaining to the trials conducted against the members of the East Asian Expeditionary Corps. The court rejected all the motions shortly before the start of proceedings.

The trial beginning on 2 December 1901 accused the journalist Robert Schmidt of insulting Major General Wilhelm von Kettler. According to an article published in *Vorwärts*, in the fall of 1900, Kettler had ordered the execution of a group of men declared to be Boxers by a Chinese child.[49] This case differed from that of the other Hun letters in that it had been initiated by the Ministry of War upon the request of the general himself after his reading the article.[50] Both he and a lieutenant took the witness stand.

When questioned, Schmidt responded that the article was the translation of a report in the American *Daily Chronicle*. Having accompanied the expedition in question, the *Chronicle* correspondent had submitted an affidavit regarding its veracity. Countering this account, Lieutenant Ulrich von Stoltzenberg responded that the expedition had been launched in response to the shooting of 200 Chinese by a group of Boxers. The French mission sent two small Chinese Christians (both of whom were easy to mistake for children) to identify the Boxers. Following an interrogation, the twenty-two "Boxer ringleaders" were convicted of the act and executed. No records were kept of the interrogation, but reports were filed in accordance with the regulations. Von Kettler confirmed this account. Addressing the court, he stated that his task had been to establish order and had merely followed the orders of Field Marshal von Waldersee: to proceed against the Boxers with all necessary severity so as to protect the peaceable population.

The second defendant, Paul John, was accused of having defamed the members of the East Asian Expeditionary Corps through publication of two Hun letters in *Vorwärts*. During cross-examination, he confirmed that he had seen one of the two originals of the Hun letters printed in his newspaper. He had sourced the other letter from other local newspapers, and named the responsible editors as witnesses to this effect.[51] The counsel for the defense again submitted a motion to take evidence in order to confirm the truth of these claims. Objecting, the prosecutor asserted that the authenticity of these letters or indeed the veracity of their contents was of no relevance to the case in hand. Accepting this argument, the court rejected the motion from the defense, arguing that the soldiers of the East Asian Expeditionary Corps had been accused universally as a plundering, thieving, and defiling horde. Such assertions represented thus not a statement of fact but a judgment; as a result, the presentation of counterproof was inadmissible. The regional court in Berlin sentenced Paul John to seven months in prison; Robert Schmidt was sent down with six months. In addition to his prison term, John was instructed to print a reply from the Ministry of War; all copies of the libelous edition were to be pulped, and its printing plates destroyed. His appeal was given a hearing, but rejected.[52]

All the Hun letter trials followed one of two patterns. The first saw the counsel for the defense attempt to demonstrate the veracity of the claims by hearing evidence from the officers involved. Once in the stand, the officers then convinced the court that they had acted in accordance with the law. They explained their conduct with reference to tactical necessity, provocation, the fog of war, and the need to maintain order so as to protect the lives of peaceable civilians and the German troops. All claimed to have acted only after careful consideration of all the options open to them. For their part, the judges were apparently prepared to place unquestioning belief in a number of far-fetched explanations. The second type of trial involved refusal on the part of the court to allow the defense to present any evidence; the accused was convicted without any examination of the case. The courts did not examine the question of either the authenticity of the letters involved or the good faith of the editors in deciding on their publication.

Combining evidence with argument, the defense sought to demonstrate that as no formal part of the German army and thus not subject to the Ministry of War, its minister was incapable of representing the East Asian Expeditionary Corps. Both the regional judges and the Imperial Court rejected such arguments. Only one defendant broached the subject of the kaiser's "Hun speech," an act provoking an immediate and impassioned response from the prosecutor. Launching into an agitated defense of Conservative Nationalist Germany, he maintained that no official record had been made of this speech; the kaiser had sought merely to warn the departing troops of the uncivilized nature of the enemy that they were about to encounter. Indeed, responsibility for the conduct of the war rested with the local commander. He continued: not only had the speech been held in front of a restricted audience, the force in China had maintained the strictest of discipline. War had always been conducted with measures of a certain stringency; the punitive nature of this campaign in defense of German honor rendered certain actions unavoidable. Had Chinese villages actually been razed, it was only on important strategic grounds and always in defense of the safety of the troops involved. Many such villages had served as arsenals for the Boxer hordes. Responding to the objections that such considerations in no way altered the putative veracity of the reports under question, the state prosecutor replied that it would have been more fitting had the defense not sought to involve the person of the kaiser.[53]

The only trial to take an unexpected turn was that of the Social Democratic parliamentarian Fritz Kunert. Arraigned in the fall of 1903 for insulting German veterans of the Chinese campaign, the Landgericht Halle postponed the hearing to give him the opportunity to augment his range of witnesses. He was also granted access to official documents pertaining to the punishment of German soldiers.[54] Taking advantage of the newly won time, he took the opportunity to make a number of calls in *Vorwärts* for the publication of a range of official material. Expecting a range of sworn statements from former members of the East Asian Expeditionary Corps regarding the atrocities perpetrated by some if its members, he also hoped for letters from China veterans or press correspondents as well as information regarding the response of the German military justice in China. In addition to German publications, he appealed to a number of press organs in France, Great Britain, America, Italy, and Austria-Hungary to assist him in his undertaking. Taking hope, the *Vorwärts* no longer wrote of the "Hun letter trials" but rather the "truth about China."[55] Nevertheless, although now able to call witnesses who confirmed the veracity of the contents of the published letters, the presiding judge ruled that the court was not interested in the truth or otherwise of the letters, rather in the charge of defaming the army. Fritz Kunert was also sent down with a prison sentence.[56]

Celebrating the outcome of the "Hun letter cases," the Conservative press reveled in the punishment handed out for the undignified obloquy to which German soldiers had recently been subject. As if speaking on behalf of such opinion, in summing up on the case of Robert Schmidt, the presiding judge of the Berlin Landgericht identified what he saw as the sad circumstances in which the editor insulted a fellow German in such terrible terms.[57] In a sharp tone, the *Vorwärts* commented that unusually, professors, pastors, and students had exercised considerable restraint in the "Hun letter affair," failing to demonstrate their flaming patriotism.[58] Even Max Liebermann von Sonnenberg, a prominent anti-Semite, commented in a parliamentary speech in 1902 that "the Chinese matter had not proceeded as smoothly as we would have hoped." His explanation: *"À la guerre comme à la guerre."*[59]

The political establishment of imperial Germany viewed the criminal justice system as the ideal instrument for the suppression of "subversive" political groupings and their actions. Employed regularly against both Roman Catholicism during the *Kulturkampf* and the representatives of the Social Democratic movement, a number of those arraigned in the Hun letter affair had already gained considerable experience of its reach and impact. Not only were the penal provisions regulating defamation very strict, the incidence of the offense was unusually dependent on the estimation of the judge.[60] The judges, many of whom were reserve officers, were dependent on the state in many more ways than for their pay. Defamation trials could take a number of forms, including lèse-majesté and defamation of the army. The Hun letter or "China" trials represented a special form of the latter.

Obscured by the question of whether the army officers had indeed been the victims of defamation lay the more far-reaching issue—which the court saw as being beyond its remit—of whether the accusations made in the letters were indeed true. The refusal of the court to be drawn into the latter debate was rooted in an inherent desire to avoid at all costs any outcome that would point to the moral culpability of the German army. However, as the government had failed to provide any proof that the Hun letters were forgeries, the Social Democrats continued their parliamentary attacks.

The Boxer War was the only of the German colonial wars with a legal aftermath. Still smarting at the government prosecutions, the press printed only those letters from the wars in German East Africa and South-West Africa for which they had access to the original. Moreover, the press was starved of information by von Trotha's assertion that it was below the honor of a Prussian soldier to report anything without the permission of his immediate superiors. The soldiers were instructed not to include anything untrue in their letters home, or indeed, anything "which you and I would have cause to discuss upon their publication." The actions of a chastened press and cautious army commanders prevented the incidence of anything approaching a second "Hun letters trial."[61]

Military Journals and Literature

The conduct of Germany's colonial campaigns not only was a topic of debate for parliamentarians but also was covered in a number of daily newspapers. With many of the publications maintaining their own reporters in the theater of war, the military establishment also provided its own press coverage. While its organs maintained only a weekly edition at best, and so were lacking in immediacy, these articles provided a good summary and assessment of recent events.

The relative importance of a conflict is often demonstrated by the attention accorded to it by military newspapers and journals. The depth of coverage of the war in German East Africa in the German, French, and British military press would indicate that it was never accorded as much significance as the conflicts in China and German South-West Africa. Devoting at least a page per week to the conflict in China, the *Militär-Wochenblatt* published only four reports on what it referred to as the "insurgency movement in German East Africa."[62] The same applied to the *Unteroffizier-Zeitung*, which dealt with the Maji Maji War in a handful of short reports. This lack of interest devoted to the conflict in German East Africa was underscored by the depth of coverage of the campaign conducted by Germany's imperial rivals.

Seeking to excuse its cursory reporting of the Herero war in 1904, the *Soldaten-Freund* indicated that the campaign in German South-West Africa had been pushed into the background by its interest in the events in East Asia—meaning the Russo-Japanese War.[63]

Despite the differences in the target audience—officers, noncommissioned officers (NCOs), and other ranks—of the various publications, the military periodicals were united in making the same appeal, calling on their readers to support the German colonial soldiers engaged in China and Africa. They called on the veterans', reservists', and Landwehr associations to organize collections for the wounded and victims of typhus in German South-West Africa. All the military periodicals contained maps locating the various engagements and provided an overview of the conflict as a whole. Maps brought the advantage that they could be easily incorporated in the article. The distances and nature of the communications involved meant that photographs could be printed only months after their being taken. Publications, such as the *Deutsche Offizierblatt*, often referred to the 1:800.000 war map from Dietrich Reimer.[64] The range of commercially available maps (a topic ignored by previous research) catered for and underlines the high level of popular interest in and support for the war.

The most important function of such illustrative material was its capacity to demonstrate the aim and thus necessity of each war, and so justify the military activity. Locating each engagement in a wider context, the maps also explained the tactics employed. Providing sufficient detail to give an impression of the conduct of the war, the maps left ample space for the projection of the readers' preconceptions.

Despite the clear similarities exhibited by the coverage of the various military periodicals of the wars, close study of the German military press also reveals considerable differences between its various organs. The *Militär-Wochenblatt*—itself used as a source by a number of domestic and international publications—focused on providing information regarding the exact strength and composition of the respective Expeditionary Corps, information regarding troop movements, matters of tactical interest, and the course of individual engagements. This focus was especially clear in its coverage of the Nama war, which included accounts of every engagement fought by each unit and the gains made. Where possible, the paper also sought to analyze the intentions of the respective commanders. All these reports were based on the combat reports dispatched to Berlin by each of the High Commands. Strongly reminiscent of the aseptic tone of the war diaries, these articles even included lists of the German and enemy dead. Maintaining a clear focus on the "art of war," the nature of life in the field was mentioned only in passing. The topics of prisoners; camp-life; executions; questions of humanity; or even criticisms from politicians, coverage of the Hun letters, and mutinies were avoided entirely. The *Militär-Wochenblatt* was interested purely in strategy and tactics.

A similar style—if not level of detail—was adopted by the *Deutsche Offizierblatt* and *Neuen Militärische Blätter,* both publications aimed at an audience of officers. Eschewing commentary, these publications restricted themselves to a depiction of the current state of the conflict. Indeed, the *Deutsche Offizierblatt* only once exhibited any level of partisanship, defending the high rate of losses suffered by officers in the battle of Ovikokorero in early 1904. The article argued that the patrol in question was composed predominantly of officers and that the performance and leadership of the troops had been underestimated by other commentators. There was absolutely no need for unease, it opined. In the final analysis, the high number of officers' deaths showed that German troops knew how to die.[65]

In contrast to the publications aimed at officers, the *Unteroffizier-Zeitung* focused less on strategy and tactics or exact data regarding the transport and arrival of reinforcements than on the individual suffering and cares to which the soldiers fighting in the colonial wars were subject. Examining topics such as the cohabitation of the various troop contingents in Peking and Tianjin and the hard life experienced by the troops in German South-West Africa, the publication did not shy from dealing with more controversial topics such as the "Hun letter debate" or the mutiny of German troops in German South-West Africa.[66] Seeking to personalize the war, its editions also included pen portraits of individual officers deemed suitable as role models, such as Ludwig von Estorff.[67] The ideological significance of this periodical was demonstrated by the end of the Estorff article: "May God [protect] and lead home this courageous God-fearing and undaunted leader from the campaign against the black beasts."[68] The *Soldaten-Freund* adopted a similar tone: the military reports from German South-West Africa focused on the "bestial cruelty" with which the natives had slaughtered settlers.[69] Following the outbreak of the Herero war in 1904, the *Soldaten-Freund* published a series of articles focusing on the Boxer War written from the perspective of a single soldier.[70] Although maintaining a constant focus on the course of the war, it did not match the level of detail provided by the *Militär-Wochenblatt* or the *Unteroffizier-Zeitung.*

Not restricting themselves to military circles, the military journals sought to address a wider audience. Even the official publication of the General Staff and Admiralty Staff vied for the attention of a wide public with specialist lectures, monographs, soldierly autobiographies, and supplements to the military periodicals. Although the war in German East Africa generated a sizeable literature, the number of treatments could not compare with the flood of publications focusing on the wars in China and German South-West Africa. The colonial military literature in general profited from the considerable popularity among the fin de siècle German middle class of novels about life in the colonies. However, the literature published immediately after 1900–1904—memoirs, diaries, novels, and children's books—reached more than a middle-class readership.

Both the General Staff and Admiralty Staff took the opportunity provided by the German colonial wars to produce an opulent commemorative volume focusing on the recent conflicts. The navy in particular exploited its role in the Boxer War to publicize its activities and escape from the shadow of its more popular sister institution. The Boxer War was the first overseas campaign in which the German navy had borne the brunt of the initial fighting. Providing a glorified account of the activities of the gunboat *Iltis*, the authors of the navy's commemorative publication then proceeded to make the case for a powerful German fleet.[71] Such profuse treatment contrasted to the navy's reticence over the African wars. It did not publish any subsequent book-length treatment of the conflicts; its output was restricted to a handful of articles in the supplements of the *Marine-Rundschau*.[72] Seeking to distance itself from what it argued must remain an essentially army role, the navy praised the performance of its naval personnel, but remained clear that the role of the navy in such colonial engagements should be restricted to an auxiliary function. In revealing its unwillingness to accept a large colonial role for the navy, the Admiralty Staff was anticipating the interservice discussion of a projected colonial army.

The significance attached to the Boxer War by the members of the Expeditionary Corps was demonstrated in 1902 by the publication of the glossy volume *Germany in China*, edited on the suggestion of von Waldersee by a number of veterans of the campaign. Opening with the fanfare "commemorating a historical event,"[73] the publication was richly illustrated by Theodor Rocholl, a military painter who had accompanied the expedition. Not concerned with the authentic reproduction of battle scenes, he took an aesthetic approach to his work. With very few depictions of battles, the volume contained a number of portraits of both German and allied soldiers as well as Chinese. These were supplemented by pictures of landscapes, temples, and other landmarks. Originally conceived of as a "book of memorial and remembrance" available only to the members of the expedition, "in view of the interest demonstrated across all classes in Germany's first overseas campaign" they extended the originally intended target audience to include a civilian readership.[74]

Opting against a thick commemorative volume for the Herero and Nama War, the General Staff chose to publish a series of smaller and more readable, richly illustrated volumes consisting of articles previously published in the *Vierteljahreshefte für Truppenführung und Heereskunde*.[75] The absence of an official treatment of the Maji Maji War meant that the memoirs of the former governor von Götzen and the Protection Force officer Ernst Nigmann achieved a semiofficial status.[76]

The unabating public interest in the Herero and Nama War was served by the publication of the memoirs of Kurd Schwabe and Maximilian Bayer, both writers and veterans of the war in German South-West Africa. The focus of their publications would suggest that they had divided the work between them: while Schwabe provided a specialist military account, Bayer addressed a wider public. Seeking to provide a "rough overview of the war,"[77] Bayer embarked on a lecture tour of thirty-five towns. Reacting to demand, he summarized his findings in book form. The jacket of the book informed its readers, "Penned by an officer of the General Staff and himself a veteran, this book provided a clear overview of the course of the war, including enthralling descriptions of the excellent performance of our troops as well as an unprejudiced account of the value of a colony and the character of the natives."[78]

Schwabe, on the other hand, expounded his view of the conflict in a number of essays published in the *Vierteljahreshefte für Truppenführung und Heeresführung* and the supplements to the *Militär-Wochenblatt* as well in a number of lectures given to the *Militärische Gesellschaft* in Berlin. Despite addressing a purely military audience, his articles always included long landscape descriptions. Making frequent recourse to notions of a "wild" nature to explain defeat or underperformance, this instrument also served to emphasize the exceptional nature of German military achievements.[79] Moreover, he masked hard geographical facts in lyrical descriptions of nature in an attempt to convince his readers of the central value of colonialism and to garner support and resources for maintaining German South-West Africa as a German colony.[80] No effort was spared to dispel the impression spread by the contributors to *Vorwärts* that "monstrous sums [of money] were being squandered on a depopulated desert of sand."[81]

Other officers from the Protection Force also penned a number of popular novels, projecting a literary treatment of their war experiences to a wide audience. Although drawing on a range of primary sources including orders and eyewitness reports, such books remained entirely fictitious in their reworking of reality and fact. One classic of this genre was the novel from 1906 and titled *Peter Moor's Journey South-West: A Campaign Report (Peter Moors Fahrt nach Südwest: Ein Feldzugsbericht).* Set in the Herero war, it was authored not by an officer but by the writer Gustav Frenssen, who was subsequently nominated for the Nobel Prize for literature. Established as set reading for all German schools in 1908, it was also used in German lessons in the United States. The author had never set foot in German South-West Africa. Indeed, firsthand experience was no precondition for writing such books, many of which merely reproduced existing motifs. With the "truth" of constructed experience being measured against the rules of the discourse on colonial warfare, it is almost impossible to differentiate between authentic and fictive literature on this topic.

All publications by soldiers, both officers and men alike, were subject to strict military censorship. Following an order issued to the corps headquarters in 1901 by Alfred von Schlieffen to secure all the documents, combat reports, and war diaries from the members of the East Asian Expeditionary Corps, he made sure to point out that any negative comments about or other sources of potential embarrassment for those holding the documents would not come to light.[82]

The officers of the Protection Forces, both active and retired, were bound by an imperial order issued in 1897 that subjected publication of their literary output to approval by the Protection Force High Command. This, in turn, was bound to the authority of the Reichskolonialamt and the imperial chancellor.[83] These prescriptions were extended in 1908 to cover all officers in colonial service, including the state police. The commander of each corps headquarters was to reach all decisions pertaining to the use of official sources in such publications and was to consult the Ministry of War and the Reichskolonialamt where necessary. Notes of events in the war already processed by the General Staff were to be presented to its chief. Texts published by soldiers in newspapers or periodicals were to be marked by the name and official position of the author. The navy practiced a similar system of censorship. All publications were to be presented to the chief of the Admiralty staff, who adjudicating "in the interests of impartiality" could withhold permission to go to print or demand changes.[84]

The treatment by the military literature of violence perpetrated away from the immediate battlefield involved a number of interpretations. While contributors to the periodicals aimed at officers managed by and large to ignore it by concentrating on strategy and tactics, both the military literature and those journals aimed at NCOs and other ranks accorded it a certain degree of attention. It is possible to identify three, often interlinking, responses to this violence: acceptance of its necessity, its justification, and an explanation of its incidence.

Violence exercised against the native population was often presented as a natural part of warfare. Thus a number of sources actively named requisitions, population displacement, shootings, and the destruction of villages perpetrated in the Boxer War without going into any great detail. Indeed, such accounts treated violence as merely one topic among a whole range of relevant subjects including descriptions of the landscape or the habits of the native population. Giving the reader the impression that overseas expeditions were nothing more than one long adventure interspersed with fighting, such accounts played down violence to such an extent that the texts soon adopted the quality of travel literature. Resting on the assumption of a Social Darwinist struggle of the cultures, the authors viewed extreme violence as an entirely legitimate option within the course of a colonial war. Silence on the matter was unnecessary.

A second approach sought to justify the actions of the German soldiers, portrayed as fighting in difficult conditions against a barbarous, underhand, and cunning enemy. Those adopting such an approach hoped to demonstrate the necessity of employing extreme measures to achieve what they portrayed as legitimate ends, arguing that those who had "not been there" consistently underestimated the difficulty of the task given to the German soldiers. The military press, in particular the *Unteroffizier-Zeitung*, adopted an even sharper tone in dealing with the allegations raised in the Reichstag. Seeking to confound Social Democratic allegations, it made repeated reference to an (unspecified) "Englishman" who was said to have attested the German soldiers an admirable level of self-control. This Englishman reportedly went on to say that the native population had not been mishandled. In a similar vein, Chancellor von Bülow emphasized the strain, anguish, thirst, and hunger to which the German soldiers had been subject, pointing out that they had shared their last drop of water with women and children.[85] Generalized and sweeping attacks were met by a response of the same nature.

In seeking to explain the necessity for the violence meted out to the civilian population of a colonial environment, proponents of such actions made recourse to the "extermination debate" prevalent in discussions of colonialism both inside and outside the Reichstag. Thus the participants of the 1905 Kolonialkongress debated at length the question as to whether the native population of German South-West Africa should be expropriated, enslaved, or exterminated.[86] Not new, this question had been subject to frequent debate. Many on both sides of the argument identified with a public debate by two authorities: Colonel Theodor Leutwein and Lothar von Trotha. Speaking out against the extermination of the Herero in his capacity as former governor of German South-West Africa, Leutwein made clear that his opinion was not the result of humanitarian consideration, but economic and military considerations. Seeking on the one hand to retain the natives as a productive labor force, he also feared provoking what he believed to be an unwinnable guerilla war.[87] A similar position was advanced by the officer Ernst Nigmann. Writing in 1911, he asserted, "While a European war must always aim at the annihilation [*Vernichtung*] of the enemy, colonial wars always dictate a certain level of restraint; in colonial contexts the destruction of the enemy depletes our most valuable possession, and amounts thus to self-damage. This explains the regularity with which commanders seek to negotiate with native soldiers, something often viewed with incomprehension by our comrades at home."[88]

Placed in the context of European military doctrine, the term "annihilation" *(Vernichtung)* of the enemy as used by Nigmann referred to the targeted killing of all those enemy soldiers deployed on the battlefield. In colonial warfare, on the other hand, it was common to differentiate between a "simple victory" *(einfacher Sieg)* and the "exploitation of the victory to the point of extermination" *(Ausnutzung des Sieges bis zur Vernichtung)*.[89] Indeed, as demonstrated in the correspondence between Leutwein and the Nama captain Hendrik Witbooi,[90] when placed in a colonial context, the word *Vernichtung*, taken to mean "extermination," could very easily culminate in the liquidation of an entire people. Assuming genocidal characteristics, such a course of action involved much more than simply "breaking the enemy resistance."[91]

Failing to differentiate between such considerations, the term *Vernichtung* proved to be far too diffuse to provide an accurate description of the type of killing involved in warfare. Such taxonomic shortcomings were of no import for a classical engagement conducted in accordance with European customs: the battle was over once the enemy had surrendered, fled, or capitulated. When placed in the context of a guerilla war, however, terms such as "victory" and "annihilation" proved to be void of any guiding principles, while at the same time licensing any degree of action. Although the term suggested a certain level of military clarity, it in fact remained a matter of complete uncertainty as to the extent to which violence should be exercised. When applied to a small ethnic grouping such as the Herero or Nama, even when no orders were issued to this end, the concept of *Vernichtung* could result in the liquidation of an entire ethnic group. Bandied about within the military and civilian discourse on colonial warfare entirely without definition, this concept could be applied to any conceivable agenda.

Forced by the parliamentary debate and the Hun letter trials to deal with this sensitive subject, the military authors emphasized that the military term *Vernichtung* was not to be confused with the term for extermination *(Ausrottung)*. The script of a lecture given by Maximilian Bayer in 1906 makes clear that "the word *vernichten* is to be understood in its military sense. [When used by] a soldier, he does not mean that everything is to be entirely razed, but that the resistance of the enemy is to be broken to such an extent that he is unable to regroup for an attack."[92]

Feeling forced to provide explanation for the concept of *Vernichtung,* the reporter for the *Militär-Wochenblatt,* Curt von François, argued that in the context of the Nama war, it did not refer to the physical killing of the entire native population, especially in view of the fact that "entire tribes cannot disappear just like that" and "a proportion of them always remain."[93] Despite this attempt to address the question of extermination, the possible aims and actual extent of the violence perpetrated by the German troops were not subject to any form of discussion. As a result, the German Empire failed to establish any binding definition of the term *Vernichtung.* Lacking any level of semantic clarity, the discussion consisted of a number of statements covering all possible variations. The meaning of the term *Vernichtung* varied according to its user and the subject under discussion. The nature of the action could not be derived from the mere use of the word to describe it.

In contrast to the uncertain and inconsistent treatment of violence unleashed on the native population, all the German-speaking military publications accorded extensive coverage of that suffered by German soldiers. Celebrating their heroism, the publications concentrated on the sacrifice of life and money and the bravery and steadfast response of the ordinary soldier to the most difficult and trying of circumstances. The readers of such accounts were assured that German soldiers, depicted as maintaining their martial spirit at all times, had not forgotten how to fight. Styling the wars in China and German South-West Africa as epic struggles, such accounts even transformed them into a success. Portraying the wars as a test of spirit and resolve, the German soldier was shown to have passed with flying colors: the previous thirty years of peace had done nothing to dim either his ardor or his pugnacity.

The Multifunctional Colonial Soldier

Although not an official publication, an illustrated history of the war in German South-West Africa published in 1907 with a foreword from Lieutenant-General von Trotha is an example of German military self-publicity, which has received comparatively little notice from historians.[94] The purpose of the book was reflected on its cover. Framed in a dark-blue cover page is a scene painted in brown tones. A mounted soldier of the Protection Force rests with his horse which, apparently tired from a long ride, is resting. Although the horse is clearly impulsive—it has thrown its head up, its eyes are gleaming, and the wind is blowing through its mane—it has obviously been tamed and is subservient to its master. Similarly broken is a kneeling native with his spear and shield lying useless alongside him. Surveying this scene is the imperial eagle. The message is clear: having subdued and cultivated nature, the white man is master of all he surveys.

This message permeates the whole book. It offers neither an introduction nor an explanation for any of the photographs. Indeed, apart from the foreword from the editor and von Trotha, the book contains no running text. The photographer is named as Feldwebel Georg Rau, a former member of the Protection Force invalided out of service. According to von Trotha, Rau was able to record both the "significant moments and main locations" of the war as well as the dangerous operations of his unit.[95] For his part, the editor dwells less on the skills of the photographer than on the significance of the publication. Intended not just as a further addition to the literature focusing on "the difficult engagements fought by our upstanding troops in German South-West Africa during the years 1904–07," the volume was intended to "help the German people—who had followed the conflict with increasing interest, as its heroic sons fought for God and kaiser and country against an enemy as cruel as it was brave—to understand the conflict through providing a photographic record."[96] The photograph was taken as an irrefutable depiction of reality requiring no further description or adornment.

The fifty-nine double pages present between six and nine black and white photographs per page. Of various formats, small, large, long, narrow, round, and square, flicking through the volume gives a very lively impression. The photographs are accompanied by small captions, and are undated. Often so small as to obscure important details, they require close study. Conditioned by the state of technology, the wide-angle camera used often gives the pictures a panoramic appearance. Details thus often become lost. The penultimate pages give close attention to a number of officers—Colonel Theodor Leutwein, Lieutenant-General Lothar von Trotha, Colonel Berthold von Deimling, Lieutenant-Colonel Erich von Redern, Major Johann Meister, Captain Maximilian Bayer, and Captain Starck are portrayed in addition to a number of black leaders including the Nama captain Hendrik Witbooi and the Herero chief Samuel Maharero. The Herero deputy-chiefs Kambazembi and Mbandjoo (Banjo) are also depicted with their families. The last pages of the volume present a number of portraits and names of the thirty-two German officers who died in German South-West Africa. Tastefully arranged, von Trotha recommends the album to all "friends of our new lands."[97]

Every page of the book is dedicated to one topic serving as a geographical or military point of orientation. Framed by the sea journey to and from the protectorate, the story unfolds through page titles such as "Departure from home," "On board the Woermann steamer 'Eleonore,'" and finally "The return home." The colony is introduced using nature photographs, with titles such as "Rock formation on the Khan Mountains" or "Vegetation in the North." The photographs present the landscape of the colony in all its forms including both the dreary subtropical lands dominated by steppe and thorn bushes and the more hilly and diverse north. Pictures of the "wilderness" are interspersed with those of cultivated nature. A number of pictures of animal husbandry and agricultural land make clear the varied form of land use and lifestyles present in the colony.

A far greater number of photographs focused on the larger settlements such as Swakopmund, Karibib, Okahandja, and Windhoek. Scenes such as "A mobile light house in the coastal town of Swakopmund," the "Mole head with a searchlight," "A ship repair yard," and "The first car train in the dried-out bed of the River Swakop" documented the progress of civilization in the colony. The impression thus generated is supplemented by images of railroads and stations, telegraph lines, and bridges from the land's interior. A particular attraction was the longest bridge in German South-West Africa (1,150 feet/350 meters) between Okahandja and Osona.

The overwhelming majority of the photographs reflected military life. Pictures such as "Scenes from military life in Windhoek," "Field telegraphy stations in the South," and "On the march from Okahandja to Otjosondu" all showed the everyday life of German colonial soldiery. The pictures captured the apparently dominating presence of the military in the colonial world: camps, field barracks, horse stalls, a command post in the communications zone, an officers' field mess, a heliographic unit, a paymaster's office, a military hospital, a field company marching, a supply column, a machine cannon section, and a horse corral. Senior officers such as Lothar von Trotha and Erich von Redern were also depicted on a reconnaissance mission.

A further series of pictures is devoted to scenes from native life. Concentrating less on the conditions of living, their customs, or habits, the photographer focused on finding pictures demonstrating the distinct harmony in which colonizer and native shared a common existence. This section was dominated by pictures showing whites and blacks working together in the garden, or the Germans distributing rations with cows and black children mingling in a nearby river. A photograph taken in the office of the field telegraph at Windhoek shows two officers, a soldier, and a black boy. The officer is leafing through a war diary.

The violent nature of the war also features in the picture sequence: "Marching to face the enemy," "Enemy in sight," "Ambush," and "Lull in combat" cover various recurring episodes of the war. The photograph "Enemy in sight" shows five soldiers among a bizarre rock formation, straining to locate an imaginary enemy. Only a number of corpses on the edge of the photograph reference the violence of war. The picture "Lull in combat" shows a number of soldiers with weapons in front of a destroyed building. Standing at an identical distance from each other, the protagonists have also assumed an identical pose. War damage is referred to in pictures such as "Buildings destroyed by the Herero" and "A damaged telegraph line." A number of soldiers' graves not only evoke the war but also are designed to comfort the bereaved.

Some of the pictures of natives also made reference to war and the inherent danger of the enemy, yet in a diluted, exotic fashion. Nevertheless, the pictures "War games from the area of Okahandja," "Hereros in war costume," and "Herero women in war jewelry" betray themselves as fantasies, as all they show are Herero in their typical everyday headwear. Further pictures included "Belligerent Herero boys" or "Herero boys playing war." Proof of their "belligerence" was provided by four young black boys standing underneath a tree holding lances, while their playmates sit on the branches with bows and arrows. On the other hand, the series of pictures "Prisoners of war" showed some forty black men, women, and children sitting in a semicircle. Sitting around waiting for the camera to take their picture, they appear both healthy and cared for and in no way indicative of the horrendous conditions in the internment camps. The picture "Transporting captive Hereros" does not show any prisoners, while the picture "Black criminals in chains" does not reveal the crime they committed.

Masking the horror and terror of war, these surreal tableaux show absolutely no injured or dead German soldiers or dying Herero prisoners. The staged pictures of this volume engender absolutely no anxiety, at best producing a little curiosity or light revulsion. Indeed, the album was published to present German South-West Africa as an emergent and prosperous country, not the reality of a colony defiled by war and mass murder. The message of the book was a simple as it was clear: this land deserved to become German, and a number of Germans had already set about the task in hand. German military commanders viewed the colonial soldier as having a double role to perform: pioneering the advance of civilization by fighting the enemies of progress, they were also to undertake the work of building the new world. The advocates of such a role were apt to draw parallels to antiquity: working in German South-West Africa, Lieutenant Ludwig von Estorff was given the soubriquet "the old Roman" for his habit of reminding everyone that the Romans had built whole roads with a pick and shovel.[98] The ideal colonial soldier, embodied by the "Protection Force Man" was not just characterized by his military virtues—fearlessness, bravery, tactical knowledge, and discipline—he was also the ideal colonizer. The multifunctional colonial soldier had been born.

To conclude, the internal German discussions of the colonial wars, especially those conducted in the Reichstag and the specialist military literature, attached far greater significance to the wars in China and German South-West Africa than the Maji Maji War in German East Africa. While the imperial government made money, men, and equipment available in ready number for these two conflicts, von Bülow realized from the outset that important financial and political considerations ruled out the conduct of the war in German East Africa on anything approaching the same scale. As the conflict was ended with the dispatch of only minimal reinforcements, the question has to be asked as to the course of action that the government would have taken following any escalation. It is safe to assume that the Reichstag would eventually have granted the necessary resources.

With the Reichstag unable to establish a cross-party consensus on the minimum standards of humanity to govern colonial warfare, the debate was dominated by heated discussion of the "national question." Despite this unfocused approach, the parliamentary exchanges revealed the rejection by the Social Democrats and some others of the level of brutality exhibited by Germany in her colonies. This matter was subject to much closer scrutiny within the framework of the Hun letter trials. Indeed, it was these processes and not—as many contend—the trials following the First World War that represented the first time that violence in war became the focus of legal proceedings. Even if this innovation was the by-product of a prosecution for defamation, the soldiers questioned were forced to address the proportionality of their response to Chinese resistance. Both the legal and the parliamentary scrutiny of Germany's colonial wars made an important contribution to sensitizing sections of German society to the realities of military violence. Despite the prevalence of racism in German society, military writers still saw themselves as required to defend the actions of the soldiers in the colonial wars.

Despite the limited legal impact of the trials, their very existence underlines the fact that even in the highly militaristic and racist nature of Wilhelmine Germany, not all military actions went unquestioned—an observation that undermines any attempt to portray the Kaiserreich as little more than a prequel to the Third Reich. However, as significant as they were, these processes and debates did little to sap the broad domestic coalition supportive of exercising regular and considerable violence as a method of colonial rule and indeed nothing to sow doubt among colonial soldiers of the validity of their role and value. Conceiving of themselves as more than the mere agents of violence, colonial soldiers ascribed themselves a multifaceted, multifunctional role involving both colonial development and destruction.

Part **III**

EVALUATION *and* MEMORY

CHAPTER 11

The Military

EXHIBITING only minor interest in learning lessons from the colonial wars, the inner circle of the German military did little to force any program of evaluation. With consultations on the matter dragging on over a number of years, the conclusions drawn from these wars were not incorporated in the planning or execution of subsequent conflicts. The efforts made to learn lessons from the campaigns in China and Africa were restricted to attempts to effect improvements in weaponry and organization. Nevertheless, in a departure from European military doctrine, German military planners did recognize the small war as a specific form of colonial warfare, but failed to provide their soldiers with any form of training pertinent to its conduct. Those charged with evaluating the conduct of the Chinese and African expeditions collated a number of disparate insights applicable to European warfare, but the Ministry of War did nothing to transform them into anything approaching binding regulations. None of the secret military reports compiled in the aftermath of the three conflicts examined in this study focused on the breach of basic rules of humanity committed by the German forces.

Reports from China and Africa:
Strategies of Annihilation and Attrition

Responsibility for evaluating the experiences of the German soldiers overseas was held by the same institutions charged with their conduct: the Protection Force High Command (part of the Imperial Colonial Office), the Ministry of

War, the Imperial Naval Office, and the General Staff. A commission set up by a cabinet order immediately after the end of the Boxer War (October 1901) was charged with "determining any necessary or desirable measures for future expeditions." Basing its deliberations on a memorandum composed by Field Marshal Alfred Graf von Waldersee, the committee sought to establish improvements to be made to any future overseas campaigns.[1]

A similar procedure was initiated following the end of the Herero and Nama War in German South-West Africa. Proposing such a course to the military cabinet in February 1908, the permanent secretary in the newly founded Imperial Colonial Office, Bernhard von Dernburg, outlined his concept of a committee to be charged with this task. Nine months later, Kaiser Wilhelm II appointed such a commission, to be chaired by Major General Erich von Gündell, quartermaster-general of the General Staff and himself a veteran of the Boxer War. Von Gündell was to appoint his committee and then evaluate "the experiences gathered in the process of dispatching reinforcements for the Protection Force to South-West-Africa."[2] The commission met a total of thirty-five times between December 1908 and March 1909.

In contrast, the war in German East-Africa was not subject to discussion by an interministerial body. However, the Imperial Naval Office and the chief of the Admiralty Staff did benefit from reading the "Report regarding the experiences gathered within the naval forces" authored by the senior naval officer in Dar es Salaam. Focusing on the climate and "particular conditions" presented in the region, the report concluded that there were no lessons to be learned from the conflict that were applicable to warfare in any other area such as German South-West Africa.[3]

The prototype for the evaluation process was provided by the memorandum drafted by von Waldersee in the aftermath of the Boxer War. Taking the form of a comprehensive error analysis, his memorandum advanced a number of explanations as to why the German expeditionary force required so much more time to organize and deploy than did its allied counterparts. A reporter in China judged that it was this delay that made the German troops unclear as to the appropriate course of action: "The incubus of aimlessness lay heavy on the hearts of all [the soldiers]."[4] The Waldersee memorandum examined problems of organization and logistics, company formation, embarkation and disembarkation, the horses available, clothing, equipment, weapons, supplies, accommodation, the medical, train, and cartographical services, the railroad troops, the practice of troop sport, and the use of interpreters.[5]

In the estimation of von Waldersee, German performance during the embarkation and disembarkation of the expeditionary force had proven to be especially bad because it had failed to enlist the help of Chinese auxiliaries or German merchants and engineers resident in China. Von Waldersee also identified serious shortcomings in German soldiers' efforts to familiarize themselves with local conditions and thus the potential resources open to them. All the other contingents, but especially the French, had proven superior in their ability "to adapt quickly to foreign conditions and exploit the resources that the land offered."[6] Reflecting on the German dependence on Chinese collaborators and German missionaries for communication with the locals, and in anticipation of the new "native troop" about to be raised in China, von Waldersee recommended improving the language skills of the Officer Corps. He discovered further deficits in matters of equipment. Reporting that the long and short arms issued to the troop—the German contingent was not equipped with machine guns—to be sufficient, he identified shortcomings with the uniforms. Too thick and not waterproof, the Khaki uniforms were not color-fast. Von Waldersee viewed the stained appearance of his soldiers with distaste. His final criticism focused on the lightweight nature of the train material which did not stand up to the demands placed on it by the Chinese environment. He recommended emulation of the British tack used for the draft animals. Despite such problems, he noted that the liaison troops and the German railroad company had performed as well as their Japanese and Russian counterparts.

Von Waldersee also considered which arms of the service were best suited to a colonial war. In keeping with conventional wisdom, he favored the deployment of mounted infantry for such purposes, arguing that their high level of mobility enabled them to overcome the intelligence system maintained by the Chinese. Such a deployment would necessitate the training of sections of the regular infantry in horsemanship. Nevertheless, von Waldersee remained convinced that the cavalry retained an important role in the colonial theater, capable as it was of performing long-range scouting, destruction, pursuit, and combat operations. His ambivalence toward this arm was echoed in the discussion conducted after 1918 of the role and relevance of the cavalry in the First World War.

Significant passages of the Waldersee memorandum were reproduced in the final report of the secret commission.[7] In the final analysis, both reports indicated that improved performance in the colonial wars required enhanced language and intercultural skills, more suitable equipment, and better preparation. The military was united in its wish to end its reliance on improvisation in colonial warfare. The assumption was that improvements in organization and technical resources would provide the route to success.

A significant conclusion emerging from this process was the identification of considerable differences in the equipment required for a colonial and a European war. The reports recommended equipping artillerymen and members of the train serving in a colonial environment with firearms so as to defend themselves against insurgents.[8] Despite identifying and discussing a number of differences between European and colonial warfare, the German military hierarchy saw no need to reconsider the strategy and tactics employed in their prosecution. Although having fought a number of engagements with regular Chinese troops from which they could have learned valuable lessons, in regarding the Chinese war as a resounding success, German planners regarded the campaign as providing vindication of the existing values and military doctrines which had been applied in what they regarded as difficult conditions. Far from being seen as requiring new military thinking, the recent success in China led many to believe that reform was unnecessary.

In keeping with this analysis, the planners' response to the Boxer campaign restricted itself to dealing with a range of practical questions such as the embarkation, disembarkation, and transit of horses and equipment.[9] No other lessons were learned that were felt to be applicable to the later war in German South-West Africa. With the long duration of the Herero and Nama War proving a source of concern, the evaluation of Germany's "African experiences" was drawn up as an error analysis, searching for the source of failure.[10] Not just focusing on organization and equipment, as part of a new development, the discussions also addressed questions of strategy and tactics.

Compared with the findings of the official interministerial commission established by the kaiser, the unofficial report from the Protection Force High Command pulled no punches in the criticism that it articulated.[11] Noting that the "European rules often failed or [at least] did not lead to complete success as would have been the case in Europe,"[12] criticism focused on the "dogma of the battle of annihilation," a concept that had not proven itself in a colonial context: "An energetic advance without consideration for the line of communications; encirclement of the enemy and a ruthless pursuit—the principle of annihilation did not have the same level of success as would be expected in Europe, or at least not within the timetable to which we aspired. The outcome was a natural result of the theater of war, enemy operations and the employment of unsuitable resources."[13]

The report highlighted the failure of the Protection Force to encircle the Herero group, even while it was weighed down with cattle, womenfolk, and children. Applied in the Nama war against a "light and unencumbered enemy," such tactics were depicted as being doomed from the outset.[14] The report implicitly accepted that women and children represented a legitimate aspect of military planning and as such, a target of action.

Close analysis of the war established that the concentric advance on the Herero position on the Waterberg had been precipitate. The report concluded that the advance should only have been ordered following the establishment of a working set of communication lines sufficient to victual the advancing army and provide enough horses with which to conduct the pursuit. Victualing required both the procurement and transport of the requisite material. As the surrounding area yielded only a little livestock and even less pasture, supplies had to be shipped from the metropole. In view of this situation, the authors of the report judged that success of the subsequent pursuit was a matter of fortune as "the enemy retreated voluntarily to an arid area in which both he and his cattle were destroyed." The pursuit in the Nama war, on the other hand, was judged to be only a partial success: the enemy had been worn down through a strategy of attrition. Not employing the conventional forms of colonial warfare (resource destruction), this new tactic represents an innovation in the arsenal of German military doctrine and tactics. Nevertheless, remaining wedded to the primacy of the battle of encirclement and annihilation, planners were reluctant to focus on what could have represented a revolution in German military thinking.[15]

This failure nevertheless marked the end of the primacy accorded by the Protection Force High Command to the doctrine of the pursuit. The adoption of the new strategy of attrition in any future conflict was rendered all the more remarkable by the contemporary attitude of the Army General Staff, which was vehement in its rejection of such an approach. It was probably no matter of chance that the official report on German South-West Africa drafted by the interministerial commission avoided any reference to a "strategy of attrition," choosing instead a considerably cagier formulation: "a final victory can often only be achieved through tenacity and unrelenting action." The commission knew that it would not accept such a direct endorsement of what amounted to a less active strategy.[16]

A further innovation contained in the report from the Protection Force was its rejection of another piece of German military orthodoxy, the primacy of the offensive. Although conceding that a small war could be won using both an offensive and a defensive strategy, it was recognized that the former required the provision of sufficient victualing and supply stations to facilitate an unremitting pursuit of the enemy. Revolving around a series of "fast, short, successful and cheap actions,"[17] an offensive strategy required a sophisticated network of logistics in order to provide the advancing troops with sufficient material with which to conduct the advance. A defensive response to an insurrection, on the other hand, was characterized by the occupation of watering holes and the seizure of livestock. This was to be supplemented by hostage taking and bribery. The report concluded that in some situations, the only option open to a colonial force was a defensive strategy, denying the enemy the experience of success.

The report advanced three further reasons for the protracted length of the war: the absence of a railroad network, the lack of parliamentary support, and the insufficient deployment of native auxiliaries. The absence of a railroad connection in the south of the protectorate between Lüderitz Bay and Keetmannshoop was seen as preventing Germany from "deploying the superior weaponry of the white man in sufficient strength and for a sufficient duration."[18] Despite recognizing that the deployment of state-of-the-art weaponry against antiquated muzzle-loaders and bows and arrow did not guarantee automatic success in colonial warfare, in focusing on the absence of a railway, the authors of the report still clung to a technological explanation. However, such a conclusion could be refuted by reference to the South African War, in which the railroads used by the British required the deployment of considerable personnel reserves to protect against sabotage.

The report was clear in singling out the lack of parliamentary support in Germany as a factor hampering the conduct of the war in German South-West Africa: "the smooth, speedy prosecution of colonial wars is more or less . . . a question of money. [Success requires that] military leaders do not have their hands tied by considerations of a pecuniary nature."[19] This reasoning established what amounted to the precursor of the "stab in the back" myth of 1918, stating that the German army had been defeated by its domestic enemies. The perversity of this argument came in its clear reversal of cause and effect—as we have seen, the Social Democratic and Center Party deputies denied further war subsidies only after it had become clear that the deficiencies in the conduct of the war had rendered its end entirely incalculable. A further weakness involved in this position was the fact that the successor parliament convened after the "Hottentot election" voted the necessary funds. The argument may well have been advanced merely to demonize the forces of domestic reform and strengthen the resolve of the antidemocratic elements at court.

In a third point, the commission report identified the lack of support among the native population as a further reason for the difficulty and costliness of the Nama war. With the exception of the Rehobother Baster, "almost all native [groupings] joined the uprising successively and we were unable to draw on any native auxiliaries."[20] In making this point, the authors of the report conceded that a war in a settler colony could not be successful without the collaboration of at least a section of the native population. Also of fundamental significance was the insight that colonial warfare required considerably greater adaptation to "foreign conditions" than was originally realized.

While the first two arguments advanced to explain the failures of the war (the absence of a railroad and the lack of parliamentary support) amount to little more than a pretext, the acknowledgment of clear failures—in particular the inadvisability of issuing the extermination proclamation and defects in military strategy—represent clear conclusions, the lessons of which could have been applied to future wars conducted in a colonial and even a European setting. Nevertheless, no such learning process was implemented; the military establishment sought to maintain the clear separation between colonial and European forms of warfare. This is demonstrated with particular clarity by the discussions surrounding the possibility of raising a colonial army.

The Colonial Army and the Lessons for Europe

In view of the scope and nature of the three wars conducted in a colonial environment, the question was raised as to whether to end the current policy of conducting colonial wars using a voluntary expeditionary corps, in favor of the establishment of a permanent colonial army with the requisite specialist training. This question was first discussed in specialist military journals before receiving consideration from the army authorities. Such calls had come as early as 1900. Writing in an article published for the *Militär-Wochenblatt*, Hermann von Wissmann argued that the long periods of training required by colonial soldiers (amounting in his view to a minimum of six months) required the formation of a number of colonial regiments to be maintained in the metropole ready for deployment at short notice as the core of a larger expeditionary corps.[21] A similar argument was advanced by

Field Marshal von Waldersee in his memorandum from 1901 in which he called for the formation of "a type of colonial army."[22] Just as the Chinese garrison had required reinforcements in 1900, Waldersee identified the distinct lack of an immediately available reserve trained for colonial operations. The former governor of German South-West Africa, Theodor Leutwein, also saw the necessity for a colonial army. Speaking in an interview held shortly after his dismissal in December 1904, he maintained that the climatic conditions presented in the colonies rendered colonial service exceptionally difficult for ordinary European soldiers and had caused a number of deaths.[23] An article published in the *Vierteljahreshefte für Truppenführung und Heereskunde* referred to the failings of the soldiers deployed in the war in German South-West Africa. Criticizing their poor firearms skills, their susceptibility to illness, their "weak character," unfamiliarity with the country, and lack of equine skills, the author identified the necessity of "special preparation[s]."[24]

The question regarding the establishment of a dedicated colonial army became a topic of intense debate in the higher echelons of the military establishment in the aftermath of the wars in German South-West Africa and German East Africa. The four institutions participating in the debate—the Imperial Colonial Office, the Imperial Naval Office, the Ministry of War, and the General Staff—not only focused on the reorganization of the Protection Force, which was to be retained as an independent force next to the army and navy, but also discussed the creation of a permanent expeditionary force, which was to provide a more suitable response to colonial emergencies, what one officer referred to as "shortcomings [registered] in unusual times."[25] While ruling out the formation of a regular colonial army on financial grounds, the debate (conducted until 1914) focused on two models. With the Reichstag usually unwilling to grant the monies for colonial undertakings, the first model concentrated on training existing military formations to equip them with the skills necessary for immediate deployment in a colonial theater. According to this model, the future expeditionary force could be formed from volunteers from the army; a further approach even foresaw the Marine Infantry constituting the core of a future colonial army. There was no interministerial lobby that could have exerted pressure for the creation of a colonial army. Instead, the arguments advanced for and against such a move reflected the interests of the institutions involved.

The Ministry of War articulated considerable disquiet regarding proposals to second specific sections of the army for training for and deployment in a colonial theater. Concerned that such a course could lead to the breakup of existing formations, planners feared their damaging absence during a European conflict. Seeking to maintain the constant availability of the army for operations in Europe, they favored a solution involving the formation of a standing colonial army of mercenaries. Despite such official opposition in military circles, the idea of a colonial expeditionary corps was never abandoned entirely, and various bodies in the ministry considered the raising of a brigade consisting of mounted infantry, a mounted machine gun section, a mounted pioneer company, and three railroad companies. Those advancing such ideas established certain restrictions on the scope of preparation that such a formation was to receive: although it was considered desirable to accord the officers, medical officers, and administrators specialist colonial training, the pressures of time involved in the mobilization of this brigade would rule out the practicality of such a step. The infantry of this new formation, on the other hand, were to be given equine training, even if only on a basic level. The Ministry of War agreed that one soldier per company was to be given training in caring for horses, but no riding lessons. All other necessary training pertinent to a colonial war was to be provided during mobilization. The ministry felt that the short periods of service to which soldiers were subject did not provide any scope for lengthier episodes of colonial training.[26]

The naval authorities were similarly wary of such proposals. Rejecting the idea of refashioning the Marine Infantry as a colonial army, the Imperial Naval Office argued that the nature of the training accorded to their soldiers did not equip them for the multifaceted tasks involved in an overseas expedition. Comprising horsemanship, marksmanship, field and patrol service, and a working knowledge of geography, ethnography, and applied gymnastics, the training required to enable the Sea Battalions to perform this role did not match the interests and functions of the navy. It would also involve the costs of establishing an equine center for every Sea Battalion with a strength of up to one hundred horses. Moreover, the navy argued that it could not spare its soldiers from the task of guarding the imperial dockyards on the Baltic and North Seas and that any short-term replacements provided by the army would not be suitable for the task. Despite conceding that the Sea Battalions could be deployed in a colonial war without additional training, the naval authorities maintained that should they again be the first to arrive in an overseas emergency, colonial military planners could not expect that they perform any mounted or specialized military operations.

Nevertheless, the Imperial Naval Office conceded (if a little reluctantly) that their battalions could be deployed as part of a colonial army without extra training.[27]

The composition of the possible expeditionary corps was not the only bone of contention between the ministries. As well as disputing the command of the possible formation, the Imperial Colonial Office and the Ministry of War were also unable to agree on the modalities of command in cases in which the corps was forced to work together with the Protection Force of a particular colony. The Protection Forces were subject to the immediate authority of the Imperial Colonial Office, a civilian authority. A number of figures in the Ministry of War considered a parallel solution in which the Protection Force would remain under this command and fight alongside the new expeditionary force, which would report to the Ministry of War.[28]

In contrast to this extensive level of discord, all those involved agreed that the current ordinances regulating European engagements—the Drill Manuals, Field Service Regulations, the Inventory of Equipment, and Administrative Ordinances—were insufficient to structure colonial campaigns. As a result, it was agreed that additional ordinances would be produced as an appendix to the existing provisions. Collated in a compendium, these would "enable every [soldier] dispatched [to the colonial theater] to establish in the shortest of time, what additional provisions apply to his training."[29] The new provisions were to be prefaced by the following address: "The domestic ordinances [continue to] provide guidance for all overseas expeditions, as far as they are not affected by the following provisions. Should these provisions prove to be insufficient, the commander of the expeditionary corps and the commanders of all its permanent and temporary formations are authorized to act on their own authority to take all necessary measures and undergo all expense to ensure that the purpose of the provisions are met."[30]

These discussions culminated in the drafting in 1912 of a secret "plan to establish a German expeditionary corps." Made up from volunteers drawn from regular formations of the army, subordinated to the imperial army and administered separately from the forces of the individual states, this formation, resembling a mixed brigade, was to be placed under the direct command of the kaiser. Consisting of mounted fighting formations, the troops were to cooperate with the command and logistics authorities as well as the line units; its brigade strength could be augmented at any time. Administered by the Prussian Ministry of War and subject to all conventional military ordinances, the force was to be provided with "Supplementary Prescriptions to

Standing Orders" and a "Field Service Ordinance Regulating War and Military Strategy in Overseas Expeditions."[31]

Despite this advance, the plan to establish an expeditionary corps included a decisive restriction, maintaining that the troops were intended exclusively for "extra-European, non-tropical areas."[32] It would appear that this caveat represented the triumph of medical considerations that doubted both the feasibility and desirability of deploying European soldiers in a tropical environment. Although European colonial troops were more reliable than native auxiliaries, their susceptibility to tropical diseases made European-manned colonial expeditions costly undertakings in terms of the money spent on medical provision.[33] The restrictions to which the deployment of white troops in a tropical colony was subject, and the short-term nature of such operations, meant that such campaigns should be conducted by formations of colored troops.[34] The planned expeditionary corps was not intended for deployment in tropical locations.[35] German East Africa was taken as an important example of a "tropical colony" in which the acclimatization and military performance of white troops posed the main problems to the conduct of a war in its territory. Lessons had been learned from this conflict.

The subtropical location and climate of German South-West Africa meant that the planned expeditionary corps could have seen service only in this German protectorate. Nevertheless, the strong reduction in the native population (the ratio of the settler population to its native counterpart was intended to be reduced to between 1:4 and 1:5) led the South-West Africa Commission to assume that the Protection Force would experience no problems in dealing with any further uprising and did not require reinforcement from the metropole. Instead, the force was intended to recruit further volunteers from the planned population surplus of what was intended to become a growing settler population. Moreover, the commission considered the proposed expeditionary corps to be inadequate for the potential tasks demanded of it. Should an uprising be sparked from revolts in neighboring colonies, then it was seen that the "struggle between the white and colored races" would be too much for the proposed expeditionary corps. Such considerations led to an agreement at the end of November 1910 between the Ministry of War, the Imperial Colonial Office, and the Imperial Naval Office, which foresaw the suspension of the medically founded restriction on operations by a white colonial army in German South-West Africa. The expeditionary corps was to be prepared for a wider overseas area of operation without restriction to a specific region or area.[36] Such considerations resulted in the conception of a globally deployable intervention force, reflecting the geopolitical aspirations of Wilhelmine World Politic *(Weltpolitik).*

The increasing radius of action accorded to the proposed expeditionary corps threatened to generate a number of political problems at the point at which the plans were to be realized. Responding to the Morocco Crisis of 1911, the minister of war, Josias von Heeringen, moved in both this and the following year—in response to the "Plan to establish a German expeditionary corps"—to request that the chancellor place the planned force on a secure legal footing. Arguing that the necessity to attain parliamentary approval for its deployment in tense situations would result in unavoidable delay, he referred to the indemnity law required in November 1900 to effect the retrospective legalization of the deployment of the East Asian Expeditionary Corps. Arguing that parliamentary sanction for such operations would not always be forthcoming, he also pointed out that such a corps could only be armed and equipped in peacetime on the basis of such a statutory footing.[37]

The German Foreign Ministry was vehement in its rejection of this argument. It would not countenance "a law containing such provisions and aimed exclusively at extra-European events which is to be passed in peacetime and not as a response to the immediate impact of events requiring [the intervention of such a force]." The ministry made a counterproposal, involving legislation aimed explicitly at the deployment of an expeditionary corps in the German protectorates. They argued that "the [probability of] the need to dispatch a large-scale expedition to a nontropical protectorate would not appear sufficient to justify [the passage] of such a law."[38]

Although there is no evidence of a response on the part of the Ministry of War, it can be assumed that this significant restriction was not received with any great enthusiasm. Although never realized, the "Plan to establish a German expeditionary corps" reveals the true intentions of the army command. Not primarily interested in colonial warfare, it sought to use the argument of colonial intervention as a covert instrument with which to extend its operational remit. The Army Command wanted a standing mandate to deploy German soldiers across the globe. The only legislative consequence of such aspirations, however, was the act passed in 1913 obliging German citizens living in the colonies to service in the local Protection Force.[39] The act also permitted servicemen from the Reich to serve their terms abroad, but only in German South-West Africa as Germany's only colony of white settlement. Further evidence of a lack of interest in matters of colonial warfare on the part of the army hierarchy was manifested in the doctrines applicable to military training developed from the reports into the wars in German South-West Africa. Representing the first long-term independent military expedition mounted by the young German state, it could be expected that the German military establishment would have sought to draw extensive lessons from its course and conduct. Although a number of investigations did reach a range of findings, they were not translated into binding directives, but instead were issued as rough-and-ready recommendations set out across three quarters of a page. Forwarded to all units by the Ministry of War, they were to be read as reporting "experiences of general value."[40] Distinguishing it from European warfare (said to be dominated by set-piece battles), the paper portrayed colonial conditions as requiring a different form of warfare. As such, so the paper argued, only a very few doctrines could be formulated from such conflicts that were transferable to Europe.

These recommendations included a number of points. First, the actions of the individual soldier were to be viewed within a wider framework encompassing the entirety of the war. Placing a greater emphasis in current training on individual initiative, it was argued, would benefit the overall performance of the troops in battle, as modern warfare placed greater demands on the personal characteristics of each individual soldier. Second, individual training for field marksmanship required urgent improvement, as soldiers were required to hit fast-moving and well-camouflaged targets. Third, improvements in field orientation were required, focusing on compass-led and astronomical orientation so as to improve patrol and reconnaissance duties. This would also benefit military operations in a European context. Fourth, the report recommended placing greater importance on field cookery and baking. Poorly prepared meals and underbaked bread had been the cause of a number of stomach complaints. Fifth, troop education should include a focus on the colonies so as to raise awareness of Germany's overseas possessions and spread eagerness among the troops for overseas service. Sixth and finally, the knowledge of the "military achievements registered by our Protection Force under the most difficult of conditions" was to be spread among the troops. Such lessons not only represented the best method of fostering an understanding of colonial matters and the nature of the warfare conducted within this context, but would "promote a sense of good soldiering and esprit de corps." Such courses of training would be of "especial benefit" during peacetime; "all the measures aiming at these ends could be recommended as serving the interests of both the Army and the Protection Force."[41] The lessons to be learned from the German colonial campaigns were thus restricted to the remedy of shortcomings recognized in the wars and the diffusion of those military and technical lessons considered to be applicable to the European theater.

The vague indication (not defined in any service regulations) made by this document of the necessity for increasing soldierly initiative meant that it could be interpreted in many different ways. Nevertheless, the considerations were important. Addressing the Military Society (Militärische Gesellschaft) in Berlin in February 1911, Ludwig von Estorff highlighted the importance of high levels of mobility, orientation, and independent initiative in winning the small wars of the future—lessons that were also applicable to the European theater.[42] No longer conducted according to well-practiced maneuvers or a single method, wars of the future would be won by those armies that succeeded in providing a flexible response to what would remain fluid situations.[43] In making this case, von Estorff had reached a set of conclusions much more far-ranging than anything produced by the Ministry of War. Returning to the nature of small wars, he argued that they required specialist troops and called for the Protection Force at the least to be accorded a correspondingly detailed course of training. He finished with reference to a set of changes from which the German army as a whole could also profit.

Seeking to improve the performance of the Protection Force of each colony, the Imperial Colonial Office had acted in 1907 to declare participation in the courses of instruction provided at the Institute of Oriental Languages as obligatory for all junior officers. For its part, however, the Ministry of War saw no need for any revision of its training and service manuals or the incorporation of small wars within its scope. The army reacted negatively to all demands for innovation, arguing that overseas wars required an entirely different approach to European conflicts. The ministry left each individual commander to draw his own lessons from the set of six recommendations drawn up after analysis of the recent colonial conflicts. This explains why the conduct of the colonial wars—which were by then overshadowed by the experience of the First World War, the loss of the colonies, and the changes undergone by the Reichswehr—did not rouse even the mildest of interest among the military establishment of the Weimar Republic. Nevertheless, the colonial wars did not vanish entirely from view, surfacing in the war games played by the newly founded Scouting movement.

CHAPTER 12

Veterans' Associations

C OLONIAL VETERANS' associations were established to share experiences and stabilize and maintain memories of the colonial wars both among their former participants and within society at large. Unreliable at best, memories never constitute an exact reproduction of experience, but rather filter all recollections through the lens of subsequent perspectives and perceptions. They also subject the past to a renewed and continuing process of reconstruction. The members of the colonial veterans' associations kept alive their memories of the wars in which they fought through a range of writings, theater productions, celebrations, pictures, monuments, anniversaries, and above all, flag consecration ceremonies. The focus of such activities rested not on the violence that its members had visited on the native populations, but that which they had experienced in their capacity as soldiers.

The former colonial soldiers were not just active in the veterans' associations; a number even acted to found the Scouting Association (Pfadfinderbewegung), the aim of which was to educate and organize the youth of the nation. In establishing the "colonial soldier" and his putative virtues as the role model for this new figure the Scout *(Pfadfinder)*, the movement not only played its part in keeping alive what amounted to an entirely artificial figure but established it as a role model for coming generations.

Colonial Veterans' Associations

Veterans' associations were a growing phenomenon in the German Empire, with its umbrella organization, the Deutscher Kriegerbund, registering a membership in excess of 1 million in 1898.[1] The success of this movement in attracting such a large membership conferred a very considerable level of influence in shaping domestic political opinion. Almost all veterans' associations maintained a militantly anti–Social Democratic, often anti-Semitic and militarist, nationalist stance. Constituting only a very small part of the wider military association movement in the German Empire, membership of a colonial veterans' association was open to all those having served in any rank of the army, navy, Protection Force, or police force of an overseas colony or as a participant in one of the colonial expeditionary forces.[2] In 1912, records registered some 2,958 members of thirty-three colonial veterans' associations.[3]

Not restricted to the large cities such as Berlin or Hamburg, the associations also grew in smaller cities such as Stuttgart, medium-sized towns such as Pforzheim, and even smaller settlements such as Waldshut (South Baden). With no uniformity in organization or appellation, many towns saw the development of separate associations for the "East Asians" and "Africans"; others such as Kiel chose to amalgamate both in an Association of Former Colonial Troops. In northern Germany, a number of special organizations were established for former members of the Marine Infantry, such as that in Kiel, which hosted the Association of Former Naval Soldiers. Characterized for some time by a high level of organizational diversity, the initiative to unify the individual groupings into an all-encompassing Confederation of Colonial Veterans came as late as 1922.

Despite the longer history of a few of the groupings incorporated in this new organizational structure—the Association of Former South-West Africans in Berlin was established as early as 1896—the majority were founded in 1907 upon the return to Germany of a great number of colonial soldiers from the war in German South-West Africa. Membership was granted following an application, either oral or in writing, to the executive board, followed by submission of military papers. While acceptance of other ranks was subject to a membership vote, the admission of former officers was automatic. With the average membership of each association registering between sixty and one hundred, the Berlin-based "Association of Former South Africans" was an exception, boasting some thirty honorary and 521 regular members.[4]

The colonial veterans' associations were established for a number of reasons. The statute of the "Association of Former East Asians and Africans" in Bremerhaven, for instance, stated five aims: First, to maintain and strengthen the love and loyalty of its members for kaiser and empire, prince and fatherland and thus also their loyalty to the memory of the time spent in the colonies on active service. Second, to celebrate holidays of national commemoration. Third, its founders sought to accompany the coffins of its deceased members to their burial with military honors. Fourth, to provide financial assistance with the burial of its deceased members as well as providing financial assistance to their bereaved dependents and, as far as the resources of the association would permit, to other of its members experiencing unexpected misfortune.[5]

The last point indicates the social function exercised by the colonial veterans' associations. Indeed, many of the bodies regarded the provision of financial assistance to its invalid members surviving on a state pension as one of its most important tasks. The Association of Former South-West Africans in Berlin advertised its provision of financial support as a way to attract new members. Examination of the number of monetary grants accorded to its members reveals a whole range of activities. These included free medical treatment from a doctor for both the member and his dependents; discounts in all chemist's stores in the greater Berlin area; free legal advice; free advice on employment, pension, and family matters; a free proof of employment; assistance for the bereaved; burial with military honors; a free subscription to the association magazine *Der Schutztruppler;* and discount access to life insurance premiums and dental treatment. The entry fees to this association amounted to a mark and the monthly fees were charged at sixty pfennigs.[6] Those members paying an extra fifty pfennigs per year were accorded a bereavement allowance in accordance with the length of their membership.

In order to guarantee the best service provision to its members, the colonial veterans' associations cooperated closely with other organizations such as the Prussian National Veterans' Associations, the Colonial Veterans' Memorial Association, the War Invalids' Memorial Association, the Board of Trustees of the German Fleet Association, the Imperial Navy Foundation, the Central Committee of the German Society of the Red Cross, the National Foundation for the Bereaved, the Women's League, the German Colonial Society, and the Imperial Committee for the War Invalids. In this way, the veterans' associations relieved the burden on the local government welfare board. The various organizations pooled information and forwarded applications. According to the annual report of the Berlin association from 1913, these welfare organizations had granted every request made with the exception of one, founded on the basis of a situation assessment conducted by the board.[7]

Established in 1909, the Colonial Veterans' Memorial Association (Kolonialkriegerdenk) was a special association dedicated to the task of assisting former soldiers to find regular employment, providing financial assistance to those experiencing hardship through no fault of their own, and providing medical assistance. Assistance was also to be provided to the families of dead soldiers and the dependents of former soldiers who had fallen ill. In certain exceptional cases, relief could also be provided to serving colonial soldiers and their immediate dependents.[8] The founder members included Major (Retd.) Kurd Schwabe and a number of well-known figures from the colonies. As the association had been established for purely charitable ends, it received recognition as a foundation in 1913.

Seeking to free itself from total dependence on donations, the Colonial Veterans' Memorial Association launched a publicity campaign and sold advertising space in its journals, the takings from which flowed into the association funds. A further source of income was the sale of the *Colonial Veterans Paperback* and from 1916, the *Colonial Veterans Memorial Almanac*, edited by Paul Rohrbach and of which 500,000 copies were sold.[9] The sale of colonial postcards and publication of a soldiers' songbook (itself also designed to provide serving troops with suitable songs for the field) also brought much-needed revenue.

The institutional life of the colonial veterans associations' involved a broad and varied program: celebrations of the kaiser's birthday, magic lantern shows regarding colonial and other themes, balls and costume parties, church services of thanksgiving, summer fetes with pyrotechnical displays, excursions and boat trips, sharpshooting competitions, charitable lotteries for needy members, and the obligatory Christmas party.[10] To maintain communication between the individual members of the various associations, the Confederation of Veterans' Associations of former Chinese and African Veterans and the Colonial Veterans' Memorial Association published the *Kolonial-Post* with a print run of 3,000 (1912), carrying reports of the monthly and annual meetings and the other activities of the association. Maintaining a close network of contacts with each other, the various colonial veterans' associations also established good and close contacts with other varieties of veterans' associations. Marking the kaiser's silver jubilee in 1913, the Veterans'

Alliance in Berlin celebrated a service of thanksgiving on the *Tempelhofer Feld* in which 180 members of the Association of South-West African Veterans participated.

Despite their militarized nature, the associations also maintained contacts with civilian sectors of Wilhelmine society; in addition to its military guests, the Association of Former African and Chinese Veterans in Bremen invited a number of representatives from prominent civilian quarters (such as the town senate and the district commander) to their service of thanksgiving to commemorate the colonial wars. Although usually declining to attend the annual play and pantomime centering on the colonial conflicts in China and Africa organized by this Bremen association, the mayor of Bremen and one of his senators decided to join the some forty serving army officers present at the celebrations in 1910 to mark the tenth anniversary of the Boxer War. The Senate also made a contribution to a fund to establish a library for the Protection Force.[11]

The colonial veterans' associations acted as a central node in a complex military-political network. Linking military and civilian groupings with an interest in the colonies, these bodies also brought together those organizations providing support for the active Protection Force and others seeking to maintain the memory of the colonial wars. Sharing such plans, the *Kolonial-Post* organized a number of monthly colonial days of remembrance, taking care to keep the commemorations as broadly focused as possible so as to integrate the largest possible range of experiences.[12]

The centerpiece of this culture of remembrance focused on the association colors and their consecration. Far more than the colorful cloth out of which it was fashioned, the colors functioned as the active symbol of togetherness, comradeship, and patriotism. They also symbolized the shared experience of suffering, pain, and want as well as a shared hope for a good future for the colonies. Although the declared aim of every association, not every such grouping was in possession of their own colors, as this was subject to strict regulation. Required to demonstrate a patriotic attitude, love and loyalty for the kaiser and Reich, the granting of the colors by the Kriegerbund was conditional upon a three-year membership of the umbrella association, the Prussian National Association of Veterans' Associations.[13] Moreover, the association statute was not only to accord with the model statutes prescribed by the Preußischer Landeskriegerverband, but required confirmation from the Prussian National Association. Permission to carry the colors was provided by the competent army district command only following a positive report from the responsible police authority. After these hurdles had been overcome, the form assumed by the colors was then subject to approval according to a set of prescriptions, any exceptions to which required imperial assent. The Association of Former Colonial Troops in Kiel wanted to fly colors depicting not only the Prussian eagle but also the arms of Bavaria, Wurttemberg, Saxony, and Kiel. Granting permission to do so, the kaiser insisted, however, that the flagstaff be decorated with black and white pennants displaying the Prussian eagle and the inscription "Prussian National Veterans' Association."[14]

The colors were consecrated within an important ceremony. The opening "prologue" involved a statement of the overarching ethos of the colonial veterans designed to address all former colonial soldiers. There was a range of prologue texts available, depending on the war or wars that the association had been established to commemorate. Thus one text referring exclusively to German South-West Africa ran, "As hot and difficult as the battle became / we happily remember all the times / in which we gave assistance / to the German eagle / to build his nest." A further exordium integrated the experiences gathered in both China and Africa: "Accompanying us in times of peace / the flag doth remember us in joy and pain / to stand for Reich and Kaiser at all times / ready to lay down our lives. / As in the Chinese realm we did hear / 'the Germans to the front' / still do we wish to build the vanguard / and show what we once could do. / In Africa, that hot and contested land / captain and men were ready always / sweltering in the dunes / to give life in that bloody fight."[15]

An ever-present focus on the colonial wars not only during the flag consecration ceremony but also in the writings of the veterans' associations, the colonial wars were not accorded a particularly realistic treatment, and a number of authors lacked any firsthand colonial experience. Ada von Liliencron (chairwoman of the Women's Colonial League) penned a number of short narratives of life and death in the protectorates despite never having set foot in any of the locations about which she wrote.[16] Other stories published in the *Kolonial-Post* or the *Kolonialkriegerdenk Kalender* gave entertaining and exciting accounts of the experiences of officers, planters, merchants, and administrators. These publications sought to disseminate a sentimental and adventurous spirit to please both veterans and a wider public.

In addition to the propagation of such sentiment, the articles published in the *Kolonial-Post* and many of the songs sung at the meetings of the associations focused on the background of the colonial soldiers and their daily routine: their answer to the call, the passage to and arrival in the colonial theater, marching and patrols, camp life, guard duty, engagements, attack and pursuit. Brief mention was given to a barbaric and cunning enemy, but there was little description, bloody or otherwise, of the battles in which the colonial veterans had fought. Instead, the songs and articles preferred to focus on the stifling heat, thirst, and hunger portrayed in such a way as to demonstrate the suffering and death of German soldiers. To forestall any charge that the sacrifices had been made in vain, deaths on the colonial battle-field (especially in German South-West Africa) were glorified as heroes' deaths for the "Homeland [*Heimat*] which we have come to love."[17] Indeed, the continued perception (even in 1935) by many of a "special bond" between the Reich and its former German settler colony was made clear by General von Epp, who presented a bag of earth from Lüderitz Bay to a national meeting of the Imperial Colonial Confederation.[18]

The colonial veterans' associations did not entirely ignore the question of the violence unleashed during the colonial wars, yet the focus rested exclusively on its experience by German soldiers. Chinese and African suffering was blended out. Serving not only a national-ideological function, this exclusive focus also exercised a sociopolitical end: enabling the veterans to justify and advance a number of contemporary claims, both material and abstract in nature. While happy to work with other veterans' associations to articulate such demands, the colonial veterans' associations made use of their experience overseas to establish a separate identity. Nevertheless, such considerations did not prevent good cooperation between the East Asian and African veterans' associations. Indeed, contemporary practices of concentrating colonial experiences within a demarcated organizational framework increased the ability of such groupings to maintain the special status of German South-West Africa among Germany's former colonies.

The Pfadfinderbewegung

Inspired by the Scouting movement established in the United Kingdom by the British general Robert Baden-Powell, former German colonial officers translated the term into German (the *Pfadfinder*) and established a similar organization. Baden-Powell was the author of *Aids to Scouting* (1899), a handbook for the British soldier. After returning from the Second South-African War, he began to formulate his ideas for a youth movement to impart the lessons that he gleaned from his wartime experiences, to boys between the ages of twelve and sixteen.[19] In this way, he opened a window for his largely urban audience into an unknown (if largely idealized) and exciting frontier world.

Formed in 1908, immediately after publication of his book *Scouting for Boys,* the Boy Scout Association sought to inculcate its members in the "universal virtues" of discipline, self-belief, frugality, selflessness, and helpfulness. Seeking to prepare them for life in the outdoors, he hoped to teach the practical skills they would need to survive in challenging environments: simple engineering skills, hut making, tree-felling, cooking, and baking. Scouts were also to be trained in orienteering, boatmanship, map-reading, and signaling. Placing great emphasis on hygiene as a component of good health, the Scouting movement did not include any aspect of military discipline, marching, or drill. Baden-Powell was entirely clear that his movement was not to serve as a premilitary organization. Instead, he hoped to use playful methods to guide his charges through a dangerous and unstable phase of youth, providing a wide range of experience-based and activity-oriented opportunities for learning.

The German Scouting movement was led by two former officers active in German South-West Africa: the medical officer Alexander Lion and Captain Maximilian Bayer, who began a career as colonial military writer while still a serving officer. Lion's decision to participate in the youth movement was motivated primarily by his interest in public health and his belief that many German deaths in the African wars could have been prevented by a rudimentary knowledge of hygiene and the practices that it entailed.[20] Following a personal meeting with Baden-Powell, Lion launched a German-English exchange program in the form of "Scout meetings" or *Pfadfinderbegegnungen.* After he lobbied the Bavarian Ministry of War and the German Foreign Ministry to meet a group of English Boy Scouts—without informing the district corps headquarters—his superiors were critical of his taking what they viewed as "South-West African liberties."[21]

The association of ex-servicemen with the *Pfadfinder* movement was not restricted to literary figures; many provided active support as participants. Such figures included Hans Paasche, the former naval officer and veteran of the Maji Maji War in East Africa. Joining the Scouting advisory board in 1912, he wrote in support of its ideals in both civilian and military life. Berthold von Deimling, another former officer who had served in German South-West Africa, joined the honorary committee of the German *Pfadfinder* association in 1914.

The first *Pfandfinder* troop was founded in Munich in 1909; this was followed in the same year by the establishment in Berlin of the association for "youth sport in the fields and woods" *(Jugendsport Feld und Wald)*. All such groupings were united in 1911 under the aegis of the German branch of the Scouting Association. The Bavarian wing of the movement retained an exceptional position within this organizational arrangement, where the Association for the Promotion of Military Strength (Verein zur Förderung der Wehrkraft) assumed control of the Scouting section. In return, the Bavarian Wehrkraftverein agreed to restrict its activities and expansion to Bavaria.[22] The year 1912 saw the establishment in Berlin of a Scouting section for girls—the Girl Guides (Pfadfinderinnen). Membership of the Pfadfinderbund advanced to 1,000 boys in its founding year, steadily growing until it reached some 90,000 youth and adult members in September 1914.[23] Scouts were to learn "the rules of a hygienic lifestyle, strengthen their body through exercise, sports and personal hygiene, avoid damaging substances (smoking, alcohol and excess) and develop the virtues of persistence and will-power."[24] Both physical and character training were viewed as indivisibly linked. A similar emphasis was placed on the observation of nature and life in the wild and camping. The Girl Guides experienced a more varied program of activities, including dancing and singing.

Contemporaries of the Scouting movement included the youth movement and progressive education movement, all of which spread a number of new ideas for the treatment of the age group fourteen to twenty. This was accompanied by the establishment of further youth organizations such as the German Wandervogel, the Young Men's Christian Association, and the youth groups of the workers' movement. Characteristic for this group of free youth movements were the "Life Reform" *(Lebensreform)* ideals and social criticism that they articulated in close association with romantic conceptions of a natural and frugal life centered around a communal ethos. These groups were accompanied by a wide selection of nationalist youth movements concentrating on sports instruction. All these groups were united by their rejection of premilitary training. As an advertising brochure from one of the Bavarian *Wehrkraftvereine* emphasized, soldierly thinking, bodily strength, agility, and performance should develop automatically.[25] This stood in stark contrast to the obviously para- and premilitary "youth forces" *(Jugendwehr)*, founded around 1896 and dedicated to military drill.

Despite the antimilitary nature of the Scouting movement, the German military authorities clearly viewed it as a provider of useful premilitary training, and accorded the movement considerable backing. The Bavarian and Prussian Ministries of War moved as early as October 1909 to order their officers and noncommissioned officers (NCOs) to provide active support to premilitary youth groups. The governments of Prussia, Bavaria, and Saxony all placed halls, parade grounds, military swimming pools, and barracks at their disposal. An order from the Prussian Ministry of Culture in 1911 laid out a range of guidelines with which to making youth work compatible with the ambitions of the military establishment.[26] The same year saw the establishment of the League of Young Germany (Jungdeutschland-Bund) on the initiative of the Imperial Ministry of War, with the clear aim of militarizing the youth sector. Aiming to prepare the German youth both mentally and physically for military service in war, the ministry sought to collect all groups of a similar outlook under the organizational aegis of the Jungdeutschland-Bund. The League of Young Germany used Scouting methods as a cover for its militaristic ends.

In contrast to this staunchly militarist and nationalist grouping, the roots of the Pfadfinderbewegung in the British Scouting movement made it vulnerable to allegations of foreign influence and "national unreliability." Such accusations were leveled against the German *Book of Scouts (Pfadfinderbuch)*. Published in 1909 with a print run of 5,000, it offered an illustrated history of the life and colonial experiences of Baden-Powell. Although intending to serve the cause of German nationalism, its critics portrayed the German Scout movement as deeply unpatriotic.[27] Seeking to counter such charges of insufficient patriotism, Lion argued that many of its founders had "recently proven a pure and noble patriotism both at home and in the colonies in the South-West African war."[28] Indeed, the first edition of the *Pfadfinderbuch* included a map of the German colonies in Africa, and the recommendations of essential reading for every Scout were drawn from the most significant examples of contemporary German colonial literature.

The *Pfadfinderbuch* also included a number of descriptions of everyday life in the Protection Force. With an extensive portrayal of the comradely aspect of field life, such accounts focused on communal activities such as cooking and baking, singing around the campfire, amateur dramatics, and acrobatics. Far from frivolous, such pastimes were described as helping to maintain morale during periods of monotony and hardship, comforting to the ill, and strengthening camaraderie and morale. The book made conscious reference to the character-building nature of colonial service: "men who have led a tough and hard life on the borders of civilization [are characterized] by their big-hearted chivalry, expressed especially toward women and the weak." It was their battle with nature that had formed them into gentlemen.[29] Written by the "Old African" Maximillian Bayer, the chapter "Service in the Field" bore a striking resemblance to the 1910 edition of the *Field Service Exercises for Colored Soldiers,* especially in its sections "Reconnaissance," "Patrol," "Meteorology," and "Intelligence."[30]

Making continual reference to the "experience of our troops in China and the colonies" and a number of "colonial practices" such as stalking or tracking, the Scout reader was instructed to emulate the example of the Africans, said to practice until they could read from the sand "as we men of culture [*Kulturmenschen*] read from a book."[31] That such "African practices" could be acquired by the diligent European was demonstrated by articles about former members of the Protection Force, who claimed proficiency in such skills themselves. In this way, the authors sought to counter the widely held view that the slow and cumbersome German troops were not equal to the challenges presented by a range of colonial environments. Acknowledging the failure of conventional European military training to prepare its soldiers for colonial service, Alexander hoped that the unique instruction imparted to Scouts would establish them as leaders in any future colonial war: "We needed to find the trail through diligence and practice; then the frugality of the primitive peoples is foreign to us. Many of us who saw service in the colonies were forced to learn these arts in the blistering steppe, dense rainforest and craggy country; in order to survive amidst hordes of cunning natives bent on revenge; finally beating them using their own cunning tricks."[32]

The *Pfadfinderbuch* sought to prepare its young readers for life in the colonies. While Bayer focused closely on warfare, Lion viewed the Scouts as possible colonists: "The German Empire needs such daring Scouts to spread German culture [*Kultur*] in our colonies, taking it to the furthest corners of the globe."[33] The same applied to those Girl Guides "seeking their path far from home in the colonies."[34]

The second edition of the *Pfadfinderbuch* (1911) saw its editor make a conscious attempt to distance himself and his movement from their British role models. "It goes without saying that the German organization is not dependent on its English counterpart, which in no way emulates it slavishly. The German organization has merely taken up its basic idea and adapted it to the German national character."[35] Expunged from the publication was not only the "ideal of a gentleman," but a whole range of practical tips stemming from the pen of Baden-Powell. A further innovation was to be found in the foreword, with its glorification of the "Father of Gymnastics," Friedrich Ludwig Jahn, in an attempt to connect the Scouting movement to both his nationalist *Turnbewegung* and the later *Wandervogel*. This interpretation recast Baden-Powell as merely reactivating a traditionally and essentially German youth movement. The examples and anecdotes of life in German South-West Africa were retained. Scout training was maintained in its essentials, but was now formulated in more technical terms. The emphasis on adventure—Baden-Powell had introduced explorers, discoverers, trappers, and bushmen as role models—largely disappeared from view.

The direction of this new trend was made clear by the incorporation of a new chapter on exercises and games included at the suggestion of the Bavarian Association for Military Preparedness (Bayerischer Wehrkraftverein). The chapter outlined a number of Scouting and war games, although the difference between these two categories was not entirely clear. Both amounted to contests between two opposing parties (Policemen and Smugglers, Protection Force Soldiers and Herero) designed to practice orientation; moving under cover and darkness; exploitation of the field; decision making; rapid yet silent movement; and the pursuit, tricking, and confusing of the "enemy."[36] The instructions involved in such games were precise: the war game should not last more than half an hour, as the development by children of skills transferable to a military context was possible only through maintenance of a certain level of tension "in combat" in the face of the "enemy." Indeed, these activities were to be treated entirely as games and were not to be given a name redolent of any military function. Despite such considerations, no games were to be conducted without the presence in some form of the "enemy," who was to be kept under close observation.[37] Such Scouting and war games were designed to sharpen the senses and train the skills necessary for service in the field.

The third edition of the German version of the *Book of Scouts*, now retitled *Young Germany's Book of Scouts (Jungdeutschlands Pfadfinderbuch)*, was published in 1912; a similar publication for Girl Guides followed in the same year.[38] The new title was the first explicit reference to the recent alliance with the Jungdeutschland-Bund. Establishing a certain degree of functional differentiation between the Scout and war games, the latter now included a separate section dealing with "small wars." Such activities were sought to impart and practice a number of military-style skills involved in colonial warfare such as sabotage, manhunts, reconnaissance, orienteering and battlefield navigation, the laying of ambushes against trackers, sabotaging telegraph lines, and organizing a "hunt for gypsies."[39] All of these games were designed to teach their participants how to reconnoiter a locality, seal off an area, break through enemy lines, or link up with allied formations across the enemy lines. Seeking to engender a feeling of realism, the "gypsies" being hunted were permitted to employ all manner of trickery, including the wearing of false uniforms, setting up fake camps, and starting fires. Similar variations of these games were outlined in the *Jungdeutschland* pocket book aimed at a readership of "young people of serviceable age [*wehrpflichtiges Jungvolk*]."[40] This publication even differentiated strongly between small wars and conventional wars, as "modern military situations" should be avoided as the context for the games. Thus seeking to avoid the impression of providing premilitary training, the military authorities also took this opportunity to maintain the special nature of the "large-scale war."[41]

The Scouting movement remained true to its founding aim of instilling a military spirit into its charges without providing military training. The colonial context in which the Scouting movement was set was always South-West Africa (and not East Africa) and the role model remained the "old African" of the white protection force. References to the "old East Asians" remained a rarity. Moreover, in focusing on the life of a Protection Force soldier, the Scouting movement concentrated almost exclusively on his life in nature; conflict with the natives assumed only a peripheral role. For the Scouts, colonial soldiers built and colonized; the violent and deadly aspect of their profession was ignored almost entirely.

The games and exercises practiced by both the German Scouting movement and other youth organizations all incorporated all the lessons learned from the colonial war that the military establishment had chosen to ignore; they provided the training and practice of skills that would equip future soldiers to fight a small war. The principles of guerilla warfare were therefore not entirely unfamiliar to the soldiers of the First World War. Although a recent study of the behavior of the German army in Belgium during the First World War draws different conclusions, not only were the German soldiers deployed in 1914 familiar with such principles; this facility was the product not of institutional military training, but of experiences gained in a more youthful and informal context: the German Scout troop.[42]

CHAPTER 13

Legacy

A LTHOUGH the German military establishment did draw a number of lessons from the experience of the colonial wars, these insights were lost amid the impact of the First World War. During the Weimar Republic, the memory of the colonial wars was kept alive only in the Scouting movement and the right-wing milieu of the colonial veterans' associations. This relative silence on the topic was conditioned by a number of factors. The international discourse on colonial warfare had undergone a fundamental change in the period after the First World War. The explicit depiction, systematization, and denunciation in the colored books of the extreme violence perpetrated in the German colonies soon established considerations of humanity and morality as the touchstone of "civilization." Following the loss of the German colonies, members of the political and military elite of the Weimar Republic joined this discourse only in as far as it was necessary to defend themselves against the range of accusations leveled against them from many quarters. For its part, the German military establishment lost interest in the internal discussion of the colonial wars. In contrast to this elite silence, the wars remained an indelible part of the individual experience of those soldiers who had fought in them.

The great majority of colonial officers returning to the metropole were initially reintegrated in infantry regiments dispersed across the service. No special regiments were created for former colonial officers. Nevertheless, around a quarter of the officers returning from colonial service were concentrated in the cavalry regiments already in existence and the technical sections of the army such as railway regiments, the field artillery, and telegraphy. At least ten officers with experience in the colonies were posted to the Great General Staff. The German army thus stood to profit from the reincorporation of skilled technicians; there is no evidence, however, to show that it sought to profit from it. Even if this had been the case, the number of such "returnees" was too low to exert a significant influence on the shared outlook and thinking of the German army. Not counting the Marine Infantry and civil servants with officer status stationed in Qingdao, a total of 341 officers were recorded as serving in the colonial Protection Forces in 1913, amounting to 1 percent of all officers in the imperial army.[1] In 1914, the army had a total strength of 800,646 men, 30,739 officers, and 105,856 noncommissioned officers.[2] A total of 2,092 officers had served in the colonies between 1897 and the outbreak of the First World War. At the outbreak of the First World War, only some 5 percent of the 31,000 officers deployed in the conflict had seen either active or peacetime service in one of the colonies. The corresponding figures for the medical corps were even lower. The year 1913 saw a total of ninety-one medical officers in the African colonies. Between 1897 and 1914, 398 medical officers had seen overseas service, compared with the 24,798 members of the Army Medical Corps.[3]

While next to nothing is known regarding the areas and services in which the other ranks of the colonial Protection Forces served, such data are available from the published biographies and autobiographies of the more well-known colonial officers.[4] These sources reveal that a number of participants in the Kapp putsch (1920), many of whom were subsequently dismissed from the Reichswehr, had extensive colonial experience. Such names include Lieutenant General Ludwig von Estorff, commander of the Protection Force in German South-West Africa between 1907 and 1911, and Major General Paul von Lettow-Vorbeck, participant in the German Africa campaign during the First World War. In contrast, the curricula vitae of the officers Hans Paasche and Berthold von Deimling present a number of unexpected turns, both culminating in conversion to the cause of pacifism.

Serving in the Maji Maji War (1905–1906), Paasche was given command of a detachment of sailors and Askari in the Rufiji area. He returned to Germany in 1909 and published a fictive travelogue entitled *Die Forschungsreise des Afrikaners Lukanga Mukara ins innerste Deutschland*. Intended as a work of social criticism in the style of Montesquieu's *Lettres Persanes*, it recounts the journey of an African explorer in Germany, thus overturning the accepted racial hierarchy. Arrested in 1917 for seeking to disseminate pacifism among sailors, he was prosecuted for "incitement to high treason" and kept in prison until the end of the war. As a member of a Workers' and Soldiers' Council, he was an active supporter of the cause of social democracy in 1918. Hans Paasche was murdered in 1920 by Reichswehr soldiers for his espousal of radical democracy and socialism.

The postcolonial record of Berthold von Deimling exhibited even greater incongruity for his higher rank. Serving in German South-West Africa between 1904 and 1906, von Deimling finished his colonial service as the commander of the Protection Force. He was promoted to General Commanding in Strasburg, in which role he held responsibility during the Zabern affair of 1913. Differences with the Supreme Army Command led to his dismissal in 1917. After 1918, he worked with the Workers' and Soldiers' Councils. Expelled from the Officers' Association following his membership in the peace movement and the republican Reichsbanner Schwarz-Rot-Gold, his represents one of the most striking cases of political radicalization within the ruling elite following a colonial experience.[5]

Following the end of the First World War, some 400,000 German soldiers, radicalized by their experience in war, defeat, revolution, and the thwarting of Germany's imperial ambitions, joined together to form some 356 paramilitary groupings referred to collectively as the Freikorps.[6] Propagating a pronounced nationalistic-racist ideology characterized by opposition to both Western democracy and Russian Bolshevism, this loose grouping of militias active in Germany, Poland, Upper Silesia, and the Baltic sought to refute the dishonor and humiliation of defeat through propagation of the "stab in the back myth" started by the Army High Command and taken up by the radical Right. A number of former colonial soldiers thronged to swell the ranks of the Freikorps, a number of whom even assumed positions of command. For example, the Ehrhardt Brigade (Marinebrigade Ehrhardt), based in the administrative area of Berlin, was named after naval lieutenant Hermann Ehrhardt, a veteran of the Nama war. Major Josef Bischoff, an "old East African," commanded the "Iron Brigade" (later renamed as the Iron Division) in the Baltic.[7] Those known to have involved themselves in the Freikorps movement included Major General Georg Maercker (Freikorps Maercker), Lieutenant General Wilhelm Faupel (Freikorps Görlitz/Faupel), General Franz von Epp (Freikorps and later the head of the Colonial Political Office of the Nationalsocialist Party), Lieutenant Waldemar Papst (Garde-Kavallerie-Schützen-Division), Naval Lieutenant Nikolaus Graf zu Dohna-Schlodien (German Freikorps for the defense of Upper Silesia), and Captain (med.) Alexander Lion (Freikorps Epp). Further research into the composition of the Freikorps and their inclusion of colonial veterans would greatly add to our understanding of the role of colonial experience in influencing the scope and nature of Freikorps violence.

The violent nature of the Freikorps movement was recognized and explained as early as the 1970s by Klaus Theweleit. Identifying the indiscriminate and extreme violence produced by this paramilitary movement as the result of a disposition to violence acquired in childhood and remodeled in adult years, he also proposed a possible connection between such prerequisites and the experience of colonial violence.[8] According to this interpretation, habitual violence gradually becomes a process that imprints on the mental and emotional world of the individual where it grows and flourishes. The readiness to commit acts of violence increases, and inhibitions diminish with every act of violence.

Other factors also offer explanations for the attractiveness of the Freikorps organization to former colonial officers. Seeking an outlet for the far greater level of independence and desire for responsibility that they had developed in the colonies, only the Freikorps presented them with the prospect of command and control—something not afforded by the staid routine of the peacetime Reichswehr. Unfettered command over a highly loyal and responsive formation of men, the life of a Freikorps leader closely resembled that of the commander of a colonial punitive expedition. The constellation of small groupings also favored the increase of violence, conditioned as they were by peer pressure, mistrust, a reduced scope for action, and the construction of borders between the in-group and the outside world.

A second factor decisive in conditioning the upward spiral of violence, at least in the Baltic lands, was a small war waged not just against the Red Army but also against the local population. Operating without any support from stronger units, supply, or the possibility of relief, the Freikorps lived from the land and often used violence to secure supplies. In such a context, ammunition was scarce and prisoners were not taken. Although fighting in an environment characterized by cold and snow, the campaign of the Baltic Freikorps was conducted amid topography very similar to that of the German colonies in general and German South-West Africa in particular: wide, apparently empty expanses of unbroken territory. Both environments had the potential to transform military operations into an existential struggle with nature.

Third, the Baltic Freikorps followed a colonizing agenda, recruiting volunteers with the promise of settlement in the Courlands after their demobilization. The Freikorps strategists envisaged a military colony on the basis of the Militärstaat Oberost established by the German Army Command in 1915 and policed by the former "Old African" Rochus Schmidt.[9] Thus, while in operation at different times, the programs followed by the German army and the Freikorps were strikingly similar. Hans Seekt advocated a similar agenda while in command of the Reichswehr during the Weimar Republic. Comparable to a colony, the military authorities viewed the "East" as a projection space for fantasies of conquest and control.

Similarities between the conduct of the war in the colonies and Eastern Europe had already been established by military publicists analyzing the South African War, who pointed out that the geographical conditions in Eastern Europe made it much easier for its population to conduct a guerilla war than was the case in the West. Further common features between Eastern Europe and the African colonies were the expanse of the apparently uninhabited territory, the range of scattered ethnic groups, the exotic rural architecture, and a German feeling of foreignness paired with cultural and civilizational superiority.

Former colonial soldiers may have viewed the "East" as providing an ideal field of operations not only on ideological grounds but also out of entirely pragmatic considerations. The requirements of action in Eastern Europe provided them with the ideal opportunity to employ and profit from the skills that they had acquired during their colonial service: tracking and orientation, improvisation and organization, frugality and endurance. The former colonial medical officers may have identified similar opportunities. Following the loss of Germany's colonies, their knowledge of tropical diseases such as malaria and dysentery may well have suggested a geographical reorientation for their further professional advancement. Despite such considerations, as we have already seen, the total number of former colonial soldiers was far too small to have formulated or articulated a special interest in the "East" within the regular military establishment. Those former colonials involved in the general drive eastward were merely part of a wider phenomenon moved by very different considerations. They cannot be regarded as its initiator. Moreover, during the period of the Weimar Republic, the energies of the majority of former colonial soldiers were channeled into the colonial movement, campaigning for a return of Germany's lost African territories. Nevertheless, such considerations do not obviate the very pressing need to investigate the number of these soldiers active in the East and how they depicted it in their publications.

With their experiences of violence gathered in the colonial wars, the First World War and—if only to a more limited extent—the Freikorps movement, the colonial soldiers represented a clear grouping within what remained an extremely heterogeneous post-1918 military milieu. As a result, there is a need for further research into the question of whether, and the extent to which, the former colonial soldiers combined with the Freikorps movement to create and propagate a new "transnational type of soldier."[10] A further question to be addressed is the extent to which elements of the multifunctional colonial soldier are to be found within this new creation.

Abbreviations

AA	Auswärtiges Amt
Att.	Attachment
BA Lichterfelde	Bundesarchiv, Lichterfelde (Berlin)
BA/MA Freiburg	Bundesarchiv/Militärarchiv, Freiburg
BayHSTA Munich	Bayrisches Hauptstaatsarchiv, Munich
ExRfdI	Exerzier-Reglement für die Infanterie
GEA	German East Africa
GLA Karlsruhe	Generallandesarchiv, Karlsruhe
GSTA PK Berlin	Geheimes Staatsarchiv Preußischer Kulturbesitz, Berlin
GSWA	German South-West Africa
HSTA Dresden	Hauptstaatsarchiv, Dresden
HSTA Stuttgart	Hauptstaatsarchiv, Stuttgart
IERMar	Infanterie-Exerzier-Reglement für die Marine
LA Schleswig-Holstein	Landesarchiv, Schleswig-Holstein
LFM	*La France Militaire*
NA London	National Archives, London
NARA Washington	National Archives and Records Administration, Washington, DC
RGB	Reichsgesetz-Blatt
SBR	Stenographische Berichte des Reichstages

SPD   Sozialdemokratische Partei Deutschlands
STA Bremen   Staatsarchiv, Bremen
TagebuchA   Tagebucharchiv, Emmendingen
USANJ   *United States Army and Navy Journal*
VolksliedA   Volksliedarchiv, Freiburg

Notes

Introduction

1. Fritz Fischer, *Germany's Aims in the First World War,* trans. Hajo Holborn and James Joll (New York: W.W. Norton, 1968) (Griff nach der Weltmacht: Die Kriegszielpolitik des kaiserlichen Deutschland 1914/18 [Düsseldorf: Droste Verlag, 1961]); Hans-Ulrich Wehler, *The German Empire: 1871–1918,* trans. Kim Traynor (Leamington Spa, Warwickshire, UK: Berg, 1985) (Das Deutsche Kaiserreich 1871–1918 [Göttingen: Vandenhoeck & Ruprecht, 1973]); Wehler, "'Deutscher Sonderweg' oder allgemeine Probleme des westlichen Kapitalismus," *Merkur: Deutsche Zeitschrift für europäisches Denken* 35, no. 5 (1981): 478–487. See also Dieter Langewiesche, "Der 'deutsche Sonderweg': Defizitgeschichte als geschichtspolitische Zukunftskonstruktion nach dem Ersten und Zweiten Weltkrieg," in *Kriegsniederlagen: Erfahrungen und Erinnerungen*, ed. Horst Carl, Hans-Henning Kortüm, Dieter Langewiesche, and Friedrich Lenger (Berlin: De Gruyter, 2004), 57–65.
2. Robert Gerwarth and Stephan Malinowski, "Hannah Arendt's Ghost: Reflections on the Disputable Path from Windhoek to Auschwitz," *Central European History* 42, no. 2 (June 2009): 279–300.
3. Hannah Arendt, *The Origins of Totalitarianism* (New York: Harcourt, Brace & World, 1966), 185–221.
4. Some examples: For China: Diana Preston, *The Boxer Rebellion: The Dramatic Story of China's War on Foreigners that Shook the World in the Summer of 1900* (New York: Walker, 2000); James L. Hevia, *English Lessons: The Pedagogy of Imperialism in Nineteenth-Century China* (Durham, NC: Duke University Press, 2003); Dietlind Wünsche, *Feldpostbriefe aus China: Wahrnehmungs- und Deutungsmuster deutscher Soldaten zur Zeit des Boxeraufstandes 1900/1901* (Berlin: Christoph Links Verlag, 2008). For German South-West Africa: Jan-Bart Gewald, *Herero Heroes: A Socio-Political History of the Herero of*

Namibia 1890–1923 (Oxford: James Currey, 1999), 141–191; Gesine Krüger, *Kriegsbewältigung und Geschichtsbewußtsein: Realität, Deutung und Verarbeitung des deutschen Kolonialkriegs in Namibia 1904 bis 1907* (Göttingen: Vandenhoeck & Ruprecht, 1999). For German East Africa: Thaddeus Sunseri, "Famine and Wild Pigs: Gender Struggles and the Outbreak of the Maji Maji War in Uzaramo (Tanzania)," *Journal of African History* 38 (1997): 235–259; Jamie Monson, "Relocating Maji Maji: The Politics of Alliance and Authority in the Southern Highlands of Tanzania, 1870–1918," ibid., 39 (1998): 95–120; Michelle Moyd, *Violent Intermediaries: African Soldiers, Conquest, and Everyday Colonialism in German East Africa* (Athens: Ohio University Press, 2014); Thoralf Klein and Frank Schumacher, eds., *Kolonialkriege: Gewalt im Zeichen des Imperialismus* (Hamburg: Hamburger Edition, 2006).

5. Benjamin Madley, "From Africa to Auschwitz: How German South-West Africa Incubated Ideas and Methods Adopted and Developed by the Nazis in Eastern Europe," *European History Quarterly* 33 (2005): 429–464; Jürgen Zimmerer, "Die Geburt des 'Ostlandes' aus dem Geiste des Kolonialismus: Die nationalsozialistische Eroberungs- und Beherrschungspolitik in (post-) kolonialer Perspektive," *Sozial.Geschichte* 19 (2004): 10–43.

6. Elizabeth Kier, *Imaging War: French and British Military Doctrine between the Wars* (Princeton, NJ: Princeton University Press, 1997), 27–28.

7. Isabel V. Hull, "Military Culture and the Production of 'Final Solutions' in the Colonies: The Example of Wilhelminian Germany," in *The Specter of Genocide: Mass Murder in Historical Perspective*, ed. Robert Gellately and Ben Kiernan (Cambridge: Cambridge University Press, 2003), 141–162; Hull, *Absolute Destruction: Military Culture and the Practices of War* (Ithaca, NY: Cornell University Press, 2005); Hull, "The Military Campaign in German Southwest Africa, 1904–1907," *Bulletin of the German Historical Institute* 37 (2005): 39–44; Madley, "From Africa to Auschwitz," 429–464; Zimmerer, "Die Geburt des 'Ostlandes' aus dem Geiste des Kolonialismus," 10–43.

8. Birthe Kundrus, "Von Windhoek nach Nürnberg? Koloniale 'Mischehenver-bote' und die Nationalsozialistische Rassengesetzgebung," in *Phantasiereiche: Zur Kulturgeschichte des deutschen Kolonialismus*, ed. Birthe Kundrus (Frankfurt am Main: Campus, 2003), 110–131.

9. The arguments are summarized in Robert Gerwarth and Stephan Malinowski, "Der Holocaust als 'kolonialer Genozid'?" *Geschichte und Gesellschaft* 33 (2007): 439–466, 444; Gerwarth and Malinowski, "Vollbrachte Hitler eine 'afrikanische' Tat? Der Herero-Krieg und der Holocaust: Zur Kritik der neuesten Sonderwegsthese," *Frankfurter Allgemeine Zeitung* (*FAZ*), 11 September 2007, no. 211, 38.

10. Second address from the Führer, unsigned, 22 August 1939: "Our strength rests in our speed and brutality. Genghis Khan happily killed millions of women and children, yet history remembers him as the great empire builder. The way in which decadent West-European civilization chooses to remember me is a matter of total indifference. I issued the order—and will have anyone

shot who speaks a word of criticism—that the aims of the war focused not on reaching any physical location but the physical extermination of the enemy [*in der physischen Vernichtung des Gegners*]." *Akten zur deutschen auswärtigen Politik 1918–1945*, series D, vol. 7 (Göttingen: Vanderhoeck & Ruprecht, 1961), doc. 193, S. 172.

11. Jürgen Osterhammel, "Kulturelle Grenzen in der Expansion Europas," in *Geschichtswissenschaft jenseits des Nationalstaats: Studien zu Beziehungsgeschichte und Zivilisationsvergleich* (Göttingen: Vanderhoeck & Ruprecht, 2001), 203–239, 223.

12. Olivier Le Cour Grandmaison, *Coloniser, Exterminer: Sur la guerre et l'État colonial* (Paris: Fayard, 2005), 18.

13. Trutz von Trotha, "Zur Soziologie der Gewalt," *Kölner Zeitschrift für Soziologie und Sozialpsychologie*, special ed. 37 (Cologne, 1997), 9–65, 20.

14. Carl von Clausewitz, *Vom Kriege* (Munich: Cormoran Verlag, 2000; Berlin: F. Dümmler, 1832), pt. 1, bk. 4, chap. 3, 214.

15. Ibid.

16. Irving Louis Horowitz, "Wissenschaft, Modernität und autorisierter Terror," in *Strukturen kollektiver Gewalt im 20. Jahrhundert,* ed. Mihran Dabag and Kristin Platt (Opladen: Leske + Budrich, 1998), 320–337, 311. Regarding the similarities and differences between war and genocide, see Helen Fein, "Genocide, Terror, Life Integrity, and War Crimes: The Case for Discrimination," in *Genocide: Conceptual and Historical Dimensions,* ed. Georges J. Andreopoulos (Philadelphia: University of Pennsylvania Press, 1997), 95–107, 99–100; Eric Markusen and David Kopf, *The Holocaust and the Strategic Bombing: Genocide and Total War in the Twentieth Century* (Boulder: Westview, 1995), 55; Martin Shaw, *War & Genocide: Organized Killing in Modern Society* (Oxford: Polity, 2006).

17. Michel Foucault, *Dispositive der Macht: Über Sexualität, Wissen und Wahrheit* (Berlin: Merve Verlag, 1978), 119–120; Michael Mann, "Das Gewaltdispositiv des modernen Kolonialismus," in *Kolonialismus: Kolonialdiskurs und Genozid,* ed. Mihran Dabag, Horst Gründer, and Uwe-K. Ketelsen (Munich: Wilhelm Fink Verlag, 2004), 111–135, 113.

18. Donald Featherstone, *Colonial Small Wars, 1837–1901* (Newton Abbot, UK: David & Charles, 1973), 5–6; Hendrik L. Wesseling, "Colonial Wars and Armed Peace, 1871–1914: A Reconnaissance," in *Imperialism and Colonialism, Essays on the History of European Expansion,* ed. H. L. Wesseling (Westport, CT: Greenwood, 1997), 12–26, 12.

19. To the Europeans and North Americans, "civilization" meant not just the achievement of a particular level of technical-scientific development but the ability or otherwise to form a government according to European standards that was strong enough to protect the lives of the whites resident in the territory. See Lawrence James, *The Savage Wars: British Campaigns in Africa, 1870–1920* (New York: St. Martin's, 1985), 13; Osterhammel, "Kulturelle Grenzen in der Expansion Europas," 203–239, 220. See also the articles

"Civilization" and "Culture" in *Dictionary of Concepts of Cultural Anthropology*, ed. Robert H. Winthrop (New York: Greenwood, 1991), 33–37, 50–61.

20. No entry in Richard Holmes, ed., *The Oxford Companion to Military History* (Oxford: Oxford University Press, 2001), and in the *Enzyklopädie Erster Weltkrieg*, ed. Gerhard Hirschfeld, Gerd Krumeich, and Irina Renz (Paderborn: Schöningh, 2014).

21. Stig Förster, Markus Pöhlmann, and Dierk Walter, eds., *Schlachten der Weltgeschichte: Von Salamis bis Sinai* (Munich: Dt. Taschenbuch-Verlag, 2005), foreword, 9.

1. The Boxer War

1. Paul A. Cohen, *History in Three Keys: The Boxers as Event, Experience, and Myth* (New York: Columbia University Press, 1997), 59–145; Joseph W. Esherick, *The Origins of the Boxer Uprising* (Berkeley: University of California Press, 1987), 96–122; Zhang Ming, "Yihetuan yishi dewenhua xiangzheng yu zhengzhi yinyu" [The cultural symbol and political metaphors in the rituals of the Boxer movement], in *Yihetuan yundong yibai zhounian guoji xueshu taolunhui lunwenji* [Selected papers from the international symposium on the 100th anniversary of the Boxer movement], vol. 1, ed. Su Weizhi and Liu Tianlu (Beijing: Shandong daxue chubanshe, 2001), 303–333.

2. Lanxin Xiang, *The Origins of the Boxer War: A Multinational Study* (London: RoutledgeCurzon, 2003), 110–113.

3. Thoralf Klein, "Aktion und Reaktion? Mission und chinesische Gesellschaft," in *Kolonialkrieg in China: Die Niederschlagung der Boxerbewegung*, ed. Mechthild Leutner and Klaus Mühlhahn (Berlin: Christoph Links Verlag, 2007), 32–42, 36. See also Klein, *Die Basler Mission in Guangdong (Südchina) 1859–1931* (Munich: Iudicium, 2002), 245.

4. A number of opinions regarding this question are presented in Klein, "Aktion und Reaktion?," 32–42; Xiang, *Origins of the Boxer War*, 31–39.

5. Wu Shiying, "Shilun Yihetuan yundong tedian ji qiyu Zhongguo jindai hua de guanxi" [The distinctive features of the Boxer movement and its relationship to Chinese modernization], in *Yihetuan yundong yibai zhounian guoji xueshu taolunhui lunwenji* [Selected papers from the international symposium on the 100th anniversary of the Boxer movement], vol. 1, ed. Su Weizhi and Liu Tianlu (Beijing: Shandong daxue chubanshe, 2001), 159–173.

6. Mou Anshi, *Yihetuan dikang lieqiang guafen shi* [The history of the Boxer resistance during the "scramble for China"] (Beijing: Jingji guanli chubanshe, 1997), 406–411.

7. Jane E. Elliott, *Some Did It for Civilization, Some Did It for Their Country: A Revised View of the Boxer War* (Hong Kong: Chinese University Press, 2002), 397–429, 515; Mark Elvin, "Mandarins and Millenarians: Reflections on the Boxer Uprising of 1899–1900," in *Another History: Essays on China from a European Perspective*, ed. Mark Elvin (Broadway, New South Wales, Aus-

tralia: Wild Peony, 1996), 219–225; Roger R. Thompson, "Military Dimensions of the 'Boxer Uprising' in Shanxi 1898–1901," in *Warfare in Chinese History*, ed. Hans van den Ven (Leiden: Brill, 2002), 288–320, 306–310; Xiang, *Origins of the Boxer War*, 275–276, 300–304.

8. A detailed discussion of the reinforcement of the legation troops is provided in Xiang, *Origins of the Boxer War*, 206–214.

9. Anon., "The Crisis in China: Attitude of the Powers," *The Times*, 2 July 1900, 7. See also the contemporary German dissertation from Friedrich Kleine, *Die Unterdrückung der Boxerunruhen in China 1900 nach ihrer völkerrechtlichen Behauptung* (Berlin: Trenkel, 1913).

10. Alfred Graf von Waldersee, *Denkwürdigkeiten des General-Feldmarschalls Alfred Grafen von Waldersee*, vol. 3, *1900–1904*, ed. Heinrich Otto Meisner (Berlin: Deutsche Verlags-Anstalt, 1923), 123.

11. Louis Kempff (Rear Admiral, United States Navy), U.S. flagship *Newark*, Dagu, 10 June 1900, to the U.S. Department of the Navy in Washington, in Annual Reports of the Navy Department (57th Cong., 1st Sess., House of Representatives), vol. 4377 (Washington, DC: U.S. Government Publishing Office, 1902), 12–13.

12. F. M. Wise (Commander of the USS *Monocacy*) to the U.S. Asian Station, 23 June 1900, ibid., 21.

13. Dietlind Wünsche, *Feldpostbriefe aus China* (Berlin: Christoph Links Verlag, 2008), 121.

14. Elihu Root (Minister of War) to President William McKinley, Washington, 30 November 1900, in Annual Reports of the War Department for the Fiscal Year Ended June 30, 1900 (56th Cong., 2nd Sess., House of Representatives), vol. 4078 (Washington, DC: U.S. Government Publishing Office, 1900), 2–14.

15. Anand Yang, "(A) Subaltern('s) Boxers: An Indian Soldier's Account of China and the World in 1900–01," in *The Boxers, China, and the World*, ed. Robert Bickers and R. C. Tiedemann (Lanham: Rowman & Littlefield, 2007), 43–65. For a general overview, see Alan Harfield, *British and Indian Armies on the China Coast 1785–1985* (London: A & J Partnership, 1990), 234. Regarding the British-Chinese Weihaiwai-Regiment, see Arthur Alison Stuart Barnes, *On Active Service with the Chinese Regiment: A Record of Operations of the First Chinese Regiment in North China from March to October 1900* (London: Grant Richards, 1902), 206–208; see also Frederick Brown, *From Tientsin to Peking with the Allied Forces* (London: C. H. Kelly, 1902), 81. Regarding the French native contingents, see Pierre Montagnard, *La France coloniale*, vol. 2 (Paris: Pygmalion, 1988), 393; Jean-François Brun, "Intervention armée en Chine: L'expédition internationale de 1900–1901," *Revue Historique des Armées* 258 (2010): 14–45.

16. Report from Major Morris C. Foote (Ninth Infantry) to the Adjutant of the Ninth Infantry, Tianjin, 25 July 1900, in Annual Reports of the War Department, vol. 4078 (Washington, DC: U.S. Government Publishing Office), 28–29; Lieutenant Colonel Chas. A. Coolidge (Ninth Infantry) to Ninth

Infantry HQ, Tianjin, 26 July 1900, ibid., 26–27: "Looting . . . seemed to be a general thing among the other troops of the allied forces."

17. Xiang, *Origins of the Boxer War*, 331–352.

18. Quoted in Bernd Sösemann, "Die sog. Hunnenrede Wilhelm II: Textkritische und interpretatorische Bemerkungen zur Ansprache des Kaisers vom 27. Juli 1900 in Bremerhaven," *Historische Zeitschrift* 222 (1976): 342–358, 349.

19. Roland Allen, *The Siege of the Peking Legations* (London: Smith, Elder, 1901), 286–287; Elvin, "Mandarins and Millenarians," 219–225. Regarding the Chinese conduct of the war, see Xiang, *Origins of the Boxer War*, 275–277, 300–304; Cohen, *History in Three Keys*, 188; Mou Anshi, *Yihetuan dikang lieqiang guafen shi*, 413–425.

20. Report from Lieutenant Colonel J. T. Dickman (Twenty-Sixth Infantry), regarding the events of August to November 1900, Peking, 5 November 1900, in Annual Reports of the War Department for the Fiscal Year Ended June 30, 1900 (57th Cong., 1st Sess., House of Representatives), vol. 4274 (Washington, DC: U.S. Government Publishing Office, 1901), 476–488, 478.

21. The diary of Colonel Grierson, 30 November 1900, NA London, WO 32/6415.

22. Report from Lieutenant Colonel J. T. Dickman (Twenty-Sixth Infantry), regarding the events of August to November 1900, Peking, 5 November 1900, Annual Reports of the War Department for the Fiscal Year Ended June 30, 1900 (57th Cong., 1st Sess., House of Representatives), vol. 4274 (Washington, DC: U.S. Government Publishing Office, 1901), 476–488, 483.

23. Laiqing Yang, "Die Ereignisse von Gaomi und der Widerstand der Bevölkerung gegen den deutschen Eisenbahnbau," in Leutner and Mühlhahn, *Kolonialkrieg in China*, 49–58, 56–57.

24. Luo Dunrong, *Gengzi guobianji* [The history of our national tragedy] (Taipei: Guangwen, 1964), 7.

25. Waldersee, *Denkwürdigkeiten*, 51.

26. John V. A. MacMurray, ed., *Treaties and Agreements with and concerning China*, vol. 1 (Manchu Period, 1894–1911) (New York: Oxford University Press, 1973, repr. of the 1921 ed.), 309.

27. Army order no. 1198, 12 November 1900, the diary of Colonel Grierson, app., 12 November 1900, NA London, WO 32/6414.

28. James L. Hevia, *English Lessons: The Pedagogy of Imperialism in Nineteenth-Century China* (Durham, NC: Duke University Press, 2003), 208–219. Hevia speaks of a "carnival of loot," 208. See also Waldersee, "Die Eroberung und Plünderung Pekings im August 1900," *Preußische Jahrbücher* 191 (1923): 193–203, 195.

29. Waldersee, *Denkwürdigkeiten*, 130.

30. Susanne Kuß, "Co-operation between German and French Troops during the Boxer War in China, 1900/01: The Punitive Expedition to Baoding," in *Imperial Co-operation and Transfer 1870–1930*, ed. Volker Barth and Roland Cvetkovski (London: Bloomsbury Academic, 2015), 197–217.

31. Report of the staff officer G. H. W. O'Sullivan regarding the Baoding expedition, Peking, 2 November 1900, Annual Reports of the War Department, vol. 4274 (Washington, DC: U.S. Government Publishing Office), 468–475, 475.

32. Regelungen des Conseil du Gouvernement Provisoire de la cité Chinoise du Tientsin: Réglements généraux d'administration de la cité chinoise de Tientsin, 1900, NARA Washington, 395/919.

33. Waldersee, *Denkwürdigkeiten*, 123.

34. Proclamation for the inhabitants of Peking with the exception of the French sector (no date, probably December 1900), published by the Committee for the Administration of Peking (excepting the French sector), NARA Washington, 395/919.

35. The following information was taken from the Committee for the Administration of Peking Protocol no. 1, 10 December 1900, points 2, 5, 6, 7, and 8.

36. Ibid., point 2.

37. Klaus Mühlhahn, *Herrschaft und Widerstand in der "Musterkolonie" Kiautschou: Interaktionen zwischen China und Deutschland 1897–1914* (Munich: Oldenbourg, 2000), 230–231.

38. *Deutschland in China*, ed. Bearbeitet von Teilnehmern an der Expedition (Düsseldorf: Druck von August Bagel, 1902), 408.

39. General adjutant H. O. S. Heistand, General Order no. 3, Peking, 11 January 1901, Annual Reports of the War Department, vol. 4274 (Washington, DC: U.S. Government Publishing Office), 527–528.

40. Report from Major General Adna R. Chaffee, Commander of U.S. forces in China, 19 January 1901, ibid., 498–505, 502.

41. Minutes from the first conference in Peking of the military medical representatives, 17 January 1901, NARA Washington, 395/919.

42. Minutes from the Committee for the Administration of Peking, no. 9, 21 January 1901, ibid.

43. Report from Lieutenant Colonel J. T. Dickman (Twenty-Sixth Infantry) regarding the events between August and November 1900, Peking, 5 November 1900, Annual Reports of the War Department, vol. 4274 (Washington, DC: U.S. Government Publishing Office), 476–488, 487.

44. Ibid., 484; see also an excerpt from a report from Major Quinton (Fourteenth Infantry), September 1900, ibid., 445.

45. Also listed were seven Italian expeditions, three Austro-Hungarian expeditions, two Japanese expeditions, one British expedition, one American expedition, one joint British-Italian expedition, one British-Japanese expedition, and one Franco-British-Japanese expedition. In Armee-Oberkommando in Ostasien, Peking, 8 May 1901: Zusammenstellung der seit dem 10. Dezember 1900 unternommenen Expeditionen (von den nichtdeutschen Kontingenten, soweit sie zur Kenntnis des Armee-Oberkommandos gekommen sind), in Fedor von Rauch, *Mit Graf Waldersee in China* (Berlin: F. Fontane, 1907), att. 11, 439–445. According to American records, of a total

of forty-four expeditions, thirty-four were purely German undertakings: Roster of all Expeditions made since 12 December 1900, Army Headquarters in East Asia, Peking, 8 May 1901, in Annual Reports of the War Department, vol. 4274 (Washington, DC: U.S. Government Publishing Office), 495–497. This also included the remark that the list was not exhaustive as they did not have access to the full information.

46. The diary of Colonel Grierson, 20 November 1900 and 8 November 1900, NA London, WO 32/6414, WO 32/6415.

47. Wünsche, *Feldpostbriefe aus China*, 347–359.

48. *Deutschland in China*, 80, 108, 110.

49. Arnold von Lequis, Schlussbericht zum Kriegstagebuch, 30 August 1901, 8a, BA/MA Freiburg, N 38/31.

50. *Deutschland in China*, 112; Army order no. 1198, 12 November 1900, the diary of Colonel Grierson, app. 12 November 1900, NA London, WO 32/6414.

51. Lequis, Handschriftlicher Bericht über Teilnahme an Expeditionen, Gefechten während der Expedition nach China, 30 August–21 November 1901, entry for 22–24 November, BA/MA Freiburg, N 38/29. Regarding reprisals for acts of resistance against the allied troops, see Claudia Ham and M. Christian Ortner, eds., *Mit SMS Zenta in China: "Mich hatte auch diesmal der Tod nicht gewollt . . ." Aus dem Tagebuch eines k.u.k. Matrosen während des Boxeraufstands* (Vienna: Verlag Österreich, 2000), 59, 75; Eugen Binder-Krieglstein, *Die Kämpfe des deutschen Expeditionskorps in China und ihre militärischen Lehren* (Berlin: Ernst Siegfried Mittler, 1902), 78–79; Frederic A. Sharf and Peter Harrington, eds., *China 1900: The Eyewitnesses Speak; The Experience of Westerners in China during the Boxer Rebellion, as Described by Participants in Letters, Diaries and Photographs* (London: Greenhill Books, 2000), 229 (reports of the American war correspondent Jasper Whiting).

52. Walther Obkircher, ed., *General Erich von Gündell: Aus seinen Tagebüchern* (Hamburg: Hanseatische Verlagsanstalt, 1939), 40.

53. Binder-Krieglstein, *Die Kämpfe des deutschen Expeditionskorps in China und ihre militärischen Lehren*, introduction, iv.

54. Lequis, Schlussbericht zum Kriegstagebuch, 30 August 1901, 14–14a, BA/MA Freiburg, N 38/31.

55. Ibid.

56. Cited in Diana Preston, *Boxer Rebellion: The Dramatic Story of China's War on Foreigners That Shook the World in the Summer of 1900* (New York: Walker, 2000), 381.

57. Heinrich Haslinde, *Tagebuch aus China 1900/1901*, ed. Marlis Ottmann (Munich: Selbstverlag Marlis Ottmann, 1990), 48–49.

58. One tael amounted to 3.16 reichsmark.

59. The diary of Colonel Grierson, 20, 21 December 1900, NA London, WO 32/6416.

60. Examples taken from Wünsche, *Feldpostbriefe aus China*, 348–349.

61. Report from Lieutenant Colonel Soulard Turner (Tenth Infantry) regarding the Baoding Expedition, 24 October 1900, in Annual Reports of the War Department, vol. 4274 (Washington, DC: U.S. Government Publishing Office), 468–475, 472. See also Sharf and Harrington, *China 1900*, 228 (report of the American war correspondent Jasper Whiting).

62. Grierson to the War Office (confidential), 9 January 1901, NA London, WO 32/6416.

63. Eugen Wolffhügel, "Der Sanitätsdienst im Berggefecht am Tschang-tschönnling 8. März 1901 mit einigen Betrachtungen über Sanitätstaktik im Gebirgskriege," *Deutsche militärärztliche Zeitschrift* 31 (1902): 393–411, 396.

64. Lequis, Handschriftlicher Bericht über Teilnahme an Expeditionen, entry for 11–18 January 1901, BA/MA Freiburg, N 38/29; Lequis, Schlussbericht zum Kriegstagebuch, 30 August 1901, 14a–15, ibid., N 38/31.

65. Report of the staff officer G. H. W. O'Sullivan regarding the Baoding expedition, Peking, 24 October 1900, Annual Reports of the War Department, vol. 4274 (Washington, DC: U.S. Government Publishing Office), 475; Général Voyron, *Rapport sur l'expédition de Chine 1900–1901* (Paris: Henri Charles-Lavauzelle, 1904), 167–172; Barnes, *On Active Service*, 177, 181.

66. Binder-Krieglstein, *Die Kämpfe des Deutschen Expeditionskorps in China und ihre militärischen Lehren*, 8.

67. Kriegstagebuch des II. Seebataillons, entry for 11 September 1900, BA/MA Freiburg, RM 121I/400.

68. Bericht des Gefreiten Naumann über seine Teilnahme an der China-Expedition, BA/MA Freiburg, RM 38/86, 10.

69. Rudolf Zabel, *Deutschland in China* (Leipzig: Verlag von Georg Wigand, 1902), 381. See also "'Hunnenbrief' eines Marineinfanteristen, Peking, 24 September 1900," *Vorwärts* 17, no. 277 (28 November 1900): 1.

70. Kriegstagebuch, I. Seebataillon, entry for 11 September 1900, BA/MA Freiburg, RM 121I/401, 69: "11.30: Lieutenant Bartsch went to the south gate with 12 men and opened fire on those trying to escape. He entered the town after it had been forced open by his troops. searching the town, the troops cooled down outside the town and after 2.15 P.M. then proceeded to set fire to the southern part of the town. At 5.00 P.M. we set off on the march back."

71. "'Hunnenbrief' des Marineinfanteristen Franz Faber, Peking," 12 September 1900, *Vorwärts* 17, no. 269 (7 November 1900): 1; "Brief eines französischen Soldaten," n.d., *Frankfurter Zeitung und Handelsblatt* 45, no. 4 (4 January 1901): Abendblatt, 2. For a comparable action by British troops, see Sharf and Harrington, *China 1900*, 231 (report of the American war correspondent Jasper Whiting).

72. Excerpt from a report from Major Quinton (Fourteenth Infantry), September 1900, in Annual Reports of the War Department, vol. 4274 (Washington, DC: U.S. Government Publishing Office), 445–446.

73. Sabine Dabringhaus, "An Army on Vacation? The German War in China, 1900–1901," in *Anticipating Total War: The German and American Experiences*,

1871–1914, ed. Manfred F. Boemeke, Roger Chickering, and Stig Förster (Cambridge: Cambridge University Press, 1999), 459–476, esp. 474–475.

74. Report from Lieutenant Colonel J. T. Dickman (Twenty-Sixth Infantry) regarding the events between August and November 1900, Peking, 5 November 1900, 484: "It was a very large expedition to accomplish a small objective, reports having greatly exaggerated the strength of the enemy."

75. The diary of Colonel Grierson, 19 November 1900, NA London, WO 32/6414.

76. Ibid., 6 November 1900, 20 November 1900.

77. Report from Captain Grote Hutcheson (Sixth Cavalry), n.d., part of a report from Major General A. R. Chaffee, commander of U.S. forces in China, 21 September 1900, Annual Reports of the War Department, vol. 4274 (Washington, DC: U.S. Government Publishing Office), 448–450, 450; Brigadier General James H. Wilson, report of an expedition against hostile Chinese in the vicinity of the River Hunhe on 18–19 September 1900, 20 September 1900, ibid., vol. 4078, 120–123, 122. See also A. S. Daggett, *America in the China Relief Expedition* (Kansas City: Hudson-Kimberly, 1903), 141–142.

78. Report of the investigation from Major E. L. Huggins (Sixth Cavalry) regarding the burning of Chinese villages, 30 October 1900, Annual Reports of the War Department, vol. 4274 (Washington, DC: U.S. Government Publishing Office), 439–440. A detailed account is provided by Lieutenant C. D. Rhodes (Sixth Cavalry), Camp of the Cavalry, Yangchuan, 30 October 1900, NARA Washington, 395/913.

79. Lord Salisbury and Sir Frank Lascelles (British ambassador to Berlin), no. 214, 2 October 1900 (Most Confidential), *British Documents on Foreign Affairs,* pt. 1, ser. E (Asia, 1860–1914), ed. Ian Nish, vol. 25 (Suppression of Boxers and Negotiations for China Settlement, August 1900–October 1900), doc. 179, 134–135. See K. L. Young, *British Policy in China* (Oxford: Clarendon Press, 1970), 157–158.

80. The diary of Colonel Grierson, 16 February 1901, NA London, WO 32/6419.

81. Ibid., 30 November 1900. See also the diary of Colonel Grierson, 20 November 1900, 30 November 1900, NA London, WO 32/6415.

82. Waldersee, *Denkwürdigkeiten,* 68.

83. Ibid., 108.

84. *Deutschland in China,* 402.

85. Waldersee, *Denkwürdigkeiten,* 119, 122.

86. Waldersee to Kaiser Wilhelm II, 22 December 1900, quoted in Obkircher, *General Erich von Gündell: Aus seinen Tagebüchern,* 37; Waldersee, *Denkwürdigkeiten,* 108.

2. The Herero and Nama War

1. Kurd Schwabe, *Der Krieg in Deutsch-Südwestafrika 1904–1906* (Berlin: C. A. Weller, 1907), foreword.

2. Gerhard Pool, *Samuel Maharero* (Windhoek, Namibia: Gamsberg Macmillan, 1991), 133–158.

3. Regarding the Herero and Nama before the German colonization, see, for example, Gesine Krüger, "Das Goldene Zeitalter der Viehzüchter: Namibia im 19. Jahrhundert," in *Völkermord in Deutsch-Südwestafrika*, ed. Jürgen Zimmerer and Joachim Zeller (Berlin: Christoph Links, 2003), 13–25; Harri Siiskonen, "The Seven Year War (1863–1870) in Namibian Historiography," in *Mission und Gewalt*, ed. Jürgen Becher and Ulrich van der Heyden (Stuttgart: Steiner, 2000), 343–355.

4. Theodor Leutwein, *Elf Jahre Gouverneur in Deutsch-Südwestafrika* (Berlin: Ernst Siegfried Mittler, 1906; repr. Windhoek: Namibia Wissenschaftliche Gesellschaft, 1997), 541.

5. For Leutwein's policy of divide and rule, see, for example, Helmut Bley, *Kolonialherrschaft und Sozialstruktur in Deutsch-Südwestafrika 1894–1914* (Hamburg: Leibniz-Verlag, 1968), 93–106.

6. For a detailed account, see Susanne Kuß, "Der Herero-Deutsche Krieg und das deutsche Militär: Kriegsursachen und Kriegsverlauf," in *Namibia—Deutschland: Eine geteilte Geschichte*, ed. Larissa Förster, Dag Henrichsen, and Michael Bollig (Cologne: Edition Minerva, 2004), 62–77, esp. 64–68.

7. For the start of the Herero rising, see Jon M. Bridgman, *The Revolt of the Hereros* (Berkeley: University of California Press, 1981), 69. The view that the uprising was due to German expectations of its incidence is advanced by Jan-Bart Gewald, *Herero Heroes: A Socio-Political History of the Herero of Namibia 1890–1923* (Oxford: James Currey, 1999), 142–156. For a contemporary account, see *Die Kämpfe der deutschen Truppen in Südwestafrika: Auf Grund amtlichen Materials bearbeitet von der Kriegsgeschichtlichen Abteilung I des Großen Generalstabes*, vol. 1, *Hereroaufstand* (Berlin: Ernst Siegfried Mittler, 1906), 24; Conrad Rust, *Krieg und Frieden im Hererolande: Aufzeichnungen aus dem Jahre 1904* (Berlin: Kommissionsverlag L.U. Kittler, 1905), 3.

8. Chief of Staff of the German Admiralty to the Staatssekretär of the Reichsmarineamt, 17 January 1904, BA/MA Freiburg, RM 2/1867.

9. The Landwehr and Landsturm were organizations of men not belonging to any regular formation of the army or navy.

10. *Die Kämpfe der deutschen Truppen in Südwestafrika*, vol. 1, 15–16; "Die Tätigkeit des Landungskorps SMS *Habicht* während des Herero-Aufstandes in Süd-West-Afrika, Januar/Februar 1904," *Marine-Rundschau* (supp. 1905): 1–31, esp. 28; Admiralstab der Marine, ed., *Das Marine-Expeditionskorps in Südwest-Afrika während des Herero-Aufstandes* (Berlin: Ernst Siegfried Mittler, 1905).

11. Gesine Krüger, *Kriegsbewältigung und Geschichtsbewußtsein* (Göttingen: Vandenhoeck & Ruprecht, 1999), 47–48.

12. *Sanitäts-Bericht über die Kaiserliche Schutztruppe für Südwestafrika während des Herero- und Hottentottenaufstandes für die Zeit vom 1. Januar 1904 bis 31. März 1907, bearb. im Kommando der Schutztruppen im Reichs-Kolonialamt*, vol. 1 (Berlin: Ernst Siegfried Mittler, 1909), 8.

13. Major General Nikolaus Ritter von Endres (Bavarian military representative in Berlin) to the Bavarian Ministry of War, 10 May 1904, BayHSTA Munich,

Mkr 803. See also Helmut Bley, *South West Africa under German Rule* (Münster: Lit, 1998), 155.

14. *Die Kämpfe der deutschen Truppen in Südwestafrika,* vol. 1, 127.

15. For the causes of the Nama uprising, see Andreas Heinrich Bühler, *Der Namaaufstand gegen die deutsche Kolonialherrschaft in Namibia von 1904–1913* (Frankfurt am Main: KO—Verl. für Interkulturelle Kommunikation, 2003), 161–174; Horst Drechsler, *Südwestafrika unter deutscher Kolonialherrschaft: Der Kampf der Herero und Nama gegen den deutschen Imperialismus (1884–1915)* (East Berlin: Akademie-Verlag, 1966), 207–210.

16. Testimony from the missionary Christian Spellmeyer made in 1905 regarding the uprising in 1904. Published in Gustav Menzel, *Widerstand und Gottesfurcht: Hendrik Witbooi—eine Biographie in zeitgenössischen Quellen* (Cologne: Rüdiger Köppe, 2000), 241–244, 243.

17. Tilman Dedering, "The Prophet's 'War against Whites': Shepherd Stuurman in Namibia and South Africa, 1904–7," *Journal of African History* 40 (1999): 1–19, esp. 3–13.

18. Walter Nuhn, *Feind überall: Guerillakrieg in Südwest; Der Große Nama-Aufstand 1904–1908* (Bonn: Bernard & Graefe, 2000), 62.

19. "Hottentott" was a term first used by the Boers to refer to the Khoi Khoi, an ethnic group to which the Nama also belonged. Perceiving their click language as a stutter, they referred to them as "the stutterers" in the northern dialect of Afrikaans: Hottentott. German settlers adopted the word with its derogatory connotations.

20. Berthold von Deimling, Kriegstagebuch, Stab 2, Feldregiment, Südfeldzug, att. 74, BA/MA Freiburg, N 559/v.7.

21. *Die Kämpfe der deutschen Truppen in Südwestafrika,* vol. 2, *Der Hottentottenkrieg* (Berlin: Ernst Siegfried Mittler, 1907), 23–24.

22. Ibid., 123.

23. Ibid., 299.

24. Paul von Lettow-Vorbeck, *Mein Leben* (Biberach: Koehler, 1957), 84.

25. *Die Kämpfe der deutschen Truppen in Südwestafrika,* vol. 2, 180.

26. Nuhn, *Feind überall,* 234–236.

27. Bühler, *Der Namaaufstand gegen die deutsche Kolonialherrschaft in Namibia,* 329–330.

28. Contemporary evaluators of the war and its course would be better advised to expend less energy in arguments over the exact number of deaths, a figure that probably can never be pinpointed exactly. See especially Bley, *Kolonialherrschaft und Sozialstruktur in Deutsch-Südwestafrika,* 191; Drechsler, *Südwestafrika unter deutscher Kolonialherrschaft,* 252; Brigitte Lau, "Uncertain Certainties: The Herero-German War of 1904," in *History and Historiographies: 4 Essays in Reprint,* ed. Brigitte Lau and Anemarie Heywood (Windhoek, Namibia: MSORP, 1995), 43–46; Lau, Letter to *Southern African Review of Books* (June–July 1990): 21. The counterposition is presented by Henning Melber, Letter to *Southern African Review of Books* (August–October 1990): 23.

29. Krüger, *Kriegsbewältigung und Geschichtsbewußtsein,* 137.

30. Gewald, *Herero Heroes,* 263–267; Gewald, "Die Beerdigung von Samuel Maharero und die Reorganisation der Herero," in Zimmerer and Zeller, *Völkermord in Deutsch-Südwestafrika,* 171–179; Gesine Krüger, "Koloniale Gewalt, Alltagserfahrungen und Überlebensstrategien," in Förster, Henrichsen, and Bollig, *Namibia—Deutschland: Eine geteilte Geschichte,* 92–105; Krüger, *Kriegsbewältigung und Geschichtsbewußtein,* 184–194, 199–203; Jürgen Zimmerer, *Deutsche Herrschaft über Afrikaner: Staatlicher Machtanspruch und Wirklichkeit im kolonialen Namibia* (Münster: Lit, 2001), 68–69, 77–84.

31. Drechsler, *Aufstände in Südwestafrika* (East Berlin: Dietz, 1984), 75–76.

32. Kirsten Zirkel, "Military Power in German Colonial Policy: The Schutz-truppen and Their Leaders in East and South-West Africa, 1888–1918," in *Guardians of Empire: The Armed Forces of the Colonial Powers c. 1700–1964,* ed. David Killingray and David Omissi (Manchester: Manchester University Press, 1999), 91–113, 100; Zirkel, *Militärische Struktur und politische Führung im Deutsch-Südwestafrika-Krieg 1904–07* (MA diss., University of Düsseldorf, 1989), 118.

33. *Die Kämpfe der deutschen Truppen in Südwestafrika,* vol. 1, 149, 150, 152, 156.

34. Ibid., 158. Regarding the course of the battle of Waterberg, see ibid., 160–165.

35. Pool, *Samuel Maharero,* 253–254.

36. Lothar von Trotha, "Direktiven für den Angriff gegen die Hereros, 4/8/1904," in *Die Kämpfe der deutschen Truppen in Südwestafrika,"* vol. 1, 156–159, 157.

37. Ibid., 179.

38. Zirkel, *Militärische Struktur und politische Führung im Deutsch-Südwestafrika-Krieg,* 124.

39. See the discussion in Walter Nuhn, *Sturm über Südwest: Der Hereroaufstand von 1904; Ein düsteres Kapitel der deutschen kolonialen Vergangenheit Namibias* (Koblenz: Bernard & Graefe, 1999), 229.

40. Ludwig von Estorff, *Wanderungen und Kämpfe in Südwestafrika, Ostafrika und Südafrika 1894–1910* (Windhoek, Namibia: Privatdruck des Herausgebers, 1968), 116. For a similar argument, see von Lequis, letter to his father, 21 August 1904, Swakopmund, BA/MA Freiburg, N 38/5.

41. Statement of the Officer of the General Staff Martin Chales de Beaulieu, printed in *Die Kämpfe der deutschen Truppen in Südwestafrika,* vol. 1, 190.

42. Trotha, order from 15 August 1904, Hamakari, BA/MA Freiburg, N 38/35.

43. Trotha, order from 20 August 1904, Okawitumbika, ibid.

44. Trotha, order from 15 August 1904, Hamakari, ibid.

45. Trotha, order from 20 August 1904, Okawitumbika, ibid.

46. Statement of the Officer of the General Staff Martin Chales de Beaulieu, printed in *Die Kämpfe der deutschen Truppen in Südwestafrika,* vol. 1, 190.

47. Such allegations were made in the "blue book" *Report on the Natives of South-West Africa and Their Treatment by Germany: Prepared in the Administrator's Office* (Windhoek, 1918), 61–67. These statements were checked by

Isabel V. Hull, *Absolute Destruction: Military Culture and the Practices of War* (Ithaca, NY: Cornell University Press, 2005), 46–50.

48. Leutwein to the Colonial Department of the Foreign Ministry, 17 May 1904, quoted in Drechsler, *Südwestafrika unter deutscher Kolonialherrschaft*, 153.

49. *Die Kämpfe der deutschen Truppen in Südwestafrika*, vol. 1, 198.

50. Ludwig von Estorff, "Kriegserlebnisse in Südwestafrika: Vortrag gehalten in der Militärischen Gesellschaft zu Berlin, 8/2/1911," *Militär-Wochenblatt* (supp. 1911): 80–101, 92. See also Estorff, *Wanderungen und Kämpfe in Südwestafrika, Ostafrika und Südafrika*, 117.

51. Lothar von Trotha, "Politik und Kriegführung," *Berliner Neueste Nachrichten* 29 (3 February 1909): 3.

52. As described in *Die Kämpfe der deutschen Truppen in Südwestafrika*, vol. 1, 202.

53. Estorff, *Wanderungen und Kämpfe in Südwestafrika, Ostafrika und Südafrika*, 117.

54. Trotha to Leutwein, 27 October 1904, cited in Drechsler, *Südwestafrika unter deutscher Kolonialherrschaft*, 164.

55. Trotha to Leutwein, 5 November 1904, cited in ibid., 180.

56. Letter from the chief of the general staff Alfred von Schlieffen to Reichskanzler Bernhard von Bülow, 23 November 1904, BA Lichterfelde, R 1001/2089, 3–4.

57. A typed text of the proclamation is held in BA/MA Freiburg, RW 51/2. An original translation into Otjiherero taken from the *Botswana National Archives* is published in Jan-Bart Gewald, "The Great General of the Kaiser," *Botswana Notes and Records* 26 (1994): 67–76, 73. On 1 January 1905, the Social Democratic *Vorwärts* printed a letter by a Wurttemberg soldier writing about an "alleged appeal to the Herero people" which von Trotha was said to have issued. The letter quoted parts of the proclamation (ibid., 22 [1 January 1905], no. 1: 2). Nevertheless, this did not ignite any discussion. Both this proclamation and a similar address to the Nama were published for the first time in the journal *Die Deutschen Kolonien* (vol. 4, no. 8: 245–246) in August 1905. Both texts were then reprinted in *Vorwärts* (15 August 1905): 3.

58. Hull, *Absolute Destruction*, 57.

59. Bley, *Kolonialherrschaft und Sozialstruktur*, 204–206.

60. See Hull, *Absolute Destruction*, 125–126. This proclamation is also printed in *Die Kämpfe der deutschen Truppen in Südwestafrika*, vol. 2, 186.

61. Nuhn, *Feind überall*, 127.

62. Joël Kotek and Pierre Rigoulot, *Das Jahrhundert der Lager: Gefangenschaft, Zwangsarbeit, Vernichtung* (Berlin: Propyläen, 2001), 45, 64–73; Jonas Kreienbaum, "Deadly Learning? Concentration Camps in Colonial Wars around 1900," in *Imperial Co-operation and Transfer, 1870–1930*, ed. Volker Barth and Roland Cvetkovski (London: Bloomsbury Academic, 2015), 219–235.

63. *Sanitäts-Bericht über die Kaiserliche Schutztruppe für Südwestafrika*, vol. 1, 141.

64. Krüger, *Kriegsbewältigung und Geschichtsbewußtsein*, 129.

65. *Sanitäts-Bericht über die Kaiserliche Schutztruppe für Südwestafrika*, vol. 1, 131.

66. Gewald, *Herero Heroes*, 186.

67. Such parallels have been drawn by Henning Melber, "Kontinuitäten totaler Herrschaft: Völkermord und Apartheid in Deutsch-Südwestafrika," in *Jahrbuch für Antisemitismusforschung,* ed. Wolfgang Benz, 1 (1992): 91–117; and Jürgen Zimmerer, "Krieg, KZ und Völkermord in Südwestafrika," in Zimmerer and Zeller, *Völkermord in Deutsch-Südwestafrika,* 45–63, 60. A contrary view is provided by Krüger in *Kriegsbewältigung und Geschichtsbewußtsein,* 134.

68. Hull, *Absolute Destruction,* 72–73.

69. This point was confirmed by the *Sanitäts-Bericht über die Kaiserliche Schutztruppe für Südwestafrika,* vol. 1, 140.

70. Ibid., 143.

71. *Sanitätsbericht für den Monat Oktober 1906, 10/11/1906,* HSTA Stuttgart, M 1/8, vol. 216; *Sanitäts-Bericht über die Kaiserliche Schutztruppe für Südwestafrika während des Herero- und Hottentottenaufstandes für die Zeit vom 1. Januar 1904 bis 31. März 1907, bearb. im Kommando der Schutztruppen im Reichs-Kolonialamt,* vol. 2, *Statistischer Teil* (Berlin: Mittler, 1920), 419.

72. Ibid., vol. 1, 142.

73. Ibid., vol. 2, 420.

74. Krüger, *Kriegsbewältigung und Geschichtsbewußtsein,* 146.

75. Zimmerer, *Deutsche Herrschaft über Afrikaner,* 46.

76. Bühler, *Der Namaaufstand gegen die deutsche Kolonialherrschaft in Namibia,* 341; Krüger, *Kriegsbewältigung und Geschichtsbewußtsein,* 166–167.

77. Estorff to the High Command of the Protection Force, 10 April 1907, BA Lichterfelde, R 1001/2140.

78. *Sanitäts-Bericht über die Kaiserliche Schutztruppe für Südwestafrika,* vol. 2, 421.

79. Zusammenstellung über die Sterblichkeit in den Kriegsgefangenenlagern in Deutsch-Südwestafrika, n.d., BA Lichterfelde, R 1001/2140, in Drechsler, *Südwestafrika unter deutscher Kolonialherrschaft,* 213.

80. Zimmerer, *Deutsche Herrschaft über Afrikaner,* 48–49.

81. Bühler, *Der Namaaufstand gegen die deutsche Kolonialherrschaft in Namibia,* 370–376. See also Wolfgang U. Eckart, "Medizin und kolonialer Rassenkrieg: Die Niederschlagung des Herero-Nama-Aufstands im Schutzgebiet Deutsch-Südwestafrika (1904–1907)," in *Kriegsverbrechen im 20. Jahrhundert,* ed. Wolfram Wette and Gerd R. Ueberschär (Darmstadt: Primus, 2001), 59–71, 66–67.

3. The Maji Maji War

1. Land use in East Africa has a long history of regional and global integration. See John Middleton, *The World of the Swahili: An African Mercantile Civilization* (New Haven, CT: Yale University Press, 1992), 20; Thomas Håkansson, Mats Wildgren, and Lowe Börjeson, "Introduction: Historical and Regional Perspectives on Landscape Transformations in Northeastern Tanzania, 1850–2000," *International Journal of African Historical Studies* 41, no. 3 (2008): 369–382.

2. John Iliffe, *A Modern History of Tanganyika* (Cambridge: Cambridge University Press, 1999), 34.

3. Jan-Georg Deutsch, "Vom Bezirksamtmann zum Mehrparteiensystem—Transformation politischer Herrschaft im kolonialen und nachkolonialen Tansania," in *Tansania: Koloniale Vergangenheit und neuer Aufbruch*, ed. Ulrich van der Heyden and Achim Oppen (Münster: Lit, 1996), 21–46, 27.

4. Iliffe, *Modern History of Tanganyika*, 168–169.

5. Marcia Wright, "Maji Maji: Prophecy and Historiography," in *Revealing Prophets: Prophecy in Eastern African History*, ed. David Anderson and Douglas H. Johnson (London: James Curry, 1995), 124–142.

6. Gustav Adolf von Götzen, *Deutsch-Ostafrika im Aufstand 1905/06* (Berlin: Dietrich Reimer, 1909), 63.

7. John Iliffe, "The Effects of the Maji Maji Rebellion on German Occupation Policy in East Africa," in *Britain and Germany in Africa: Imperial Rivalry and Colonial Rule*, ed. Prosser Gifford and Wm. Roger Louis (New Haven, CT: Yale University Press 1967), 557–575, esp. 560–561. Jamie Monson adopts this stance in her argument against the "nationalist Dar es Salam" school in Monson, "Relocating Maji Maji: The Politics of Alliance and Authority in the Southern Highlands of Tanzania, 1870–1918," *Journal of African History* 39 (1998): 95–120. Taking a different focus is Thaddeus Sunseri, "Famine and Wild Pigs: Gender Struggles and the Outbreak of the Maji Maji War in Uzaramo (Tanzania)," *Journal of African History* 38 (1997): 235–259.

8. Gilbert C. K. Gwassa, "African Methods of Warfare during the Maji Maji War 1905–1907," in *War and Society in Africa*, ed. Bethwell A. Ogot (London: F. Cass, 1972), 122–147, 136–137.

9. Otto Stollowsky, "On the Background of the Rebellion in German East Africa in 1905/06," trans. John W. East, *International Journal of African History* 21 (1988): 677–696, 686.

10. Felicitas Becker, "Von der Feldschlacht zum Guerillakrieg: Der Verlauf des Krieges und seine Schauplätze," in *Der Maji-Maji-Krieg in Deutsch-Ostafrika 1905–1907*, ed. Felicitas Becker and Jigal Beez (Berlin: Christoph Links Verlag, 2005), 74–86, esp. 76.

11. Juhani Koponen, *Development for Exploitation: German Colonial Policies in Mainland Tanzania, 1884–1914* (Helsinki: SHS, 1995), 230.

12. Götzen, *Deutsch-Ostafrika im Aufstand 1905/06*, 65. The following figures are taken from ibid., 135.

13. Ibid., 78.

14. This subdivision of the Maji Maji War into four phases according to its expansion follows a suggestion from Detlef Bald, "Afrikanischer Kampf gegen koloniale Herrschaft: Der Maji-Maji-Aufstand in Ostafrika," *Militärgeschichtliche Mitteilungen* 1 (1976): 23–50.

15. Telegram from Merker (in Samanga) to the government, 3 August 1905, BA/MA Freiburg, RM 121I/445.

16. Gwassa, "African Methods of Warfare," 122–147, 138–139.

17. Ibid., 142–143; Iliffe, *Modern History of Tanganyika*, 180.
18. Telegram from Götzen to the Foreign Office, 21 October 1905, BA/MA Freiburg, RM 121I/438.
19. Detlef Bald, "Afrikanischer Kampf gegen koloniale Herrschaft," *Militärgeschichtliche Mitteilungen* 1 (1976): 23–50, 37.
20. Denkschrift über die Entwickelung der Schutzgebiete in Afrika und der Südsee im Jahre 1906/07, Teil B: Deutsch-Ostafrika, SBR, XII. Legislaturperiode, 1st Sess., 1907–09, vol. 245, 3689–3824, esp. 3693.
21. These were the findings of Gilbert Gwassa, *The Outbreak and Development of the Maji Maji War 1905–1907* (Cologne: R. Köppe, 2005), 219. A wide consensus has accepted the figures that he presents. See also Iliffe, *Modern History of Tanganyika*, 200.
22. Ludger Wimmelbücker, "Verbrannte Erde: Zu den Bevölkerungsverlusten als Folge des Maji-Maji-Krieges," in Becker and Beez, *Der Maji-Maji-Krieg in Deutsch-Ostafrika*, 87–99, esp. 92.
23. "Zusammenstellung der Verluste in Deutsch-Ostafrika," *Deutsches Kolonialblatt* 8 (1907): 333.
24. Helge Kjekshus, *Ecology Control and Economic Development in East African History: The Case of Tanganyika 1850–1950* (Berkeley: University of California Press, 1977), 150–151.
25. Detlef Bald, *Deutsch-Ostafrika 1900–1914: Eine Studie über Verwaltung, Interessengruppen und wirtschaftliche Erschließung* (Munich: Weltforum Verlag, 1970); Hartmut Pogge von Strandmann, *Imperialismus vom Grünen Tisch: Deutsche Kolonialpolitik zwischen wirtschaftlicher Ausbeutung und "zivilisatorischen" Bemühungen* (Berlin: Christoph Links Verlag, 2009), 434–435.
26. Bernhard Dernburg, *Zielpunkte des Deutschen Kolonialwesens: Vortrag auf Veranlassung des Deutschen Handelstages am 11. Januar 1907* (Berlin: Ernst Siegfried Mittler, 1907), 14. See also Koponen, *Development for Exploitation*, 261.
27. Bernhard Dernburg, "Fragen der Eingeborenenpolitik: Rede seiner Exzellenz des Herrn Staatssekretärs des Reichs-Kolonialamts Dernburg in der Sitzung der Budgetkommission des Reichstages vom 18. Februar 1908," *Deutsches Kolonialblatt* 19, no. 18 (1908): 216–231, 226.
28. War Diary Abteilung Paasche, entry for 6 August 1905, BA/MA Freiburg, RM 121I/452; War Diary Abteilung Lindi, kept by Oberleutnant zur See von Wernecke, introductory remarks, ibid., RM 121I/448. See also *Die Tätigkeit der Marine während der Niederwerfung des Eingeborenen-Aufstandes in Ostafrika 1905/06*, ed. Admiralstab der Marine (Beiheft zur Marine-Rundschau; Berlin: Ernst Siegfried Mittler, 1907), 16–18.
29. Übersicht über die Verteilung der Seestreitkräfte in Ostafrika, ibid., RM 121I/447. See also Hans Paasche, *"Im Morgenlicht" Kriegs-, Jagd- und Reise-Erlebnisse in Ostafrika* (Berlin: C. A. Schwetschke und Sohn, 1907), 77.
30. Keudel to Friedrich-Wilhelm Back, 6 August 1905, BA/MA Freiburg, RM 121I/445.

31. *Die Tätigkeit der Marine während der Niederwerfung des Eingeborenen-Aufstandes in Ostafrika 1905/06,* 7. All the following information is taken from ibid., 10, 16, 17, 18.

32. Ibid., 9.

33. Ibid., 14. See also Bericht des Oberleutnant zur See Paasche über den Vormarsch am Rufiji vom 15. bis 27. August 1905, entry for 19 August, BA/MA Freiburg, RM 121I/448: "Without water, we were forced to return." And War Diary Abteilung Paasche, entry for 22 August, ibid., RM 121I/452: "Upon receiving a message from Mtansa, informing us that the insurgents had broken formation in a wild retreat, I ordered the return . . . as I lack all provisions for the Europeans."

34. *Die Tätigkeit der Marine während der Niederwerfung des Eingeborenen-Aufstandes in Ofrika 1905/06,* 243, 245. See also Moritz Merker, "Ueber die Aufstandsbewegung in Deutsch-Ostafrika," *Militär-Wochenblatt* 91, no. 46 (12 April 1906): cols. 1085–1092, esp. 1086.

35. Antwort des Oberleutnants zur See Paasche vom Detachement Mtansa auf die geheime Umfrage des ältesten Offiziers der ostafrikanischen Station an die Führer der Marinedetachements (Umfrage 9), 15 November 1905, BA/MA Freiburg, RM 121I/460.

36. The following descriptions are taken from *Die Tätigkeit der Marine während der Niederwerfung des Eingeborenen-Aufstandes in Ostafrika 1905/06,* 9, 12, 18; Paasche, *"Im Morgenlicht,"* 102; Merker in *Militär-Wochenblatt* 91, no. 6 (1906): cols. 1085–1092, 1086; War Diary Abteilung Paasche, entry for 17 August 1905, BA/MA Freiburg, 121I/452; ibid., entry for 23 August 1905; ibid., entry for 27 October 1905; Bericht des Oberleutnants zur See Paasche über den Vormarsch am Rufiji vom 15. bis 27, August 1905, BA/MA Freiburg, RM 121I/448; Militärpolitischer Bericht, att. 3 (Bericht des Oblt. z.S. Paasche über die Tätigkeit der Rufiji-Expeditionsabteilung vom 25.10. bis 23.11.), ibid., RM 3/4317.

37. *Die Tätigkeit der Marine während der Niederwerfung des Eingeborenen-Aufstandes in Ostafrika 1905/06,* 13; Antwort des Hauptmanns von Schlichting vom Detachement Massassi auf die geheime Umfrage des ältesten Offiziers der ostafrikanischen Station an die Marinedetachementsführer (Umfrage 6), 12 December 1905, BA/MA Freiburg, RM 121I/460.

38. Runderlass von Gouverneur Götzen an sämtliche Bezirksämter, Bezirks-Nebenämter, Militär-Stationen und Militär-Posten, 13 November 1905, BA Lichterfelde, R 1001/728. Sections in Götzen to the Kolonialabteilung des Auswärtigen Amts, 7 December 1905, ibid., R 1001/723.

39. Examples for the collection of taxes, in War Diary Abteilung Paasche, entry for 4 September 1905, 31 October 1905, BA/MA Freiburg, RM 121I/452.

40. Regarding the death of the sailor Gramkau, see Merker in *Militär-Wochenblatt* 91, no. 46 (1906): cols. 1085–1092, 1089.

41. *Die Tätigkeit der Marine während der Niederwerfung des Eingeborenen-Aufstandes in Ostafrika 1905/06,* 20.

42. Ibid., 235–236.

43. Geheimer Fragebogen des ältesten Offiziers der ostafrikanischen Station an die Führer der Marinedetachements, 15 November 1905, BA/MA Freiburg, RM 121I/460, point 3: "Is it the view of the detachment leader that concessions should be made to the natives in order to put a swift end to the uprising. If yes, which? Or is it too early for such a course? When is the optimal time for such measures?"

44. Zusammenfassung der Urteile der Marine-Detachementführer auf den Fragebogen des ältesten Offiziers der ostafrikanischen Station, von Hauptmann von Schlichting, 15 November 1905, ibid.; Antwort Oberleutnant Sommerfeldt vom Detachement Mtingi auf die geheime Umfrage des ältesten Offiziers der ostafrikanischen Station an die Marinedetachementsführer (Umfrage7), ibid.

45. War Diary Abteilung Paasche, entry for 1 November 1905, ibid., RM 121I/452; Militärpolitischer Bericht III über die Tätigkeit der in Ostafrika befindlichen Kreuzer und Marinetruppen (Monat Dezember 1905), Dar es Salaam, 7 December 1905, ibid., RM 3/4317.

46. Iliffe, *Modern History of Tanganyika*, 193. See also the statement by Governor Götzen: "As in all wars conducted against savage peoples, . . . this war also required the infliction of planned damage to the property and possessions of the enemy population. The destruction of all economic assets such as the burning of villages and provisions may appear barbaric to the outsider. However, consideration of the speed with which the negro huts were rebuilt and the rich nature of the fruits yielded by the tropical environment, leads to an understanding of this 'dira necessitas.'" Götzen, *Deutsch-Ostafrika im Aufstand 1905/06*, 247–248.

47. Wangenheim to Götzen, 22 February 1905, quoted in Götzen, *Deutsch-Ostafrika im Aufstand 1905/06*, 149.

48. For a discussion of the term "scorched earth policy" which Gilbert Gwassa first introduced to describe the tactics employed in German East Africa, see Gilbert C. K. Gwassa, "German Intervention and African Resistance in Tanzania," in *A History of Tanzania*, ed. Isaria N. Kimambo and J. T. Arnold (Nairobi: East African Pub., 1969), 85–112, 102.

49. Militärpolitischer Bericht, att. 3 (Bericht des Oberleutnant zur See Paasche über die Tätigkeit der Rufiji-Expeditionsabteilung vom 25.10. bis 23.11.1905), BA/MA Freiburg, RM 3/4317.

50. Stengel to the senior officer at the East African station, 20 November 1905, ibid. : "So many supplies taken to the camps, that a proportion had to be burned because they could not be transported."

51. Bericht von Hauptmann Curt Wangenheim, Militärstation Mahenge, betr. die politischen Verhältnisse im Bezirk nach dem Aufstand, 27 July 1906, BA Lichterfelde, R 1001/1045.

52. Militärpolitischer Bericht III über die Tätigkeit der in Ostafrika befindlichen Kreuzer und Marinetruppen (Monat Dezember 1905), Dar es Salaam, 7 December 1905, BA/MA Freiburg, RM 3/4317.

53. War Diary Abteilung Paasche, 17 January 1900, ibid., RM 121I/452. The following information is taken from War Diary Abteilung Paasche, entry for

23 November 1905; War Diary Abteilung Paasche, letter from the district officer Keudel, 17 August 1905, ibid., 7 August 1905; War Diary Marineinfanterie-Detachement Kilwa, entry Hauptmann von Schlichting, 26 October 1905, ibid., RM 121I/449; Bericht von Hauptmann Wangenheim, Militärstation Mahenge, betr. die politischen Verhältnisse im Bezirk nach dem Aufstand, 27 July 1906, BA Lichterfelde, R 1001/1045.

54. Richard Kalkhof, *Reisebriefe von einer Parlamentarischen Studienreise nach Deutsch-Ostafrika* (Berlin: Dietrich Reimer, 1907), 39–40.

55. Bericht von Hauptmann Kurt von Schleinitz, betr. die Erfahrungen aus dem letzten Eingeborenen-Aufstand, 1 June 1907, BA/MA Freiburg, RM 5/6036.

56. *Die Tätigkeit der Marine während der Niederwerfung des Eingeborenen-Aufstandes in Ostafrika 1905/06*, 26.

57. Paasche, *"Im Morgenlicht,"* 124.

58. Martin Baer and Olaf Schröter, *Eine Kopfjagd: Deutsche in Ostafrika* (Berlin: Christoph Links, 2001), 99–100; Götzen to the Colonial Department of the Foreign Office, 12 December 1905, BA Lichterfelde, R 1001/723.

59. Deutsch-Ostafrikanische Zeitung, 2 December 1905. The appendix from Militärpolitischer Bericht IV über die Tätigkeit der in Ostafrika befindlichen Kreuzer und Marinetruppen (1/1 bis 6/2/1906) des ältesten Offiziers der ostafrikanischen Station, BA/MA Freiburg, RM 3/4317.

60. *Jahresbericht über die Entwickelung der deutschen Schutzgebiete in Afrika und in der Südsee 1906/07* (Berlin: Ernst Siegfried Mittler, 1908), 3–4; report from Hauptmann Wangenheim, Militärstation Mahenge, 27 July 1906, betr. die politischen Verhältnisse im Bezirk nach dem Aufstand, BA Lichterfelde, R 1001/1045.

61. Monson, "Relocating Maji Maji," 117–118; Ingrid Laurien, "'That Homa Homa Was Worse Child!' Berichte afrikanischer Zeitzeugen über den Maji Maji Aufstand in Deutsch-Ostafrika," in *Studien zur Geschichte des deutschen Kolonialismus in Afrika,* ed. Peter Heine, Peter Sebald, and Ulrich van der Heyden (Pfaffenweiler: Centaurus, 1995), 350–367.

62. Kjekshus, *Ecology Control and Economic Development in East African History,* 150. See also Wimmelbücker, "Verbrannte Erde," in Becker and Beez, *Der Maji-Maji-Krieg in Deutsch-Ostafrika 1905–1907,* 89–91.

4. The Motivation of White and Native Colonial Soldiers

1. The term "colonial soldier" is used here to refer to both white and nonwhite soldiers.

2. The Protection Force in German East Africa was established on 22 March 1891 (*Reichsgesetz-Blatt* 1891: 53–57), its counterparts in German South-West Africa and Cameroon on 9 June 1895 (ibid. 1895: 258–259).

3. Gesetz, betreffend die Kaiserlichen Schutztruppen in den Afrikanischen Schutzgebieten und die Wehrpflicht daselbst, 18 July 1896 (ibid. 1896: 653–659), sec. 1. See also *Organisatorische Bestimmungen für die Kaiserlichen*

Schutztruppen in Afrika (Schutztruppen-Ordnung) (Berlin, 1898), mit Berichtigungen vom Februar 1907 (Etatsmäßige Druckvorschrift 347, BA/MA Freiburg, printed in *Deutsches Kolonialblatt* [supp. to 1898], no. 20: sec. 1).

4. *Reichsgesetz-Blatt* 1907: 239.

5. *Schutztruppen-Ordnung*, sec. 2.

6. Ibid., sec. 7.

7. Carl Freiherr von Horn to Königliches Generalkommando, I., II. und III. Armeekorps, 16 June 1910, BayHSTA Munich, Kriegsarchiv Mkr 778.

8. Hans Rafalski, *Vom Niemandsland zum Ordnungsstaat: Geschichte der ehemaligen Kaiserlichen Landespolizei für Deutsch-Südwestafrika* (Berlin: Wernik, 1930), 39, 48; Sven Schepp, *Unter dem Kreuz des Südens: auf Spuren der Kaiserlichen Landespolizei von Deutsch-Südwestafrika* (Frankfurt am Main: Verlag für Polizeiwissenschaft, 2009); Jakob Zollmann, *Koloniale Herrschaft und ihre Grenzen: Die Kolonialpolizei in Deutsch-Südwestafrika, 1894–1915* (Göttingen: Vandenhoeck & Ruprecht, 2010).

9. *Schutztruppen-Ordnung*, sec. 7.

10. Wolfgang Petter, "Das Offizierkorps der deutschen Kolonialtruppen 1889–1918," in *Das deutsche Offizierkorps 1860–1960*, ed. Hans Hubert Hoffmann (Boppard: Harald Boldt, 1980), 163–174, 164–169.

11. Gesetz über die Pensionierung der Offiziere, III. Teil: Kaiserliche Schutztruppe in den afrikanischen Schutzgebieten, secs. 62–77, *Gesetz über die Pensionierung der Offiziere einschließlich der Sanitätsoffiziere des Reichsheeres, der Kaiserlichen Marine und der Kaiserlichen* Schutztruppen, 31 May 1906 (Berlin: J. Guttentag, Verlagsbuchhandlung, 1907), 244–276.

12. The following figures are taken from the database of colonial officers drawn from the list of ranks of the Royal Prussian Army and the Thirteenth Royal Württemberg Army Corps 1897–1914. Two qualifications should be made. First, the practice of recording only the surnames produces a number of unclear identities in the case of identical names. Second, the military set the midyear as the limit of detection for the number of officers in the colonies. As a result, it is not always clear exactly when an officer left a particular protectorate. Nevertheless, the resulting deviations amount to between 2 and 3 percent and do not have a significant impact on the data. Cameroon was included in the data pool to take into account the move of personnel to this destination.

13. These figures relate to both officers in the Protection Forces and volunteers. Clear differentiation between these two groups is possible only for China. Anyone attempting to ascertain the number of officers serving in more than one of the colonial wars needs to consider those serving in China.

14. The officers Georg Rudolf Maercker and Rochus Schmidt, both of whom served in German South-West Africa, ended their careers as major generals. Other officers, such as Eduard von Liebert in German East Africa and Lothar von Trotha in German South-West Africa, had either entered colonial service with this rank or achieved it after a qualifying period. Others were promoted upon quitting active service, such as Theodor Leutwein and Viktor

Franke. Ludwig von Estorff required almost fifteen years of colonial service before being promoted to the rank of general upon retirement in 1910.

15. Gesine Krüger, *Kriegsbewältigung und Geschichtsbewußtsein: Realität, Deutung und Verarbeitung des deutschen Kolonialkriegs in Namibia 1904 bis 1907* (Güttingen: Vandenhoeck & Ruprecht, 1999), 92.

16. Victor Franke, *Die Tagebücher des Schutztruppenoffiziers Victor Franke*, vol. 1, *Tagebuchaufzeichnungen vom 26.05.1896–27.05.1904* (Berlin: Verlag für Literatur über die Kolonial- und Mandatszeit Südwestafrikas, 2002). The entry for March 1904: "The Freiherr von Erffa shot another two of the enemy; the man has begun killing a few too many Herero for my taste since leaving my command." Ibid., 358.

17. Birthe Kundrus, *Moderne Imperialisten: Das Kaiserreich im Spiegel seiner Kolonien* (Cologne: Böhlau, 2009), 129–137.

18. Preußisches Kriegsministerium, Medizinal-Abteilung, to the Korps-Generalärzte des Garde, I.–IX., XIV. und XV. Armeekorps, 7 February 1891, GLA Karlsruhe 456, F 113/21.

19. In 1900, the figure amounted only to medical officers, supplemented by a handful of government doctors. The largest single body of medical officers (twenty-two) was that attached to the Protection Force for German East Africa, itself representing one third of the total military personnel. See the colonial officers' database and Wolfgang U. Eckart, *Medizin und Kolonialimperialismus: Deutschland 1884–1945* (Paderborn: Schöningh, 1997), 113–114.

20. See *Unteroffizier-Zeitung* 32, no. 30 (27 July 1906): 476; Gustav Adolf von Götzen, *Deutsch-Ostafrika im Aufstand 1905/06* (Berlin: Dietrich Reimer, 1909), 195–196.

21. Robert Schian, "Die Bekämpfung des Typhus unter der Schutztruppe in Südwestafrika im Hererofeldzug 1904/05," *Deutsche militärärztliche Zeitschrift* 34 (1905): 593–604, 604.

22. Werner Steuber, "Tropenkrankheiten und koloniale Medizin: Mittheilungen aus dem Sanitätswesen von Deutsch-Ostafrika," *Deutsche medizinische Wochenschrift* 29, no. 19 (7 May 1903): 340–342, 340.

23. Preußisches Kriegsministerium, Medizinal-Abteilung, to the Korps-Generalärzte des Garde-, I.–IX, XIV. und XV. Armeekorps, 12 September 1887, GLA Karlsruhe, 456, F 113/21.

24. Passed especially for the Protection Force: Bestimmungen zum Einführungsgesetze zur Militärstrafgerichtsordnung, 23 July 1900, Reichskanzler Chlodwig Fürst zu Hohenlohe, BayHSTA Munich, Kriegsarchiv, Mkr 777.

25. Ernst Nigmann, *Geschichte der kaiserlichen Schutztruppe für Deutsch-Ostafrika* (Berlin: Ernst Siegfried Mittler, 1911), 82.

26. Preußisches Kriegsministerium, Medizinal-Abteilung, to the Korps-Generalärzte des Garde, I.–IX., XIV. und XV. Armeekorps, 7 February 1891, GLA Karlsruhe, 456, F 113/21.

27. Emil Steudel, "Der ärztliche Dienst in den deutschen Schutzgebieten," *Archiv für Schiffs- und Tropenhygiene* 12 (1908, supp. 6): 17–31, 17.

28. Generalkommandos, XIV. Armeekorps to all Königliche Generalkommandos, 10 December 1895, GLA Karlsruhe, 456, F113 / 21. There were vacancies for both medical officers and orderlies.

29. Anforderungen an die körperlichen Eigenschaften der in den afrikanischen Dienst einzustellenden Militärpersonen, att. 3 *Schutztruppen-Ordnung* (see n3); and Anl. 2a für den Übertritt von Mannschaften und Unteroffizieren in die südwestafrikanische Schutztruppe.

30. Preußisches Kriegsministerium to all Königliche Generalkommandos, 2 July 1904, BayHSTA Munich, Kriegsarchiv, Mkr 785.

31. Generalkommandos XIV. Armeekorps to all Königliche Generalkommandos, 28 May 1904, GLA Karlsruhe, 456, F 41 / 38; telegram Preußisches Kriegsministerium to the Württembergisches Kriegsministerium Stuttgart, 25 June 1904, HSTA Stuttgart, M 1 / 4, Bd. 536.

32. Soldier from the Protection Force in Aais (GSWA), 30 June 1895, *Unteroffizier-Zeitung* 22, no. 40 (4 October 1895): 601.

33. Leutwein to the District officers, 23 July 1896, in *Deutsches Kolonialblatt* 7 (1896): 644.

34. *Die Tagebücher des Schutztruppenoffiziers Victor Franke,* vol. 1, 275, 289, 290, 310, 311, 312.

35. Anon., "Zum Aufstand in Südwestafrika (CXVII)," *Unteroffizier-Zeitung* 33, no. 19 (11 May 1906): 299.

36. This and all following information is taken from Stammrolle II der Feuerwerker, Unteroffiziere, Lazarettgehilfen und Buchsenmacher der Schutztruppe (1898–1914), BA Lichterfelde, R 1001 / 9586. This is a self-contained data set which has been subject to statistical evaluation. The list comprises 158 data sets, yet duplications and omissions mean that entries have been found for only 154 NCOs recruited to the Protection Force between February 1898 and December 1908 and deployed in German East Africa between April 1898 and the First World War.

37. Eugen Binder-Krieglstein, *Die Kämpfe des deutschen Expeditionskorps in China und ihre militärischen Lehren* (Berlin: Ernst Siegfried Mittler, 1902), 6.

38. Ueberblick über die in den Kommissionsberathungen über die Ostasiatische Expedition zu erörternden Fragen. Allgemeines Kriegs-Departement, 1 November 1901, HSTA Stuttgart, M1 / 4, Bd. 535. All the following information is taken from pp. 4 and 5.

39. *Die Tagebücher des Schutztruppenoffiziers Victor Franke,* vol. 1, 353.

40. Bestimmungen für Aufstellung und Entsendung von Verstärkungen der Schutztruppe für Südwest-Afrika, 13 May 1904, 7, HSTA Stuttgart, M 635 / 1, vol. 854.

41. Erfahrungen gelegentlich des Aufstandes in Südwestafrika: Grundzüge für die Stellungnahme des Kriegsministeriums, November 1908, BA / MA Freiburg, RM 3 / 4323, 68–83, 71.

42. *Die Kämpfe der deutschen Truppen in Südwestafrika: Auf Grund amtlichen Materials bearbeitet von der Kriegsgeschichtlichen Abteilung I des Großen Generalstabes,* vol. 1, *Hereroaufstand* (Berlin: Ernst Siegfried Mittler, 1906), 134.

43. Regarding the "classic" gunboat diplomacy in China, see Jürgen Oster-hammel, *China und die Weltgesellschaft: Vom 18. Jahrhundert bis in unsere Zeit* (Munich: C. H. Beck, 1989), 157.

44. Gesetz über die Pensionierung der Offiziere, II. Teil: Kaiserliche Marine, sec. 53, in *Gesetz über die Pensionierung der Offiziere* (31 May 1906), 222. See also Thomas Scheerer, *Die Marineoffiziere der Kaiserlichen Marine: Sozialisation und Konflikte* (Bochum: Verlag Dr. Dieter Winkler, 2002), 119.

45. Bericht über die mit den Marinetruppen in Ostafrika gewonnenen Erfah-rungen, verfasst von Ludwig Glatzel, ältester Offizier der ostafrikanischen Station, 23 March 1906, 6, BA/MA Freiburg, RM 3/4323.

46. Hans Paasche, *"Im Morgenlicht," Kriegs-, Jagd- und Reise-Erlebnisse in Ostafrika* (Berlin: C. A. Schwetschke und Sohn, 1907), 75.

47. G. Auer and M. Unterbeck, eds., *In Südwestafrika gegen die Hereros: Nach den Kriegs-Tagebüchern des Obermatrosen G. Auer* (Berlin: Ernst Hofmann, 1911), 15.

48. Ibid., 28.

49. *Sanitätsbericht über die Marine-Expeditionskorps in Südwestafrika 1904/05 und in Ostafrika 1905/06,* bearb. in der Medizinal-Abteilung des Reichs-Marine-Amts (Berlin: Ernst Siegfried Mittler, 1908), 8.

50. Alfred von Tirpitz, Staatssekretär im Reichsmarineamt, to Bayrisches Staatsministerium des Königlichen Hauses & des Äußern, Berlin, 7 June 1906, BayHSTA Munich, Kriegsarchiv, Mkr 756. Regarding the infantry training accorded to naval personnel, see *Reichsmarineamt*, ed., *Infanterie-Exerzier-Reglement für die Marine (ausschließlich Marineinfanterie)* (Berlin: Ernst Siegfried Mittler, 1907).

51. Inspektion der Marineinfanterie (Hauptmann von Schlichting, Kom-paniechef im I. Seebataillon), Stellungnahme zu dem Bericht des Major von Schleinitz, 20 August 1908, BA/MA Freiburg, RM 3/4317.

52. Ibid.

53. See Reinhard, "Zum 50jährigen Jubiläum der deutschen Marineinfanterie," *Marine-Rundschau* (13 January–June 1902): 527–536, 535–536.

54. Denkschrift des Oberst Karl Dürr über die Entsendung des Marine-Expeditionskorps und die in Südwestafrika gesammelten Erfahrungen, BA Lichterfelde, R 1001/2116, 3.

55. Christian Rogge, *Deutsche Seesoldaten bei der Belagerung der Gesandtschaften in Peking* (Berlin, Ernst Siegfried Mittler, 1902), 2.

56. Max von Prittwitz und Gaffron, *Geschichte des I. Seebataillons* (Oldenburg: Stalling, 1912), 88.

57. Heinrich von Goßler to all Königlichen Generalkommandos, Berlin, 19 July 1900, GLA Karlsruhe, 456 F 41, 38.

58. Denkschrift des Oberst Dürr über die Entsendung des Marine-Expeditionskorps und die in Südwestafrika gesammelten Erfahrungen, BA Lichterfelde, R 1001/2116, 3.

59. *Sanitätsbericht über die Marine-Expeditionskorps in Südwestafrika 1904/05 und in Ostafrika 1905/06,* 8.

60. Admiralstab der Marine, ed., *Das Marine-Expeditionskorps in Südwest-Afrika während des Herero-Aufstandes* (Berlin: Ernst Siegfried Mittler, 1905), 95.

61. Inspector of Marine Infantry to the Imperial Command of the Baltic Station regarding the return of the Naval Expeditionary Corps 1904, 29 April 1904, printed in Walter Nuhn, *Kolonialpolitik und Marine: Die Rolle der Kaiserlichen Marine bei der Gründung und Sicherung des deutschen Kolonialreichs 1889–1914* (Bonn: Bernard & Graefe, 2002), 304–305.

62. Prittwitz und Gaffron, *Geschichte des I. Seebataillons,* 58.

63. Denkschrift des Oberst Dürr, BA Lichterfelde, R 1001/2116, 3.

64. Both quotations in *Tagebücher des Schutztruppenoffiziers Victor Franke,* vol. 1, 352, 354.

65. Militärpolitischer Bericht von Major Kurt von Schleinitz, 1 June 1907, 11, BA/MA Freiburg, RM 3/4317.

66. Next three quotations in Denkschrift des Oberst Dürr, BA Lichterfelde, R 1001/2116, 17, 10.

67. *Das Marine-Expeditionskorps in Südwest-Afrika während des Herero-Aufstandes,* 3.

68. Att. 4 zum Geheimbericht des Gouverneurs Paul Jaeschke an den Staats-sekretär Alfred von Tirpitz, Reichsmarineamt, betr. Organisation chine-sischer Versuchstruppen, 9 March 1899, 28–40, esp. 28–29, BA/MA Freiburg, RM 3/6792. For British practice, see *The Chinese Regiment: Soldier's Pocket Book* (Shanghai: Brewer, 1905), 5.

69. Fu-teh Huang, *Qingdao: Chinesen unter deutscher Herrschaft 1897–1914* (Bochum: Edition Cathay, 1999), 141.

70. Bestimmungen über Anwerbung von chinesischen Soldaten, 21 July 1899, point 1, 98, BA/MA Freiburg, RM 3/6792.

71. Att. 4 zum Geheimbericht von Jaeschke an Tirpitz, betr. Organisation chinesischer Versuchstruppen, 9 March 1899, 28–40, 34, ibid., RM 3/6792.

72. Ibid., 30.

73. Monatsbericht des Kompaniechefs Erich von Falkenhayn für Gouverneur Jaeschke, 1 November 1899, 38–40, ibid., RM 3/6745.

74. Jahresbericht des Kompaniechefs von Schöler, 24 September 1900, 181–187, 181–183, ibid., RM 3/6792.

75. Ibid., 184. See also Jaeschke to Tirpitz, 5 November 1900, 172–174, ibid., RM 3/6745.

76. Gedanken über die Notwendigkeit der Aufstellung von Chinesentruppen im Kiautschou-Gebiet, ibid., 241–245. For further details regarding O. v. Truppel's plan, see Leitsätze nebst Begründungen und Erläuterungen über Organisation einer Chinesentruppe, 21 July 1904, ibid., 272–283.

77. Jaeschke to Tirpitz, 5 November 1900, ibid., 172.

78. *Praktische Erfahrungen aus Deutsch-Südwestafrika* (Berlin: Reichsdruck, 1904), 25, point 21, HSTA Stuttgart, M 660/083, Bü 4.

79. *Sanitäts-Bericht über die Kaiserliche Schutztruppe für Südwestafrika während des Herero- und Hottentottenaufstandes für die Zeit vom 1. Januar 1904 bis 31. März*

1907, bearb. im Kommando der Schutztruppen im Reichs-Kolonialamt, vol. 1. (Berlin: Ernst Siegfried Mittler, 1909), 139. See Dag Henrichsen, *"Ozombambus* and *Ovasolondate:* Everyday Military Life and African Service Personnel in German South West Africa," in *Hues between Black and White: Historical Photography from Colonial Namibia 1860s to 1915,* ed. Wolfram Hartmann (Windhoek, Namibia: Out of Africa Publishers, 2004), 161–184.

80. For further information regarding the Baster, see Theodor Leutwein, *Elf Jahre Gouverneur in Deutsch-Südwestafrika* (Berlin: Ernst Siegfried Mittler, 1906; repr. Windhoek: Namibia Wissenschaftliche Gesellschaft, 1997), 217–218.

81. Georg Maercker, *Unsere Schutztruppe in Ostafrika* (Berlin: K. Siegismund, 1893), 61, 68–70. A detailed account is provided in Michael von Herff, *"They Walk through the Fire Like the Blondest German": African Soldiers Serving the Kaiser in German East Africa, 1888–1914* (Montreal: McGill University, 1991), 48–68; Michelle R. Moyd, *Violent Intermediaries: African Soldiers, Conquest, and Everyday Colonialism in German East Africa* (Athens: Ohio University Press, 2014), 108–111.

82. Organisatorische Bestimmungen für die Kaiserliche Schutztruppe in Deutsch-Ostafrika, 9 April 1891, sec. 2, point 2, BayHSTA Munich, Kriegsarchiv, Mkr 776.

83. Militärpolitischer Bericht von Major Schleinitz, 1 June 1907, 30, BA/MA Freiburg, RM 3/4317.

84. Ernst Nigmann, *Felddienstübungen für farbige (ostafrikanische) Truppen* (Dar es Salaam: Deutsch-Ostafrikanische Zeitung, 1910), ix–x.

85. Marianne Bechhaus-Gerst, *Treu bis in den Tod: Von Deutsch-Ostafrika nach Sachsenhausen—Eine Lebensgeschichte* (Berlin: Christoph Links Verlag, 2007), 39–50; Eckart Michels, "Deutschlands bekanntester 'Kolonialheld' und seine 'Askari': Paul von Lettow-Vorbeck und der Feldzug in Ostafrika im Ersten Weltkrieg," *Revue d'Allemagne et des pays de langue allemande* 38 (2006), 541–554, 552.

86. Stefanie Michels, *Schwarze deutsche Kolonialsoldaten: Mehrdeutige Repräsentationsräume und früher Kosmopolitismus in Afrika* (Bielefeld: Transcript, 2009), 52–54.

87. Detlef Bald, "Afrikanischer Kampf gegen koloniale Herrschaft: Der Maji-Maji-Aufstand in Ostafrika," *Militärgeschichtliche Mitteilungen* 1 (1976): 43; Jamie Monson, "Relocating Maji Maji: The Politics of Alliance and Authority in the Southern Highlands of Tanzania, 1870–1918," *Journal of African History* 39 (1998): 115; Ingrid Laurien, " 'That Homa Homa Was Worse Child!' Berichte afrikanischer Zeitzeugen über den Maji Maji Aufstand in Deutsch-Ostafrika," in *Studien zur Geschichte des Kolonialismus in Afrika,* ed. Peter Heine, Peter Sebald, and Ulrich van der Heyden (Pfaffenweiler: Centaurus, 1995), 350–367, 356, 363.

88. Heinrich von Bülow, *Deutschlands Kolonien und Kolonialkriege* (Dresden: E. Pierson, 1900), 18.

89. Antwort Oberleutnant Sommerfeldt vom Detachement Mtingi auf die geheime Umfrage des ältesten Offiziers der ostafrikanischen Station an die Marinedetachementsführer (Umfrage 7), BA/MA Freiburg, RM 121I/460.

5. Training and Weaponry

1. Heinrich Rohne, *Schießlehre für die Infanterie unter besonderer Berücksichtigung des Gewehrs 98 mit S-Munition der Maschinengewehre und Schießvorschrift für die Infanterie vom 2. November 1905*, 2nd ed. (Berlin: Ernst Siegfried Mittler, 1906), 1.

2. Richard Wille, *Waffenlehre* (Berlin: R. Eisenschmidt, 1896; repr. Hamburg: Andraeas, 1969), 38.

3. Rohne, *Schießlehre für die Infanterie*, 69. Leitfaden betreffend das Gewehr und Seitengewehr 98 from 19 January 1899 (Berlin, 1902), point 126.

4. Hans Paasche, *"Im Morgenlicht" Kriegs-, Jagd- und Reise-Erlebnisse in Ostafrika* (Berlin: C. A. Schwetschke und Sohn, 1907), 115.

5. Schlick, "Meine kriegschirurgischen Erfahrungen während der chinesischen Wirren im Juni bis Oktober 1900," *Deutsche militärärztliche Zeitschrift* 30 (1901): 450–488, 477.

6. Rohne, *Schießlehre für die Infanterie*, 69.

7. Friedrich Schaefer, "Moderne Bewaffnung und Kriegssanitätsdienst," *Militär-Wochenblatt* (supp. 1907): 93–117, 96.

8. *Unsere Truppen in Ostasien: Enthaltend 12 Tafeln mit 78 Abbildungen nebst ausführlicher Liste der Offiziere etc.* (Leipzig: Ruhl, 1900; repr. Starnberg: LTR Verlag GMBH, 1989), 21.

9. For China: Karl Herhold, "Über die während der ostasiatischen Expedition im Feldlazareth IV (Paotingfu) beobachteten Schussverletzungen," *Deutsche Militärärztliche Zeitschrift* 30 (1901): 603–621, 603. For Africa: Moritz Merker, "Ueber die Aufstandsbewegung in Deutsch-Ostafrika," *Militär-Wochenblatt* 91, no. 46 (12 April 1906): cols. 1085–1092, 1086. For a detailed consideration of the weapons used by the Nama, see Andreas Heinrich Bühler, *Der Namaaufstand gegen die deutsche Kolonialherrschaft in Namibia von 1904–1913* (Frankfurt am Main: KO—Verl. für Interkulturelle Kommunikation, 2003), 184–187.

10. See Max Boot, *War Made New: Technology, Warfare, and the Course of History 1500 to Today* (New York: Gotham Books, 2006), 152.

11. Estimations taken from Gustav Adolf von Götzen, *Deutsch-Ostafrika im Aufstand 1905/06* (Berlin: Dietrich Reimer, 1909), 110; Walter Nuhn, *Flammen über Deutschost: Der Maji-Maji-Aufstand in Deustch-Ostafrika 1905–1906, die erste gemeinsame Erhebung schwarzafrikanischer Völker gegen weiße Kolonialherrschaft* (Bonn: Bernard & Graefe, 1998). *Der Maji-Maji-Aufstand*, 112, on the other hand, speaks of between 20,000 and 25,000 attackers.

12. Götzen, *Deutsch-Ostafrika im Aufstand 1905/06*, 110.

13. For China: Vorschläge der durch Allerhöchste Kabinets-Order vom 31/10/1901 berufenen Kommission zur Berathung der für etwaige künftige Expeditionen

erforderlichen oder wünschenwerthen Maßnahmen (Expeditions-Vorschläge), Geheim, 1901, point 16, BA/MA Freiburg, RM 3/7727. See also Ueberblick über die in den Kommissionsberathungen über die Ostasiatische Expedition zu erörternden Fragen: Allgemeines Kriegs-Departement, 01 November 1901, 8, 16, HSTA Stuttgart, M1/4, vol. 535. For GSWA: "Die Maschinengewehre in Deutsch-Südwestafrika," *Militär-Wochenblatt* 89, no. 146 (29 November 1904): cols. 3460–3462, 3460. For GEA: Vertheilungsplan der Schutztruppe und Landespolizei von Deutsch-Ostafrika am 31/01/1896, printed in *Deutsches Kolonialblatt* 7, no. 6 (1896): 55 and 157.

14. *Exerzier-Reglement für die Infanterie* (ExRfdI), 29 May 1906 (Berlin: Ernst Siegfried Mittler, 1906), sec. 265a.

15. Friedrich von Merkatz, *Unterrichtsbuch für die Maschinengewehr-Abteilungen* (Berlin: Eisenschmidt, 1906), introduction.

16. Excerpt from the War Diary, II. Bataillon, 4. Ostasiatisches Infanterie-Regiment, pt. 4, entry for 17 February 1901, BayHSTA Munich, Kriegsarchiv, B 1485.

17. Heinrich Rohne, "Ein Beitrag zum Studium der Kolonialartillerie," *Viertel-jahreshefte für Truppenführung und Heereskunde* 3 (1906): 422–429, 422.

18. Denkschrift über Erfahrungen in China, field marshal Waldersee, 1901, BayHSTA Munich, Kriegsarchiv, 3. Pi.Btl., vol. 962; HSTA Stuttgart, M1/4, vol. 535. Sections of the memorandum are published in Bernd-Felix Schulte, *Die deutsche Armee 1900–1914: zwischen Beharren u. Verändern* (Düsseldorf: Droste, 1977), 169–173.

19. Hans Fromming, "Die Bewaffnung der kaiserlichen Schutztruppe von Südwest-Afrika," *Deutsches Waffen-Journal* 2 (1966): 42–47, 44; *Leitfaden betreffend das Gewehr und Seitengewehr 98 vom 19/1/1899* (Berlin: Ernst Siegfried Mittler, 1902), points 115–125a.

20. Überblick über die in den Kommissionsberathungen über die Ostasiatische Expedition zu erörternden Fragen, 1 November 1901, 8, HSTA Stuttgart, M1/4, vol. 535.

21. Denkschrift über Erfahrungen in China, field marshal Waldersee, 1901, BayHSTA Munich, Kriegsarchiv, 3. Pi.Btl., vol. 962; also in HSTA Stuttgart, M1/4, vol. 535.

22. "Hunnenbrief" from 1 September 1900, *Vorwärts* 17, no. 255 (1 November 1900): 2.

23. Bestimmungen für Aufstellung und Entsendung von Verstärkungen der Schutztruppe für Südwest-Afrika, 13 May 1904, HSTA Stuttgart, M 635/1, vol. 854.

24. Ibid., 9–10.

25. Jahresbericht der Marineakademie 1905–1906, Kiel, 1 September 1906, BA/MA Freiburg, RM 27I/v.44. See also Thomas Scheerer, *Die Marineof-fiziere der Kaiserlichen Marine: Sozialisation und Konflikte* (Bochum: Verlag Dr. Dieter Winkler, 2000), 63.

26. Unterlagen zu den Vorlesungen über Geschichte und Erdkunde an der Kriegsakademie, 1905–1908. Here: Erdkunde, vol. 2: Wasser, Erde, Luft,

Pflanzen, Tiere, Mensch in ihren Wechselbeziehungen und nach ihrer räumlichen Anordnung, BA/MA Freiburg, PH 21/5.

27. Ibid., 181, 189.

28. Draft of a letter from the director of the Institute for Oriental Languages, Eduard Sachau, to Reichskanzler Bernhard von Bülow, 19 September 1909, in GSTA PK Berlin, Rep. 208a/409.

29. As the foreseen period of study amounted to two semesters, these numbers should be reduced by between a half and a third.

30. Kommando des I. Seebataillons, secret letter from Karl Dürr (Commander), Kiel, 12 January 1897; Kommando des II. Seebataillons, letter from Oskar v. Lossow (Commander), Entwurf. Ausbildungsplan für die Marineinfanterie, 12 February 1897, BA/MA Freiburg, RM 121I/233.

31. Max von Prittwitz und Gaffron, *Geschichte des I. Seebataillons* (Oldenburg: Stalling, 1912), 74.

32. *Felddienst-Ordnung*, 1 January 1900 (previous ed.: 20 July 1894; the fundamental concepts and main points remained unchanged); *Exerzier-Reglement für die Infanterie* (ExRfdI), 29 May 1906 (previous ed.: 01 September 1889); *Infanterie-Exerzier-Reglement für die Marine* (IERMar), 22 July 1907. See also the continually revised *Leitfaden für den Unterricht in der Taktik auf den Königlichen Kriegsschulen* (Berlin: Ernst Siegfried Mittler, 1906).

33. ExRfdI, 1889, introduction, point 1; ExRfdI, 1906, introduction, point 3; IERMar, 1907, introduction, point 3.

34. ExRfdI, 1889, pt. 2, point 84; ExRfdI, 1906, sec. 392; IERMar, 1907, sec. 393.

35. Theodor Leutwein, *Elf Jahre Gouverneur in Deutsch-Südwestafrika* (Berlin: Ernst Siegfried Mittler, 1906; repr. Windhoek, Namibia: Wissenschaftliche Gesellschaft, 1997), 535.

36. ExRfdI, 1906, sec. 421; IERMar, 1907, sec. 422. Still not so drastic: ExRfdI, 1889, pt. 2, point 83.

37. ExRfdI, 1906, sec. 424; IERMar, 1907, sec. 425.

38. *Exerzier-Reglement für die Kavallerie* (named after the Prussian service regulations of the same name, Munich 1895, printed in the Bavarian War ministry (Königlich Bayerisches Kriegsministerium) (ExRfdI), point 377.

39. *Leitfaden für den Unterricht in der Taktik auf den Königlichen Kriegsschulen*, pt. 1, point 553, 82.

40. Stig Förster, "Der deutsche Generalstab und die Illusion des kurzen Krieges, 1871–1914: Metakritik eines Mythos," *Militärgeschichtliche Mitteilungen* 54 (1995): 61–95, 80. The most well-known account is provided by Gerhard Ritter, *Der Schlieffenplan: Kritik eines Mythos* (Munich: R. Oldenbourg, 1956). See also Jehuda L. Wallach, *The Dogma of the Battle of Annihilation: The Theories of Clausewitz and Schlieffen and Their Impact on the German Conduct of the Two World Wars* (Westport, CT: Greenwood, 1986) (*Das Dogma der Vernichtungsschlacht*, Nördlingen 1970, 1st ed. Frankfurt am Main, 1967), 62–108; Arden Bucholz, *Moltke, Schlieffen and Prussian War Planning* (New York: Berg, 1991),

158–213; Gunther E. Rothenberg, "Moltke, Schlieffen, and the Doctrine of Strategic Envelopment," in *Makers of Modern Strategy: From Machiavelli to the Nuclear Age,* ed. Peter Paret (Princeton, NJ: Princeton University Press, 1986), 296–325.

41. *Praktische Erfahrungen aus Deutsch-Südwestafrika* (Berlin: Reichsdruck, 1904), HSTA Stuttgart, M 660/083, Bue 4.

42. ExRfdI 1906, sec. 326; IERMar 1907, sec. 327.

43. Maximilian Bayer, *Der Krieg in Südwestafrika und seine Bedeutung für die Entwicklung der Kolonie* (Leipzig: Engelmann, 1906), 41.

44. *Deutschlands koloniale Wehrmacht in ihrer gegenwärtigen Organisation und Schlagfähigkeit: Auf Grund der neusten amtlichen Dokumente bearbeitet von einem höheren Offizier,* no name, but the author was Hermann von Wissmann (Berlin: R. v. Decker, 1906), 80.

45. *Praktische Erfahrungen aus Deutsch-Südwestafrika* (Berlin: Reichsdruck, 1904), point 43, HSTA Stuttgart, M 660/083, Bue 4.

46. Carl von Clausewitz, *Vom Kriege: Hinterlassenes Werk des Generals Carl von Clausewitz* (Munich: Cormoran, 2000; Berlin: F. Dümmler, 1832), pt. 2, bk. 6, chap. 26, 529.

47. *Leitfaden für den Unterricht in der Taktik auf den Königlichen Kriegsschulen,* pt. 2, point 162, 140–141.

48. Ibid., 141.

49. Carl Peters, *Gefechtsweise und Expeditionsführung in Afrika* (Berlin: Walther, 1892), 6; Peters, *Gesammelte Schriften,* vol. 2 (Munich: C. H. Beck, 1943), 515–528, 519; Georg Maercker, "Kriegführung in Ostafrika: Vortrag, gehalten in der Militärischen Gesellschaft zu Berlin am 15/11/1893," *Militär-Wochenblatt* (supp. 1894): 149–177, 168–171 (Ausführung und Führung krieger-ischer Expeditionen); Maercker, *Der Aufstand in Deutsch-Ostafrika und die Wissmann'sche Schutztruppe: Vortrag gehalten zu Karlsruhe, 13/12/1889* (Karlsruhe: Druck der G. Braunschen Hofbuchdruckerei, 1890); Hermann von Wissmann, *Afrika: Schilderungen und Rathschläge zur Vorbereitung für den Aufenthalt und den Dienst in den Deutschen Schutzgebieten* (Berlin: Ernst Siegfried Mittler, 1895, 2nd ed. 1903, repr. from the *Militär-Wochenblatt,* 1894); Friedrich von Schele, "Ueber die Organisation der Kaiserlichen Schutztruppe in Deutsch-Ostafrika und die kriegerischen Operationen daselbst während der Jahre 1893/94," *Militär-Wochenblatt* (supp. 1896): 441–478; Lothar von Trotha, *Meine Bereisung von Deutsch-Ostafrika: Vortrag gehalten in der Sitzung der Gesellschaft für Erdkunde am 12. Juni 1897* (Berlin: Brigl, 1897); Theodor Leutwein, "Die Kämpfe der Kaiserlichen Schutz-truppe in Deutsch-Südwestafrika in den Jahren 1894–96, sowie die sich hieraus für uns ergebenden Lehren: Vortrag gehalten in der Militärischen Gesellschaft zu Berlin am 19. Februar 1898," *Militär-Wochenblatt* (supp. 1899): 1–30.

50. "Major v. Wissmann published a series of articles in the *Militär-Wochenblatt* focusing on warfare in Africa. We would like to focus on . . . the following,"

printed in *Unteroffizier-Zeitung* 21, no. 44 (2 November 1894): 646–674, 646; "'Ueber die Ausbildung unserer Schutztruppe': Briefe des Major v. Wissmann, part 1," ibid., 22, no. 19 (10 May 1895): 291–291, pt. 2: ibid., 22, no. 40 (4 October 1895): 602; Kommando des II. Seebataillons, Otto von Lossow (Kommandeur), Entwurf: Ausbildungsplan für die Marineinfanterie, 12 February 1897, BA/MA Freiburg, RM 121I/233.

51. Unteroffizier-Vorschule in Neubreisach (Alsace, today France): Spielplan für die Festvorstellung am Geburtstage Seiner Majestät des Kaisers und Königs, 27 January 1901, GLA Karlsruhe, 456/F 141–2.

52. Peters, *Gefechtsweise und Expeditionsführung in Afrika*, 7. All the following quotations and summaries are taken from 9, 13, 14.

53. Wissmann, *Afrika*, 18. All the following quotations and summaries are taken from 17, 23–24, 33.

54. Trotha, *Meine Bereisung von Deutsch-Ostafrika*, 85.

55. Leutwein, "Die Kämpfe der Kaiserlichen Schutztruppe in Deutsch-Südwestafrika in den Jahren 1894–96," 1–30, 29.

56. Wissmann, *Afrika*, 17.

57. Charles Edward Callwell, *Small Wars: Their Principles & Practice* (London, printed for H. M. Stationery Office, 1896, 3rd ed. 1906), 61, 93, 130, 255.

58. Wissmann, *Afrika*, 1–2, 1.

59. Arthur Forbes Montanaro, *Hints for a Bush Campaign of 1900* (London: Sands, 1901) (*Winke für Expeditionen im afrikanischen Busch: Übersetzt von H. Glauning, Hauptmann und Kompaniechef in der Kaiserlichen Schutztruppe für Kamerun*, Berlin: Ernst Siegfried Mittler, 1905). Colonel Montanaro had fought in the Ashanti expedition (1895–1896) to West Africa and was appointed commander of the troops in South Nigeria in 1903.

60. Katalog der Haupt-Bibliothek der Kaiserlichen Marine-Akademie und Schule, Kiel, 1907./Nachtrag zum Katalog der Hauptbibliothek des Bildungswesens der Marine, enthaltend die in Zugang gekommenen Bücher vom 1/4/1907 bis 31/7/1908, Kiel 1908. Includes Montanaro, *Winke für Expeditionen im afrikanischen Busch;* Callwell, *Small Wars;* Général Gallieni, *Neuf ans à Madagascar: Ouvrage illustré* (Paris: Hachette, 1908); Garnet J. Wolseley, *Narrative of the War with China in 1860* (London: Longman, 1862); Wolseley, *The Story of a Soldiers Life* (Westminster: A. Constable, 1903). The library of the Great General Staff (*Katalog der Bibliothek des Königlich-Preußischen Großen Generalstabes* [Berlin: Ernst Siegfried Mittler, 1912]) also held the volume from A. F. Montanaro and Callwell's *Small Wars* (but in French translation: *Petites Guerres,* 1899) as well as the third edition of G. J. Wolseley, *The Soldier's Pocket-Book for Field Service* (London: Macmillan, 1869) from 1874 and his *The Story of a Soldier's Life,* 2 vol. (Westminster: A. Constabel, 1903). Also available from the library was Thomas Robert Bugeaud, *L'Algérie: Des Moyens de conserver et d'utiliser cette conquête* (Paris: Dentu, 1842). On the other hand, there were no publications from either Gallieni or Lyautey, except a treatment of firing tactics

61. Kommando des II. Seebataillons, Brief von Otto von Lossow (Kommandeur) an das Oberkommando der Marine, 10 January 1897, BA/MA Freiburg, RM 121I/233.

62. Bericht des Kriegsministeriums: Erfahrungen gelegentlich des Aufstandes in Südwestafrika; Grundzüge für die Stellungnahme des Kriegsministeriums, 21 November 1908, ibid., RM 3/4323, 69–83, 74.

63. Callwell, *Small Wars*, 151. Translated into French: *Petites guerres: Leurs principes et leur exécution, par le major C.-E. Callwell, traduit et annoté par le lieutenant-colonel breveté Septans de l'infanterie de marine* (Paris: Henri Charles-Lavauzelle, 1899, 2nd ed. 1910).

64. Wolseley, *The Soldier's Pocket-Book for Field Service*.

65. George John Younghusband, *Indian Frontier Warfare* (London: K. Paul, Trench, Trübner, 1898). It was published in the "Wolseley Series," intending to educate officers; Harry Lumsden, *Frontier Thoughts and Frontier Requirements* (1861). Republished as *Lumsden of the Guides: A Sketch of the Life of Lieut.-Gen. Sir Harry Burnett Lumsden K.C.S.I., C.B., with Selections from His Correspondence and Occasional Papers,* ed. by General Sir Peter Lumsden and George R. Elsmie (London: John Murray, 1899), 291–315.

66. Callwell, *Small Wars*, 40.

67. As did the foreword from Captain Walter H. James, xv, to Younghusband, *Indian Frontier Warfare.*

68. Callwell, *Small Wars*, 147.

69. G. J. Wolseley, *The Soldier's Pocket-Book for Field Service*, 5th ed. (London, 1886), 243.

70. Ibid., 414.

71. Ibid., 413.

72. A classic account is provided by Thomas Robert Bugeaud, *De la stratégie, de la tactique, des retraites et du passage des défilés dans les montagnes des Kabyles* (Algiers: Imprimerie du Gouvernement, 1850), 5–6. See also Jean-Pierre Bois, *Bugeaud* (Paris: Fayard, 1997), 274–275; Douglas Porch, "Bugeaud, Gallieni, Lyautey: The Development of French Colonial Warfare," in Paret, *Makers of Modern Strategy,* 376–407, 378–379.

73. Louis Hubert Lyautey, "Du rôle colonial de l'Armée," *Revue des deux mondes* 70 (1900): 308–328, 324–325. For a general treatment of Louis Hubert Lyautey, see Marc Ferro, *Colonization: A Global History* (London: Routledge, 1997), 87–89; Arnaud Teyssier, *Lyautey: Un saharien atypique* (Paris: Perrin, 2004), 47–49; William A. Hoisington, *Lyautey and the French Conquest of Morocco* (London: Macmillan, 1995), 21–39.

74. Joseph-Simon Gallieni, Auszug aus dem Rapport von 1905 über Instruktionen zur Bekämpfung eines Aufstandes, der in der Nacht vom 17. auf den 18. November 1904 im Südosten von Madagaskar ausgebrochen war, 83. Partially reprinted in *Gallieni: Pacificateur; Écrits coloniaux de Gallieni,* ed. Hubert Deschamps and Paul Chauvet (Paris: Presses universitaires de France, 1949), 361–362, 361; Gallieni, *Rapport d'ensemble sur la pacification, l'organisation et la*

colonisation de Madagascar 8 octobre 1896 à mars 1899 (Paris: Henri Charles-Lavauzelle, 1900).

75. In response to the war in Morocco, the *Section Historique de l'État-Major de l'Armée* published a number of books in 1908: Jean Jules Henri Mordacq, *La guerre en Afrique: Tactique des grosses colonnes; Enseignements de l'expédition contre les Beni Snassen (1859)* (Paris, 1908), 83–84; René-Jules Frisch, *Guerre d'Afrique: Guide-annexe des règlements sur le service en campagne et de manœuvres* (Paris, 1908).

76. Quoted according to Prager, "Ein französisches Reglement für die Kriegführung in Afrika," *Vierteljahreshefte für Truppenführung und Heereskunde* 6 (1909): 475–492, 478; Callwell, *Small Wars,* 40.

77. Erick J. Mann, *Mikono ya damu: "Hands of Blood"; African Mercenaries and the Politics of Conflict in German East Africa, 1888–1904* (Frankfurt am Main: P. Lang, 2002), 81.

78. Victor G. Kiernan, *Colonial Empires and Armies 1815–1960* (Montreal: McGill-Queen's University Press, 1998), 160.

79. Georg Maercker, *Unsere Schutztruppe in Ostafrika* (Berlin: K. Siegismund, 1893), 201.

80. Disziplinar-Strafordnung für das Heer, 31 October 1872, in *Kompendium über Militärrecht,* ed. Königlich Preußisches Kriegsministerium (Berlin: Ernst Siegfried Mittler, 1911), 223–247. For the navy: *Disziplinar-Strafordnung für die Kaiserliche Marine* (Berlin: Ernst Siegfried Mittler, 1914); Militärstrafgesetzbuch für das Deutsche Reich, 20 June 1872, in *Kompendium über Militärrecht,* 156–200, pt. 4: Zusatzbestimmungen für die Marine, ibid., 199–200; Militärstrafgerichtsordnung vom 01/12/1898, ibid., 1–150 (Marine, secs. 5, 6). Nevertheless, the Military Tribunals Ordinance first took effect on 1 October 1900 for the whole German army and navy. As a result, it was introduced for the East Asian Expedition Corps from the day it left home waters. Reichskanzler Hohenlohe to the Bundesrat, 12 August 1900, BA/MA, RM 3/7595. See also "Einführung der deutschen Militärstrafgesetze in den afrikanischen Schutzgebieten," 26 July 1896 (RGB, 669).

81. Disziplinar-Strafordnung für das Heer, 31 December 1872, secs. 1, 3. See also Kriegsartikel für das Heer, 22 September 1902, art. 5: "All those soldiers neglecting their duties will receive the just punishment," *Armee-Verordnungsblatt* 16, no. 29 (27 September 1902): 279–284.

82. Einführungsgesetz zum Militärstrafgesetzbuch für das Deutsche Reich, 20 June 1872, in *Kompendium über Militärrecht,* 153–155.

83. *Einführungsgesetz zur Militärstrafgerichtsordnung,* 01 December 1898, ibid., 3–15.

84. Order from Wilhelm II to Second Lieutenant Curt von François, 26 April 1889, forwarded to the Foreign Office on 16 May 1889, GLA Karlsruhe, 456, F 113/21.

85. Verordnung, betreffend das strafgerichtliche Verfahren gegen Militärpersonen der Kaiserlichen Schutztruppen, 26 June 1896, RGB 1896, 670–676, BayHSTA Munich, Kriegsarchiv, Mkr 777.

86. Appended to the imperial prescription from 2 November 1909 was a list of civil prisons to which all members of the Protection Force in Africa convicted by a court-martial convened by the Protection Force were to be transferred.

87. Anon., "betr. Überführung von Strafgefangenen aus Südwestafrika nach Deutschland," *Unteroffizier-Zeitung* 33, no. 26 (29 June 1906): 409.

88. Bestimmungen zum Einführungsgesetze zur Militärstrafgerichtsordnung, 23 July 1900, Reichskanzler Hohenlohe, BayHSTA Munich, Kriegsarchiv, Mkr 777. See also Kaiserliche Verordnung from 18 July 1900 (RGB 1900, 831), replaced by the Kaiserliche Verordnung from 2 November 1909 (RGB 1909, 943).

89. *Sanitäts-Bericht über die Kaiserliche Schutztruppe für Südwestafrika während des Herero- und Hottentottenaufstandes für die Zeit vom 1. Januar 1904 bis 31. März 1907, bearb. im Kommando der Schutztruppen im Reichs-Kolonialamt,* vol. 2, 257.

90. Anon., "betr. Bestrafungen," *Unteroffizier-Zeitung* 32, no. 43 (27 October 1905): 669.

91. The kaiser's "Hun speech" quoted in Bernd Sösemann, "Die sog. Hunnenrede Wilhelm II: Textkritische und interpretatorische Bemerkungen zur Ansprache des Kaisers vom 27. Juli 1900 in Bremerhaven," *Historische Zeitschrift* 222 (1976): 342–358, 350.

92. Zusammenfassung des Berichts der durch Allerhöchste Order vom 14/11/1908 berufenen Kommission zur Beratung aufgrund der bei der Entsendung von Verstärkungen in Südwestafrika gesammelten Erfahrungen, 28 May 1909, 16, BA/MA Freiburg, RM 3/4323, BayHSTA Munich Kriegsarchiv, Mkr 814.

93. Assault: *Reichsstrafgesetzbuch,* secs. 223, 230, 232. Rape: secs. 176, 179, 182.

94. Allerhöchste Verordnung über die Einführung neuer Kriegsartikel für das Heer, 22 September 1902, art. 17: "The soldier in the field is to remember at all times that war is being conducted against the armed formations of the enemy. The property of his civilian population, the wounded, sick and prisoners of war enjoy the special protection of the law, just as does the property of the members of the German or allied troops." "The plundering and malicious or wanton damage or destruction of the belongings of others and the suppression of the native population will be punished with the strictest of sanctions. *Plundering* does not involve the acquisition of foodstuffs, medicines, fuel, fodder and the means of transport to satisfy immediate requirements." Italics in text.

95. *Leitfaden für den Unterricht über Truppendienst (Dienstkenntnis) auf den Königlichen Kriegsschulen: Auf Veranlassung der General-Inspektion des Militär-Erziehungs- und Bildungswesens ausgearbeitet* (Berlin: Ernst Siegfried Mittler, 1907), 9, War articles, art. 17, repr. in *Der Soldaten-Freund* 70, no. 4 (16 October 1902): 193–199.

96. *Militärstrafgesetzbuch für das Deutsche Reich,* 20 June 1872, sec. 147.

97. *Manual of Military Law* (London: Stationery Office, 1884). Further eds.: 1887/1888/1894/1899; *Nouveaux codes français et lois usuelles civiles et militaires: Recueil spécialement destiné à la Gendarmerie et à l'Armée* (Paris: Henri Charles-Lavauzelle, 1895); *The Military Laws of the United States*

(Washington, DC: Government Printing Office, 1901, 4th ed.), doc. 545. *Government Publications* (56th Cong., 2d Sess., House of Representatives), vol. 4197, chap. 47: "The Articles of War," 962–1008, art. 58: "In time of war, insurrection, or rebellion, larceny, robbery, burglary, arson, mayhem, manslaughter, murder, assault and battery with an intent to kill, wounding, by shooting or stabbing, with an intent to commit murder, rape, or assault and battery with an intent to commit rape, shall be punishable by the sentence of a general court-martial, when committed by persons in the military service of the United States, and the punishment in any such case shall not be less than the punishment provided, for the like offense, by the laws of the State, Territory, or district in which such offense may have been committed," 990–991.

98. Frisch, *Guerre d'Afrique*, art. 45, 51.

99. Summary report from Captain G. Hutcheson, Sixth Cavalry, Peking, 19 May 1901, Annual Reports of the War Department, *Government Publications*, vol. 4274, 510–513.

100. General Orders, no. 13, Peking, 6 September 1900, Private Stephan Dwyar, I Company, Ninth Infantry, NA Washington, RG 395/929.

101. See letter from the Kriegsministerium to the Reichskanzler and the Reichsjustizamt, 1 July 1902, BA Lichterfelde, R 3001/5266.

102. Regarding the punishment for plunderers: Alfred Graf von Waldersee, *Denkwürdigkeiten des General-Feldmarschalls Alfred Grafen von Waldersee*, vol. 3 (1900–1904), ed. Heinrich Otto Meisner (Berlin: Deutsche Verlags-Anstalt, 1923), 47; Georg Wegener, *Zur Kriegszeit durch China 1900/1901* (Berlin: Allgemeiner Verlag für deutsche Litteratur, 1902), 159.

103. Bericht über die mit den Marinetruppen in Ostafrika gemachten Erfahrungen, verfasst von L. Glatzel, ältester Offizier der ostafrikanischen Station, 23 March 1906, 16, BA/MA Freiburg, RM 3/4323.

104. Announced in *Armee-Verordnungsblatt*, 24 July 1900. See Bestimmungen über die Militär-Rechtspflege beim Ostasiatischen Expeditionskorps, 15 July 1900, BA/MA Freiburg, RM 2/1859.

105. Sec. 18: "The preceding stipulations do not affect the powers of the commanding officer to treat foreign nationals caught red handed in committing actions with the aim of undermining the German or allied war effort in accordance with the customs of war and without prior trial." Printed in Theophil Ahrends, *Die Bestrafung der auf dem Kriegsschauplatz und im besetzten Feindesgebiet begangenen Delikte und die Kommandogewalt* (Borna-Leipzig: Noske, 1916), 56–65, 65. The imperial ordinance was issued as a legal ordinance and was thus not a Reich law. As such it was not printed in the RGB. The kaiser authorized the Ministry of War to publish the ordinance in the case of general mobilization, which was performed on 2 August 1914. Only then did it acquire the status of an army ordinance and thus a standing regulation. Ibid., 24–28.

106. Bestimmungen für das Militärgerichts-Verfahren etc. während des Kriegszustandes in Deutsch-Südwest-Afrika, 11 June 1904, erlassen von Trotha,

BA/MA Freiburg, RW 51/12. The following quotations are all drawn from this document.

107. Jürgen Zimmerer interprets the legal regulation of the situation as evidence "that Lieutenant General von Trotha . . . possessed a clear conception of a racial war which had no place in the humane treatment of prisoners of war and which had to culminate in the extermination of the prisoners." Zimmerer, "Kriegsgefangene im Kolonialkrieg," in *In der Hand des Feindes: Kriegsgefangenschaft von der Antike bis zum Zweiten Weltkrieg,* ed. Rüdiger Overmans (Cologne: Böhlau, 1999), 277–294, 282.

108. Julius von Hartmann, "Militärische Notwendigkeit und Humanität: Ein kritischer Versuch I," *Deutsche Rundschau* 13 (1877): 111–128; Hartmann, "Ein kritischer Versuch II," ibid., 450–471; "Ein kritischer Versuch III," ibid. 14 (1878): 71–91. Published as a book: von Hartmann, *Kritische Versuche: Militärische Nothwendigkeit und Humanität* (Berlin: Paetel, 1878).

109. Isabel V. Hull, *Absolute Destruction: Military Culture and the Practices of War* (Ithaca, NY: Cornell University Press, 2005), 123–124; taking a different perspective: Geoffrey Best, "How Right Is Might? Some Aspects of the International Debate about How to Fight Wars and How to Win Them," in *War, Economy and the Military Mind,* ed. Geoffrey Best and Andrew Wheatcroft (London: Croom Helm, 1976), 120–135.

110. Julius von Hartmann, "Über den modernen Krieg," *Preußische Jahrbücher* 44 (1879): 223–245, 333–370, 348.

111. Hartmann, "Ein kritischer Versuch II," 452.

112. Hartmann, "Über den modernen Krieg," 350.

113. Hull, *Absolute Destruction,* 119–121.

6. Ideology and Passage to War

1. H. U. Wehler, *Deutsche Gesellschaftsgeschichte,* vol. 3: *Von der "Deutschen Doppelrevolution" bis zum Beginn des Ersten Weltkrieges 1849–1914* (Munich: C. H. Beck, 1995), 1066–1085, 1066. See also Geoff Eley, *Society, Culture and the State in Germany, 1870–1930* (Ann Arbor: University of Michigan Press, 1996).

2. Mechthild Leutner, "Deutsche Vorstellungen über China und Chinesen," in *Von der Kolonialpolitik zur Kooperation: Studium zu den deutsch-chinesischen Beziehungen,* ed. Heng-yü Kuo (Munich: Minerva Publikation, 1986), 401–442, 411.

3. Peter Martin, *Schwarze Teufel, edle Mohren: Afrikaner in Bewusstsein und Geschichte der Deutschen* (Hamburg: Junius, 1993), 198–200; Matthias Fiedler, *Zwischen Abenteuer, Wissenschaft und Kolonialismus: Der deutsche Afrikadiskurs im 18. und 19. Jahrhundert* (Cologne: Böhlau, 2005), 55–56.

4. Hermann von Wissmann, *Afrika: Schilderungen und Rathschläge zur Vorbereitung für den Aufenthalt und den Dienst in den deutschen Schutzgebieten* (Berlin: Ernst Siegfried Mittler, 1895, 2nd ed. 1903, repr. Militär-Wochenblatt, 1894), 67–69.

5. *Praktische Erfahrungen aus Deutsch-Südwestafrika* (Berlin: Reichsdruck, 1904), point 21, 25, HSTA Stuttgart, M 660/083, Bue 4.

6. Examples provided in Horst Gründer, ed., *"Da und dort ein junges Deutschland gründen": Rassismus, Kolonien und kolonialer Gedanke vom 16. bis zum 20. Jahrhundert* (Munich: Deutscher Taschenbuch Verlag, 1999), 222–297.

7. Christian Geulen, *Geschichte des Rassismus* (Munich: C. H. Beck, 2007), 80.

8. Heinz Gollwitzer, *Die Gelbe Gefahr: Geschichte eines Schlagwortes* (Göttingen: Vandenhoeck & Ruprecht, 1962), 43–44.

9. Maximilian Yorck von Wartenburg, *Weltgeschichte in Umrissen*, 4th ed. (Berlin: Ernst Siegfried Mittler, 1901), 503; Wichard Graf von Wilamowitz-Moellendorf, *Besteht eine gelbe Gefahr?* (Potsdam: A. Stein, 1905). Wilamowitz-Moellendorf was another veteran of the Boxer war; Friedrich von der Goltz, *Die gelbe Gefahr im Lichte der Geschichte* (Leipzig: Engelmann, 1907).

10. See also Geoff Eley, *Die Umformierung der Rechten: Der radikale Nationalismus und der Deutsche Flottenverein 1898–1908*, in Eley, *Wilhelminismus, Nationalismus, Faschismus: Zur historischen Kontinuität in Deutschland* (Munster: Verlag Westfälisches Dampfboot, 1991), 144–173.

11. All quotations taken from Johann Ernst, ed., *Reden des Kaisers: Ansprachen, Predigten und Trinksprüche Wilhelms II* (Munich: Deutscher Taschenbuch Verlag, 1966), 87, 89, 93.

12. Cited according to Bernd Sösemann, "Die sog. Hunnenrede Wilhelm II: Textkritische und interpretatorische Bemerkungen zur Ansprache des Kaisers vom 27. Juli 1900 in Bremerhaven," *Historische Zeitschrift* 222 (1976): 350. Despite the existence of a number of different versions of the kaiser's speech, the authenticity of these words should not be doubted, even if a consensus has yet to be reached regarding their political instrumentalization by both the kaiser's immediate circle and the press.

13. Ernst, *Reden des Kaisers*, 91.

14. Dietlind Wünsche, *"Jeden Zehnten mindestens Kopf ab in den aufrührerischen Gegenden . . . ,"* in *Kolonialkrieg in China: Die Niederschlagung der Boxerbewegung,* ed. Mechthild Leutner and Klaus Mühlhahn (Berlin: Christoph Links Verlag, 2007), 153–161, 158.

15. Reinhard, *Mit dem II. Seebataillon nach China!* (Berlin, 1902), 12.

16. Sösemann, "Die sog. Hunnenrede Wilhelm II," 345.

17. G. Auer and M. Unterbeck, eds., *In Südwestafrika gegen die Hereros: Nach den Kriegs-Tagebüchern des Obermatrosen G. Auer* (Berlin: Ernst Hofmann, 1911), 62. Similar formulations can be found in a number of soldiers' letters later published in the SPD newspaper *Vorwärts,* and others. See anon., "Pardon wird nicht gegeben," in *Vorwärts* 21, no. 64 (16 March 1904): 3.

18. Brandhorst to the Harbour Office Bremerhaven, 1 September 1900, in which he requested the further dissemination of the song, to which end he included two copies. A note on the letter indicates that a copy had been taken from the file to serve as instruction material for the troops. STA Bremen 4, 20 1019/112.

19. All emphasis in original.

20. An allusion to the British base at Weihaiwei.

21. The soldiers' song "Was blasen die Trompeten? Husaren heraus!" told of the "Battle of the Nations" at Leipzig, 1813. The text was written by Ernst Moritz Arndt (1813). The melody was that of the song "Frisch auf ihr Tiroler, wir müssen ins Feld" (1809).

22. Günter Ullrich, *Soldatenlieder im Wandel der Zeit: Darstellung, Wertung und Interpretation* (Beckum: Vogel-Druck, 1989), 135.

23. August Bebel, 16 March 1901, SBR, X. Legislaturperiode, 2nd Sess., vol. 180, 1919. He referred to a song dedicated to the two sea battalions embarking the ships *Wittekind* and *Frankfurt* leaving from Wilhelmshaven on 03 July 1900. The text: "Thunder and lightning in the East / We will repay those miserable Chinese / No quarter for murderers / You will be done by as your actions speak, / Laughing at the law, / we will take more than just your pigtails / you will enter heaven without your head." Quoted from (according to Bebel) *Zehnte Ausgabe zu dem Buche: Fest- und Marschklänge für Kameraden in und außer Dienst von Richard Liesendahl.*

24. Freifrau Ada von Liliencron, *Kriegsklänge der Kaiserlichen Schutztruppe in Deutsch-Süd-West-Afrika. Illustrations from the Former Mounted Soldiers Franz Spenker et al.* (Hamburg: Spenker, 1905). Also in Arne Schöfert, ed., *Deutsche Koloniallyrik: Lieder und Gedichte* (Saarbrücken: Fines-Mundi-Verlag, 2006). A number of songs are found in Liedtypmappen: Kolonien Deutschlands im 19. Jahrhundert. VolksliedA Freiburg.

25. Corresponding reports of the setup of tents and booths in Bremerhaven are found in STA Bremen, 4, 20 1020 / 112.

26. War Diary, II. Seebataillon, 4. Ostasiatisches Infanterieregiment, entries for 6 August 1900, 10 August 1900, 12 August 1900, 13 August 1900, 14 August 1900, BayHSTA Munich Kriegsarchiv, B 1485; Reinhard, *Mit dem II. Seebataillon nach China!,* 19–20; Ludwig von Estorff, *Wanderungen und Kämpfe in Südwestafrika, Ostafrika und Südafrika 1894–1910* (Windhoek: Privatdruck des Herausgebers, 1968), 18; Kurd Schwabe, *Dienst und Kriegführung in den Kolonien und auf überseeischen Expeditionen* (Berlin: Ernst Siefried Mittler, 1903), 35.

27. Bericht von Hauptmann Grube (Transportführer) über die Erfahrungen während der Seereise an Bord der Gertrud Woermann, HSTA Stuttgart M 1/4, vol. 535.

28. Emil Lessel, *Böhmen, Frankreich, China 1866–1901: Erinnrungen eines preußischen Offiziers* (Cologne: Grote, 1981), 181; Georg Hillebrecht, diary entry from 7 July–8 July 1904, printed in *"S'ist ein übles Land hier": Zur Historiographie eines umstrittenen Kolonialkrieges; Tagebuchaufzeichnungen aus dem Herero-Krieg in Deutsch-Südwestafrika von Georg Hillebrecht und Franz Ritter von Epp,* ed. Andreas S. Eckl (Cologne: Köppe, 2005), 82.

29. Das Tagebuch des Chinafahrers Heinrich Müller: Artillerist im Expeditionskorps zur Bekämpfung des Boxer-Aufstandes in China 1900–1901, entry for September 1900, 25. TagebuchA Emmendingen, 671 / 1.

30. Michel Foucault, "Andere Räume," in *Aisthesis: Wahrnehmung heute oder Perspektiven einer anderen Ästhetik: Essais,* ed. Karlheinz Barck et al. (Leipzig: Reclam, 1991), 34–46, 46.

7. Environment and Enemy

1. See John K. Noyes, *Colonial Space: Spatiality in the Discourse of German South West Africa 1884–1915* (Chur, Switzerland: Harwood Academic Publishers, 1992), 126.

2. Denkschrift, betr. die Entwicklung des Kiautschou-Gebiets in der Zeit vom Oktober 1898 bis Oktober 1899 (Berlin, 1899), 30–32, BayHSTA Munich, Kriegsarchiv, Mkr 760.

3. Taken from the papers of the officer Arnold von Lequis, BA / MA Freiburg, N 38 / 31. Sections of this material have been printed as an appendix to Susanne Kuß, "Deutsche Strafexpeditionen im Boxerkrieg," in *Kolonialkrieg in China: Die Niedserschlagung der Boxerbewegung,* ed. Mechthild Leutner and Klaus Mühlhahn (Berlin: Christoph Links Verlag, 2007), 135–146, 145.

4. Report of Staff Officer G. H. W. O'Sullivan regarding the Baoding expedition, Peking, 2 November 1900, Annual Reports of the War Department for the Fiscal Year Ended June 30, 1900, *Government Publications* (57th Cong., 1st Sess., House of Representatives), vol. 4274 (Washington, DC: Government Printing Office, 1901), 476–488, 478.

5. Curt von François, "Zu den Unruhen im Gebiete der Bondelzwarts," *Militär-Wochenblatt* 88, no. 136 (3 December 1903): cols. 3223–3230, 3226.

6. Dietrich Reimer (Publishing House and Cartographical Institute) to Wilhelm Stuebel (director of the Colonial Department of the *Auswärtiges Amt*), 1 March 1904, BA Lichterfelde, R 1001 / 1503.

7. Theobald von Schäfer, "Kriegskunst," in *Handbuch der neuzeitlichen Wehrwissenschaften,* vol. 1, *Wehrpolitik und Kriegführung,* ed. Hermann Franke (Berlin: de Gruyter, 1936), 180–227, 222.

8. Hermann von Wissmann, *Afrika: Schilderungen und Rathschläge zur Vorbereitung für den Aufenthalt und den Dienst in den Deutschen Schutzgebieten* (Berlin: Ernst Siegfried Mittler, 1895, 2nd ed. 1903, repr. Militär-Wochenblatt, 1894), 84 and 86.

9. Leutwein to the Imperial Government in German South-West Africa, Windhoek, 2 August 1901, BA Lichterfelde, R 1001 / 1503.

10. Trotha to the Colonial Department of the Foreign Office, 2 September 1897; Foreign Office to Wilhelm von Hahnke, Chief of the Military Cabinet 11 October 1897; Hahnke to the Foreign Office, 16 November 1897, BA Lichterfelde, R 1001 / 307.

11. Alfred von Schlieffen, Chief of the Army General Staff to the Colonial Department of the Foreign Office, 22 April 1903, ibid.

12. Governor Rechenberg to all District Offices, Residences, Military Stations, Subsidiaries and Military Posts, 6 August 1910, ibid.

13. Major Estorff (deputizing for the governor) to the Colonial Department of the Foreign Office, 9 January 1902, ibid., R 1001/1503.

14. *Militärisches Orientierungsheft für Deutsch-Ostafrika, Entwurf,* (Dar es Salaam: Deutsch-Ostafrikanische Rundschau, 1911), *Beilage: 9 Wegekarten.*

15. Heinrich von Goßler, minister of war, to the Reichstag, 16 March 1901, SBR, X. Legislaturperiode, II. Sess., vol. 180, 1913.

16. It was assumed that they would have fewer qualms in policing an area to which they had no family ties.

17. Lieutenant Colonel Konrad von Burgsdorff (Gibeon District) to the Imperial Governor Major Theodor Leutwein, 22 December 1895, BA Lichterfelde, R 151/82086, emphasis in text.

18. Second Lieutenant Lampe, Gobabis, to the Imperial Governor's office, Windhoek, 29 November 1895, BA Lichterfelde, R 151/82086.

19. Report from Lieutenant Otto Eggers, Okahandja, regarding the recruitment of the Hereros as soldiers, Windhoek, 3 January 1895, ibid.

20. Regarding the construct of the "martial races," see David Killingray, "Guardians of Empire," in *Guardians of Empire: The Armed Forces of the Colonial Powers c. 1700–1964,* ed. David Killingray and David E. Omissi (Manchester: Manchester University Press, 1999), 1–24, 14–16; Killingray, "Race and Rank in the British Army in the Twentieth Century," *Ethnic and Racial Studies* 10 (1987): 276–290; Anthony H. M. Kirk-Greene, "'Damnosa Hereditas': Ethnic Ranking and the Martial Races Imperative in Africa," ibid., 3 (1980): 393–414; Sir George MacMunn, *The Martial Races of India* (Quetta: Gosha-e-Adab, 1934), 2; Sarah Womack, "Ethnicity and Martial Races: The Garde Indigene of Cambodia in the 1880s and 1890s," in *Colonial Armies in Southeast Asia,* ed. Karl Hack and Tobias Rettig (Oxford: Routledge, 2006), 106–125, 112.

21. The description of the individual districts and the "nature of the information" had caused significant difficulty. This led the editors of the *Orientation Manual* to publish it only in draft form to be superseded after three years by a revised edition. *Militärisches Orientierungsheft für Deutsch-Ostafrika,* foreword by Major Kurt von Schleinitz, Commander of the Protection Force. The following information is taken from this manual, 4–7.

22. *A Handbook of German East Africa: Compiled by the Geographical Section of the Naval Intelligence Division, Naval Staff, Admiralty* (London: H. M. Stat. Off., 1920).

23. The definitive study is provided by Trutz von Trotha, *Koloniale Herrschaft: Zur soziologischen Theorie der Staatsentstehung am Beispiel des "Schutzgebietes Togo"* (Tübingen: J. C. B. Mohr, 1994), 58–85, 62–63.

24. Dorothy Middleton, ed., *The Diary of Arthur Jeremy Mounteney Jephson: Emin Pasha Relief Expedition 1887–1889* (Cambridge: Cambridge University Press, 1969), 78.

25. Rochus Schmidt, *Deutschlands Kolonien: Ihre Gestaltung, Entwicklung und Hilfsquellen* (Berlin, 1898, repr. Augsburg: Verlag des Vereins der Bücherfreunde, 1999), 23.

26. Regarding Peters, see Arne Perras, *Carl Peters and German Imperialism 1856–1918: A Political Biography* (Oxford: Oxford University Press, 2004), 112–167.

27. Wolfgang Riegel, *Aufgaben des Sanitätsdienstes bei Landungen und bei Expeditionen in tropische und subtropische Gebieten* (Berlin: Ernst Siegfried Mittler, 1910), 2.

28. Lothar von Trotha, "Genozidaler Pazifizierungskrieg: Anmerkungen zum Konzept des Genozids am Beispiel des Kolonialkrieges in Deutsch-Südwestafrika, 1904–1907," *Zeitschrift für Genozidforschung* 2 (2003): 30–57, 45; Trotha, "'The Fellows Can Just Starve': On Wars of 'Pacification' in the African Colonies of Imperial Germany and the Concept of 'Total War,'" in *Anticipating Total War: The German and American Experiences, 1871–1914*, ed. Manfred F. Boemeke, Roger Chickering, and Stig Förster (Cambridge: Cambridge University Press, 1999), 415–435.

29. Michael Pesek, *Koloniale Herrschaft in Deutsch-Ostafrika: Expeditionen, Militär, Verwaltung seit 1880* (Frankfurt am Main: Campus, 2005), 204.

30. Georg Richelmann, "Die Besiegung der Feinde vom Rufiji bis zum Urumba," in *Hermann von Wissmann*, ed. Conradin von Perbandt, Georg Richelmann, and Rochus Schmidt (Berlin: Verlagsbuchhandlung, 1906), 202–252, 247.

31. Runderlaß an alle Bezirksämter, Bezirksnebenämter, Militär-Stationen und Offizierposten: Vertraulich, Dar es Salaam, 17 January 1903. Der Kaiserliche Gouverneur, in Vertretung, BA Lichterfelde, R 151/82077.

32. Ibid.

33. Circular ordinance from Oskar Stuebel, Foreign Office (Colonial Department) to the Imperial Government in Dar es Salaam, 3 April 1903, ibid.

34. That is, the Mueda plateau.

35. Circular ordinance from Oskar Stuebel, Foreign Office (Colonial Department) to the Imperial Government in Dar es Salaam, 3 April 1903, BA Lichterfelde, R 151/82077.

36. Handwritten remarks from Governor Leutwein, Windhoek, 17 August 1903, ibid.

37. Pesek, *Koloniale Herrschaft in Deutsch-Ostafrika*, 255.

38. Such reasons given included not wishing to join the expedition, failure to adapt to the conditions in the expedition, providing incorrect information regarding the route, or lying. These examples were taken from Josef Weinberger, *Ein bayerischer Unteroffizier als Sergeant bei der Kaiserlichen Schutztruppe in Deutsch-Ostafrika, Tagebücher 1891–1896: Zusammenfassung aller übertragenen Tagebücher und Notizen; Das Hauptbuch* (Haßloch: W. Hubach, 2004). Diary entries for 4 June 1894, 5 June 1894, 27 July 1894, 1 August 1894, 12 August 1894, 15 August 1894, 21 August 1894, 24 August 1894, 28 August 1894, 5 November 1894, and 4 January 1895.

39. Erich von Salzmann, *Im Kampfe gegen die Herero*, 3rd ed. (Berlin: Dietrich Reimer, 1905), 77.

40. Gilbert Clement Kamana Gwassa, *The Outbreak and Development of the Maji Maji War 1905–1907* (Dar es Salaam, 1973), ed. Wolfgang Apelt (Cologne: Köppe, 2005), 188.

41. Wissmann, *Afrika*, 23.

42. Paul Schlieper, *Meine Kriegs-Erlebnisse in China: Die Expedition Seymour im Juni 1900* (Minden: Köhler, 1902), 84.

43. Major Kurt von Schönberg to the King of Saxony, Shanhaikuan, 23 October 1900, HSTA Dresden, 11248/9597.

44. *Deutschland in China 1900–1901*, ed. Bearbeitet von den Teilnehmern an der Expedition (Düsseldorf: Druck von August Bagel, 1902), 408.

45. Götzen, Governor of GSWA to the Foreign Office, Colonial Department, 12 December 1905, BA Lichterfelde, R 1001/723.

46. Kuß, "Deutsche Strafexpeditionen im Boxerkrieg," 134–146, 144.

47. A close description is provided by Gwassa, *Outbreak and Development of the Maji Maji War 1905–1907*, 185–186.

48. Lothar von Trotha, "Genozidaler Pazifizierungskrieg," *Zeitschrift für Genozidforschung* 2 (2003): 30–57, 56.

49. Zweite Ergänzung zum Entwurfe des Haushalts-Etats für die Schutzgebiete auf das Rechnungsjahr 1907, Südwestafrika. A total of 1,500,000 marks was earmarked for the supply, clothing, etc. of prisoners of war. HSTA Stuttgart, E 130, a Bue 895.

50. China in 1900: Figures taken from a speech by Heinrich von Goßler, minister of war, 16 March 1901, SBR, X. Legislaturperiode, 2nd Sess., vol. 180, 1913 [calculations of the author].

51. Lequis, Schlussbericht zum Kriegstagebuch, 15, BA/MA Freiburg, N 38/31.

52. *Die Kämpfe der deutschen Truppen in Südwestafrika: Auf Grund amtlichen Materials bearbeitet von der Kriegsgeschichtlichen Abteilung I des Großen Generalstabes*, vol. 1: *Der Hereroaufstand* (Berlin: Ernst Siegfried Mittler, 1906), 10.

53. Maximilian Bayer, *Mit dem Hauptquartier in Südwest-Afrika* (Berlin: Weicher, 1909), 65–66.

54. Kurd Schwabe, *Der Krieg in Südwest-Afrika 1904–1906* (Berlin: C. A. Weller, 1907), 219.

55. Curt von François, *Kriegführung in Süd-Afrika* (Berlin: Dietrich Reimer, 1900), 7.

56. Ibid., 11.

57. Curt von François, "Der Hottentotten-Aufstand," *Militär-Wochenblatt* 90, no. 65 (30 May 1905): cols. 1542–1548, 1542, emphasis in text. See also *Die Kämpfe der deutschen Truppen in Südwestafrika*, vol. 2: *Der Hottentottenkrieg*, 299. Further examples in Gesine Krüger, *Kriegsbewältigung und Geschichtsbewußtsein: Realität, Deutung und Verarbeitung des deutschen Kolonialkriegs in Namibia 1904 bis 1907* (Göttingen: Vandenhoeck & Ruprecht, 1999), 98–99.

58. Bestimmungen für das Militärgerichts-Verfahren etc. während des Kriegszustandes in Deutsch-Südwest-Afrika, 11. Juni 1904, erlassen von Trotha, point 8.

59. *In Südwestafrika gegen die Hereros: Nach den Kriegs-Tagebüchern des Ober-matrosen G. Auer*, 106–107; Hans Paasche, *"Im Morgenlicht," Kriegs-, Jagd- und Reise-Erlebnisse in Ostafrika* (Berlin: C. A. Schwetschke und Sohn, 1907), 102.

60. Portionslisten vom 14.6. und 1.8.1904. *Sanitäts-Bericht über die Kaiserliche Schutztruppe für Südwestafrika während des Herero- und Hottentottenaufstandes für die Zeit vom 1. Januar 1904 bis 31. März 1907, bearb. im Kommando der Schutztruppen im Reichs-Kolonialamt*, vol. 1 (Berlin: Ernst Siegfried Mittler, 1909), 64 and 68–70.

61. *Praktische Erfahrungen aus Deutsch-Südwestafrika* (Berlin, Reichdruck 1904), point 33, 36, HSTA Stuttgart, M 660/083, Bue 4; see also G. J. Wolseley, *The Soldier's Pocket-Book for Field Service* (London: Macmillan, 1869) pt. 3, paragraph "War with Savage Nations," 412: "In grassy countries like the Natal, the American prairies &c., beware of being burnt out."

62. *Die Kämpfe der deutschen Truppen in Südwestafrika*, vol. 2: *Der Hottentotten-krieg*, 290–291.

63. Ergebnis der durch Allerhöchste Kabinettsorder vom 14. November 1908 berufenen Kommission zur Beratung auf Grund der bei der Entsendung in Südwestafrika gesammelten Erfahrungen, Inhaltsverzeichnis, BA/MA, Freiburg, RM 3/7728; *Die Kämpfe der deutschen Truppen in Südwestafrika*, vol. 2: *Der Hottentottenkrieg*, 302–303.

64. Hans von Haeften, "Eine deutsche Kolonialarmee," *Vierteljahreshefte für Truppenführung und Heereskunde* 2 (1905), 610–631, 627; see also Carl Peters, *Gefechtsweise und Expeditionsführung in Afrika* (Berlin: Walther, 1892), 16.

65. How many soldiers took advantage of this offer is unknown.

66. *Die Kämpfe der deutschen Truppen in Südwestafrika*, vol. 1: *Der Feldzug gegen die Hereros*, 207.

67. Friedrich Ratzel, *Deutschland: Einführung in die Heimatkunde*, 2nd ed. (Leipzig: F. W. Grunow, 1907), 255.

68. Emer de Vattel, *The Law of Nations* (1758), ed. Béla Kapossy and Richard Whatmore (Indianapolis, IN: Liberty Fund, 2008), 129–130 (I. vii. 81). For the debate, see David Armitage, "John Locke, Theorist of Empire?," in *Empire and Modern Political Thought*, ed. Sankar Muthu (Cambridge: Cambridge University Press, 2012), 84–111.

69. Moritz Merker, "Ueber die Aufstandsbewegung in Deutsch-Ostafrika," *Militär Wochenblatt* 91, no. 46 (12 April 1906): cols. 1085–1092, 1085.

70. Militärpolitischer Bericht von Hauptmann Kurt von Schleinitz, 1 June 1907, 25–26, BA/MA, Freiburg, RM 5/6036.

71. Birthe Kundrus, *Moderne Imperialisten: Das Kaiserreich im Spiegel seiner Kolonien* (Cologne: Böhlau, 2009), 145.

8. Diseases and Injuries

1. Robert Schian, "Die Bekämpfung des Typhus unter der Schutztruppe in Südwestafrika im Hererofeldzug 1904/05," *Deutsche militärärztliche Zeitschrift* 34 (1905): 593–604, 594.

2. *Sanitätsbericht über das Kaiserliche Ostasiatische Expeditionskorps für den Berichtzeitraum vom 1. Juli 1900 bis 30. Juni 1901 und die Ostasiatische Besatzungsbrigade für den Berichtzeitraum vom 10. Juni 1901 bis 30. September 1902* (Berlin: Ernst Siegfried Mittler, 1904), 24.

3. Krosta, "Ueberblick über die Thätigkeit der Sanitäts-Formationen beim Ostasiatischen Expeditionskorps," *Deutsche militärärztliche Zeitschrift* 30 (1901): 321–327, 325.

4. Sanitätsordnung während des Kriegszustandes in Deutsch-Südwest-Afrika, 1 July 1904, sec. 1, HSTA Stuttgart, M 660/083, Bue 4.

5. Ibid., sec. 5.

6. Karl Herhold, "Ueber die während der ostasiatischen Expedition im Feldlazareth IV (Paotingfu) beobachteten Schussverletzungen," *Deutsche militärärztliche Zeitschrift* 30 (1901): 603–621, 603; Eugen Wolffhügel, "Der Sanitätsdienst im Berggefecht am Tschang-tschönn-ling 8. März 1901 mit einigen Betrachtungen über Sanitätstaktik im Gebirgskriege," ibid., 31 (1902): 393–411, 409, 411.

7. Philatheles Kuhn, "Ueber das Militär-Sanitätswesen in Südwestafrika während des Eingeborenen-Aufstandes 1904/05," pt. 1, *Militär-Wochenblatt* 85, no. 71 (15 June 1905): cols. 1669–1678, esp. 1676.

8. *Sanitätsbericht über das Kaiserliche Ostasiatische Expeditionskorps,* 47.

9. Werner Steuber, "Tropenkrankheiten und koloniale Medizin: Mittheilungen aus dem Sanitätswesen von Deutsch-Ostafrika," *Deutsche medizinische Wochenschrift* 29, no. 19 (7 May 1903): 340–342, 340.

10. Georg Mayer, *Hygienische Studien aus China* (Leipzig: Barth, 1904). A summary publication of a number of articles about the water situation in Peking, originally published in the Munich-based *Medizinische Wochenschrift*.

11. For China: *Sanitätsbericht über das Kaiserliche Ostasiatische Expeditionskorps,* 47. For Africa: *Sanitäts-Bericht über die Kaiserliche Schutztruppe für Südwest-Afrika während des Herero- und Hottentottenaufstandes für die Zeit vom 1. Januar 1904 bis 31. März 1907, bearb. im Kommando der Schutztruppen im Reichs-Kolonialamt,* vol. 1 (Berlin: Ernst Siegfried Mittler, 1909), 152.

12. Hugo Bofinger, "Einige Mitteilungen über Skorbut," *Deutsche militärärztliche Zeitschrift* 39 (5 August 1910): 569–582, 574, 576.

13. *Sanitäts-Bericht über die Kaiserliche Schutztruppe für Südwest-Afrika,* 142; Julius Morgenroth et al., "Bericht über die im bakteriologischen und chemischen Laboratorium zu Tientsin in der Zeit vom 1. Oktober 1900 bis 1. März 1901 ausgeführten Arbeiten," *Deutsche Militärärztliche Zeitschrift* 30 (1901): 548–559, 552.

14. Otto Nägele, Vorschläge zur Hebung des Gesundheitszustands der Eingeborenen, 9 November 1908. From the Government in GSWA to the Reichskolonialamt Berlin, BA Lichterfelde, R 1001/6042.

15. Protokoll über die Besprechung des Gouverneurs mit den Vorleuten der "Eingeborenen" in Windhuk (signed Hintrager), 28 November 1908, BA Lichterfelde, R 1001/6040.

16. Governor of GSWA (signed Hintrager) to the Reichskolonialamt Berlin, 31 August 1908. Letter following the inquiry from Prof. Dr. Klaatsch, Breslau, as to whether Herero skulls could be obtained from the protectorate for his collection, BA Lichterfelde, R 1001 / 6112.

17. Wolfgang U. Eckart, "Medizin und kolonialer Rassenkrieg: Die Niederschlagung des Herero-Nama-Aufstands im Schutzgebiet Deutsch-Südwestafrika (1904–1907)," in *Kriegsverbrechen im 20. Jahrhundert,* ed. Wolfram Wette and Gerd R. Ueberschär (Darmstadt: Primus, 2001), 59–71.

18. Otto Nägele, Vorschläge zur Hebung des Gesundheitszustandes der Eingeborenen; Vorschläge zur Errichtung eines massiven Eingeborenenlazaretts in Windhuk, n.d., sent to the Reichskolonialamt in November 1908, BA Lichterfelde, R 1001 / 6042.

19. Governor of GSWA (signed Hintrager) to the Reichskolonialamt Berlin, 9 November 1908, ibid.

20. The regulations for the Protection Forces were laid out in Schutztruppen-Ordnung, att. 3, sec. 7.

21. Emil Steudel, "Die Untersuchung auf Tauglichkeit zum Dienst in den Kaiserlichen Schutztruppen," *Deutscher militärärztlicher Kalender 1903* (Hamburg, 1903), supp., 317–322, 318, GSTA PK Berlin, Rep. 208a / 144I. See also the leaflet *Untersuchung auf Tropendiensttauglichkeit* (no date), HSTA Dresden, 11351, no. 816.

22. See Gutachten für Josef Müller, 8 April 1904, Würzburg, von Oberstabsarzt Somning, BayHSTA Munich, Kriegsarchiv, Mkr 790.

23. T. zur Verth, "Zur Hygiene europäischer Truppen bei tropischen Feldzügen," *Archiv für Schiffs- und Tropenhygiene* 13, supp. 1 (1909): 5–73, 11; Wolfgang Riegel, *Aufgaben des Sanitätsdienstes bei Landungen und Expeditionen in tropischen und subtropischen Gebieten* (Berlin: Ernst Siegfried Mittler, 1910), 15–18.

24. Emil Steudel, "Kann der Deutsche sich in den Tropen akklimatisieren?," *Archiv für Schiffsund Tropenhygiene* 12, supp. 4 (1908): 5–22, 7.

25. "Gesundheitsbelehrungen für das Ostasiatische Expeditionskorps," *Sanitätsbericht über das Kaiserliche Ostasiatische Expeditionskorps,* 8–10, 8.

26. Verth, "Zur Hygiene europäischer Truppen bei tropischen Feldzügen," 5–73, 43–49; Steuber, "Über die Verwendbarkeit europäischer Truppen in tropischen Kolonien vom gesundheitlichen Standpunkte," *Vierteljahreshefte für Truppenführung und Heereskunde* 4 (1907): 232–268, 251.

27. Alexander Lion, *Tropenhygienische Ratschläge* (Munich: Gmelin, 1907), 13; Bernhard Nocht speaking at the Colonial Congress 1902, Ausschuß des Reichs-Gesundheitsrats für Schiffs- und Tropenhygiene, 14 February 1908, 8, STA Bremen, 3-R.1.g.no. 43.

28. A seminal study, repeatedly cited by contemporaries: Ferdinand Hueppe, "Über die modernen Kolonisationsbestrebungen und die Anpassungsmöglichkeit der Europäer in den Tropen, part I," *Berliner klinische Wochenschrift* 38 (7 January 1901): 7–11; pt. 2, ibid.: 46–51.

29. Karl Däubler, *Die Grundzüge der Tropenhygiene* (Berlin: O. Enslin, 1900), 2; Steuber, "Tropenkrankheiten und koloniale Medizin: Mittheilungen aus dem Sanitätswesen von Deutsch-Ostafrika," 340–342, 340.

30. Arnold von Lequis, Schlussbericht zum Kriegstagebuch, 15a, BA/MA Freiburg, N 38/31.

31. Karl Herhold, "Über die bei der II. Brigade des Ostasiatischen Expeditionskorps vorzugsweise vorgekommenen Krankheiten mit Bezug auf Klima und Boden der Provinz Petchili in China," *Deutsche militärärztliche Zeitschrift* 30 (1901): 641–655, 644. The following considerations are also drawn from this essay.

32. Alfred Graf von Waldersee, *Denkwürdigkeiten des General-Feldmarschalls Alfred Grafen von Waldersee*, vol. 3 (1900–1904), ed. Heinrich Otto Meisner (Berlin: Deutsche Verlags-Anstalt, 1923), 122.

33. Lion, *Tropenhygienische Ratschläge*, 12.

34. *Sanitäts-Bericht über die Kaiserliche Schutztruppe für Südwestafrika während des Herero- und Hottentottenaufstandes für die Zeit vom 1. Januar 1904 bis 31. März 1907, bearb. im Kommando der Schutztruppen im Reichs-Kolonialamt*, vol. 2, *Statistischer Teil* (Berlin: Mittler, 1920), 268–270. The figures for the Home Army (excluding Bavaria) amounted to 0.1 percent in the military years 1903/04–1906/07.

35. *Sanitätsbericht über das Kaiserliche Ostasiatische Expeditionskorps*, 40.

36. *Sanitätsbericht über die Marine-Expeditionskorps in Südwestafrika 1904/05 und Ostafrika 1905/06*, bearb. in der Medizinal-Abteilung des Reichs-Marine-Amts (Berlin: Ernst Siegfried Mittler, 1908), 83.

37. *Sanitäts-Bericht über die Kaiserliche Schutztruppe für Südwestafrika*, vol. 2, 285.

38. Ibid.

39. Inspektion der Marineinfanterie (gez. Wyneken), geheimer Inspektionsbe-fehl, 23 March 1906, BA/MA Freiburg, RM 121I/128.

40. *Sanitäts-Bericht über die Kaiserliche Schutztruppe für Südwestafrika*, vol. 2, 257.

41. Richard Carow, *Die Kaiserliche Schutztruppe in Deutsch-Südwest-Afrika* (Leipzig: G. Freund, 1898), 49.

42. "Im Herero-Aufstand: Aus dem Tagebuch eines Schutztrupplers, Epukiro, 20/10/1904," *Berliner Tageblatt* 33, no. 656 (25 December 1904), Sunday ed.: 6. supp.

43. Philatheles Kuhn, "Alkohol in den Tropen I u. II," *Deutsche Kolonialpost* 3, no. 10–11 (October–November 1908): 1–3, 1–4. A similar text with slight variation is reproduced in Kuhn, "Alkohol in den Tropen," 1910.

44. Eugen Wolffhügel, "Truppenhygienische Erfahrungen in China," *Münchner Medizinische Wochenschrift* 50 (1 December 1903): 2105–2108, 2105.

45. *Sanitäts-Bericht über die Kaiserliche Schutztruppe für Südwestafrika während des Herero- und Hottentottenaufstandes für die Zeit vom 1. Januar 1904 bis 31. März 1907, bearb. im Kommando der Schutztruppen im Reichs-Kolonialamt*, vol. 1 (Berlin: Ernst Siegfried Mittler, 1909), 79.

46. Ibid., vol. 2, 262.

47. Die Entwickelung der Alkoholverpflegung bei der Schutztruppe, 30 September 1908. Zusammengestellt von Uhlmann, Kalkulaturvorsteher, BA Lichterfelde, R 151/82379.

48. *Sanitäts-Bericht über die Kaiserliche Schutztruppe für Südwestafrika,* vol. 2, 258.

49. Victor Franke, *Die Tagebücher des Schutztruppenoffiziers Victor Franke,* vol. 1, *Tagebuchaufzeichnungen vom 26.05.1896–27.05.1904* (Berlin: Verlag für Literatur über die Kolonial- und Mandatszeit Südwestafrikas, 2002), 276, 315.

50. *Sanitäts-Bericht über die Kaiserliche Schutztruppe für Südwestafrika,* vol. 2, 262.

51. Werner Steuber, *Arzt und Soldat in drei Erdteilen* (Berlin: Schlegel, 1940), 38–39.

52. *Militärischer Suaheli-Sprachführer für Deutsch-Ostafrika* (Dar es Salaam: Deutsch-Ostafrikanische Rundschau, 1911), 34.

53. Robert Koch, *Die Bekämpfung des Typhus: Vortrag, gehalten in der Sitzung des wissenschaftlichen Senats bei der Kaiser Wilhelms-Akademie, gehalten am 28. November 1902* (Berlin: Hirschwald, 1903).

54. Schian, "Die Bekämpfung des Typhus unter der Schutztruppe in Südwestafrika im Hererofeldzug 1904/05," *Deutsche Militärärztliche Zeitschrift* 34 (1905): 593–604, here 594.

55. *Sanitätsordnung während des Kriegszustandes in Deutsch-Südwest-Afrika,* 1 July 1904, sec. 14, emphasis in the original.

56. Medizinal-Abteilung des Königlich Preussischen Kriegsministeriums, ed., *Beiträge zur Schutzimpfung gegen Typhus: Veröffentlichungen aus dem Gebiete des Militär-Sanitätswesens,* vol. 28 (Berlin: Hirschwald, 1905), 2–5; *Sanitäts-Bericht für die Kaiserliche Schutztruppe über Südwest-Afrika,* vol. 2, 255, Schian, "Die Bekämpfung des Typhus unter der Schutztruppe in Südwestafrika im Hererofeldzug 1904/05," 593–604, 602. Regarding the experience made with the vaccination, see Eichholz, "Einige Erfahrungen über den Typhusverlauf bei geimpften und nichtgeimpften Mannschaften der Schutztruppe für Deutsch-Südwest-Afrika," *Münchner medizinische Wochenschrift* 54, no. 16 (16 April 1907): 777–779; "Beobachtungen über Ergebnisse der Typhusschutzimpfung in der Schutztruppe für Südwestafrika: Mitgeteilt vom Oberkommando der Schutztruppe," *Archiv für Schiffs- und Tropenhygiene* 9 (1905): 527–529.

57. Philatheles Kuhn, "Über das Militär-Sanitätswesen in Südwestafrika während des Eingeborenen-Aufstandes 1904/05, part 2," *Militär-Wochenblatt* 85, no. 72 (17 June 1905): cols. 1708–1714, 1711.

58. *Sanitätsbericht über die Marine-Expeditionskorps in Südwestafrika 1904/05 und Ostafrika 1905/06,* 40.

59. *Sanitäts-Bericht über die Kaiserliche Schutztruppe in Deutsch-Südwestafrika,* vol. 2, 90.

60. Ibid., 108.

61. Kuhn, "Über das Militär-Sanitätswesen in Südwestafrika während des Eingeborenen-Aufstandes 1904/05, part 2," cols. 1708–1714, 1712.

62. Ernst Kaerger, *Der Typhus in Südwestafrika: Februar 1904 bis März 1905* (Kiel: Druck von Schmidt & Klaunig, 1905), 7–10.

63. *Sanitätsbericht über die Marine-Expeditionskorps in Südwestafrika 1904/05 und Ostafrika 1905/06,* 17.

64. Emil Steudel, "Über die Entstehung und Verbreitung des Typhus in Süd-westafrika, sowie über die bisher erzielten Erfolge der Schutzimpfung," *Verhandlungen des deutschen Kolonialkongresses 1905,* 191–199, 196, GSTA PK Berlin, Rep. 208a/144I.

65. *Sanitäts-Bericht über die Kaiserliche Schutztruppe für Deutsch-Südwestafrika,* vol. 2, 117, 216: "Any explanation of the development of the typhus epidemic in German South-West does not require assumption that the infection came from the watering holes previously occupied by the Herero and contaminated with typhus."

66. Ernst Nigmann, *Geschichte der kaiserlichen Schutztruppe für Deutsch-Ostafrika* (Berlin: Ernst Siegfried Mittler, 1911), 82.

67. *Sanitäts-Bericht über die Kaiserliche Schutztruppe für Südwestafrika,* vol. 2, 340.

68. Denkschrift zur Bekämpfung der Geschlechtskrankheiten im Südwestafri-kanischen Schutzgebiet: Kaiserliches Gouvernement für Deutsch-Südwestafrika; Windhuk, 5 November 1908, BA Lichterfelde, R 1001/6040; *Sanitätsbericht über das Kaiserliche Ostasiatische Expeditionskorps,* 43; *Sanitäts-Bericht über die Kaiserliche Schutztruppe für Südwestafrika,* vol. 2, 457; *Sanitätsbericht über die Marine-Expeditionskorps in Südwestafrika 1904/05 und Ostafrika 1905/06,* 52, 88.

69. *Sanitätsbericht über das Kaiserliche Ostasiatische Expeditionskorps,* 43.

70. Ibid.

71. *Sanitätsbericht über die Marine-Expeditionskorps in Südwestafrika 1904/05 und Ostafrika 1905/06,* 70, 84.

72. Karl Herhold, "Über die bei der II. Brigade des Ostasiatischen Expeditions-korps vorzugsweise vorgekommenen Krankheiten mit Bezug auf Klima und Boden der Provinz Petchili in China," *Deutsche Militärärztliche Zeitschrift* 30, no. 12 (1901): 641–655, 654. See also Herhold, *Die Hygiene bei überseeischen Expeditionen nach den während der Expedition nach Ostasien gemachten Erfah-rungen* (Berlin: Ernst Siegfried Mittler, 1903), 39–40.

73. *Sanitäts-Bericht über die Kaiserliche Schutztruppe für Südwestafrika,* vol. 2, 343.

74. Denkschrift zur Bekämpfung der Geschlechtskrankheiten im Südwestafri-kanischen Schutzgebiet, 5 November 1908, BA Lichterfelde, R 1001/6040.

75. Werner Bauer, *Geschichte des Marinesanitätswesens bis 1945* (Berlin: Ernst Siegfried Mittler, 1958), 76; Heinrich Ruge, *Die Bekämpfung der Geschlechts-krankheiten in der deutschen Marine mit besonderer Berücksichtigung der Jahre 1920–25* (Berlin: Ernst Siegfried Mittler, 1927).

76. *Sanitäts-Bericht über die Kaiserliche Schutztruppe für Südwestafrika,* vol. 2, 342–343; Sanitätsbericht für den Monat Oktober 1905, Sanitätsamt Windhuk (gez. H. Plagge), 16 November 1905, HSTA Stuttgart, M 1/8, vol. 216.

77. *Sanitätsbericht über die Marine-Expeditionskorps in Südwestafrika 1904/05 und Ostafrika 1905/06,* 84.

78. Komitee für die Verwaltung der Stadt Peking, 21 January 1901, NARA Washington, RG 395/919.

79. Eugen Wolffhügel, "Truppenhygienische Erfahrungen in China (Schluss)," *Münchner Medizinische Wochenschrift* 50, no. 49 (8 December 1903): 2149–2151, esp. 2150.

80. *Sanitätsbericht der Kaiserlich Deutschen Marine für den Zeitraum vom 1.4.1899 bis 30.9.1901,* ed. Medizinal-Abteilung des Reichsmarineamtes (Berlin: Ernst Siegfried Mittler, 1903), 363.

81. Protokoll der 1. Militär-Sanitäts-Vertreter-Konferenz (Komitee für die Verwaltung der Stadt Peking, Nr. 41), Peking, 17 January 1901, NARA Washington, RG 395/919.

82. *Sanitäts-Bericht über die Kaiserliche Schutztruppe für Südwestafrika,* vol. 1, 131.

83. Ibid., 141.

84. Denkschrift zur Bekämpfung der Geschlechtskrankheiten im Südwestafrikanischen Schutzgebiet, 05 November 1908, BA Lichterfelde, R 1001/6040.

85. *Sanitäts-Bericht über die Kaiserliche Schutztruppe für Südwestafrika,* vol. 1, 139.

86. Trotha to Schlieffen, Okatarobaka, 4 October 1904, BA Lichterfelde, R 1001/2089. Printed in Isabel V. Hull, *Absolute Destruction: Military Culture and the Practices of War* (Ithaca, NY: Cornell University Press, 2005), 59.

87. Hugo Bofinger, "Einige Mitteilungen über Skorbut," *Deutsche Militärärztliche Zeitschrift* 39 (5 August 1910): 569–582, 576.

88. *Sanitäts-Bericht über die Kaiserliche Schutztruppe für Südwestafrika,* vol. 1, 105.

89. Examples in Gesine Krüger, "Bestien und Opfer: Frauen im Kolonialkrieg," in *Völkermord in Deutsch-Südwestafrika,* ed. Jürgen Zimmerer and Joachim Zeller (Berlin: Christoph Links, 2003), 141–159, 154.

90. Information is provided in a memorandum from 1908: Denkschrift zur Bekämpfung der Geschlechtskrankheiten im Südwestafrikanischen Schutzgebiet, 5 November 1908, BA Lichterfelde, R 1001/6040.

91. Protokoll über die Besprechung des Gouverneurs mit den Vorleuten der Eingeborenen in Windhuk, 17 October 1908, betr. Bekämpfung von Geschlechtskrankheiten. Schelle responded to the protocol on 23 November 1908 Stellung. In BA Lichterfelde, R 1001/6042.

92. Denkschrift zur Bekämpfung der Geschlechtskrankheiten im Südwestafrikanischen Schutzgebiet, 5 November 1908, BA Lichterfelde, R 1001/6040.

93. Susanne Kuß, "Sonderzone Eingeborenenlazarett. Geschlechtskranke Frauen im Kriegsgefangenenlager Windhuk in Deutsch-Südwestafrika 1906," in *Lager vor Auschwitz: Gewalt und Integration im 20. Jahrhundert,* ed. Christoph Jahr and Jens Thiel (Berlin: Metropol-Verlag, 2013), 84–98.

94. It is worth noting that the statistical section of the Military Report for German South-West Africa was published in 1920. *Sanitäts-Bericht über die Kaiserliche Schutztruppe für Südwestafrika,* vol. 2.

95. From 1 July 1900 to 30 June 1901. This involved 8,171 (44.5 percent) of hospital-bound sick. See *Sanitätsbericht über das Kaiserliche Ostasiatische Expeditionskorps,* 26.

96. Ibid., 29, 33, 34, 38, 39, 40, 41, 42, 43.

97. Ibid., 28.

98. Ibid., 350, 352.

99. III. Seebataillon from Qingdao (333 men): fifty-one injured (15.3 percent); Seymour Corps (512 men): seventy-five injured (14.6 percent). *Sanitätsbericht über die Kaiserlich Deutsche Marine für den Zeitraum vom 1. April 1899 bis 30. September 1901*, 349.

100. *Sanitäts-Bericht über die Kaiserliche Schutztruppe für Südwestafrika*, vol. 2, 2, 402.

101. Ibid., 211, 406.

102. *Sanitätsbericht über die Marine-Expeditionskorps in Südwestafrika 1904/05 und Ostafrika 1905/06*, 33–34, 40, 42.

103. Ibid., 36.

104. Ibid., 74, 75, 77, 86.

105. *Deutschlands koloniale Wehrmacht in ihrer gegenwärtigen Organisation und Schlagfähigkeit: Auf Grund der neusten amtlichen Dokumente bearbeitet von einem höheren Offizier*, no name, but written by Hermann von Wissmann (Berlin: R. v. Decker, 1906), 94.

106. The case of the U.S. war with Cuba (1898) provides an interesting point of comparison: of the 400 soldiers lost in the campaign, only 300 died in or following combat. J. T. H. Connor, "'Before the World in Concealed Disgrace': Physicians, Professionalization and the 1898 Cuban Campaign of the Spanish American War," in *Medicine and Modern Warfare*, ed. Roger Cooter, Mark Harrison, and Steve Sturdy (Atlanta, GA: Rodopi, 1999), 29–59, 31. For further examples, see Philip D. Curtin, *Disease and Empire: The Health of European Troops in the Conquest of Africa* (Cambridge: Cambridge University Press, 1998).

9. Reaction from the Foreign Powers

1. An example: Report on the Allied Expedition to Kalgan. Commanded by Colonel Yorck von Wartenburg, which marched from Peking on 12th November 1900, by Lieut.-Col. Powell, NA London, WO 32/6147. This expedition was composed of German, Austrian, and Italian troops with a small British contingent of infantry and cavalry.

2. Report on the Organisation of the German Contingent with the China Expeditionary Force, by Col. J. M. Grierson, in Miscellaneous Reports regarding the China Expeditionary Force, Foreign Contingents, 1901, 28–60, 47, National Library, London, IOR, L/Mil/17/20/14. The following summaries are taken from p. 60 of this report.

3. Ibid., 60.

4. Ibid.

5. Report on the German Troops in North China, by Lieut.-Col. J. T. Dickman, Peking, 10 November 1900, NARA Washington 395/913.

6. Report on the Organisation of the French Contingent with the China Expeditionary Force, by Col. J. M. Grierson, in Miscellaneous Reports regarding the China Expeditionary Force, Foreign Contingents, National Library, London, IOR, L/Mil/17/20/14, 19–23, 22; Report on the Organ-

isation of the Italian Contingent with the China Expeditionary Force, by Col. J. M. Grierson, ibid., 66–69, 66.

7. Anand Yang "(A) Subaltern('s) Boxers: An Indian Soldier's Account of China and the World in 1900–01," in *The Boxers, China, and the World,* ed. Robert Bickers and R. C. Tiedemann (Lanham, MD: Rowman & Littlefield, 2007), 43–65, 57.

8. Arnold von Lequis, Schlussbericht zum Kriegstagebuch, 30 August 1901, Notizen über fremde Kolonien, n.d., BA/MA Freiburg, N 38/31.

9. Report on the British Troops in North China, by Lieut.-Col. J. T. Dickman, Peking, 1 November 1900, NARA Washington 395/913. See also Mj. W. E. Craighill, Report on the French Troops in North China, Peking, 30 October 1900, ibid.

10. Report on the Russian Troops in North China, by Mj. W. E. Craighill, Peking, 15 October 1900, ibid.

11. Miscellaneous Reports regarding the China Expeditionary Force, Foreign Contingents, 1901, 66–69, 66, National Library, London, IOR, L/Mil/17/20/14.

12. Report on the Organisation of the Italian Contingent with the China Expeditionary Force, by Col. J. M. Grierson, ibid.

13. Report on the Japanese Troops in North China, by Maj. Charles H. Muir, 24 October 1900, NARA Washington 395/913. Similar: Record of Events, Lieut.-Col. J. T. Dickman, Twenty-Sixth Infantry, 5 November 1900, Annual Reports of the [U.S.] War Department (Washington, DC, Government Publishing Office), vol. 4274, 476–488, 481.

14. Reports from Lieut.-Col. A. G. Churchill: Relief of the Peking Legations Operations of the Japanese Contingent, July–August 1900, NA London, WO 32/6145.

15. Arthur Alison Stuart Barnes, *On Active Service with the Chinese Regiment: A Record of Operations of the First Chinese Regiment in north China from March to October 1900* (London: Grant Richards, 1902), 207: "Personally I found the Russians more docile and less brutal than the soldiers of at any rate two other nations boasting a higher type of intelligence and civilization, and throughout my humble efforts I have tried not to be led away from what convictions I was forced to by my own observations."

16. Anon., "France and Germany," *United States Army and Navy Journal (USANJ)* 38, no. 1 (1 September 1900): 36.

17. Silbermann, "Journal de marche d'un soldat colonial en Chine," pt. 1, *Revue des troupes coloniales* 5 (1906): 547–578, 571.

18. The term "South African War" is preferable to that of the "Boer War." More comprehensive, it encompasses the black African population.

19. Cord Eberspächer, "'Albion zal hier ditmal zijn Moskou vinden!' Der Burenkrieg (1899–1902)," in *Kolonialkriege: Militärische Gewalt im Zeichen des Imperialismus,* ed. Thoralf Klein and Frank Schumacher (Hamburg: Hamburger Edition, 2006), 182–207, 192. For a general introduction to the South

African War, see Michael Barthorp, *The Anglo-Boer Wars: The British and the Afrikaners 1815–1902* (Poole: Blandford, 1987); Byron Farwell, *The Great Boer War* (London: A. Lane, 1977); Fred R. Hartesveldt, *The Boer War: Historiography and Annotated Bibliography* (Westport, CT: Greenwood, 2000); Martin Marix Evans, *Encyclopedia of the Boer War* (Santa Barbara, CA: ABC-CLIO, 2000); William Nasson, *The South African War, 1899–1902* (London: Edward Arnold, 1999). Regarding the phase of the guerilla war and the British policy of imprisonment, see Howard Bailes, "Military Aspects of the War," in *The South African War: The Anglo-Boer War 1899–1902*, ed. Peter Warwick (London: Longman, 1980), 65–102, 95–101. Examples for Boer guerilla actions against the British are provided in Arthur Campbell, *Guerillas: A History and Analysis* (London: Barker, 1967), 29–41. A contemporary account: Christiaan Rudolf de Wet, *Der Kampf zwischen Bur und Brite (Der dreijährige Krieg)* (Katowice: Siwinna, 1903).

20. William Nasson, "Africans at War," in *The Boer War: Direction, Experience, and Image*, ed. John Gooch (London: Frank Cass, 2000), 126–140, 127; Peter Warwick, *Black People and the South African War 1899–1902* (Cambridge: Cambridge University Press, 1983).

21. Failing to point to this difference, Hull allows the impression to develop that the British public opinion was equally concerned for the plight of the inmates of both "black" and "white" camps. Isabel V. Hull, *Absolute Destruction: Military Culture and the Practices of War* (Ithaca, NY: Cornell University Press, 2005), 182–187.

22. Nasson, "Africans at War," 126–140, 126.

23. Ludwig von Estorff, *Der Burenkrieg in Südafrika* (Berlin: Ernst Siegfried Mittler, 1901). The book had already appeared in a shortened form in 1900. Anon. review, *Militär-Wochenblatt* 85, no. 24 (14 March 1900): col. 607. *Wanderungen und Kämpfe in Südwestafrika, Ostafrika und Südafrika* was published in 1968.

24. Estorff, *Der Burenkrieg in Südafrika*, 276, emphasis in text.

25. Ibid.

26. Estorff, *Wanderungen und Kämpfe in Südwestafrika, Ostafrika und Südafrika*, 93.

27. Ibid., 94–95.

28. Ibid., 96.

29. Anon., "Der Buren-Krieg und die Europäische Kriegskunst," pt. 1, *Militär-Wochenblatt* 85, no. 18 (21 February 1900), col. 451–457, col. 451; Kurt von Lindenau, "Was lehrt uns der Burenkrieg für unseren Infanterieangriff?," ibid., supp. 1902, 133–177.

30. *Aus dem südafrikanischen Kriege 1899 bis 1902*, ed. Great General Staff, Kriegsgeschichtliche Abteilung I *(Erfahrungen außereuropäischer Kriege neuester Zeit)*, vol. 32 *(1. Colenso—Magersfontein)* (Berlin: Ernst Siegfried Mittler, 1903), no. 33 *(2. Operationen unter Lord Roberts bis zur Einnahme von Bloemfontein)* (Berlin: Ernst Siegfried Mittler, 1904), 66.

31. Colmar von der Goltz, "Was können wir aus dem Burenkriege lernen?," *Deutsche Revue* 27 (1902): 129–136, 132.

32. Ibid. The groundbreaking study of tactical doctrine by Jakob Meckel, the well-known German officer and since 1885 tutor at the Japanese Staff Academy. See Jakob Meckel, *Grundriß der Taktik* (Berlin: Ernst Siegfried Mittler, 1895), 281.

33. Military Report on German South-West Africa, 1906. Addendum 1: May 1908, 6, NA London, WO 33/416.

34. Michael Fröhlich, *Von Konfrontation zur Koexistenz: Die deutsch-englischen Kolonialbeziehungen in Südafrika 1884 und 1914* (Bochum: N. Brockmeyer, 1990), 239–240; Horst Bernhard, "Der Aufstand gegen die Herrenmenschen," in *Philosophie der Eroberer und koloniale Wirklichkeit: Ostafrika 1884–1918*, ed. Kurt Büttner and Heinrich Loth (East Berlin: Akademie-Verlag, 1981), 251–302, 291.

35. Cap. H. C. Lowther, 18 January 1904, Notes on the Herero Rising in German South West Afrika, 18 January 1904–6 May 1904, NA London, WO 106/265. Lowther was replaced by Captain Eardley Eardley-Russell in September 1904.

36. Militärattaché Lieut.-Col. Gleichen to J. B. Whitehead (British Embassy in Berlin), 7 July 1904, ibid.

37. John C. Cleverly (Office of the Residence Magistrate, Walvis Bay) to the Native Department (Cape Town), no. 80, Confidential, 20 January 1904, ibid.

38. Lieut.-Commander Alan Bruce on board the *Partridge*, 20 August 1904, ibid.

39. Anonymous report, Boer communication during the late war, 8 March 1904, ibid.

40. Ibid.

41. Friedrich Freiherr von Nettelbladt, Herero Rebellion in GSWAfrica, n.d. (probably July 1904), NA London, WO 106/265.

42. Anonymous report, Boer communication during the late war, 8 March 1904, ibid.

43. Ensward (War Office) to the British Foreign Minister Lord Lansdowne (Foreign Office), 6 March 1905, NA London, FO 64/1646.

44. Albrecht von Bernstorff (German Embassy in Cape Town) to the British Foreign Minister Lord Lansdowne (Foreign Office), 20 April 1904, ibid.

45. F. J. A. Trench to the War Office, 1 August 1905, ibid., FO 64/1647.

46. Military Report on German South-West Africa. Confidential. Third Edition. Prepared by the General Staff, War Office, December 1906. (A.1131. This report supersedes A.906, dated 1904, which should be immediately destroyed.) Including Addendum 1: May 1908 to the Military Report on German South West Africa, 1906. Addendum 2: October 1910 to the Military Report on German South West Africa, 1906. NA London, WO 33/416.

47. Ibid., app. 10: List of Principal Authorities Consulted, 208: Rochus Schmidt, *Deutschlands Kolonien: Ihre Gestaltung, Entwicklung und Hilfsquellen* (Berlin: Verlag des Vereins der Bücherfreunde, 1898); Organisatorische Bestimmungen

für die Kaiserlichen Schutztruppen; Kurd Schwabe, *Mit Schwert und Pflug in Deutsch-Südwestafrika: Vier Kriegs- und Wanderjahre* (Berlin: Ernst Siegfried Mittler, 1899); Hugo von François, ed., *Nama- und Damara: Deutsch-Südwestafrika* (Magdeburg: E. Baensch, 1895); Curt von François, *Deutsch-Südwest-Afrika: Geschichte der Kolonisation bis zum Ausbruch des Krieges mit Witbooi April 1893* (Berlin: Dietrich Reimer, 1899); Gerding, *Die Bahn Swakopmund-Windhoek* (Berlin: Süsserott, 1902); Hermann Friedrich Ortloff, *Landungsverhältnisse an der Küste Deutsch-Südwest-Afrika* (Berlin, 1902); Colonial Army Systems, War Dept., United States / Harry Hamilton Johnston, *A History of the Colonization of Africa by Alien Races* (Cambridge: Cambridge University Press, 1899); Report on German Colonies 1900–01, Foreign Office; Reports on German Colonies by Various British Officers; Jahresberichte über die Entwickelung der deutschen Schutzgebiete in Afrika und in der Südsee 1900–05; André Chéradame, *La colonisation et les colonies* (Paris: Plon-Nourrit, 1905); *Deutsches Kolonialblatt; Deutsche Kolonialzeitung; Deutscher Kolonialkalender 1906;* and various magazines and papers.

48. Military Report on German East Africa. Compiled in the Intelligence Department, War Office, by Maj. J. H. V. Crowe, 1902, NA London, WO 33 / 259. / Military Report on German East Africa. Confidential. Prepared by the General Staff, War Office, 1905 (A.956). Including Addendum 1, May 1906; Addendum 2, May 1907; Addendum 3, May 1908, ibid., WO 33 / 336. Authored by Major H. C. Lowther, who had also composed the reports on the Herero uprising, initially commissioned by the War Office. App. 6,72: List of Principal Authorities Consulted: Jahresberichte (1893 to 1903), German Official; German Annual Estimates, German Official; Friedl Martin, *Unsere Kolonien, deren Verwaltung und Werth: Kritische Abhandlung* (Munich: Schupp, 1902); Moritz Ruhl, *Die deutsche Schutztruppe für Südwest-Afrika: 44 Abb. Von Offizieren und Soldaten* (Leipzig: Ruhl, 1894); Rudolf Fitzner, *Deutsches Kolonial-Handbuch*, 2nd ed. (Berlin: Paetel, 1901); Gustav Meinecke, *Deutscher Kolonial-Kalender* (Berlin), 1898–1899. / Henri Hauser, *Colonies allemandes impériales et spontanées* (Paris: Nony, 1900); Colonial Army Systems, War Dept., United States / J. E. S. Moore, *To the Mountains of the Moon: Being an Account of the Modern Aspect of Central Africa, and of Some Little Known Regions Traversed by the Tanganyika Expedition in 1899 and 1900* (London: Hurst and Blackett, 1901); Ferdinand Wohltmann, *Deutsch Ost-Afrika. Bericht über die Ergebnisse seiner Reise, ausgeführt im Auftrag der Kolonialabteilung des Auswärtigen Amts, Winter 1897/98* (Berlin: Telge, 1898); Afrika Pilot., pt. 2, Admirality. / Board of Trade Journal. / C. Peters, *Das Deutsch-Ostafrikanische Schutzgebiet* (Munich: Oldenbourg, 1895).

49. Military Report on German East Africa, 1905, table of contents; Military Report on German South-West Africa, 1906, table of contents.

50. Military Report on German South-West Africa, 1906, 86; Military Report on German East Africa, 1905, 21.

51. Ibid., Addendum 1: May 1908, 3.

52. Ibid., 28.

53. Military Report on German East Africa, 1905, 13.

54. Intelligence Department, War Office, 23 February 1904, Secret: I. The military resources of Germany, and probable method of their employment in a war between Germany and England. II. Memorandum on the military policy to be adopted in a war with Germany. NA London, WO 106/46, E 2/2.

55. War with Germany, Col. Drake, 1905, ibid., E 2/1.

56. Scheme for operations against German East Africa 1897, Secret, ibid., E 2/3.

57. War with Germany, Col. Drake, 1905. See also ibid., War with Germany. List of preparations to be made forthwith, n.d., anonymous.

58. Dominik Geppert, *Pressekriege: Öffentlichkeit und Diplomatie in den deutsch-britischen Beziehungen (1896–1912)* (Munich: Oldenbourg, 2007), 72–77.

59. Anon., "Army Foreign," *Army and Navy Gazette (ANG)* 45 (23 January 1904): 80.

60. Anon., "The Germans in Africa," ibid., 45 (7 May 1904), 435.

61. Anon., "On the Nama War," ibid., 46 (23 May 1905), 891.

62. Anon., "Conditions of Colonial Success," *USANJ* 41, no. 39 (28 May 1904): 1030–1031; Anon., "On the Nama war," ibid., 42, no. 42 (17 June 1905): 1135.

63. "Foreign Bulletins: Allemagne," *La France Militaire (LFM)* (15 December 1904): 2; Dispatches under "Étranger: Allemagne," ibid. (13 April 1905): 2; Anon., "Allemagne/Étranger Allemagne," ibid. (19 March 1904): 2; Anon., "Étranger: Allemagne," ibid. (27 May 1905): 2.

64. Anon., "Army Foreign," *ANG* 45 (10 December 1904): 1184.

65. Anon., "Étranger: Allemagne," *LFM* (20 January 1904): 2.

66. Anon., "Étranger: Allemagne Résumé de la situation dans l'Afrique sud-occidentale," ibid. (03 June 1904): 2.

67. Ibid. (11 October 1904): 2.

68. Ibid. (18 October 1904): 2.

69. Ibid. (22 October 1904): 2.

70. A number of examples: anon., "La révolte du Sud-Ouest africain allemande," *Revue des troupes coloniales* 3 (July–December 1904): 100–101, 522, 624: "The operations against the Hereros remained inconclusive"; anon., "La révolte du Sud-Ouest africain allemande," ibid. 5 (July–December 1905): 88.

71. Military Report on German South-West Africa, 1906, 4.

72. Charles Edward Callwell, *Small Wars: Their Principles & Practice* (London: H. M. Stationery Office, 1896, 3rd ed. 1906), 93, 130.

73. Anon., "The Rising in German South-West Africa," *The Times* (14 November 1904): 4.

74. Anon., "Dans l'Afrique Allemande," *Le Temps* (17 October 1904): 2; anon., "La révolte des Herreros," ibid. (08 August 1905): 1.

75. Anon., "La révolte des Herreros," ibid. (17 August 1905): 2. The *Times* did not print Trotha's Herero proclamation but did print the Nama proclamation in May 1905: anon., "The Rising in German South-West Africa," *The Times* (19

May 1905): 5. See also anon., "German Colonial Troubles," ibid. (07 August 1905): 3.

76. Anon., *ANG* 45 (7 May 1904): 435.

77. *Military Report on German East Africa*, 1905, 28.

78. "Conditions of Colonial Success," *USANJ* 41, no. 39 (28 May 1904): 1030–1031. The article also contains a great deal of incorrect information more applicable to German East Africa. For example, estimating the population figures in GSWA at between four and five million, the article spoke of 2,000 German native auxiliaries, of which many were said to have deserted.

79. Ibid. This position was also given further expression in another article focusing on the Nama war (ibid., 42, no. 42 [17 June 1905]: 1135). See also *USANJ*, anon. note, 41, no. 43 (25 June 1904): 1121.

80. *Die Kolonialdeutschen aus Deutsch-Ostafrika in belgischer Gefangenschaft*, ed. Reichskolonialamt (Berlin: Reichsdruckerei, 1918); Reichskolonialamt, *Die Kolonialdeutschen aus Kamerun und Togo in französischer Gefangenschaft* (Berlin: Reichsdruckerei, 1917); Reichskolonialamt, *Verhalten der englischen und unter englischem Oberbefehl stehenden französischen Truppen gegen die weiße Bevölkerung der deutschen Schutzgebiete Kamerun und Togo* (Berlin: Reichsdruckerei, 1917).

81. *Die Kolonialdeutschen aus Kamerun und Togo in französischer Gefangenschaft*, introduction.

82. *Report on the Natives of South-West Africa and Their Treatment by Germany: Prepared in the Administrator's Office* (Windhoek, 1918).

83. Martin Donandt *(Senatskommission für Reichs- und auswärtige Angelegenheiten)* to the Reichskanzler, Bremen, 21 September 1918, STA Bremen, J-M.2.h2. no.123.

84. *The Treatment of Native and Other Populations in the Colonial Possessions of Germany and England: An Answer to the English Blue Book of August 1918; Published by the German Colonial Office* (Berlin: Engelmann, 1919). (German Translation: *Die Behandlung der einheimischen Bevölkerung in den kolonialen Besitzungen Deutschlands und Englands.*)

85. Ibid., 2.

86. Heinrich Schnee, *Die koloniale Schuldlüge* (Munich: Oldenbourg, 1924). Published in 1926, the English edition bore the title *German Colonization Past and Future*. See also Schnee, *Braucht Deutschland Kolonien?* (Leipzig: Quelle & Meyer, 1921).

87. *Report on the Natives of South-West Africa and Their Treatment by Germany*, introduction, 5.

88. *A Handbook of German East Africa, Compiled by the Geographical Section of the Naval Intelligence Division, Naval Staff, Admirality* (London: H. M. Stationery Office, 1920). The following summaries are taken from pp. 211, 212, and 215 of the handbook.

89. Ibid., 212.

90. Ibid., 1.

91. *The Treatment of Native and Other Populations in the Colonial Possessions of Germany and England*, introduction.

92. *Report on the Natives of South-West Africa and Their Treatment by Germany*, 5.

93. *The Treatment of Native and Other Populations in the Colonial Possessions of Germany and England*, 309.

94. Ibid., 308.

95. Denkschriften der Kriegsgeschichtlichen Abteilung 3 des Großen Generalstabes, 7. Zerstörungen und Behandlung der Landeseinwohner durch die englischen Truppen im Burenkrieg 1899–1902, BA/MA Freiburg, PH 3/133.

96. Ibid., *alphabetisches Sachregister.*

10. Parliament and the Military Press

1. Thomas Nipperdey, *Deutsche Geschichte 1866–1918*, vol. 2, *Machtstaat vor Demokratie* (Munich: C. H. Beck, 1998), 574; H. U. Wehler, *Deutsche Gesellschaftsgeschichte*, vol. 3, *1849–1914* (Munich: C. H. Beck, 2008), 864. See also Gordon A. Craig, *Germany 1866–1945* (New York: Oxford University Press, 1978), 43–54.

2. Reichsverfassung from 16 April 1871, art. 69, http://www.dhm.de/lemo/html/dokumente/verfassungkai/index. Html (accessed 30 November 2015).

3. For a discussion of party attitudes to colonial questions, see Horst Gründer, *Geschichte der deutschen Kolonien*, 3rd ed. (Paderborn: Schöningh, 1995), 63–78.

4. Entwurf eines Gesetzes, betr. die Feststellung eines dritten Nachtrags zum Reichshaushalts-Etat für das Rechnungsjahr 1900, 14 November 1900; Etat für die Expedition nach Ostasien auf das Rechnungsjahr 1900, BA Lichterfelde, R 3001/5266.

5. Anon., "Vierzig Millionen für China," *Vorwärts* 18, no. 282 (3 December 1901): 2.

6. Entwurf eines Gesetzes, betr. die Feststellung eines zweiten Nachtrags zum Haushalts-Etat für die Schutzgebiete auf das Rechnungsjahr 1904, n.d. Sowie für die Aufführung der Gesamtausgaben: Denkschrift, betr. die Rechnungslegung und Rechnungsprüfung über die Aufstandsausgaben in Deutsch-Südwestafrika, 1912, HSTA Stuttgart, E 130, a Bue 895.

7. Handwritten note from the Reichsjustizamt for Reichskanzler Bülow, 16 November 1905. Similar: Secret Report for the Reichskanzler, 22 August 1905, BA Lichterfelde, R 3001/5268.

8. Reichskanzler Bülow to the *Auswärtiges Amt*, 21 August 1905, ibid.

9. Entwurf eines Gesetzes betr. die Feststellung eines dritten Nachtrags zum Reichshaushalts-Etat für das Rechnungsjahr 1905, 7 December 1905, att. 3, ibid.

10. Bericht der Kommission für den Reichshaushalts-Etat betreffend die Feststellung eines dritten Nachtrags zum Reichshaushalts-Etat für das Rechnungsjahr 1905, 08 February 1906, ibid.

11. See Telegram Götzen to the *Auswärtiges Amt*, 26 August 1905; draft of a telegram from Reichskanzler Bülow to Götzen, 28 August 1905, BA/MA Freiburg, RM 5/6035.

12. Gerd Fesser, *Reichskanzler Fürst von Bülow: Architekt der deutschen Weltpolitik* (Leipzig: Militzke, 2003), 123–125.

13. August Bebel (Social Democrat), 13 March 1906, SBR, XI. Legislaturperiode, 2nd Sess., vol. 216, 1986–1987. All records of the debates in the Reichstag are available at http://www.reichtagsprotokolle.de.

14. Bebel (Social Democrat), 19 November 1900, SBR, X. Legislaturperiode, 2nd Sess., vol. 179, 29, 30, emphasis in original.

15. Heinrich von Goßler (Minister of War), 19 November 1900, ibid., 29, 38.

16. Eugen Richter (Left Liberal), 20 November 1900, ibid., 54–56.

17. Philipp Lieber (Center), 19 November 1900, ibid., 20.

18. Ernst Bassermann (National Liberal), 20 November 1900, ibid., 48.

19. Albert von Levetzow (Conservative), 20 November 1900, ibid., 52.

20. Bebel (Social Democrat), 17 March 1904, ibid., XI. Legislaturperiode, 1st Sess., vol. 199, 1891. Both letters (specifying full names) had previously been published in the *Halleschen Zeitung* and the *Triererischen Volksfreund*. The first, dispatched on 22 February 1904, included the following passage: "Prisoners are being taken every day and either hanged or shot. The latest order has forbidden the taking of prisoners, i.e. we are to shoot them [out of hand]." A further letter stated, "We have been instructed not to take any prisoners. Everything alive and black is to be shot."

21. Georg Ledebour (Social Democrat), 6 April 1905, ibid., XI. Legislaturperiode, 1st Sess., vol. 204, 5888. Similar: August Bebel, 17 March 1904, ibid., vol. 199, 1891.

22. Ludwig Graf zu Reventlow (German Social Party / Anti-Semites), 17 March 1904, ibid., 1900.

23. Ledebour (Social Democrat), 25 May 1905, ibid., 6159.

24. Ibid. The French newspaper *Le Temps* translated these words freely in its anonymous article "La révolte des Herreros," ibid. (17 August 1905): 2.

25. Matthias Erzberger (Center), 25 May 1905, ibid., XI. Legislaturperiode, 1st Sess., vol. 204, 6182.

26. Ibid.

27. Ibid.

28. Erzberger (Center), 2 October 1905, ibid., XII. Legislaturperiode, 2nd Sess., vol. 214, 80.

29. Colonel Berthold von Deimling, 2 December 1905, ibid., 95. See Kirsten Zirkel, *Vom Militaristen zum Pazifisten: General Berthold von Deimling—eine politische Biographie* (Essen: Klartext, 2008), 60–62; Berthold von Deimling, *Aus der alten in die neue Zeit: Lebenserinnerungen* (Berlin: Ullstein, 1930), 101–110.

30. Berthold von Deimling, 19 March 1906, SBR, XII. Legislaturperiode, 2nd Sess., vol. 216, 2126–2127.

31. Deimling, 26 May 1906, ibid., vol. 217, 3538.

32. Bassermann (National Liberal), 20 November 1900, ibid., X. Legislaturperiode, 1st Sess., vol. 179, 44; Adolf Stoecker (German Conservative Party), 15

February 1901, ibid., X. Legislaturperiode, 2nd Sess., vol. 180, 1377. The Taiping uprising (1850–1864) was a civil war in China, in which some twenty million people were killed.

33. Richter (Left Liberal), 20 November 1900, SBR, vol. 179, 66.

34. Ledebour (Social Democrat), 15 March 1906, ibid., XII. Legislaturperiode, 2nd Sess., vol. 216, 2044.

35. Bebel (Social Democrat), 19 November 1900, SBR, X. Legislaturperiode, 2nd Sess., vol. 179, 11.

36. A number of details are provided in Frank Oliver Sobich, 'Schwarze Bestien, rote Gefahr': Rassismus und Antisozialismus im deutschen Kaiserreich (Frankfurt am Main: Campus, 2006), 261–316.

37. Bebel (Social Democrat), 15 February 1901, SBR, X Legislaturperiode, 2nd Sess., vol. 180, 1374.

38. In a speech made on 19 November 1900, Bebel quoted passages from twelve letters. Ibid., vol. 179, 26, 29.

39. Ibid., 30.

40. This question is dealt with in considerable detail by Ute Wielandt and Michael Kaschner, "Die Reichstagsdebatten über den deutschen Kriegseinsatz in China: August Bebel und die 'Hunnenbriefe,'" in Das Deutsche Reich und der Boxeraufstand, ed. Susanne Kuß and Bernd Martin (Munich: Iudicium, 2002), 183–201, 195–198. A summary is provided in Dietlind Wünsche, Feldpostbriefe aus China (Berlin: Christoph Links Verlag, 2008), 69–72. For a contemporary treatment, see Rudolph Zabel, Deutschland in China (Leipzig: Wigand, 1902), 379, 381.

41. Goßler (Minister of War), 15 February 1901, SBR, X Legislaturperiode, 2nd Sess., vol. 180, 1376; Bebel (Social Democrats), 11 January 1902, ibid., vol. 182, 3314.

42. Goßler, 19 November 1900, ibid., 1st Sess., vol. 179, 38.

43. Bebel, 23 November 1900, ibid., 386, emphasis in original.

44. Ibid.

45. Goßler, 15 February 1901, ibid., X. Legislaturperiode, 2nd Sess., vol. 180, 1377; see also anon., "Zur China-Vorlage," Unteroffizier-Zeitung 27, no. 8 (22 February 1901): 120–122, 121.

46. Goßler, 16 March 1901, SBR, X. Legislaturperiode, 2nd Sess., vol. 180, 1916.

47. The only (albeit very brief) reference to the trial was that from Michael Kaschner. See Wielandt and Kaschner, "Die Reichstagsdebatten über den deutschen Kriegseinsatz in China," 183–201, 189. As yet, it has proven impossible to locate the trial documents of either the regional or the imperial courts hearing these cases. Nevertheless, working on the basis of newspaper articles (the majority of which were written by court reporters) and a number of private telegrams and dispatches from the Wolff telegraphic office, it was possible to outline the following process. In a trial before the Landgericht Stuttgart of the Wurttemberg State Parliament Liberal Party against the deputy and editor in chief of the Stuttgarter Beobachter, Karl Schmidt, one

witness called was Lieutenant General von Lessel. Schmidt was cleared of all charges; Freund was sentenced to four weeks in prison. The next case to come to court was that of Berthold Hegmann, editor of the satirical weekly *Wahrer Jacob,* heard before the Landgericht Stuttgart on 7 November 1901. Hegmann was sentenced to payment of a fine of 200 reichsmarks. The case against the Social Democratic journalist Mark Quarck was heard by the Landgericht Frankfurt (Main) on 8 November 1901. Not tried for publication of a Hun letter, he was arraigned for an article commenting on their publication. The trial saw the imposition of a witness statement order against August Bebel. Quarck was sentenced to a prison term of four weeks. The date 2 December 1901 saw the opening in the Landgericht Berlin of the trial of three of the editors of *Vorwärts:* Robert Schmidt, Paul John, and Wilhelm Schröder (postponed). Schmidt and John, who had been sentenced to a number of months in prison, appealed their conviction in the Imperial Court in Leipzig. The date 17 July 1902 saw the start of the trial of Wilhelm Schröder in the Landgericht Berlin. The dates 23 October 1903 and 16 June 1905 saw the trial before the Landgericht Halle of the Social Democratic Reichstag deputy Wilhelm Kunert, who had held a speech in 1903 deemed to be insulting to the East African Expeditionary Corps. Kunert was sentenced to three months in prison, and his appeal was rejected by the Imperial Court. These trials were supplemented by a hearing held on 18 April 1904 in Essen against Fiedler, a former member of the East Asian Expeditionary Corps who was tried for insulting two officers, not during the war in China but rather in early 1904, during the course of a workers' assembly in Essen. Found guilty, Fiedler was handed down a prison sentence. Compiled from the following articles: anon., "Der erste der Chinaprozesse," *Vorwärts* 18, no. 258 (3 November 1901): 1–2; anon., "Der Stuttgarter China-Prozeß," ibid., 1st supp.; anon., "Zwei Hunnenprozesse," ibid., 18, no. 264 (11 November 1901): 1–2; August Bebel, "Die Hunnenbriefe," ibid., 18, no. 265 (19 November 1901): 1; anon., "Ein Chinaprozeß," ibid., 21, no. 64 (16 March 1904): 3; anon., "Die Vertagung der China-Wahrheit," ibid., 21, no. 70 (23 March 1904): 2; anon., "China-Prozeß / Essen," ibid., 21, no. 92 (20 April 1904): 4; anon., "Der China-Prozeß gegen den Stuttgarter Beobachter," *Frankfurter Zeitung und Handelsblatt* 46, no. 304 (2 November 1901): 2nd morning iss., 2; anon., "Gerichtszeitung," ibid., 46, no. 310 (8 November 1901): evening ed., 2; anon., "Gerichtsverhandlung" *Kreuz-Zeitung* 18, no. 564 (2 December 1901): evening ed.: 2; anon., "Gerichtsverhandlung," ibid., 18, no. 565 (3 December 1901): morning ed., 2nd supp.

48. Haase, to the Landgericht, Strafkammer 8, Berlin, 11 June 1901, printed in *Vorwärts* 18, no. 284 (5 December 1901): 5.

49. Anon., "Geradezu viehische Bestialitäten," *Vorwärts* 17, no. 283 (5 December 1900): 1.

50. On 6 February 1901. Anon., "Gerichtsverhandlung," *Kreuz-Zeitung* 18, no. 564 (2 December 1901), evening ed.: 2.

51. Anon., "Gerichtsverhandlung," ibid., 18, no. 565 (3 December 1901), morning ed., 2nd supp.

52. Anon., "Gerichtsverhandlung," ibid., 19, no. 330 (17 July 1902), evening ed.: 2.

53. Anon., "Zwei Hunnenprozesse," *Vorwärts* 18, no. 264 (11 November 1901): 1–2.

54. Anon., "Die China-Wahrheit," ibid., 20, no. 253 (29 October 1903): 2; anon., "Halle am 23.10.1903," *Unteroffizier-Zeitung* 30, no. 44 (30 October 1903): 689.

55. Anon., "Die China-Wahrheit," ibid., 20, no. 256 (1 November 1903): 3.

56. Fritz Kunert (Social Democrat), 23 February 1906, SBR, XI. Legislaturperiode, 2nd Sess., vol. 215, 1537–1542.

57. Anon., "Gerichtsverhandlung," *Kreuz-Zeitung* 19, no. 330 (17 July 1902), evening ed.: 2.

58. Anon., "Hunnenfreude," *Vorwärts* 18, no. 285 (6 December 1901): 1.

59. Max Liebermann von Sonnenberg, 10 January 1902. SBR, X. Legislaturperiode, 2nd Session, vol. 182, 3275.

60. *Reichsstrafgesetzbuch* secs. 185, 186. Sec. 185: "Defamation is to be punished with a fine of up to six hundred Marks or with a prison sentence of up to one year. If defamation involved physical assault, it is to be punished by a fine of up to 1,500 Marks or a prison sentence of up to two years."

61. Letter from Trotha to the "Rheinisch-Westfälische Zeitung," 1 December 1904, printed in the article anon., "Bekenntnisse Trothas," *Vorwärts* 22, no. 6 (7 January 1905): 2.

62. Moritz Merker, "Ueber die Aufstandsbewegung in Deutsch-Ostafrika," *Militär-Wochenblatt* 91, no. 45 (10 April 1906): cols. 1021–1030; no. 46 (12 April 1906): cols. 1085–1092; no. 47 (14 April 1906): cols. 1119–1126; no. 65 (26 May 1906): cols. 1530–1538.

63. Anonymous, "Über Südwestafrika," *Soldaten-Freund* 71, no. 9 (March 1904): 565.

64. Review of the map by von Zobel (Genmj. Ret.) in *Deutsches Offizierblatt* 9, no. 5 (31 January 1905): 1; "Kriegskarte von Deutsch-Südwestafrika in 1:800.000. Blatt Zesfontein, Owambo, Andara, Keetmanshoop, Warmbad, Verlag von Dietrich Reimer, Berlin, Preis pro Blatt 1 Mark," *Unteroffizier-Zeitung* 31, no. 15 (8 April 1904): 237.

65. Anon., "Zur Würdigung der augenblicklichen Kriegslage in Deutsch-Südwestafrika," *Deutsches Offizierblatt* 8, no. 19 (10 May 1904): 266–267.

66. Anon., "Zum Aufstand der Hereros in SWA (XV)," *Unteroffizier-Zeitung* 31, no. 18 (29 April 1904): 280; anon., "Zum Aufstand in Südwestafrika (CXXIII)," ibid., 33, no. 25 (22 June 1906): 392.

67. Richard Carow, "Oberstleutnant v. Estorff," ibid., 33, no. 23 (8 June 1906): 362.

68. Ibid.

69. Anon., "Der Aufstand in Deutsch-Südwestafrika," *Soldaten-Freund* 71, no. 10 (April 1904): 629–631, 631.

70. "Im alten Wunderlande China: Reiseskizzen eines deutschen Soldaten 1900–1901," pt. 8 (Wieder in Tongkou), pt. 9 (Tientsin), pt. 10 (Von Tientsin

bis nach Peking), ibid., no. 9 (March 1904): 528–540; pt. 11 (Eine Expedition nach Kalgan), ibid., no. 10 (April 1904): 611–614.

71. Admiralstab der Marine, ed., *Die Kaiserliche Marine während der Wirren in China 1900–1901* (Berlin: Ernst Siegfried Mittler, 1903).

72. These articles were supplemented by Admiralstab der Marine, ed., "Die Tätigkeit des Landungskorps SMS 'Habicht' während des Herero-Aufstandes in Süd-West-Afrika, Januar/Februar 1904," *Marine-Rundschau,* supp. 1905: 1–31.

73. Bearbeitet von den Teilnehmern an der Expedition, ed., *Deutschland in China 1900–1902* (Düsseldorf: Druck von August Bagel, 1902), introduction.

74. Ibid.

75. *Die Kämpfe der deutschen Truppen in Südwestafrika,* vol. 1: *Hereroaufstand* (Berlin: Ernst Siegfried Mittler, 1906); vol. 2: *Der Hottentottenkrieg* (Berlin: Ernst Siegfried Mittler, 1907); Maximilian Bayer, "Südwestafrika und die öffentliche Meinung," *Militär-Wochenblatt* 41, no. 34 (25 August 1906): cols. 330–331, 331.

76. The most well-known: Gustav Adolf von Götzen, *Deutsch-Ostafrika im Aufstand 1905/06* (Berlin: Dietrich Reimer, 1909); Ernst Nigmann, *Geschichte der kaiserlichen Schutztruppe für Deutsch-Ostafrika* (Berlin: Ernst Siegfried Mittler, 1911); Hans Paasche, *"Im Morgenlicht" Kriegs-, Jagd- und Reise-Erlebnisse in Ostafrika* (Berlin: C. A. Schwetschke und Sohn, 1907).

77. Maximilian Bayer, *Der Krieg in Südwestafrika und seine Bedeutung für die Entwicklung der Kolonie* (Leipzig: Engelmann, 1906), foreword, 3.

78. Friedrich Engelamm (Leipzig, July 1906) to the Saxon Generalkommando, HSTA Dresden, 11347/673.

79. Kurt Schwabe, "Einige Lehren aus dem Kriege in Deutsch-Südwestafrika," *Vierteljahreshefte für Truppenführung und Heereskunde* 1 (1904): 461–480, 462.

80. Kurd Schwabe, "Deutsch-Südwestafrika: Historisch-geographische, militärische und wirtschaftliche Studien; Vortrag gehalten in der Militärischen Gesellschaft zu Berlin am 15.3.1905," *Militär-Wochenblatt,* supp. 1905, 213–239, 232.

81. Anon., "Ein dritter Nachtragsetat für Südwestafrika," *Vorwärts* 22, no. 54 (4 March 1905): 3.

82. Alfred von Schlieffen, Chief of the General Staff to all Armeekorps, 15 June 1901. 7. Badisches Infanterieregiment no. 142. This information was passed on to all officers and other ranks and all members of the expedition on 28 June 1901. GLA Karlsruhe, 456 F 41, 38.

83. Order from 23 January 1897 (*Armee-Verordnungsblatt* 1897, 36). Mentioned in a letter from Kaiser Wilhelm II to Reichskanzler Bülow (Protection Force High Command), 11 December 1900, BayHSTA Munich, Kriegsarchiv, Mkr 4954.

84. Kaiser Wilhelm II to Reichskanzler Hohenlohe, 16 October 1899, BA/MA Freiburg, RM 1/v.1021.

85. Anon., "Reichskanzler Bülow in der Reichstagssitzung vom 9.12.," ibid., 32 (15 December 1905), 782.

86. Georg Hartmann, *Der wirtschaftliche Wiederaufbau Deutsch-Sudwestafrikas Vortrag in Sektion V. Verhandlungen des Deutschen Kolonialkongresses am 5., 6. und 7. Oktober 1905* (Berlin, 1906), 651–682, with a discussion up to page 698: "It would be both foolish and short-sighted if we were not to take discussion of the native question to [its logical conclusion]: extermination."

87. Theodor Leutwein, *Elf Jahre Gouverneur in Deutsch-Südwestafrika* (Berlin: Ernst Siegfried Mittler, 1906, repr. Windhoek: Namibia Wissenschaftliche Gesellschaft, 1997), 524–525.

88. Nigmann, *Geschichte der kaiserlichen Schutztruppe für Deutsch-Ostafrika*, iv.

89. Heliographic exchange between Estorff and Leutwein, June 1904, War Diary, 2. Feldkompanie 1904 in Deutsch-Südwestafrika, BA / MA Freiburg, RM 121I / 431, 50–51.

90. Leutwein once wrote to Witbooi, "I have made entirely clear that you have no choice other than the unconditional capitulation to the will of his Majesty the German King, or to suffer war until your extermination [*Vernichtung*]." In doing so, Leutwein threatened him with far more than the death of all his fighting men in battle. Three months later, Witbooi made his position clear: "During your attacks, I have realized that you seek to exterminate my entire people. Taken as guilty [by association] my entire people is locked into this war." Leutwein to Witbooi, 5 May 1894; Witbooi to Leutwein, 23 August 1894; Leutwein, *Elf Jahre Gouverneur*, 34–35; Hendrik Witbooi, *Afrika den Afrikanern! Aufzeichnungen eines Nama-Häuptlings aus der Zeit der deutschen Eroberung Südwestafrikas 1884 bis 1894*, ed. Wolfgang Reinhard (Berlin: J. H. W. Dietz, 1982), 179 180, 198 199.

91. Bayer, *Der Krieg in Südwestafrika und seine Bedeutung für die Entwicklung der Kolonie*, 23.

92. Ibid. Bayer informed the Saxon Ministry of War of this lecture by dispatch of the script, which was sent together with a prospectus showing the Herero prisoners with their belongings and a quote from the lecture: "Speaking from a human perspective, I seek . . . merely to say that in war, the entire nation suffers." App. to a letter from Friedrich Engelamm (Leipzig, July 1906) to the Saxon Generalkommando, HSTA Dresden, 11347 / 673.

93. Curt von François, "Die Kämpfe unserer Schutztruppe gegen Simon Kopper und Manasse Noroseb," *Militär-Wochenblatt* 91, no. 106 (28 August 1906): cols. 2452–2460, 2460.

94. Georg Rau, *Deutsch-Süd-West-Afrika: Bilder aus den Kriegen gegen die Hereros und Hottentotten; Mit einem Geleitwort Sr. Exzellenz des Generalleutnants z.D. von Trotha* (Berlin: Stern & Schiele, 1907). Reproduced in black and white *Völkermord in Deutsch-Südwestafrika*, ed. Jürgen Zimmerer and Joachim Zeller (Berlin: Christoph Links, 2003), 95.

95. Trotha, "Geleitwort," *Deutsch-Süd-West-Afrika*.

96. Ibid., foreword.

97. Trotha, "Geleitwort," ibid.

98. Carow, "Oberstleutnant v. Estorff," 362.

11. The Military

1. Vorschläge der durch Allerhöchste Kabinetts-Order vom 31/10/1901 berufenen Kommission zur Berathung der für etwaige künftige Expeditionen erforderlichen oder wünschenwerthen Maßnahmen (Expeditions— Vorschläge), Geheim, BA/MA Freiburg, RM 3/7727.
2. Wilhelm II to the Reichskanzler, 14 November 1908, ibid. The committee consisted of Colonel Franz Georg v. Glasenapp and Lieutenant Colonel L.v. Estorff (commander of the Protection Force in German South-West-Africa), Major Arnold von Lequis, General Prof. Dr. Werner Steuber (both in the Protection Force High Command at the Reichskolonialamt), the Geheimer Regierungsrat Nachtigall (Vortragender Rat im Reichskolonialamt, Protection Force High Command), and three unnamed representatives, each from the Kriegsministerium, the Great General Staff and the Reichsmarineamt.
3. Bericht des ältesten Offiziers der ostafrikanischen Station, L. Glatzel, an den Staatssekretär des Reichsmarineamtes, 23 March 1906, ibid.
4. Eugen Binder-Krieglstein, *Die Kämpfe des deutschen Expeditionskorps in China und ihre militärischen Lehren* (Berlin: Ernst Siegfried Mittler, 1902), 229.
5. Alfred von Waldersee, Denkschrift über Erfahrungen in China, October 1901 (subsequently referred to as Denkschrift Waldersee), BayHSTA Munich, Kriegsarchiv. 3. Pi.Btl., vol. 962. Also in HSTA Stuttgart, M1/4, vol. 535. The memorandum is partially reproduced in Bernd-Felix Schulte, *Die deutsche Armee 1900–1914: Zwischen Beharren u. Verändern* (Düsseldorf: Droste, 1977), 169–173. The following quotations are taken from pp. 1, 11, 6, and 5.
6. Ibid., 8.
7. Expeditions-Vorschläge, Geheim, 69.
8. Ibid., 5.
9. Corresponding reports regarding the transport of horses to China and German South-West Africa, HSTA Stuttgart, M 1/4, vol. 535.
10. Ergebnis der Arbeiten der durch Allerhöchste Kabinettsorder vom 14. November 1908 berufenen Kommission zur Beratung auf Grund der bei der Entsendung von Verstärkungen für die Schutztruppe in Südwestafrika gesammelten Erfahrungen (subsequently referred to as Bericht GSWA), BA/MA Freiburg, RM 3/4323, also ibid., RM 3/7728, 84. See Bericht von Gündell für den Kaiser, der das Ergebnis der Arbeiten der Kommission zusammenfasst, 28 March 1909 (subsequently referred to as Bericht Gündell), BayHSTA Munich, Kriegsarchiv, Mkr 814.
11. Geheimer Bericht des Reichskolonialamtes, Kommando der Schutztruppe. Überblick über die bei der Entsendung von Verstärkungen für die Schutztruppe in Südwestafrika gesammelten Erfahrungen und die in den Kommissionsberatungen zu erörternden Fragen, 1 November 1908 (subsequently referred to as Geheimbericht Reichskolonialamt), ibid. One hundred fifty copies were distributed among the members of the committee; the Ministry

of War; the General Staff; the military cabinet; Reichsmarineamt; the royal Bavarian, Saxon, and Wurttemberg Ministries of War; and the High Command of the Protection Force.

12. Ibid., 127.

13. Ibid., 125.

14. Ibid., 127.

15. Ibid.

16. Bericht GSWA, 84.

17. Geheimbericht Reichskolonialamt, 127.

18. Ibid., 125.

19. Ibid., 126.

20. Bericht GSWA, 88; Geheimbericht Reichskolonialamt, 125.

21. Hermann von Wissmann, "Schaffung einer Kolonial-Reservetruppe," *Militär-Wochenblatt* 85, no. 72 (4 August 1900): cols. 1731–1735.

22. Denkschrift Waldersee, 11.

23. "Theodor Leutwein über Südwestafrika: Ein Interview," *Berliner Tageblatt* 33 (31 December 1904), no. 665, morning ed. A summary is provided in LFM, Étranger: Allemagne, 6 January 1905: 3.

24. Hans von Haeften, "Eine deutsche Kolonialarmee," *Vierteljahreshefte für Truppenführung und Heereskunde* 2 (1905), 610–631, 614, emphasis in the original.

25. Ibid., 611.

26. Bericht Gündell, 8–9.

27. Ausführungen des Korvettenkapitäns Heinrich Löhlein in der Sitzung, 17 February 1909, betr. Frage der Verwendung der Marineinfanterie als Expeditionstruppe; Vorschläge der SWA-Kommission, 28 March 1909, 5–7, BA/MA Freiburg, RM 3/4323. See also Bericht Gündell, 7.

28. Hans von Haeften, "Eine deutsche Kolonialarmee," *Vierteljahreshefte für Truppenführung und Heereskunde* 2 (1905): 610–631, 629. See also Curt Morgen, Eine deutsche Kolonialarmee, BA/MA Freiburg, NL 38/31.

29. Bericht Gündell, 10.

30. Ibid., 22.

31. Protokoll der Sitzung von Vertretern des Kriegsministeriums, Reichskolonialamts und Reichsmarineamts über die Ausführung des Südwestafrika-Berichts am 30. November 1910, vormittags 10½ Uhr, 21, ibid., RM 3/4323. This ordinance was to be drafted by a commission chaired by the quarter-master general, Major General Graf Maximilian von Montgelas. No such document has been found in the archives.

32. Erfahrungen, betr. Südwest- und Ostafrika Expedition. Vorarbeiten für Entsendung eines Marine-Expeditionskorps, point 2, BA/MA Freiburg, RM 3/4324.

33. Werner Steuber, "Über die Verwendbarkeit europäischer Truppen in tropischen Kolonien vom gesundheitlichen Standpunkte," *Vierteljahreshefte für Truppenführung und Heereskunde* 4 (1907): 232–268.

34. Vorschläge der Südwestafrika-Kommission, 28 March 1909, 13–14, BA/MA Freiburg, RM 3/4323.
35. Protokoll der Sitzung von Vertretern des Kriegsministeriums, Reichskolonialamts und Reichsmarineamts über die Ausführung des Südwestafrika-Berichts am 30. November 1910, vormittags 10½ Uhr, 10, ibid.
36. Ibid.
37. Secret letter of the minister of war Josias von Heeringen to Reichskanzler Bethmann Hollweg, 2 August 1911, regarding the creation of a legal basis for overseas campaigns; secret letter of Heeringen to Bethmann-Hollweg, 6 May 1912, regarding the plan to establish a German expeditionary corps, BA Lichterfelde, R 3001/3602.
38. Secret letter of Heeringen to Bethmann-Hollweg, 8 March 1913, ibid. See also letter of the war minister Falkenhayn to the Reichsmarineamt, 7 May 1914, BA/MA Freiburg, RM 3/4325.
39. "Wehrgesetz für die Schutzgebiete 22/07/1913," *Reichsgesetz-Blatt* 1913, 610–615.
40. Heeringen to all units, 29 April 1910, BA/MA Freiburg, RM 3/4323. Bayrisches Kriegsministerium, Armeeabteilung I, 19 May 1910 to all units, BayHSTA, Kriegsarchiv Munich, Mkr 778.
41. Ibid.
42. Ludwig von Estorff, "Kriegserlebnisse in Südwestafrika: Vortrag gehalten in der Militärischen Gesellschaft zu Berlin, 8.2.1911" (Berlin: Ernst Siegfried Mittler, 1911). Also printed in *Militärwochenblatt* (1911), supp.: 80–101.
43. Estorff, "Kriegserlebnisse in Südwestafrika."

12. Veterans' Associations

1. H. U. Wehler, *Deutsche Gesellschaftsgeschichte*, vol. 3 (1849–1914), 884. For greater detail, see Thomas Rohkrämer, *Der Militarismus der "kleinen Leute": Die Kriegervereine im Deutschen Kaiserreich 1871–1914* (Munich: Oldenbourg, 1990), 27–37.
2. Satzungen des Kolonialkriegerdanks, sec. 2, 16 March 1913, HSTA Stuttgart, E 130, a Bue 637. See also Satzungen des Kolonialkriegerdanks, 27 December 1909, BA Lichterfelde, R 151 F, 82385.
3. Taken from the *Kolonial-Post* 7, no. 8 (1 August 1912): 1. Consisting of only those associations that had submitted their data to the *Kolonial-Post*, this list remains incomplete. The actual number is probably considerably higher.
4. *Jahresbericht des Vereins südwestafrikanischer Krieger zu Berlin für das Jahr 1913 und Mitglieder-Verzeichnis* (Berlin: Verein Sudwestafrikanischer Krieger, 1914), 7.
5. Satzungen des Vereins ehemaliger Ostasiaten und Afrikaner an der Unterweser in Bremerhaven, sec. 1: Zweck des Vereins, STA Bremen, 3-V.2.no. 746.
6. *Jahresbericht des Vereins südwestafrikanischer Krieger zu Berlin für das Jahr 1913 und Mitglieder Verzeichnis*, 12. The welfare services of the association were used regularly. Eighty-nine members and their dependents received free medical attention from a doctor, 54 members were given free legal advice, 104 free proof of employment, and 344 free advice and information.

7. Ibid., 6.

8. Satzungen des Kolonialkriegerdanks, sec. 2, 16 March 1913, HSTA Stuttgart, E 130, a Bue 637. And Satzungen des Kolonialkriegerdanks, 27 December 1909, BA Lichterfelde, R 151/82385.

9. Regarding the *Colonial Veterans' Memorial Almanac*, see *Kolonialkriegerdank-Kalender für das Jahr 1917, Jahresbericht für 1915*, 3. *Der Jahresbericht für 1915* (Berlin), 30 April 1916, also in HSTA Stuttgart, E 130, a Bue 637.

10. Examples for the activities of one year: *Jahresbericht des Vereins südwestafrikanischer Krieger zu Berlin für das Jahr 1913*.

11. Polizei-Distrikt, Bremen to the Senat, 30 July 1909, STA Bremen, 3-V.2.no.831.26; Brief des Vereins ehemaliger Afrika- und China-Krieger zu Bremen, an den Senat, 8 August 1910, handwritten note on the rear, 13 August 1910; Brief der Ada von Liliencron an den Senat der Stadt Bremen, über: Beihilfe zu der Einrichtung von Büchereien für die Kolonialtruppen, 6 June 1910, *Deutsche-Kolonialzeitung*, vol. 45, 1909, 752–753; Senats-Protokolle, 15 July 1910, 645, STA Bremen, 3-V.2.no.831.26.

12. An example is provided in *Kolonial-Post* 7, vol. 1 (1 January 1912): 1.

13. Satzungen des Preußischen Landes-Kriegerverbandes in der auf dem Abgeordnetentage zu Weißenfels am 8./9. Juli 1898 beschlossenen Fassung. Genehmigt durch Allerhöchste Kabinettsorder vom 21/12/1898 (Berlin, 1899), LA Schleswig-Holstein, 301/1874.

14. Oberpräsident to the Regierungspräsident Schleswig, 22 May 1912. Verbatim report of the Prussian minister of the interior, 15 April 1912, ibid., 309/16820.

15. M. H., "Prolog zur Fahnenweihe," in *Rathjen's Kolonial-Liederbuch: Speziell für die Vereine ehemaliger Kolonial-Krieger in Deutschland, als auch für ehemalige und aktive Schutztruppler in den Kolonien*, ed. Heinrich Rathjen (Hamburg-Rissen: Heinrich Rathjen, 1913); Arne Schöfert, ed., *Deutsche Koloniallyrik: Lieder und Gedichte* (Saarbrücken: Fines-Mundi-Verlag, 2006); *Prolog zur Fahnenweihe, von Carl Goedecke, Kriegsveteran*, ibid., 85.

16. Liliencron, "Letzter Gruß," *Kolonial-Post* 7 (1 August 1912), vol. 8: 86.

17. Rathjen, *Rathjen's Kolonial-Liederbuch*.

18. Anon., "Die Bundestagung in Freiburg," *Kolonial-Post* 29 (1935): 125–132, 129.

19. Robert Baden-Powell, *Aids for Scouting* (London: Gale & Polden, 1899), and Baden-Powell, *Scouting for Boys: A Handbook for Instruction in Good Citizenship* (London: C. Arthur Pearson, 1908). While *Aids for Scouting* was not published in German, a number of German-language versions were published after 1909. The *Kleines Späherbuch* (Leipzig: Grethlein, 1912) edited by Karl Hellwig was, however, a translation of *Scouting for Boys*.

20. Alexander Lion, *Die Pfadfinder- und Wehrkraftbewegung und ihre Ursachen* (Munich: Gmelin, 1913), 28; Lion, "Ernst im Spiel," *Die Woche* 11 (10 April 1909), vol. 15: 640–642.

21. Generalkommando, II Armeekorps to the Bavarian Ministry of War, 10 July 1909, BayHSTA Munich, Kriegsarchiv, Mkr 4916.

22. Hermann Giehrl, *Nationale Wehrkraft in England: Vortrag gehalten in München*, 13.2.1910. *Werbemappe des Vereins Wehrkraft (e.V.)*. Including a letter from the Munich Ministry of War (Freiherr von Horn) to all subordinate offices, 30 November 1909, BayHSTA Munich, Kriegsarchiv, Mkr 4916.

23. Christoph Schubert-Weller, "*'Kein schönrer Tod . . .'. Die Militarisierung der männlichen Jugend und ihr Einsatz im Weltkrieg 1890–1918*" (Weinheim: Juventa, 1998), 154–155.

24. Alexander Lion, *Das Pfadfinderbuch: Nach General Baden-Powells Scouting for Boys; Unter Mitwirkung von Offizieren und Schulmännern* (Munich: Gmelin, 1909, repr. 1987), foreword, v. In the original text, the whole paragraph is italicized.

25. Werbemappe des Vereins Wehrkraft (e.V.). Includes Freiherr von Horn (Ministry of War) to all immediately subordinate officers, BayHSTA Munich, Kriegsarchiv, Mkr 4916.

26. *Das Pfadfinderbuch* (2nd ed., Munich, 1911), foreword, xii, and Erlaß des Ministers der geistlichen, Unterrichts- und Medizinal-Angelegenheiten vom 18. Januar 1911 betreffend Jugendpflege (Berlin), 1911.

27. Lion, *Das Pfadfinderbuch*, 304–307.

28. Ibid., 22, emphasis in the original.

29. Ibid., 138.

30. Maximilian Bayer, "Felddienst," ibid., 137–173; Ernst Nigmann, *Felddienstübungen für farbige (ostafrikanische) Truppen*.

31. *Pfadfinderbuch* (1st ed. 1909), 57.

32. Alexander Lion, *Die deutsche Pfadfinderbewegung und Wehrkraftbewegung und ihre Ursachen* (Munich: Gmelin, 1913), 15.

33. Ibid., 14.

34. Publicity for the book: Elise Bake, *Schwere Zeiten: Schicksale eines deutschen Mädchens in Südwestafrika* (Munich: Gmelin, 1913). Max Bayer in the *Pfadfinder* 1913. Editor of the *Der Pfadfinder* was Maximilian Bayer. *Die Pfadfinderin*, published monthly after 1914, was aimed at the Girl Guides.

35. The second edition bore the title *Das Pfadfinderbuch*, hg. von Stabsarzt Dr. A. Lion (Munich: Verlag der Ärztlichen Rundschau Gmelin, 1911), ix.

36. Ibid., 222–235.

37. Ibid., 238.

38. M. Bayer and A. Lion, *Jungdeutschlands Pfadfinderbuch* (Munich: Gmelin, 1912); Elise von Hopffgarten, *Das Pfadfinderbuch für junge Mädchen: Ein anregender, praktischer Leitfaden für die heranwachsende, vorwärtsstrebende weibliche Jugend* (Munich: Gmelin, 1912).

39. *Jungdeutschlands Pfadfinderbuch*, 3rd new ed., 1912, 199–203.

40. Oberstleutnant von Hoff, ed., *Jungdeutschland-Taschenbuch für Führer, Unterführer und Jungmannschaften* (Stuttgart: Union Deutsche Verlagsgesellschaft, 1913), 94.

41. Ibid., 94.

42. John Horne and Alan Kramer, *German Atrocities, 1914: A History of Denial* (New Haven, CT: Yale University Press, 2001), 140–153.

13. Legacy

1. See colonial officer data base.
2. http://www.germanhistorydocs.ghi-dc.org/pdf/deu617, accessed 15 March 2016.
3. See the colonial officer data base and the *Sanitätsbericht über das Deutsche Heer (Deutsches Feld- und Besatzungsheer) im Weltkrieg 1914/18*, vol. 1, *Gliederung des Heeressanitätswesens* (Berlin: Ernst Siegfried Mittler, 1935), 30. It is safe to assume that some 2 percent of all medical officers deployed in the First World War possessed colonial experience.
4. Contemporary accounts are provided in Ludwig R. Maercker, *Vom Kaiserheer zur Reichswehr* (Leipzig: Koehler, 1921); Berthold von Deimling, *Aus der alten in die neue Zeit* (Berlin: Ullstein, 1930). See also Eckard Michels, *Paul von Lettow-Vorbeck* (Paderborn: Ferdinand Schöningh, 2008); Uwe Schulte-Varendorff, *Kolonialheld für Kaiser und Führer: General Lettow-Vorbeck— Mythos und Wirklichkeit* (Berlin: Links, 2008); Katja Wächter, *Die Macht der Ohnmacht: Leben und Politik des Franz Xaver Ritter von Epp 1868–1946* (Frankfurt am Main: P. Lang, 1999); Kirsten Zirkel, *Vom Militaristen zum Pazifisten: General Berthold von Deimling—eine politische Biographie* (Essen: Klartext, 2008). We lack studies of less well-known colonial officers.
5. Regarding Paasche, see Peter W. Lange, *Hans Paasche: Das verlorene Afrika; Ansichten vom Lebensweg eines Kolonialoffiziers zum Pazifisten und Revolutionär* (Berlin: trafo Wissenschaftsverlag, 2008), introduction, 9–41. Regarding Deimling, see Zirkel, *Vom Militaristen zum Pazifisten*, 120–137.
6. H. U. Wehler, *Deutsche Gesellschaftsgeschichte*, vol. 4, *Vom Beginn des Ersten Weltkriegs bis zur Gründung der beiden deutschen Staaten 1914–1949* (Munich: C. H. Beck, 2003), 385–387; David Stone, *Fighting for the Fatherland: The Story of the German Soldier from 1648 to the Present Day* (London: Bloomsbury, 2006), 295–300; Robert G. L. Waite, *Vanguard of Nazism: The Free Corps Movement in Postwar Germany, 1928–1923* (Cambridge, MA: Harvard University Press, 1952).
7. Hagen Schulze, *Freikorps und Republik* (Boppard am Rhein: H. Boldt, 1969), 257; Bernhard Sauer, "Vom 'Mythos eines ewigen Soldatentums.' Der Feldzug deutscher Freikorps im Baltikum im Jahre 1919," *Zeitschrift für Geschichte* 43 (1995): 869–902, 873–874.
8. Klaus Theweleit, *Männerphantasien*, vol. 2 (Frankfurt am Main: Piper, 2005), 343–309, 391–392. For a discussion, see Richard J. Evans, *Rereading German History: From Unification to Reunification* (London: Routledge, 1997).
9. Gabriel Vejas Liulevicius, *War Land on the Eastern Front: Culture, National Identity and German Occupation in World War I* (Cambridge: Cambridge University Press, 2000), 78.
10. Robert Gerwarth, "The Central European Counter-Revolution: Paramilitary Violence in Germany, Austria and Hungary after the Great War," *Past and Present* 200 (2008): 175–209, 179.

Acknowledgments

This book would not have been possible without the help of a number of people. I should particularly like to thank William Kirby (Harvard) and Mechthild Leutner (Berlin) for their unstinting support, encouragement, and stimulus. William Kirby especially enabled me to work in the Widener Library at Harvard. I profited greatly from a number of discussions with Dieter Langewiesche (Tubingen) and would like to thank him for his suggestions on how to make the transition from a German Habilitation to an English book. I am also grateful to Stig Förster (Bern), Gerd Krumeich (Düsseldorf), and Bernd Martin (Freiburg) for our ongoing discussions about the German military in the nineteenth century. Similarly, I have profited greatly from many discussions about the German colonial empire with friends from my Freiburg and Berlin undergraduate days—Stefan Knirsch, Friedrich Dreves, Christoph Jahr, and Jürgen Förster. I have also profited from the perspective of Huang Fude (Taibei), Zhou Xin and André Maertens (Gaoxiong), and Germain-Hervé Mbia Yebega (Paris/Jaunde). Michael Berger (Freiburg) spent countless hours collecting and ordering data about the German military in the colonies, for which I extend my thanks. The help of Patrick Loos (Düsseldorf) was indispensable in its statistical evaluation. He also rendered invaluable services in a range of technical matters. I should also like to thank Peter Palm (Berlin) for producing the maps used in this book. Sabine Schmidt (Freiburg), Jacqueline Specht (Hagen), Christa Klein (Freiburg), and Stefanie Harder (Freiburg) read and commented on various drafts of this book, in both German and English.

    This translation would not have been possible without the financial assistance of the Börsenverein des Deutschen Buchhandels and their translation prize. I should also like to thank my German publisher, Christoph Links (Berlin), and his staff for their support and kindness. At Harvard University Press, I was always able to rely on Kathleen McDermott for her assistance and suggestions in producing the English edition. I should also like to thank the anonymous reviewers for their comments, which proved vital in the genesis of this book. My translator, Andrew Smith, was instrumental in highlighting the differences between the German academic and military cultures. Tom Akehurst and Brian Smith proved to be more than vigilant in reading and correcting various drafts of the translation. My thanks go also to Pamela Nelson and Ellen Lohmann for the standardization of the text and the notes.

Projects of this scale tend to have a long genesis. Started in Freiburg at the end of the 1990s with the support of the German Research Foundation, the work was eventually accepted as a Habilitation thesis by the University of Bern (Switzerland) in 2012. During this time, I have become convinced of the impossibility of tracing a line of continuity between the colonial wars at the turn of the twentieth century and the barbarism unleashed during the wars of the National Socialist state. What Cecil Blackbourn and Geoffrey Eley established for Germany as a whole must also apply to its wars: human action cannot be explained by reference only to the structures that produced it, however plausible such an approach may appear.

Index